2 30

W9-AEF-494

A THEOLOGY READER

A Theology
READER

EDITED BY

Robert W. Gleason, S. J.

THE MACMILLAN COMPANY · *NEW YORK*

COLLIER-MACMILLAN LIMITED · *LONDON*

FIRST PRINTING

The Macmillan Company, New York

Collier-Macmillan Canada, Ltd.,

Toronto, Ontario

Library of Congress catalog card number: 66–14691

Printed in the United States of America

Acknowledgments

T HE AUTHOR GRATEFULLY acknowledges permission from the following publishers and individuals to reproduce copyrighted material: *Theology Digest* for "The Theology of Mysteries" by Clement Tierney, 1959; "Literary Genres in the Bible" by Pierre Lobez, 1956; "The Sacraments: An Encounter With God" by Edward H. Schillebeeckx, O.P., 1960; "Functional Christology in the New Testament" by Léopold Malevez, S.J., 1962; "Faith: Personal Encounter With God" by René Latourelle, S.J., 1962; "The Preambles of Faith" by Guy De Broglie, S.J., 1959; "St. Paul and a Mystical Redemption" by Stanislas Lyonnet, S.J., 1960; "The Gift of Self-Redemption" by August Brunner, S.J., 1958; "Ritual and Grace in the Sacraments" by Pieter Smulders, S.J., 1961; "The Apostolate of Laymen" by Karl Rahner, S.J., 1957. *Theological Studies* for "The Conception of our Gospels as Salvation History" by David M. Stanley, S.J., 1959, and used with the permission of The Newman Press, Westminster, Maryland, from their forthcoming book by David M. Stanley, *The Apostolic Church in the New Testament*. The Macmillan Company for "Miracles and Contemporary Theology" by Robert W. Gleason, S.J., from the book *The Encounter With God* edited by Joseph E. O'Neill, S.J., © The Macmillan Company 1960, 1961, 1962. *Lumen Vitae* for "Towards a Psychology of Divine Grace" by Piet Fransen, 1958. *Cross Currents* for "Death: A Test for Love, A Condition of Freedom" by Roger Troisfontaines, 1957.

CONTENTS

Introduction

The last two decades have witnessed a remarkable renaissance of all branches of Catholic theology. Sacred Scripture, too, has seen a flourishing revival since the publication in 1948 of the Encyclical *Divino Afflante Spiritu*. As a result of recent investigations, new perspectives on old problems have been opened up and theology has also posed new problems requiring extensive speculation. There is scarcely an area of theological thinking which has not been in some way affected by the wave of new speculation and research.

As a result, the entire approach to faith and revelation has received a different emphasis today. If in the past the Catholic apologist sometimes presented his claims for the credibility of the Christian message in terms that sounded almost rationalistic, this is certainly no longer true. The credentials of faith—miracles and prophecies—have been subjected to extensive reinvestigation and today the sign-value of the miracle is emphasized more than sheer physical transcendence of "natural law." The inner moral and religious dispositions required for the recognition of a supernatural event are underscored by today's theologians. This question is of course tied in very closely with the whole theology of faith and here again advances have been made, reorientations which are at once new and a partial return to a more primitive and biblical way of looking at things. After the Council of Trent the intellectual aspects of faith had received a heavy emphasis. Today this aspect is integrated into a more concrete approach which studies also the volitional and affective elements entering into a total commitment of faith. A phenomenology of the very special type of knowledge that faith represents has distinguished it from a chill intellectual assent to a "proposition" and reintegrated the notion of trust and total disposition of oneself with regard to Jesus Christ. As a result, revelation is seen as more than a series of dogmatic statements. God's *actions* in history are underscored today and history is seen as a communication of God to man. The new studies in Scripture have sought for an ever closer understanding of the literal sense of Scripture, that intended by the sacred author. The study of Semitic thought patterns, of the literary forms used in the ancient Near East has illuminated the Bible which no longer appears as an isolated document but is better able to be understood through parallels in profane literature.

The advances of "form criticism" have pointed up the importance of primitive tradition and in many cases have helped the scholar come to a closer grasp of the original setting of the Gospels' narratives and statements. Recent biblical research has also stimulated new reflection on perennial problems of theology and often a considerable shift of interest and perspective can be noted. There has been a restudy of the relationship between tradition and sacred Scripture and this restudy has often clarified the meaning of tradition itself.

Hardly a field in dogmatic theology has been untouched by these new currents of thought. The Church, for so long treated from a heavily juridical point of view, is now studied under the many biblical images, the people of God, the Mystical Body, etc., with the result that there is more emphasis on her inner life than on her institutional structure in today's writings. The emergence of the layman has resulted in large part from reflection on the nature of the Church as the prolongation of the Incarnate Christ in space and time.

In Christology, long preoccupied with metaphysical questions concerning the Hypostatic Union, a renewed interest in the *psychology* of Christ—His knowledge and consciousness—has made itself felt. The work of Christ in the redemption of the human race has been subjected to continued reinvestigation and less juridical approaches have resulted from Scriptural and historical studies of that dogma. Insights from the Oriental Church and from Protestant theology have been incorporated into much of the modern thinking on this dogma and others.

The whole meaning of the supernatural has been subjected also to restudy, thus illuminating the differences which divide Protestant and Catholic Christendom as well as assisting to a far greater understanding of nature itself. The meaning and value of terrestrial realities, of marriage, of the flesh, have been explored more fully in the present century than ever before. Such studies could not but profoundly affect one's concept of a theology of morals, and Christian ethics have seen a definite reorientation in the direction of a refocusing on biblical categories, especially love or charity. A fuller appreciation of the secular dimension in life has aided in the newer approaches to the problem of religious liberty, the relationship between Church and State and the tension between freedom and authority.

In the area of grace, another era was much preoccupied with the questions of actual grace and the eternal problem of reconciling man's liberty with God's grace. This century has seen a renewal of interest in the divinization of man by grace, in a more dynamic concept of grace, and in the workings of grace with human psychology. The relationship of grace to the Mystical Body—to the grace of the Head, Christ—has been the subject of new studies.

Contemporary atheism has also stimulated a wealth of new investigations into the old and new sources of atheism and into the question as to what human reason can and cannot do in coming to a certain knowledge of the existence of God. Here again modern psychology and post-Kantian philosophy have been put to interesting use by contemporary theologians.

With the emergence of many "theologies" of history there has come a renewal of interest in the transformation of the universe by Christ and in the study of the last things. Eschatology has become in many ways the storm center of theology today, with new theories on the meaning of death, of the relationship of man after death to the cosmos, etc.

Sacramental theology has seen challenging and often controversial development. The "mystery-theory," the theology of encounter, the role of symbol, the insistence upon the sacraments as actions, have had a great influence not only in speculative thought but in the contemporary development of the liturgy.

Obviously, not all of these questions could be covered in one book. Yet a surprising number of these new orientations are visible in the selections incorporated here, and in every case these questions are treated with a remarkable clarity and competence. It is a pleasure to present so many distinguished thinkers in one volume, and to be able to present so broad a spectrum of contemporary theological opinion.

A special word of thanks is due to the Reverend Gerald Van Ackeren, S.J., President of the Catholic Theological Association of America and Dean of St. Mary's College, St. Mary's, Kansas. As Editor of *Theology Digest,* Father Van Ackeren graciously gave permission for the use of a number of the selections in this volume. Because of the compactness of these excellent digests, many topics have been incorporated which could not otherwise have been dealt with. We wish also to express our appreciation to the authors for their generous cooperation and to the editors of the various reviews who permitted reprinting of articles.

A THEOLOGY READER

1 Literary Genres in the Bible*

PIERRE LOBEZ

God Himself speaks to us in His Scriptures, but He does so through the sacred writers. This means that His word comes to us clothed in the concepts and styles of these writers. By treating the Bible as though it were all scientific history, many have concluded that it contains historical errors. However, modern research into oriental languages and history enables the scholar to determine which of the literary forms peculiar to their time and place the sacred writers used. Knowledge of the form in turn helps the scholar to evaluate the content.

IN MODERN TIMES literary genres go by such names as novel, play, essay, short story, poetry. They are simply the various forms of literature used by writers to make known their ideas.

Literary genres existed in biblical times, too; and a current theory of interpreting the Bible gives them a place of fundamental importance. In fact, not only the scripture scholar but also the ordinary reader must have some acquaintance with literary genres if he is to understand at all what is happening in the study of the Bible today.

While it is true that God is the principal author of the Bible, still He made use of human authors; and they have left their personal mark on their work. Being human, they were naturally influenced by their secular contemporaries. Hence, if we want to understand fully what the inspired writers wrote we must understand the ways or genres in which their secular contemporaries wrote.

A NEW APPROACH

Although both St. Jerome and St. Thomas refer to literary genres, actually the question has been studied only during the past half century. New advances in ancient history and related fields began to pose many problems, and Catholic scholars attempted to

---

* "Les 'Genres litteraires' dans la Bible," *L'Ami du Clergé,* October 27, 1955.

offer solutions. Cardinal Newman's theory of "remarks made in passing" and Monsignor d'Hulst's false distinction between "inspiration" and "inerrancy" were two such early attempts.

A fundamental principle was laid down by Leo XIII, who stressed the absolute inerrancy of all the parts of Scripture in his encyclical *Providentissimus Deus*. After Leo XIII had spoken there was no more mention of "biblical errors," but instead such expressions as "relative truth," "Bible legends," "popular traditions," began to be used. Modernism was in full sway, and the authority of the Church had to step in. Pius X saved the Church from danger by promulgating rules of interpretation which necessarily restricted the liberty of Scripture scholars, and the Biblical Commission began to hand down decrees to correct the mistakes made by some writers.

FURTHER ATTEMPTS AT SOLUTIONS

Father Prat, S.J., proposed the theory of "implicit quotations" from non-inspired authors to account for apparent errors in the Bible. The Biblical Commission replied that such a solution could be employed only in exceptional cases. Father Hummelauer, S.J., proposed a theory of "narratives historical only in appearance." This theory was not entirely false, but in substance it was rejected by the Biblical Commission.

Later attempts gave rise to the theory of literary genres. The theory was made possible by the study of the ancient literatures of the Near East. Its basic principle is that "the type of truth and the degree of truth of a book depend mainly on the end envisioned by the writer, and this end can usually be determined by the literary genre adopted."

The first Catholic scholars who seem to have treated the subject were Fathers Hummelauer and Prat and M.-J. Lagrange, O.P.

LIST OF GENRES

According to Father Hummelauer, many literary genres can be recognized in the Bible:

(1) The *fable* is a fictional account to illustrate a teaching (e.g., Jud. 9:8-15).

(2) The *parable* is a type of teaching sufficiently known from the gospel, differing from the fable by being realistic.

(3) In *epic history* the writer begins from an historical foundation, but to dress up his account he thinks up new characters and more or less adapts events to his purpose (e.g., the description of the plagues of Egypt in Wisd. 16-19).

(4) In *religious history* the writer intends to edify and chooses for this end whatever historical facts are pertinent, not hesitating to modify the words and deeds of his characters to obtain a better result.

(5) *Ancient history* is true history, but conceived according to the manner of antiquity, in which little care was taken to make a critical examination. Modern historical method aims at exactness in everything, while ancient historical writing involved much more freedom.

(6) *Popular tradition* consists in a core of historical truth about which have accumulated traces of legends. The first eleven chapters of Genesis seem to belong to this genre. In 1909 the Biblical Commission pointed out a certain number of details in these chapters which must be held as historical, though it admitted that not everything need be taken in a literal sense and that one should not look for specific precision. In its *Letter to Cardinal Suhard* in 1948 the Commission further admitted that not all the problems raised by these chapters can be solved at the present time.

(7) In a *free account* or *romance* the author selects certain historical facts and adds a fictional account to help him. Cardinal Wiseman's *Fabiola* is a modern example. The books of Tobias, Judith, and Esther have been placed in this genre by some Catholic scholars.

(8) The *midrash haggada* is a moral instruction based on facts of biblical history, with the account more or less approximating the historical facts. According to some, this is the genre of Paralipomenon and of Daniel, 1-6.

(9) *Poetry.* Poets have traditionally enjoyed a certain freedom, and people realize that one should not look to them for historical exactness. In the Bible there is *lyric poetry* (in which the poet sets forth his inmost feelings, as in many of the Psalms) and *didactic*

poetry (which has teaching in view—Proverbs and Ecclesiastes, for example).

(10) *Prophecy.* The proverbial obscurity of the prophets arises from such causes as the use of poetry and imagery from contemporary life. In revealing the future they give vague descriptions which permit events to be recognized only after they occur. Above all, they lack "perspective": events which are distant and events which are close at hand seem on the same scale. It is this use of language without perspective which Our Lord used in His discourse on the destruction of Jerusalem and the end of the world (Matt. 24 f.).

(11) *Apocalyptic writings.* The general idea of this difficult genre is that in the course of (or following on) a revelation, the author touches on various subjects and especially on things future and eschatological. The main signs of this genre are pseudonym, symbolism in imagery, symbolism in the use of numbers, and vague language. Apocalyptic writing can be found in Isaiah (24-26); Ezechiel (37-39); Daniel (7-12); Joel; Zacharias (9-14); Matthew (24); Apocalypse of St. John.

(12) *Mythology* may be added to the list if the term is correctly understood as referring to a familiar way of speaking about things that are true, though it is probably better to drop the term altogether. On the other hand, there is no reason why the inspired writers could not make reference to myths, provided they did not maintain that they were true.

DETERMINING GENRES

This catalogue can be quite useful, but one must not forget the remark of Pius XII in *Divino Afflante Spiritu* that literary genres can be determined only after careful study of the ancient literatures of the East.

The entire contents of a book need not belong to the same literary genre. There are apocalyptic sections in the Prophets, historical books, and Gospels. There is poetry in Exodus (15:1-18) and Isaias (5:12; 12:1-6, etc.). Unanimity among scripture scholars is a good indication of the genre of a given passage, though the final word, of course, belongs to the Church.

What does the Church think of genres? *Providentissimus Deus* (1893) makes no mention of them. A reply of the Biblical Commission in 1905 was cautious in allowing the possibility of their existence. Benedict XV in *Spiritus Paraclitus* recognizes the legitimacy of the principle of literary genres, but condemns those which are incompatible with divine speech.

PIUS XII ON GENRES

Pius XII in *Divino Afflante Spiritu* gives unequivocal approval to literary genres provided they conflict in no way with the "sanctity or veracity of God." He not only authorizes research in the genres but says:

. . . let the Catholic scripture scholar make prudent use of this aid [literary genres]. Let him try to discover how . . . the literary genre . . . can result in a true and precise interpretation. He should be convinced that he cannot neglect this part of his work without great harm to Catholic scriptural study.

In 1948 the Biblical Commission addressed a *Letter to Cardinal Suhard* on the first eleven chapters of Genesis. The letter assures scripture scholars of the most complete freedom within the limits of the teaching of the Church, calls for the interpretation of its earlier decrees in the light of *Divino Afflante Spiritu,* and ends by encouraging the study of literary genres.

FREEDOM OF SCHOLARS TODAY

In *Humani Generis* (1950), Pius XII warned of a tendency to place popularized accounts on the same level with mythologies, but despite this warning it is clear that today's scholars enjoy much more freedom than their predecessors. This is easily explained by the change in circumstances, for in a very real sense biblical questions today breathe in an atmosphere much more serene than formerly. Most non-Catholics have abandoned extreme positions; and the Church, for its part, freed from the danger of Modernism, is able to allow her scholars more freedom in using the findings of modern studies.

According to Pius XII, only those literary genres must be excluded from Scripture which are "incompatible with the sanctity or veracity of God." Incompatible with God's sanctity would be erotic poetry, although powerful descriptions of human love, such as the Canticle of Canticles and the twenty-third chapter of Ezechiel are "not unworthy of the Holy Spirit." Myth is obviously against the veracity of God, but in the case of other genres the question is more involved.

"TRUTH" IN SCRIPTURE

The difficulty comes from the definition of "truth." The peoples of the ancient East neither thought nor expressed themselves exactly as we do. "One must study at close hand . . . their very concept of historical truth," as the *Letter to Cardinal Suhard* puts it.

One must look to see what the human author intended to express in his words, for truth is found in them in the sense which their author intended to give them. Thus the axiom: "each literary genre has its proper type of truth."

According to St. Thomas, truth is a "correspondence of reality and intellect" found only in the formal judgment. The mind considers its object only under a particular aspect; hence an initial qualification, *from the standpoint of the object known.* For this reason the Bible is not a book of astronomy.

On the other hand, the mind does not always affirm things with the same degree of certainty; hence a second qualification, *from the standpoint of the knowing subject.*

The author can also adopt an artificial manner of speaking with the intention of not being taken literally. These are the fictional genres.

Thus all the different qualifications of truth are carefully indicated by the choice of literary genre made by the author.

IDENTIFYING GENRES

Generally speaking, the literary genre cannot be indicated in an a priori manner but only scientifically by persistent philological study and by minute comparison with other books, sacred and profane.

Comparison with the other sacred books suggests itself at once. This is the "Method of Parallelism" recently proposed by Robert and adopted by Feuillet. This method is based on the fact that later books of the Bible frequently quote earlier books, or at least make allusions to them. When these parallelisms abound one can be guided by this agreement in deciding the literary genre of the more recent work.

Comparison with profane works is particularly necessary for the historical books in general and more especially for the accounts of the "beginning," since we have no other sacred books which relate the same events.

EXAMPLES

The following are examples of solutions to problems of biblical exegesis made with the theory of literary genres:

(1) *Accounts about the beginning of the world and of man.* According to Roland de Vaux, O.P., the first eleven chapters of Genesis give a popularized account of the beginning of the human race. Similar accounts can be traced in neighboring peoples and ultimately back to the traditions of Upper Mesopotamia, the place from which Abraham set out. The history of the patriarchs is a popularized history of a family and often neglects what seems essential to a modern historian. It is a religious history and facts are introduced to make a religious point. But the accounts are historical in the sense that they tell of real events.

(2) In general, the *Mosaic Legislation* must be placed in parallel with the legislative codes of the East. Deuteronomy must be compared with earlier books such as Exodus. The editor of Deuteronomy is not merely a legislator who makes an abstract promulgation; he is a preacher who exhorts his hearers to observe the Law.

(3) The book of Josue contains the famous difficulty about the stopping of the sun above Gabaon (Jos. 10:12-14). One simple solution is that there are two accounts: one in prose (10:7-11) describing a storm coming up miraculously and blotting out the sky with a violent fall of hail; the other in poetry (10:12-14) drawn from the "Book of the Just."

(4) The books of Paralipomenon are so recent that they are often said to belong to the genre of *midrash haggada*. The author uses secular documents and whole chapters from Kings. With great freedom, he fits the borrowed texts to the demands of his theme

(the justification of the liturgical customs of his day). An analogous situation is the "rabbinical" argumentation of St. Paul (e.g., Rom. 10:18; 2 Cor. 3:7-28; Ephes. 4:8, etc.).

(5) Among the didactic books the Canticle of Canticles is regarded as one of the most difficult. It has been classified in many genres. Robert and Feuillet have recently described it as an allegory. Using parallelism, they show that most of the images and expressions are found in earlier books, especially the Prophets. The bridegroom and bride do not signify human beings, but Yahweh and His people. Human love is allegorically described to represent the infinitely deeper divine love.

(6) Present exegesis inclines more and more to regard the book of Jonas as a piece of didactic fiction. The main reasons are the number of improbabilities and the silence in both biblical and secular history on the sudden conversion of a city of such importance as Nineveh. The author might well have (1) borrowed the name of his heroes from IV Kings 14:25; (2) drawn his teaching from Jeremias and Ezechiel; (3) used his account to show that God does not make good His threats when sinners repent.

CONCLUSION

In *Divino Afflante Spiritu* Pius XII requests that scripture scholars who devote themselves to settling difficult questions be judged with fairness, justice, and charity. And he asks that the other sons of the Church be on the watch "against that zeal—anything but prudent—which thinks it must attack or hold in suspicion everything that is new." Not every difficulty in the Bible can be solved by the theory of literary genres; but, as the Sovereign Pontiff goes on to say, "Thanks to the knowledge and the true appreciation of the manners and ways of speaking and writing among the men of antiquity, many of the objections raised against the truth and the historical value of these Divine Pages can be answered."

2 The Conception of Our Gospels as Salvation History

DAVID MICHAEL STANLEY

The search for the "historical Jesus" has given way to a deeper analysis of the specific literary genre represented by our Gospels.

For some time now it has been evident that in the domain of Catholic biblical studies a new breeze has been blowing. "The breeze blows wherever it pleases," St. John informs us; and the breeze, which for well over a decade has begun to spring up to revivify Catholic scholarly endeavor, has been felt in almost every branch of scriptural research. Biblical inspiration and inerrancy,[1] the Mosaic authorship of the Pentateuch,[2] the "prehistory" of the first eleven chapters of Genesis,[3] all these questions have been given quite new solutions. Among the problems that have undergone a reorientation in New Testament studies, that of the historical character of the Gospels[4] has enjoyed a certain preeminence. Catholic exegetes now appear to be permitted to voice opinions upon this subject which fifty, even twenty-five, years ago would have caused considerable concern, if not condemnation.

While the professional student of Scripture rejoices at the new impetus thus given his work through the present day liberal attitude of the magisterium,[5] he is also conscious that, on the part of some within the Church, there has already been a reaction to many of the views he now feels free to express. He would be foolish indeed to ignore the fact that a certain malaise has manifested itself on the part of some theologians. They are not so sure as their biblical colleagues that the effects of the twentieth-century scriptural renaissance can be called progress. There are undoubtedly some who feel, even though perhaps they do not express their fears too openly,[6] that the old ghost of Modernism, which Pius X was thought to have laid within the household of the faith, has staged a reappearance, this time as a poltergeist.

And nowhere, I believe, is this uneasiness so strongly felt as it is with regard to the exegetes' new conception of what has always been known as the "historicity" of the Gospels. Even some of those who have come to recognize the validity of certain principles of Form-Criticism, let us say, when they are applied to the Old Testament books, can scarcely repress a shudder when these same principles are allowed to operate in the study of the Gospels. The truth is, of course, that if these principles have real, universal validity, then it ought to be not only possible but necessary to apply them (due regard being had for the variety that obtains in biblical historical narrative) no less in the New than in the Old Testament.

Let me say at once, on the other hand, that there is some reasonableness in this somewhat conservative reaction we are speaking of. It is only too obvious, for instance, that between the antiquity and folkloric character of many oral traditions incorporated in the Old Testament and the relatively short lived and well substantiated oral traditions forming the basis of the written Gospels, there is a vast and easily discernible difference. Anyone can surely see that there were no human eyewitnesses to the creation. By contrast, the Evangelists could have found a not inconsiderable number of serious-minded, sincere men to testify to the sayings and doings of Jesus of Nazareth.[7]

We do not wish to minimize this attitude of reserve which, though rarely vocal, is certainly present in some Catholic minds. It is based really upon a fear that, because certain long established props have been pulled out from under the structure of Catholic apologetics by the new methods, the whole edifice is in danger of collapse. I find no difficulty in granting that such a fear (undoubtedly unfounded, as I believe) has been partly caused by a few of the Catholic exegetes themselves. It is most regrettable that occasionally the scripture scholar has, in the exuberance of experiencing his new found freedom, displayed an entirely too negative attitude in approaching the question of the Gospels' historical character.[8] I do not mean merely that some scholars have succumbed to the temptation to play the *enfant terrible,* shocking the genuine, if ill-informed, piety of earnest Christians. I refer rather to the iconoclastic tendency occasionally displayed by biblical experts to devote themselves to the demolition of outmoded solutions to scriptural difficulties without sufficiently calling attention to the positive values found in the explanations which they seek to substitute for them. Not all New Testament critics have shouldered their new responsibility of developing a much needed New Testament biblical theology.

FUNDAMENTALISM

Still, granting that the new Catholic approach to Gospel criticism has not always been conducted with the delicacy and prudence it requires,[9] we must admit that the causes for the opposition to it cannot be laid entirely at the exegetes' door. A factor which we cannot afford to overlook is an attitude which, though characteristically Protestant, has influenced the thinking of not a few Catholics: I mean, of course, biblical fundamentalism. Fundamentalism's adherents have been chiefly found amongst certain non-Catholic sects, for the very good reason that Bible reading has been more commonly practiced by them than by Catholics. In addition, the fundamentalist viewpoint has developed partly as a corollary of the Protestant dogma of "private interpretation," partly as a repudiation by sincere (and too often uneducated) Christians of that "historicism" to which nineteenth-century Protestant rationalism lent its patronage. Historicism which, applied to the Gospels, was known as the "quest of the historical Jesus," never won any support in Catholic scholarship.[10]

Can we define fundamentalism?[11] Essentially, it consists of a conscious and deliberate "literal-mindedness"[12] in accepting the affirmations of biblical writers without regard to the idiom, the context, or the literary form through which they are expressed. Fundamentalism is, in fact, a misguided determination to cling to a superficial meaning of the Bible at all costs—even the cost of real understanding. A form of anti-intellectualism, it is quite out of harmony with that spirit of religious inquiry (*fides quaerens intellectum*) which the Catholic Church has always sought to encourage in the faithful, and which is the ideal and the guiding principle of Catholic theology.

One pernicious effect of the fundamentalist mentality is to expose the Scriptures to serious misunderstanding and even ridicule by those who do not possess Christian faith. It can, moreover, create a harmful dichotomy between faith and reason among Christians in whom a well developed literary or scientific education is combined with religious instruction that is uncritical and intellectually deficient.[13] Indeed, fundamentalism has been known to lead to a kind of "illuminism." I am thinking of the injudicious attack by an Italian priest, Dolindo Ruotolo, made in 1941 upon Catholic biblical scholarship through a pamphlet that had to be censured by the Biblical Commission.[14] Ruotolo (or "Dain Cohenel," as he signed himself) advocated, for a proper comprehension of the Bible, giving free rein to the Spirit, "as though" (to cite the Church's condemnation of his ideas) "all were in personal communion with the divine Wisdom and received from the Holy Spirit special personal illumination. . . ."[15]

DIVINO AFFLANTE SPIRITU

In his Encyclical of 1943, *Divino Afflante Spiritu,* Pope Pius XII "unequivocally repudiated fundamentalism in Catholic exegesis."[16] This statement of John L. McKenzie, S.J., requires some amplification, since the fundamentalist attitude had, over a long period, become fairly firmly entrenched in Catholic thinking, particularly as regards the Gospels. It may, then, not be out of place here to recall briefly those directives of Pius XII which can provide norms for the desirable, indeed necessary, Catholic approach to Gospel studies.

Pius lays down two principles of paramount importance, which run directly counter to the fundamentalist position: (1) "the supreme law of interpretation is that by which we discover and determine what the writer meant to say";[17] (2) there are only very few texts of the Bible "whose meaning has been declared by the Church's authority, nor are those more numerous about which there is a unanimous opinion of the holy Fathers."[18] It may be helpful to examine the scope of these two norms, which are applicable to the study of the Gospels, in greater detail.

How does one, according to Pius XII, determine the sacred writer's meaning? It is, in the first place, by discerning "the distinctive genius of the sacred writer."[19] The papal insistence upon the human character of the Bible is noteworthy.[20] The Encyclical makes it very clear that belief in God's primary authorship of the sacred books must not be misunderstood, so that, for example, we attempt implausible "harmonizations" of various Gospel accounts of the same episode, forcing them to agree where they actually differ in detail.[21] The proper method, we are told, entails careful research into the inspired author's background and culture, as well as his manner of writing (sources used, literary forms employed). We must not allow ourselves to overlook the profound differences separating our modern Occidental point of view from that of the ancient Near East. "Frequently the literal sense" of the biblical writer, the Pope warns, "is not so obvious" to us today.[22] Consequently, to grasp the author's meaning the rules of grammar and philology are not always sufficient. We must invoke the aid of history, archeology, ethnology,[23] and even psychology.[24] Most important of all, we must study the types of literature which have survived in Near Eastern literary remains of all kinds, in order to master the modes of expression through which the sacred writers set down "what they had in mind."[25]

As regards the variety of historical writing to be found in the Bible, the interpreter must constantly bear in mind "the special purpose, the religious purpose, of biblical history."[26] We shall return to a consideration of this remark when we discuss the special character of the Gospels as salvation-history.

Speaking more generally of the great richness of biblical literary forms, Pius XII states that "the sacred books need not exclude any of the ancient Near Eastern forms of expression in human language, provided they are compatible with the divine sanctity and veracity."[27] Thus that ingenuous a priorism habitually found in the fundamentalist interpretation of the Bible is effectively ruled out. The exegete "must ask himself how far this form of expression or literary genre employed by the sacred writer may contribute to the true and genuine interpretation."[28]

The second basic principle of Catholic hermeneutics, viz., that only a tiny sector of the many affirmations in the Bible has received any authoritative interpretation, has been called "perhaps the most important statement of the encyclical."[29] The Pope asserts that the Catholic exegete must be given full liberty in his search for solutions to "many important questions"[30] which admit free discussion within the limits of orthodoxy. Not infrequently we meet the tendency on the part of some Catholics to cling doggedly to what they consider to be the "traditional" explanation of a scriptural passage.[31] They sincerely feel that in this way they are being most orthodox, when in point of fact there is no such tradition, I mean, theologically significant tradition, existing.[32]

Another point clarified by this papal directive is the concept of "private interpretation." Provided it does not conflict with Catholic doctrine, any explanation of the great bulk of scriptural texts is as good or bad as the reasons given for it, and this holds good equally for the majority of the patristic opinions or those given by theologians, however ancient, as for the suggestions of modern exegetes. Indeed, today's biblical scholar may quite conceivably provide a far more satisfactory explanation of a scriptural difficulty than his predecessors.[33] Moreover, he is, through this Encyclical, invited to attempt to do so; nor is the term "new" to be used by those who differ as though it were a stigma.[34]

With the insight provided by these hermeneutical norms, we must now examine what is meant by the historical character of our Gospels.

HISTORICAL CHARACTER OF THE GOSPEL NARRATIVES

The modern concept of history goes back ultimately to the Greeks,[35] who classed it among the arts under the patronage of the muse Clio. In our day, inasmuch as it is the product of the historical method, history is classed as a social science. However, the writing of history remains an art, involving as it inevitably does the selection and interpretation and expression in some literary form of the "remembered past."[36] More basically, history in the modern sense is to be identified with the ancient Greeks' view of it because the intelligibility sought by the contemporary as by the classical historian is a *human* intelligibility. Both share the conviction that there is a pattern discernible in the events of the past which sprang ultimately from the mind of man, a pattern, consequently, which is recoverable by the application of the historical method (a process invented by the mind of man) and which can be represented by the art of historical writing.

"Historical writing," says C. H. Dodd, "is not merely a record of occurrences as such. It is, at least implicitly, a record of the interest and meaning they bore for those who took part in them, or were affected by them. . . ."[37] And he concludes: "Thus the events which make up history are relative to the human mind which is active in those events."[38] Dodd then defines history "as consisting of events which are of the nature of occurrences *plus* meaning."[39]

If we accept Dodd's definition it becomes clear that the task of selecting and interpreting the facts to be chronicled is an essential part of the historian's function. While the exercise of these two will vary according as he writes cultural, political, or economic history, the historian must choose and he must interpret. Assuming, for instance, it were possible to film a battle completely, such a newsreel record would not be history but only a source for history.

Selection and interpretation of course presuppose some criterion of judgment. The very choice of sources will be governed by the type of history to be written. The political historian will find much of his data in government archives; the cultural historian discovers valuable material in folklore, local customs, family traditions, even legends.[40] The historian's work will ultimately be judged by the correctness of his interpretation of the evidence he has unearthed. In some instances he will be led to highlight an event which in itself, or at the time of its occurrence, may have been almost insignificant. Thus the historian of the Counter Reformation will direct attention to the battle of Pamplona, a tiny incident in a series of border skirmishes, because an impoverished Basque nobleman, Iñigo de Loyola, there received the wound which led to his "conversion" and eventually to the founding of the Society of Jesus.

But before he selects and interprets the events about which he intends to write, the historian must satisfy himself as to their situation in space and time. "When" and "where" are two of the historian's most elementary queries. John L. McKenzie has called chronology and geography "the eyes of history." "If," he adds, "the modern historian cannot tell you when and where something happened, he will not call it a historical event, although he does not thereby deny that it happened."[41] To anticipate our discussion of the historical nature of the Gospels, we wish to state at once that the Evangelists show a strongly marked tendency to dissociate most of the episodes constituting Jesus' public life which they record, from both time and place. While the significance of this phenomenon will appear later in this essay, it must be noted here as one indication of the distance which separates the Gospels from modern historical writing. The Evangelists' lack of interest in the specific geographical or chronological settings of many of their narratives unquestionably sets a limitation upon our attempts to prove these events "historical" in the modern sense.[42] Jesus' earthly life, to be sure, is located in Palestine; His birth occurred "in diebus regis Herodis," his death "sub Pontio Pilato"; the dates of both events are known only approximately. As for His public ministry, the impression given by the Synoptic Gospels is that it lasted about six months.

What, then, is the biblical conception of history, and how do our Gospels differ from "history" in the modern acceptation of the word? The biblical notion of history rests upon the belief that God has, in the past, revealed Himself in a special way within the cadre of human affairs.[43] Through specific events, personalities, and human utterances, God has intervened in the world of man. From this point of view, it is clear that the intelligibility to be seen in the biblical narratives is essentially that of a divine, not a human, pattern.[44] It is best described as "a Mystery," in the Pauline[45] (and Johannine[46]) sense, viz., as God's revelation, in time, to men of His eternal plan for the world's salvation. This Mystery was disclosed to mankind in two stages: one incomplete and rudimentary to God's chosen people in the Old Testament; the second, complete and definitive through His only Son, Jesus Christ, to the Church of the New Testament. This genre of history, which we call salvation-history or *Heilsgeschichte*, is the story of God's self-revelation to us; and its aim is obviously very different from that modern scientific history which is written without reference to the divine point of view.

Here, in fact, we have touched upon one of the profound differences between the *Weltanschauung* of modern man, the product of a distinctively Greek culture, and the ancient Semitic mentality. Where we moderns habitually discuss the meaning of happenings in terms of secondary or finite causality, the Semitic genius interested itself principally in God, the First Cause of all things. The attitude may strike us as somewhat naïve. How many priests, for instance, after smiling indulgently at the explanation, offered by Psalm 28, of the thunderstorm as the "Voice of Yahweh," turn to the newspaper or television broadcast for an analysis of the weather? They find, we must admit, that the meteorologists' pronunciamentos, couched in mythological terms of "high- and low-pressure areas," are eminently more satisfying than the insight of the Psalmist. Yet if, as the priest surely believes, God causes the weather as He causes everything else, which explanation touches the reality more profoundly? The example illustrates, at any rate, the radical difference between the two viewpoints.[47]

The Evangelists propose in their written accounts of Jesus' life upon earth to give their readers not merely an exposition based upon ocular testimony. They aim at writing salvation history. They offer an insight into the meaning of the Mystery of Jesus Christ, i.e., they disclose to the reader (in whom they presuppose Christian faith) something which cannot be seen with the eye or perceived by the ear: the *propter nos et propter nostram salutem*.[48] And this, we should not forget, is their primary intention. They claim to be not only eyewitnesses, but witnesses to the Good News of salvation, since their message like the rest of the Bible is addressed not simply to man's intellect for his information, but to the whole man for his salvation.

The twofold nature of this apostolic testimony to Jesus Christ is already consciously present in Peter's sermon to Cornelius' household at Caesarea (Acts 10:34–43).[49] The apostolic preachers are, in the first place, "witnesses of all He [Jesus] did in the country of the Jews and Jerusalem" (v. 38), or "witnesses appointed beforehand by God, who ate and drank with Him after His resurrection from death" (v. 41). But they have the office of witnessing in a deeper, more important sense, because they have received a mandate from the risen Lord "to preach to the people and to bear witness that He is the Judge of living and dead, constituted by God and Father" (v. 42).

This same double purpose is manifest in our written Gospels. Mark, whose account reflects perhaps more strikingly than any other Gospel the influence of an observant eyewitness[50] has entitled his book "the Good News of Jesus Christ, Son of God" (Mark 1:1).[51] This intention of providing us with a profounder realization of Christ's divinity, with a grasp of a supernatural truth which does not fall under the observation of the senses, implies something more than ocular testimony. Even Luke, whose prologue reveals a spirit not unacquainted with "historical method," manifests to his aristocratic convert, Theophilus, his aim of writing salvation-history. True, he has "investigated it all carefully from the beginning"; he has "decided to write a connected account of it." But both the thorough examination of his sources and the ordering of his narrative have been carried out "in order that you may more clearly grasp the authentic character of the oral instructions you have received" (Luke 1:4). The term we have translated as "the authentic character" (*asphaleia*) meant "security" in the contemporary commercial and military usage.[52] Since he is writing for a man who is already a believer, Luke aims at more than establishing the historical character of the events and sayings he records. He means to interpret their Christological significance, as indeed the whole of his two-volume work reveals.[53] The author of the fourth Gospel declares as he reaches the conclusion of his book that "these things have been written in order that you may persevere in your belief[54] that Jesus is the Messias, the son of God, and that persevering in this belief you may possess life in His Name" (John 20:31). John has, in the scene he has just described between the doubter Thomas and the risen Lord, brought out clearly the relative value of eyewitness experience and the intelligibility apprehended by Christian faith. It is obvious from Christ's insistence that Thomas touch Him and so have the reality of his Lord's risen Body impinge upon his senses, that there can be no doubt of the necessity for eyewitness testimony. But Jesus also points out to His disciple that belief implies much more than mere seeing with bodily eyes: "Is it because you have seen me that you have believed?" Faith belongs to a higher order, providing the superior perceptiveness expressed in Thomas' "My Lord and my God." Accordingly, Jesus pronounces a new beatitude upon all future generations of Christians: "Happy those who, though they did not see, yet become believers" (John 20:28–29). In the eyes of the Evangelist we of a later age are at no disadvantage in comparison with the disciples who saw and heard Jesus: we possess the *unum necessarium,* that perception of the salvific character of Jesus' earthly life through Christian faith which, if it reposes upon the Apostles' eyewitness testimony, grasps quite as accurately as they the supernatural meaning of that life, which is beyond the reach of mere historical investigation.

How do the Evangelists convey this "fourth-dimensional" quality of the salvation history they write? We can only find the answer to this question (1) by appreciating the very personal manner in which each of the Evangelists has conceived the Good News of salvation in Jesus Christ (2) by investigating how he employs the various kinds of materials that have gone into the making of his book, and finally (3) by determining the manifold literary genera[55] through which he has expressed what he wishes to tell us.

Before attempting to illustrate our answers to these three aspects of the problem by concrete examples, we wish to make several observations of a general nature. First, it must be evident that to treat these questions thoroughly demands exact and detailed literary and historical analysis which would be out of place here. Secondly, we must not allow ourselves to forget that there is no rule-of-thumb solution to the question of the Gospels' historicity: each narrative must be examined for itself and for the problem it presents. Thirdly, if we are to avoid the fundamentalist mentality, we must be on our guard against the superficial conclusion that, because one is forced to admit that certain details in an Evangelist's narrative (or even its general framework) are due to the literary form used or to his specific purpose, the whole story has been invented. Such a "black-or-white" attitude is simply due to the failure of a modern Occidental mind to comprehend the Semitic view evinced by the Evangelist. Finally, it will not infrequently happen that, after the most patient literary analysis, we cannot decide with any certainty "what actually happened,"[56] and we must content ourselves with such imprecision.[57]

"THE DISTINCTIVE GENIUS" OF OUR FOUR EVANGELISTS

The ancient titles which tradition has given the Gospels show that from a very early period the Christian Church was conscious that, while there is only one Gospel (*to euaggēlion*), still each of the four Evangelists has presented it according to his personal understanding (*kata Matthaion,* etc.) of it by means of those aspects of the person and mission of Jesus which struck him particularly. In fact, we may say that our four Evangelists present us with four different Christologies, if, as Oscar Cullmann has recently reminded us, we do not forget that this Christology is inseparable from the Christian *Heilsgeschichte*. Dr. Cullmann insists that "the question of Jesus in primitive Christianity was answered, not on the basis of a ready made myth, but of a series of real facts, which occurred during the first century of our era, facts which went unnoticed by the 'history-makers' of the time . . . but which, for all that, are no less historical: the life, mission, and death of Jesus of Nazareth. . . ."[58]

Such a Christological interpretation of the history of Jesus is seen already operative in the Marcan Gospel, in many respects the least artistically conceived of the four—adhering as it does so closely to the Petrine version of the primitive preaching.[59] Mark's principal theme is that the incarnate Son of God, Jesus Christ, has, in His public life, His death and resurrection, realized His vocation as the Servant of God. It is in terms of the Deutero-Isaian Suffering and Glorified *Ebed Yahweh* that Mark has couched the Gospel message. At Jesus' first appearance in his book, on the occasion of His baptism by John, the heavenly Voice proclaims Him Son of God who is also the Suffering Servant: "You are my beloved Son. In you I take delight" (Mark 1:11). The words contain an allusion to the first Servant Song (Isa. 42:1). Rightly called the Gospel of the Passion, Mark's book announces Jesus' death as early as the third chapter (Mark 3:6); and the passion-account occupies a proportionally large place in this shortest of the Gospels. The characteristically Marcan statement by Jesus of His life's work is expressed in terms of the Servant theme: "Why, even the Son of Man has come to act as a servant, not to be served, and to lay down His life as a ransom for all the rest of men" (Mark 10:45; cf. Isa. 53:5–8). Another echo of this theme is perceptible in the Transfiguration episode, which forms the literary center of Mark's Gospel:[60] "This is my beloved Son. Pay heed to Him" (Mark 9:7). Jesus' triple prophecy of His future passion is stated in terms of the Servant's mission.[61]

Since it is as *incarnate* Son that Jesus acts as the Servant on Mark's view, his narrative underscores the reality of Jesus' human nature to the point where the reader is almost disconcerted.[62] Jesus can become impatient, angry, sharp in His rebukes, sensitive to His hearers' reactions, surprised at the turn of events. Yet Mark presents undeniable evidence of Jesus' divinity, while admitting

implicitly that the reality of Jesus' adoption of the Servant's role
hid this profound truth during His public life from all, even His
chosen followers, until at His death even a pagan centurion could
be moved to confess, "This man was really God's Son!" (Mark
15:39).[63] The Christian reader, however, is provided with in-
controvertible testimony that Jesus is Son of God: in His forgiving
of sins (Mark 2:1–11), His assertion of authority over the Sabbath
(Mark 2:28), His control of even inanimate nature (Mark 4:35–
41). Thus the second Gospel gives us an unmistakable picture of
the Son of God who "despoiled Himself by taking on the Servant's
character" and "carried self-abasement, through obedience, right
up to death" (Phil. 2:7–8).

The conception of Jesus and His redemptive work which domi-
nates the Matthean Gospel is connected with the mystery of the
Church, in which the Evangelist sees realized God's dominion in
this world as the divine or "heavenly Kingdom." Emmanuel is
Matthew's characteristic title for Jesus—a name foretold by Isaiah
in his prediction of the virginal conception (Isa. 7:14) and explained at the outset of this Gospel as meaning "with us is God"
(Matt. 1:24). At the very close of his book, Matthew records the
promise of the glorified Christ upon His departure from this
world: "And remember, *I am with you* all the time until the end of
the world" (Matt. 28:20).[64] Matthew's version of Jesus' public
life is so constructed as to bring home to us the truth that, in His
Galilean ministry—particularly by His preaching[65]—Jesus has
begun to found that Church through which He will remain with us
until the end of time. Behind the immediate reality of five long
instructions, into which Matthew has grouped Jesus' sayings, we
are given a glimpse of the future Church. The sermon on the
mount (Matt. 5–7) is an expression of the Church's spirit and her
function; the missionary discourse (Matt. 10), particularly its second half, is a prophecy of the evangelizing activities of the Church
in the apostolic age (cf. Matt. 10:17–42);[65a] the instruction in
parables (Matt. 13) discloses the mystery of the Church, the
added explanations of the sower[65b] (Matt. 13:19–23) and of the
cockle (Matt. 13:36–43) reflecting the experience of the apostolic
Church; the community discourse (Matt. 18) prescribes the
mutual relations of the Church's members; and the prophetic description of the ruin of the Temple (Matt. 24–25) gives a preview
of the Church's ultimate liberation from Judaism as the necessary

consequence of Jesus' exaltation through His passion and resurrection.[65e] This Emmanuel-Christology is the fundamental significance for Matthew of the earthly life of Jesus Christ.

For Luke, Jesus is primarily the Saviour,[66] whose message of mercy and salvation provides the God-given answer to the religious aspirations of that Hellenistic world for which Luke writes. Luke sees all the events of Jesus' life as orientated towards Jerusalem, the scene of man's salvation.[67] The Lucan Infancy narratives revolve about Jerusalem and its Temple; and almost ten chapters of this book are devoted to Jesus' last journey to the Holy City (Luke 9:51—19:27). Arrived there, Luke insinuates, the disciples "tarry in the city" (Luke 24:49) until the coming of the Holy Spirit. There are no Galilean appearances of the risen Christ in Luke's story.

John's Gospel is markedly different in spirit and style, as in the episodes narrated, from the first three. John is absorbed in the contemplation of God's Son, the divine Word, or perfect expression of the Father, who becomes man to "interpret" to us the God whom "no man has ever seen" (John 1:18). It is most of all the sacramental quality of Jesus' actions during His public life which has impressed John: Christ speaks to us of God, not only by what He says, but even more forcibly by the symbolic character of His actions. His miracles are "signs" which have a supernatural meaning for the eyes and ears of faith. They are so many symbols of the Christian sacraments: of baptism, in the cure of the blind man, for instance (John 9:1–41), who washes in a pool bearing Christ's name, "the One sent" (John 9:7); of the Eucharist, in the multiplication of loaves (John 6:1–13).[68] John's message, in brief, directed as we have seen to those Christians who have believed without having seen Jesus upon earth, is that the glorified Christ, who lives on in the Church and in her sacraments, is the same Jesus of Nazareth whose "signs" to men revealed His unseen Father.

THE EVANGELISTS' USE OF THEIR SOURCES

An examination of how the Evangelists used the data about Jesus furnished them by tradition will reveal their utter fidelity to the reality of the sacred history, while employing considerable freedom in their expression of it. Thus, while Matthew and Luke present Jesus' temptations in the desert as a rejection of the false messianic ideal, Mark, who devotes but a single verse to the episode, portrays Jesus in the episode as the New Adam in the New Paradise.[69] The Lucan account of Jesus' visit to Nazareth, which is probably a synthesis of three visits, or of three distinct scenes connected with one visit, forms the solemn introduction to Jesus' public life in the third Gospel.[70] Again, Luke has assembled, in his well-developed travel-story of the last journey to Jerusalem (Luke 9:51—19:27), the bulk of the materials which his own independent research had unearthed.[71]

Characteristic of Matthew is his compressing of his narratives. He interests himself principally in highlighting their religious meaning without too much regard for details he considers insignificant.[72] Thus, the centurion seeking a cure for his sick "boy" comes in person to make his request (Matt. 8:5–13), while Luke's version shows that the petition was actually made through two groups of intermediaries without the centurion's appearing at all (Luke 7:1–10). This same Matthean tendency to abbreviation is seen operative in the story of the raising of Jairus' daughter,[73] as in the incident of the cursing of the fig tree.[74]

Not infrequently, we see an Evangelist assemble materials preserved in several distinct traditions and create a new literary unity out of them. John, for instance, presents in his first chapter a series of testimonies by the disciples, where we can discern a Christological rather than a simple historical purpose. By means of seven different titles given to Jesus (the Prophet, the Lamb of God, the Son of God, Rabbi, the Anointed, King of Israel, Son of Man), John sums up for us the disciples' conception of their master. At the same time, an examination of this passage shows that John here records much valuable data, viz., that Peter, Andrew, John, Nathanael, and Philip, even Jesus Himself, had originally been followers of the Baptist.[75] The synthetic character of this series of vignettes is, however, obvious from what the Synoptics, notably Mark, tell us of the disciples' slowness and difficulty in recognizing Jesus as the Messias.

THE EVANGELISTS' USE OF LITERARY FORMS

Considered as a whole, each of our Gospels belongs to a special literary form which arose from the oral form of the apostolic preaching. This kerygma was a proclamation to nonbelievers of

Jesus' work of universal redemption through His passion and resurrection, to which certain episodes and sayings from His public life
were added. The written Gospel, as we have seen, was, on the
contrary, meant for Christian readers to provide a more profound
understanding of the mysteries of the faith.[76] Like the preaching,
however, it attempts to express that reality which surpasses the
limits of our time-space world and its experiences. Indeed, it may
be said that the external historical events it records are subordinate
to the infinitely more important, less easily perceptible fact that
God has, in Jesus Christ, personally entered our human history.
The historical happenings recorded by the Gospels are not set
down solely (nor primarily) for the sake of the history they contain, but for their Christological signification. To assess fully the
evangelical *genus litterarium*, we must attend above all to the
dialogue between the inspired author and his Christian reader, that
witnessing to Christ which, as Paul characterizes it, is "from faith
to faith" (Rom. 1:17), which makes the Gospel "God's power
unto salvation for every believer" (Rom. 1:16). Only when this is
borne in mind can the historical character of the Gospels be rightly
evaluated.

Incorporated under this specific form, the Gospel form, which
we have called salvation history, we can discern many other literary forms which aid us in grasping the meaning of the Gospels'
historical character. At this point it may not be inopportune to
recall Pius XII's insistence upon the very wide variety of historical
literary forms found in the Bible, all perfectly consonant with the
divine veracity and dignity. To decide just how God should (or
should not) have transmitted His revelation to us, without first
putting ourselves to school to His inspired writers, is scarcely a
reverent approach to the scriptural Word. No sincere Christian
should attempt an apology for the divine choice of certain means
of God's self-revelation.

Let me put this another way. The problem posed by the presence of certain literary forms in our Gospels is in no sense to be
regarded as one of reconciling the "history" with the Christology.
Once we grant the supreme truth of the Incarnation with all its
consequences, the Christology *is* the history.[77]

Among the subordinate literary forms found in the gospel narratives, we might enumerate the genealogy,[78] the eyewitness ac-

count,[79] popular traditions,[80] family reminiscences,[81] externalized representations of interior experiences,[82] and finally the *midrash*.[83] With regard to sayings and sermons of Jesus, there are some logia which undoubtedly retain the form and idiom of the speaker.[84] But there are also discourses which the Evangelist himself has constructed from Jesus' sayings and sermons; and these can even be expressed (as in the fourth Gospel) in the author's own style and terminology. There are parables which in the course of oral tradition have undergone a certain historicization[85] or allegorization.[86] At times we find liturgical texts which enshrine pronouncements of Jesus dealing with the ritual or sacramental life of His future Church.[87]

While this list is by no means exhaustive, it exemplifies sufficiently the great variety of literary forms which our Gospels contain. In an essay that is already lengthy, there is room to discuss only one or two of these genres. However, a brief consideration of the genealogy and of the eyewitness account may serve to illustrate the statement of Pius XII, already referred to, that, prescinding from divine inspiration, the pre-eminence of the Israelites in historical writing lies in the *religious* character of the history they wrote.[88]

The age-old attempt to "reconcile" the genealogies of Jesus given by Matthew (Matt. 1:17) and by Luke (Luke 3:23-38), a celebrated *crux interpretum* since the patristic age, is largely the result of a failure to understand the nature of this important biblical *genus litterarium*.[89] Once it is recognized that these genealogical tables are deliberately incomplete[90] and that, moreover, it is impossible to corroborate or explain the variations in the names of Jesus' immediate ancestry, we are in a position to ask the real question: What religious message is expressed through this obviously artificial literary construction?

Luke, who uses the ascending order, tells us at the start that people thought Jesus was Joseph's son. In reality, however—and this is what Luke is attempting to convey—Jesus was the Son of God. Luke's use of the Greek genealogical phrase, "X who was of Y," permits him to employ the same expression for Adam's relationship to God as for Seth's relationship to Adam. Accordingly the theological significance of the whole structure becomes clear. Jesus, who is "of God" in a way infinitely superior to Adam, is the

New Adam whose redemptive act far surpasses in its universality Adam's sinful act and its effect upon the entire human race.

The chief purpose of the Matthean genealogy is to show the link between Jesus and the salvation history of His people. It descends from Abraham, and employs the biblical term "generated." Matthew can thus state that Jesus is that "seed of Abraham" (cf. Gal. 3:16) who inherits the divine promise made to that patriarch. He is, moreover, that member of the Davidic dynasty in whom the promise made to David (II Sam. 7:12 ff.) is realized. The extraordinary inclusion of four women in this family tree (Thamar, Rahab, Ruth, and Bethsabee, all probably of non-Jewish origin) reveals Matthew's interest in the salvation of the Gentiles.

Mark's Gospel abounds in narratives that clearly repose upon eyewitness testimony. Characteristic of such passages is their explicit reference to time and place, together with the vivid quality of their descriptive details. The story of twenty-four hours in Jesus' public life (Mark 1:21–39), that of the storm on the lake (Mark 4:35–41), or the feeding of the five thousand (Mark 6:34–44) are striking examples of eyewitness accounts. A brief but very graphic instance, which we quote here, depicts the reactions of the crowds who seek cures.

Because there was such a crowd, He told His disciples to have a rowboat ready for Him, to prevent their pushing up against Him. He had cured many, so all who had ailments kept thrusting themselves towards Him in order to touch Him. And the impure spirits, when they caught sight of Him, would fling themselves down at His feet and scream, "You are the Son of God!", while He kept ordering them vehemently not to reveal who He was (Mark 3:9–12).

As we read the passage, we receive the unmistakable impression of a report obtained at first hand. At the same time, this eyewitness is testifying to a supernatural reality which he knows by something more than the testimony of his senses: the divine mystery of Jesus' person. Thus we see that the Evangelists in their use of this type of material, no less than by those literary genres like the genealogy which are more artificially contrived, are engaged upon their predominating purpose, the record of the Good News about Jesus Christ, which is salvation history.

By way of conclusion, I should like to refer to an episode in the fourth Gospel which, I believe, illustrates in a striking way this conception of New Testament salvation history. I have in mind the scene in which a baffled Sanhedrin is resolving to put Jesus effectively out of the way. "If we permit Him to go on this way, everybody will find faith in Him. Besides the Romans will intervene and do away with both the Temple and the Nation" (John 11:48). To them in their quandary, Caiaphas, "as high priest of that year" (of the accomplishment of man's redemption), addresses an inspired pronouncement: "You have completely misunderstood the case. You do not realize that it is better that one man die for the people, and that the whole nation should not perish" (John 11:50). This remark is designated as "prophecy" by the sacred writer, not in the sense of a mere prediction of Jesus' approaching death, but in the sense of an utterance which voices the divine verdict about the nature of that death. On John's view, Caiaphas here becomes God's official spokesman. Accordingly the high priest gives expression (whether unwittingly or not, John does not tell us) to the *propter nos et propter nostram salutem*. The Evangelist's reflections upon the true significance of Caiaphas' words are of interest to our study, since they imply not only his own awareness as an inspired writer of the nature of salvation history, but also a conviction that, to deliver such a statement, a special divine charism is at work: "He did not say this on his own. But, as high priest of that year, he prophesied that Jesus was destined to die for the nation—indeed, not only for the nation, but that He might reunite God's dispersed children" (John 11:51–52).

NOTES

1. Among the recent studies on these subjects, the following are noteworthy: P. Synave and P. Benoit, *La prophétie* (*Somme théologique*, ed. Revue des Jeunes; Paris, 1947); P. Benoit, "L'Inspiration," in Robert-Tricot, *Initiation biblique* (3rd ed.; Paris, 1954), pp. 6–45; *idem*, "Note complémentaire sur l'inspiration," *Revue biblique* 63 (1956) 416–22; Karl Rahner, "Über die Schriftinspiration," *Zeitschrift für katholische Theologie* 78 (1956), 137–68; J. Coppens, "L'Inspiration et l'inerrance biblique," *Ephemerides theologicae Lovanienses* 33 (1957) 36–57; Johannes Schildenberger, *Vom Geheimnis des Gotteswortes: Einführung in das Verständnis der heiligen Schrift* (Heidel-

berg, 1950). I have attempted to review and evaluate the more significant contributions in a recent paper, "The Concept of Biblical Inspiration," in *Catholic Theological Society of America: Proceedings of the Thirteenth Annual Convention, 1958* (New York, 1959), pp. 65–89.

2. Bruce Vawter, *A Path through Genesis* (New York, 1956); R. de Vaux, *La Genèse (Bible de Jérusalem;* Paris, 1951).

3. Charles Hauret, *Origines de l'univers et de l'homme d'après la Bible* (2nd ed.; Paris, 1950); R. A. F. MacKenzie, "Before Abraham Was . . . ," *Catholic Biblical Quarterly* 15 (1953) 131–40.

4. These developments have been recently reviewed in a most effective way by B. Rigaux, "L'Historicité de Jésus devant l'exégèse récente," *Revue biblique* 65 (1958) 481–522.

5. John L. McKenzie, "Problems of Hermeneutics in Roman Catholic Exegesis," *Journal of Biblical Literature* 77 (1958) 197–204.

6. *Ibid.,* p. 198: "At the present writing, fifteen years after the publication of the encyclical [*Divino Afflante Spiritu*], opposition to creative biblical scholarship speaks only in whispers, and it no longer inhibits original work which goes beyond commonly accepted theological opinion."

7. That they actually did so has been convincingly demonstrated by C. H. Dodd, *History and the Gospel* (London, 1938), "The Historical Tradition in the New Testament," pp 41–74.

8. The most balanced and penetrating criticism of such a regrettable outlook has been made by a modern English scripture scholar: Thomas Worden, "Is Scripture to Remain the Cinderella of Catholic Theology?", *Scripture* 8 (1956) 2–12.

9. Prudence does not here mean a refuge in conservatism which borders upon obscurantism. The proper approach is well expressed by J. Cambier, "Historicité des évangiles synoptiques et Formgeschichte," *La formation des évangiles* (Bruges, 1957) p. 196:

L'importance, comme aussi la délicatesse du problème littéraire, obligent à une grande prudence. L'emploi judicieux et nuancé de cette méthode littéraire plus perfectionnée dans l'étude des évangiles synoptiques oblige à constater certaines libertés que les évangélistes ont prises avec l'histoire, au sens critique et moderne du mot. Nous pensons que, et pour une intelligence plus nuancée de l'histoire sacrée, et pour épargner une crise inutile de scepticisme à nos élèves de séminaires et aux chrétiens cultivés, il faut s'essayer à leur faire prendre une conscience plus nette du problème.

More recently, this same Catholic attitude has been expressed serenely by L. Alonso-Schökel, professor of the Pontifical Biblical Institute, in a trenchant review of an Old Testament Introduction whose author, to say the least, has not "moved with the times"; cf. *Biblica* 39 (1958) 502:

Cogitare videtur Auctor progressum solum vel praesertim in eo consistere debere, ut sententiae confirmentur, quae 'traditionales' ei vocare libet. Absque dubio persuasum habet, se sic fidelius Ecclesiae servire, securiorem doctrinam docere. Sed sententiae rigidiores non semper sunt securiores. Discipuli secundum spiritum huius voluminis formati, ministerium sacerdotale aggredientur muniti argumentis in illo exhibitis; ea fidelibus proponent, inter quos laici docti et intelligentes aderunt, qui cum audierint has sententias ob eiusmodi argumenta cum fide cohaerere, nonne et fides eorum in periculum adduci, vel saltem dubia in eis suscitari poterunt, quae facile evitari potuissent?

I might point out here that the commentaries in the *Bible de Jérusalem* series on St. Matthew and St. John, by P. Benoit and D. Mollat, are fine examples of modern Catholic work on the Gospels. To them apply most appositely the remarks of my colleague, R. A. F. MacKenzie, in a review in *Theological Studies* 14 (1953) 465 of several Old Testament fascicules in this same collection:

> These Catholic scholars, free of polemical preoccupations, are going about their own proper work, in the calm assurance that they are carrying on the centuries-old exegetical tradition of the Church, and that, in the light of faith, they can safely and profitably use modern discoveries, to achieve that fuller understanding of Sacred Scripture which the Holy See hopes and expects of them.

10. McKenzie, *art. cit.* (supra n. 5) p. 200: "The revolt against historicism and the demand for a biblical theology in the Protestant churches has had a parallel in the Catholic Church. Here there was no revolt against historicism, because there never had been any historicism against which to revolt. But there was a stout affirmation of the 'historical character' of the Bible without any attention whatever to the study of literary forms. The purely defensive and almost entirely controversial scholarship of the era of the siege mentality had by 1943 proved its sterility beyond all question."

11. John L. McKenzie, *The Two-Edged Sword* (Milwaukee, 1956) p. 105, defines it as "the crass literal interpretation of the Bible without regard for literary forms and literary background."

12. I say "conscious and deliberate," in order to exclude the simple faithful who, despite an unconsciously ingenuous attitude towards much in the Bible, do reach the real message of the sacred text.

13. Worden, *art. cit.* (supra n. 8) p. 7.

14. The pamphlet, entitled "Un gravissimo pericolo per la Chiesa e per le anime. Il sistema critico-scientifico nello studio e nell'interpretazione della Sacra Scrittura, le sue deviazioni funeste e le sue aberrazioni," was roundly condemned in a letter to the Italian hierarchy, August 20, 1941; *AAS* 33 (1941) 465–72. Its author was judged lacking in "judgment, prudence, and reverence."

15. ". . . quasi che ognuno fosse in personale communione con la divina Sapienza, e ricevesse dallo Spirito Santo speciali lumi individuali, come pretesero i primitivi protestanti."

16. McKenzie, *art. cit.* (supra n. 5) p. 198.

17. *AAS* 35 (1943) 314: "Neque enim quemquam latet summam interpretandi normam eam esse, qua perspiciatur et definiatur, quid scriptor dicere intenderit, ut egregie Sanctus Athanasius monet: 'Hic, ut in omnibus aliis divinae Scripturae locis agere convenit, observandum est, qua occasione locutus sit Apostolus, quae sit persona, quae res cuius gratia scripsit, accurate et fideliter attendendum est, ne quis illa ignorans, aut aliud praeter ea intellegens, a vera aberret sententia.'"

18. *Ibid.*, p. 319: "Illud enim imprimis ante oculos habeant, in normis ac legiblus ab Ecclesia datis, de fidei morumque doctrina agi; atque intermulta illa, quae in Sacris Libris, egalibus, historicis, sapientialibus et propheticis pro-

ponuntur, pauca tantum esse quorum sensus ab Ecclesiae auctoritate declaratus
sit, neque plura ea esse, de quibus unanimis Sanctorum Patrum sit sententia.
Multa igitur remanent, eaque gravissima, in quibus edisserendis et explanandis
catholicorum interpretum acumen et ingenium libere exerceri potest ac debet,
ut ad omnium utilitatem, ad maiorem in dies doctrinae sacrae profectum,
et ad Ecclesiae defensionem et honorem ex suo quisque viritim conferat."

19. *Ibid.*, p. 314: "Interpres igitur omni cum cura, ac nulla quam
recentiores pervestigationes attulerint luce neglecta, dispicere enitatur, quae
propria fuerit sacri scriptoris indoles ac vitae condicio, qua floruerit aetate,
quos fontes adhibuerit sive scriptos sive ore traditos, quibusque sit usus
formis dicendi. Sic enim satius cognoscere poterit quis hagiographus fuerit,
quidque scribendo significare voluerit."

20. The last citation makes this clear. Also to be noted in Pius XII's repeated emphasis upon the primacy of the *sensus litteralis*. The Encyclical
Humani generis added a further important nuance; see *AAS* 42 (1950) 569:

> Immo perperam loquutur de sensu humano Sacrorum Librorum sub quo
> sensus eorum divinus lateat, quem solum infallibilem declarant.

P. 570:

> Ac praeterea sensus literalis Sacrae Scripturae eiusque expositio a tot
> tantisque exegetis, vigilante Ecclesia, elaborata, ex commenticiis eorum
> placitis, novae cedere debent exegesi, quam symbolicam ac spiritualem
> appellant. . . .

Gustave Lambert remarked in his commentary on this Encyclical,
"L'Encyclique 'Humani Generis' et l'écriture sainte," *Nouvelle revue
théologique* 73 (1951) 226:

> L'Encyclique 'Divino afflante Spiritu' avait cependant insisté avec toute la
> clarté désirable sur le *seul sens qui se trouve partout dans l'Ecriture et*
> qui est *le sens littéral*. Ce sens littéral, qui est aussi *le sens théologique* des
> textes sacrés, est celui qui a été connu et voulu *conjointement* par l'auteur
> principal qui est Dieu et par la cause instrumentale (intelligente et libre) qui
> est l'hagiographe humain. . . . L'hagiographe, en écrivant à la manière
> humaine, a exprimé une pensée divine.

21. To quote but two examples: (1) While the Synoptics agree in placing
Jesus' cleansing of the Temple at the close of His public life, indeed in its
last week (Matt. 21:12–13; Mark 11:15–17, where it occurs the day *after*
Jesus' messianic entry; Luke 19:45–46), John 2:13–22 employs the episode as
the inaugural act of Jesus' Jerusalem ministry. However one wishes to explain these variations (e.g., the first time Jesus comes to Jerusalem in the
Synoptic Gospels, which depict His public life as a Galilean ministry chiefly,
is in the last ten days before His death; hence they must insert it where they
do. John on the other hand, whose Gospel might be considered as a commentary on Jesus' logion in Luke 13:34 par., may well be following a
chronological order), the postulating of *two* cleansings of the Temple is
really no explanation at all. (2) The two stories of Judas' end (Matt. 27:3–10;
Acts 1:18–19) differ on three important details: Did Judas commit suicide
(Matt.) or die of some mysterious accident or disease (Acts)? Did the
Sanhedrin purchase the "potter's field" (Matt.) or did Judas himself buy it as
a farm (Acts)? Whose blood led to the naming of the area Haceldama,

Jesus' (Matt.) or Judas' (Acts)? It seems clear that two somewhat independent traditions of the Judas story have been preserved in the New Testament; nor does the Vulgate's ingenious harmonizing translation of Acts 1:18, "suspensus crepuit medius," resolve the problem.

22. *AAS* 35 (1943) 314: "Quisnam autem sit *litteralis* sensus, in veterum Orientalium auctorum verbis et scriptis saepenumero non ita in aperto est, ut apud nostrae aetatis scriptores"—an admirable example of papal understatement. Matt. 23:9 is a good illustration of what the Pope means: "And do not call anyone on earth your father. Only one is your Father, and He is in heaven." This text, which makes many a non-Catholic scrupulous about calling a priest "Father," is probably a warning to the disciples not to imitate the scribes and Pharisees, who delighted in assuming high sounding titles, assimilating themselves to "the Fathers," i.e., the patriarchs and other famous Jewish forbears.

23. *AAS* 35 (1943) 314: "Nam quid illi verbis significare voluerint, non solis grammaticae, vel philologiae legibus, nec solo sermonis contextu determinatur; omnino oportet mente quasi redeat interpres ad remota illa Orientis saecula, ut subsidiis historiae, archaeologiae, ethnologiae aliarumque disciplinarum rite adiutus, discernat atque perspiciat, quaenam litteraria, ut aiunt, genera vetustae illius aetatis scriptores adhibere voluerint, ac reapse adhibuerint."

24. A fine example of attention to the psychological differences between the Western and the Semitic mentality may be found in Célestin Charlier, "Méthode historique et lecture spirituelle des écritures," *Bible et vie chrétienne* 18 (1957) 7–26.

25. *AAS* 35 (1943) 315: "Veteres enim Orientales, ut quod in mente haberent exprimerent, non semper iisdem formis iisdemque dicendi modis utebantur, quibus nos hodie, sed illis potius, qui apud suorum temporum et locorum homines usu erant recepti. Hi quinam fuerint, exegeta non quasi in antecessum statuere potest, sed accurata tantummodo antiquarum Orientis litterarum pervestigatione. Haec porro, postremis hisce decenniis maiore, quam antea, cura et diligentia peracta, clarius manifestavit, quaenam dicendi formae antiquis illis temporibue adhibitae sint, sive in rebus poëtice describendis, sive in vitae normis et legibus proponendis, sive denique in enarrandis historiate factis atque eventibus."

26. *Ibid.*, p. 315: "Haec eadem pervestigatio id quoque iam lucide comprobavit, israëliticum populum inter ceteras Orientis veteres nationes in historia rite scribenda, tam ob antiquitatem, quam ob fidelem rerum gestarum relationem singulariter praestitisse; quod quidem ex divinae inspirationis charismate atque ex peculiari historiae biblicae fine, qui ad religionem pertinet, profecto eruitur."

27. *Ibid.*, p. 315: "A Libris enim Sacris nulla aliena est illarum loquendi rationum, quibus apud veteres gentes, praesertim apud Orientales, humanus sermo ad sententiam exprimendam uti solebat, ea tamen condicione, ut adhibitum dicendi genus Dei sanctitati et veritati haudquaquam repugnet...."

28. *Ibid.*, p. 316: "Qua propter catholicus exegeta, ut hodiernis rei biblicae necessitatibus rite satisfaciat, in exponenda Scriptura Sacra, in eademque ab omni errore immuni ostendenda et comprobanda, eo quoque prudenter subsidio utatur, ut perquirat quid dicendi forma seu litterarum genus, ab hagiographo adhibitum, ad veram et genuinam conferat interpretationem; ac sibi persuadeat hanc officii sui partem sine magno catholicae exegeseos detrimento neglegi non posse."

29. McKenzie, *art. cit.* (supra n. 5) p. 198.

30. *AAS* 35 (1943) 319: "Hac tamen in rerum condicione catholicus interpres . . . neutiquam retineri debet, quominus difficiles quaestiones, hùcusque nondum enodatas, iterum atque iterum aggrediatur, non modo ut, quae ab adversariis opponantur, propulset, sed ut solidam etiam explicationem reperire enitatur, quae et cum Ecclesiae doctrina, cum iisque nominatim, quae de Sacra Scriptura ab omni errore immuni tradita sunt, fideliter concordet, et certis quoque profanarum disciplinarum conclusionibus debito modo satisfaciat."

31. If I may be forgiven a reference to a personal experience, I should like to cite the official summary of a discussion following a paper in the introduction to which I attempted to show that the disciples had no clear realization of Christ's divinity until after they received the revelation through the gift of the Holy Spirit. "To many, even of those present, the possibility that the apostles did not realize the divinity of Christ during His public life came as a novelty and a surprise. Concern was voiced that students might be led to conclude from this that Christ did not reveal His divinity at all. One group asked about the theological certitude of Father's position and wondered what theological note would be assigned to it. Some felt that more unanimous concurrence and greater certitude on the theological level would be necessary before such a position could be taught in class"; *Society of Catholic College Teachers of Sacred Doctrine: Proceedings of the Fourth Annual Convention, 1958* (Notre Dame, Ind.), p. 36.

32. To cite one example, Stanislas Lyonnet has pointed out in his interpretation of the Pentecostal glossolalia as ecstatic prayer, "De glossolalia Pentecostes eiusque significatione," *Verbum domini* 24 (1944) 65–75, that the rather common patristic opinion (viz., that the gift bestowed the power to speak foreign languages in a miraculous way) was based upon the demonstrably erroneous view that the charism was given for preaching.

33. One recent and striking instance is the interpretation of Matt. 1:18–22 by Xavier Léon-Dufour, "L'Annonce à Joseph," *Mélanges bibliques rédigés en l'honneur de André Robert* (Paris, 1957) pp. 390–97. Another is Alberto Vaccari's brilliantly simple solution of the Matthean divorce logia, "La clausola sul divorzio in Matteo 5,32; 19,9," *Rivista biblica* 3 (1955) 97–119.

34. *AAS* 35 (1943) 319: "Horum autem strenuorum in vinea Domini operariorum conatus non solummodo aequo iustoque animo, sed summa etiam cum caritate iudicandos esse ceteri omnes Ecclesiae filii meminerint; qui quidem ab illo haud satis prudenti studio abhorrere debent, quo quidquid novum est, ob hoc ipsum censetur esse impugnandum, aut in suspicionem adducendum."

35. Erich Dinkler, "Earliest Christianity," *The Idea of History in the Ancient Near East* (New Haven–London, 1955) p. 172: "The concept of history has been given to us by Greek science and to this very day is employed by us in a Greek sense. From Thucydides to Toynbee the common and connecting assumption has been that history is a rational, intelligible continuity, an integrated nexus or concatenation, operating in a unified world, capable of investigation and illumination by historical method."

36. McKenzie, *op. cit.* (supra n. 11) p. 60.

37. Dodd, *op. cit.* (supra n. 7) pp. 26–27.

38. *Ibid.*, p. 27.

39. *Ibid.*, p. 36.

40. Hippolyte Delehaye, *Les légendes hagiographiques* (3rd ed.; Brussels,

1927) p. 10: "La légende est, primitivement, l'histoire qu'il faut lire le jour de la féte du saint, *legenda*." It is the fashion, at least in clerical circles, to smile superiorly at the stories occasionally found in the second nocturns of the Roman Breviary (e.g., the heroic fasts of the infant St. Nicholas, or the marvelous prayer-feats of St. Patrick), and, indeed, in the future revision of the divine office we can expect that many of these *legenda* will be excised. However, it must be remembered that these stories constitute (and this not despite but because of their incredible character) the essential proof of the people's belief in the sanctity of these saints, and as such represent historical reality. *Vox populi, vox Dei*, in the age before official canonization, was the principle which justified the cultus paid to the saints. These legendary tales are the popular expression of the people's belief in the heroic sanctity of these heroes of God.

41. McKenzie, *op. cit.* (supra n. 11) p. 62.

42. Thus the "historicity" of the Gospel narratives is not as simple as some apologetics manual would lead us to think. The Evangelists' purpose was quite different from that of the historian: their aim primarily was to testify to the divine-human fact of God's intervention in human history which brought man salvation in Jesus Christ. The means they chose to express this vary from parables to eyewitness accounts; hence the supreme importance of careful attention to the subsidiary literary forms found in the Gospels. If our apologetics is to be valid, we must make it clear that the Magi story, for instance, is not "historical" in the sense in which the narrative of the crucifixion may be called "historical."

43. Dodd, *op. cit.* (supra n. 7) p. 30: "This is in fact the assertion which Christianity makes. It takes the series of events recorded or reflected in the Bible, from the call of Abraham to the emergence of the Church, and declares that in this series the ultimate reality of all history, which is the purpose of God, is finally revealed, because the series is itself controlled by the supreme event of all—the life, death and resurrection of Jesus Christ." Cf. also Jean Daniélou's recension of Herbert Butterfield's "Christianity and History" in *Downside Review* 68 (1950) 182–90.

44. It is this viewpoint which distinguishes all biblical history from the profane, or so-called scientific history and indeed constitutes its superiority vis-à-vis "history" as we understand it today. This is what Pius XII has pointed out so masterfully in the passage of *Divino Afflante Spiritu* cited in n. 26.

45. That is, the divine plan of salvation as revealed in the historical process which Paul and other sacred writers call "the last times": cf. Rom. 16:25; Col. 1:26–27; Eph. 3:8–13, etc.

46. L. Bouyer, *Le quatrième évangile* (2nd ed.; Tournai-Paris, 1955) p. 19: "*Pour lui* [Jean]*, l'histoire est un mystère et la raconter c'est nécessairement exposer en même temps ce mystère* . . . le déroulement de l'histoire humaine nous révèle le geste de la main divine qui l'accompagne et le produit."

47. Here one may well ask upon what grounds the validity of this supra-human interpretation rests, if, as we have asserted, salvation history is simply God's revelation of Himself. Obviously it cannot be proven (or disproven) *solely* by the use of modern historical method. For while it is quite possible to demonstrate scientifically the "historical" (in our modern sense) character of the Gospels, still the fact that God has spoken to men through books written by men is an object of faith. Faith's guarantee that these writers have infallibly expressed the revelation of Jesus Christ as incarnate Son and uni-

versal Redeemer is founded upon the supernatural fact of *scriptural inspiration*. Thus for an adequate comprehension of the Evangelists' testimony we must realize that it possesses not merely the authority of reliable eyewitnesses, but the authority of God Himself.

48. A careful reading of 1 John 1:1–2 will reveal this viewpoint of the sacred writers.

49. Another striking example is to be found in Acts 2:22 ff.

50. A study of this Gospel reveals that its author, while providing us with some of the most vivid and detailed scenes of Jesus' public life, was innocent of anything like literary art or a creative imagination. This strange combination of two apparently contradictory qualities happily vouches for the authenticity of the early testimony of Papias that while Mark was not a disciple of Jesus himself, he "wrote down accurately all that he remembered" of Peter's preaching. Thus the liveliness of the Marcan narratives, so rich in minute detail, goes back to Peter's all-seeing eye.

51. We accept these words as authentically Marcan; cf. Vincent Taylor, *The Gospel According to St. Mark* (London, 1952) p. 152.

52. Cf., *s.v.*, Moulton-Milligan, *The Vocabulary of the Greek Testament Illustrated from the Papyri and Other Non-Literary Sources* (London, 1949).

53. Etienne Trocmé, *Le "Livre des Actes" et l'histoire* (Paris, 1957) pp. 38–75.

54. Note the use here of the present subjunctive, which denotes not the beginning but the continuance of an action.

55. To those who still need to be convinced that certain literary forms are actually to be found in the Bible, we recommend Jean Levie, *La Bible: Parole humaine et message de Dieu* (Paris–Louvain, 1958) pp. 241–75.

56. That is, "what actually happened" from our modern point of view. For the early Christians, "what actually happened" was what was recorded upon the sacred page. *Dabar* in Hebrew means both "word" and "event." It is true that frequently we can, by an investigation of the original *Sitz im Leben* of a scriptural passage, satisfy our curiosity or refute certain tendentious arguments proposed by those who content themselves with a merely natural view of the Gospels. However useful such investigation may be, it must not be forgotten that it is the meaning intended by the inspired author that has the primacy.

57. J. Cambier, *art. cit.* (supra n. 9) p. 211: "Mais il est important de ne pas oublier que l'analyse littéraire d'une narration ne permet pas de conclure sans plus à l'affirmation ou à la négation de sa valeur historique. Celle-ci dépend d'autres facteurs, et en tout premier lieu, pour ce qui est de nos évangiles, de la qualité des témoins et de la nature de la tradition qui rapporte les dits et les faits du Christ. Le problème de l'historicité de nos évangiles est plus intimement lié à celui de la tradition qu'à la méthode des formes littéraires."

58. Oscar Cullmann, *Die Christologie des Neuen Testaments* (Tübingen, 1957) pp. 326–27: "Die mit der Vielheit der christologischen Würdetitel und Lösungen gegebene mannigfaltigkeit, die Feststellung, dass jede der zeitlich verschiedenen christologischen Funktionen zunächst Gegenstand eines *besonderen* Titels sein kann, dass erst allmählich die Verbindung zu den andern ins Blickfeld tritt und damit dann eine *heilsgeschichtliche* Perspektive entsteht, beweist, dass die Jesusfrage im Urchristentum nicht von einem fertigen Mythus, sondern von einer Reihe realer Tatsachen aus beantwortet wurde, die sich im ersten Jahrhundert unserer Zeitrechnung ereignet haben,

Tatsachen, welche von denen, die damals 'Geschichte machten,' unbeachtet blieben und noch heute verschieden interpretiert werden können, aber deswegen nicht weniger geschichtlich sind: das Leben, Wirken und Sterben Jesu von Nazareth; das Erleben seiner Gegenwart und seines Weiterwirkens über den Tod hinaus innerhalb der Gemeinschaft seiner Jünger."

59. Taylor, *op. cit.* (supra n. 51) p. 148.

60. Mark 8:27–9:32, connected as it is by a chronological reference (a rare phenomenon in the Synoptic Gospels), probably pre-existed this Gospel in a written form. Dom Willibald Michaux in his analysis of the plan of this Gospel, "Cahier de Bible: L'Evangile selon Marc," *Bible et vie chrétienne* 1 (1953) 78–97, has made use of this fact to show that this complex forms the literary center of Mark.

61. Mark 8:31; 9:31 = Isa. 53:10–11; Mark 10:33 = Isa. 50:6.

62. The re-editing of many Marcan episodes by Greek Matthew in the interests of edification suggests that the author was also disconcerted: compare Mark 4:38 with Matt. 8:25; Mark 6:5–6 with Matt. 13:58; Mark 5:30–31 omitted by Matt. 9:22.

63. On the meaning of this confession, cf. "Balaam's Ass, or a Problem in New Testament Hermeneutics," *Catholic Biblical Quarterly* 20 (1958) 55–56.

64. Thus we have an *inclusio*, which gives the spirit of the whole work.

65. Matthew's chief interest is in the logia of Jesus. For the first Evangelist, the incident is of importance only for the doctrinal message it contains— an illustration of *dabar* as word event.

65a. The wider perspective of this second part can be seen in the heightened opposition to the Gospel (16–17) both in Palestine itself (17) and in the Diaspora (18). The disciples now possess the Pentecostal Spirit (20). Mention is made of the coming of "the Son of Man" in the destruction of the Temple, 70 A.D. (23): the apostolic kerygma is preached universally (27), for the apostles have now, in the primitive Christian Church, assumed the office of the prophets (41).

65b. The point of the sower centers upon the harvest, i.e., the eschatological judgment: the future judgment will reveal what is decided in the present (represented by the varying fortunes of the seed). In the explanation, the original point of the sower is overshadowed by a psychological allegorization, which dwells upon the reception of the *logos* (the apostolic kerygma) by various classes of men. One type is *proskairos*, a term found elsewhere only in the Pauline writings (21), which implies an organized community against which persecution is directed (*thlipsis, diōgmos*) such as Acts 8:1 describes. Another type is led to abandon the Christian faith by the *merimna tou aionos* or the *apatē tou ploutou* (22): such will be Ananias and Sapphira (Acts 5:1–11). Thus it seems probable we are dealing here with an application to her own experiences by the apostolic Church of the Lord's teaching.—Only Matthew records the explanation of the cockle. Here again, while the point of the parable (the eschatological judgment, as is indicated by the unnatural command to collect the cockle *first* (30), which contradicts the normal Palestinian practice) has been kept in the explanation, still it appears we are again dealing with an allegorical application to the Church of the apostolic age. The universal nature of the preaching here is opposed to Jesus' habitual practice of addressing Himslf only to Jews in His lifetime (38: *ho de agros estin ho kosmos:* cf. Matt. 15:24). Also the good seed is taken as a symbol of the members of the Christian Church (38b: *hoi huioi tēs basileias*), which is distinguished (43) from heaven (*basileia tou patros autōn*), a distinction characteristic of the Pauline letters.—Thus in these explanations recorded by Matthew we have a most valuable piece of scriptural evidence that the Church of the apostolic age was already doing what the Church has ever claimed the right to do, viz., render explicit the doctrinal implications of her Master's teaching.

65c. That this discourse applies directly and *in toto* to the events of the year 70 A.D., and only typically to the end of the world, has been shown by A. Feuillet, "La synthèse eschatologique de saint Matthieu (XXIV–XXV)," *Revue biblique* 56 (1949) 340–64; 57 (1950) 62–91, 180–211.

66. Luke alone of the Synoptics gives Jesus the title *sōtēr* (Luke 2:11; cf. also 1:69, 71, 77; 19:9; 2:30; 3:6).

67. E. Osty, *Les évangiles synoptiques* (Paris, 1947) p. liv: "Il a représenté tous les événements de la vie du Seigneur comme *emportés par une force mystique vers Jérusalem*, le théâtre de sa passion et de son triomphet."

68. John gives a popular etymology for the place-name Siloë (which really means a conduit) in order to indicate the pool as a type of the baptismal font. —The Johannine modifications of the incident of the multiplication of loaves have been dictated by the Eucharistic significance he has perceived in it: cf. "The Bread of Life," *Worship* 32 (1957–58) 477–88.

69. This interpretation appears to me to be at least as probable as that which interprets the allusion to "wild beasts" as an indication of evil. Cf. Taylor, *op. cit.* (supra n. 51) p. 164.

70. Matthew in fact mentions two visits, one at the beginning of the public life (4:12–13), another later (13:54–58). Luke 4:16–30 is probable a composite picture, of which 16–22a corresponds to Matt. 4:12–13; 22b–24 corresponds to Matt. 13:54–58, Mark 6:1–6; and 25–30 is from a source not used by Matt.-Mark. Cf. E. Osty, *op. cit.* (supra n. 67) p. lvi; in a different sense, Ronald Knox, *A New Testament Commentary* 1: *The Four Gospels* (London, 1953) pp. 131–32.

71. L. Vaganay, *Le Problème synoptique* (Paris–Tournai–New York–Rome, 1954) p. 253.

72. This tendency to abbreviate narrative is probably to be explained by Matthew's inclusion of so many logia of Jesus, on the one hand, and by the material limitations of the ordinary scroll on which he wrote. At times, Matthean brevity leads to obscurity: to understand Matt. 9:2b ("Jesus seeing their faith") one must read Mark 2:4; similarly, the incomprehensible "I repeat" of Matt. 19:24 is clarified by Mark 10:23–24.

73. Compare Matt. 9:18–24 with Mark 5:21–43, where, by having Jairus come to say his daughter "has just died," Matt. eliminates the Marcan messengers who give Jairus (who has in Mark told Jesus his daughter "was dying") news of his daughter's death.

74. In Matt. 21:19 the fig tree withers up "instantaneously"; for quite a different version, cf. Mark 11:12–14, 20–25.

75. Another important detail: John 1:42 agrees with Mark 3:10 and Luke 6:14 in assigning the change of Simon's name to Peter to a quite early stage of the public ministry. Hence it becomes probable that the scene at Caesarea Philippi, as recorded by Matt. 16:13–20, is a synthesis of several diverse elements.

76. Thus it is a particular genre of that religious history of which Pius XII speaks in *Divino Afflante Spiritu*: cf. n. 26.

77. Cullmann, *op. cit.* (supra n. 58) p. 328: "Auf doppelte Weise bildet

vielmehr schon das Leben Jesu den Ausgangspunkt allen christologischen Denkens: in Jesu eigenem Selbstbewusstsein und in der konkreten Ahnung, die seine Person und sein Werk in den Jüngern und im Volke wachriefen." Here we must also mention another question frequently put to the Catholic critic when he is discussing the literary form of certain Gospel narratives: "Where do you stop?" If we accept the incarnational view of Sacred Scripture proposed by *Divino Afflante Spiritu*, viz., "Dei verba, humanis linguis expressa, quoad omnia humano sermoni assimilia facta sunt, excepto errore" (*AAS* 35 [1943] 316), then the answer is clear enough. We "stop" when we have been satisfied that we understand completely the words of the inspired writer, since then we know we have grasped the divine message intended for us in this biblical passage.

78. Matt. 1:1–17; Luke 3:23–38. Note that the biblical genealogy (of such doctrinal importance in the Old Testament because of the messianic idea held by Israel) is an *art form*; hence it is not to be confused with those family trees found in modern histories or biographies, which profess to trace *all* the ancestors of a given individual back through many generations. The biblical genealogy has a religious purpose which must be discovered, in each instance, by careful analysis.

79. Amongst the Evangelists, Mark, the faithful recorder of what the observant eye of Peter noted, has perhaps preserved the greatest number of eyewitness descriptions of scenes. Matthew is rightly regarded as having, the most frequently, transcribed the logia of Jesus so as to keep their original Semitic flavor and idiom.

80. By popular traditions here is meant the type of story told, especially in the ancient Near East, among the people. By the nature of things, there is much more of this genre in the Old Testament than in the New Testament; but they do exist in the New Testament, e.g., the story of the Magi (Matt. 2:1–12), the two stories of Judas' death referred to above, possibly also the story of the strange happenings in Jerusalem after Jesus' death (Matt. 27:51–53). For those who boggle at the suggestion that God has condescended to use "the story" as a vehicle of His revelation, we recommend John L. McKenzie's masterly discussion of "The Hebrew Story," *op. cit.* (supra n. 11) pp. 60 ff.

81. To this class, I believe, belong certain elements in the Matthean and Lucan Infancy narratives; also, perhaps, the strange story preserved in Mark 3:21–22.

82. E.g., the heavenly Voice at Jesus' baptism, apparently heard by no one else (Matt. 3:16 ff. par.); Jesus' triple temptation (Matt. 4:1–11), which in Luke 4:1–13 is more "spiritual"; possibly also the Lucan annunciations to Zachary (1:11–22) and to our Lady (1:26–38)—the case of Joseph's dream is clearer (Matt. 1:20–21). Related to this genre are attempts to describe supernatural phenomena which defy human expression: e.g., Acts 2:3: the Pentecostal "tongues *as if* of fire"; Luke 22:44b: "His sweat became *as it were* clots of blood. . . ."

83. Cf. the interesting discussion by René Laurentin, *Structure et théologie de Luc I–II* (Paris, 1957), pp. 93 ff., of the midrashic examples in the Lucan Infancy narrative.

84. These can be determined by comparing the various forms in which the saying may be represented in the evangelical tradition: the simplest and most obvious example, perhaps, is Matt. 5:40; cf. Luke 6:29b.

85. For instance, the Matthean parable of the wedding feast (Matt. 22:1–

14): the detail in v. 7 is probably a reference to the destruction of Jerusalem under Titus in 70 A.D., while the addition by Matthew of the guest without a wedding garment (v. 11 ff.), intended as a warning to the Gentile Christians, probably reflects the constitution of the Church which Matthew knew at the time of writing (*ca.* 80 A.D.).

86. It is a delicate question to determine how much or how little allegory was present in many of the parables as Jesus Himself gave them. However, it is probable that the three Matthean parables, the steward (Matt. 24:45–51), the virgins (Matt. 25:1–13), the talents (Matt. 24:14–30), reflect the organization of the Church at the time this Gospel was written, and represent the hierarchical authorities, groups of consecrated women, and the body of the faithful.

87. E.g., Matt. 28:18–19, Mark 14:22–24, John 9:35–38, like Acts 8:34 ff., appear to reflect the pre-baptismal interrogation. Cf. "Liturgical Influences on the Formation of the Four Gospels," *Catholic Biblical Quarterly* 21 (1959) 24–38.

88. Cf. n. 26 above.—This quality distinguishes the literature of Israel from that of her neighbors and explains the remarkable way in which the sacred writers were able to take over literary forms and even myths from their pagan contemporaries and transform them into apt vehicles which express the divine revelation.

89. No solution that is entirely satisfactory has ever been discovered, even though some are highly ingenious: e.g., (1) Matthew gives Joseph's, Luke Mary's Davidic ancestry; (2) both give Joseph's descent: Matthan (Matt.) and Melchi (Luke) married the same woman in turn; then Jacob, Heli's half-brother, married Jacob's childless widow, Joseph being the issue of this union; (3) Matthew gives legal Davidic descent, Luke Joseph's real ancestry; eventually, of Matthat's two sons, Jacob was father of our Lady, Heli of Joseph, who thus inherited the title, since his uncle had no male offspring, etc., etc.

90. The Matthean genealogy is schematized to obtain three series of fourteen each: in the second group, three kings, Ochozias, Joas, Amasias, are omitted (practice of *erasio nominis?*); and it is conceivable that similar omissions occur in the third list.

3 The Historicity of The Gospels*

MYLES M. BOURKE

An account of modern Catholic scripturists working in the "new" manner but with the old goal: that understanding had by the first-century Christians.

LIKE JUDAISM, CHRISTIANITY is a religion for which history is of the utmost importance. It is founded on the belief that God has acted in human history, and that by His acts salvation has been brought to men. It is impossible, then, for the Christian to be indifferent to the reality of those acts which are believed to constitute the divine intervention. A religion which is concerned only with "timeless truths" which do not depend on God's acting in history would be in no way affected if it were shown that such acts had never taken place; for the Christian, on the contrary, to deny the sacred history is to deny his faith. Consequently, the historical reliability of the Gospels is a matter of importance for him, and a discussion of the question is especially pertinent in these times when the charge has been made that the Gospel interpretation of many contemporary Catholic scholars is lessening and even destroying the historical value of those priceless documents.[1]

Let us concede at the outset that the type of history, the "literary genus," which those scholars believe the Gospels represent is not the same as that represented by scientific historiography, in which the historian arranges the facts pertinent to his subject in proper order of time and place, and in which his purpose is to

---

* This article is a revised form of an address delivered originally to the Third National Conference on Convert Work now known as the Conference on Doctrine and Ecumenism.

39

produce as faithful a picture of "what really happened" as his materials allow. But can anyone read the Gospels, particularly can anyone compare the Gospels with each other, and fail to see that the evangelists did not have those concerns? Apart from a certain broad outline, the synoptic Gospels are almost indifferent to the time and place of the events which they narrate, and the synoptic outline gives the reader an impression of the chronology and topography of Jesus' ministry quite different from that which he gets from the Gospel of St. John. And the instances in which the Gospels differ in their record of the same event or saying are so numerous that one cannot think that exact reproduction of the past was a prime consideration of the authors.

Yet up to a point, even the most "conservative" proponents of the historicity of the Gospels will admit all that. What, then, are the major differences between these adherents of the older views and the majority of Catholic exegetes? We cannot speak of all of them; one important difference which we shall not discuss, at least directly, is the way in which either group conceives of the relation between our canonical Gospels and the authors to whom tradition assigns them.[2] The two points which we have chosen for consideration here are the ones which are principally responsible for the uneasiness felt by some about the direction which the "new scripture" is taking. First, its proponents believe that since the literary genus to which the Gospels belong is theologically interpreted history, the factual data (whether events or sayings) which had been related by the eyewitnesses of the events and the hearers of the words may have been modified and added to in the course of their transmission and in their being committed to writing by the evangelists, in order that their deep significance and their application to the Church might be brought out. Secondly, these exegetes find it quite natural that when a story of an event has been passed down by oral tradition, the event may have been recounted in such ways that differences which defy convincing harmonization have been introduced into the various accounts; they also find no difficulty in supposing that the evangelists, or those who dealt with the traditional material before the evangelists, may have combined into a unit elements of the tradition which originally referred to disparate incidents. Consequently they believe that some of the events of the Gospels did not take place in the way in which we find them recorded.[3]

It is surely correct to call such an approach to the Gospel "new," if by that we mean that it is different from the one taken for centuries by scholars both within and outside of the Catholic Church. But the new approach has as its goal something ancient, namely, the same understanding of the Gospels as that which the Christians of the first century had. There is good reason to think that modern biblical scholarship has come far toward achieving that goal.

THE GOSPELS AS THEOLOGICALLY INTERPRETED HISTORY

It is now generally admitted that there is no history in which the historian does not interpret the facts which he records. At a very minimum, his selection of the facts which he considers worth recording and his omission of others involves a value judgment which is itself an interpretation. According to the nineteenth-century ideal, an ideal associated principally with the name of Leopold von Ranke, the historian was a collector and recorder of facts which he scrupulously refrained from interpreting, thus showing himself completely impartial. A more recent judgment is that such an ideal is impossible: ". . . the theory that an historian could be impartial seems to us today one of manifest buckram. We wonder that anyone troubled to destroy it. . . . Not only do we repudiate the ideal of Ranke that history should be colourless, new and impartial. We do not even suggest that it is desirable."[4] The now prevalent concept of history has been well expressed by C. H. Dodd, who writes: "We might indeed say that an historical 'event' is an occurrence *plus* the interest and meaning which the occurrence possessed for the people involved in it, and by which the record is determined."[5] And T. A. Roberts who objects to Dodd's definition on other grounds admits that "there can be no objection to the Gospels as historical documents because they blend fact and interpretation."[6] Interpreting facts does not mean falsifying them; it does mean, of course, that the historian is presenting his interpretation as the one which gives them their true meaning.

In the case of the Gospels, the facts were interpreted in the light of the belief that in Jesus the decisive intervention of God in history had taken place, that the Final Age, the *eschaton,* had arrived, that Jesus of Nazareth was the Messiah of Israel and the Son of God. The confession "Jesus is Lord"—expression of the

Easter faith of the early Christians—is the classical summary of the belief which cast light upon all the memories which the apostles and the other eyewitnesses had of what they had seen and heard during the public life of their Master. It was by a community which shared the faith of those who had seen the risen Lord that those recollections were passed down, and by evangelists who shared that faith that our Gospels were written in the form in which we know them.

The Gospels are, in fact, a development of the apostolic preaching, the kerygma[7]—a development which interprets Jesus' ministry in the light of the central truth of that preaching, namely, that through Jesus salvation has been given to men. Christ's public ministry was one of the points of the preaching (cf. Acts 10:38–39a), but so far as that kerygma can be reconstructed from the discourses of the first part of Acts (1:1–15:35) the ministry was given relatively little importance. That is understandable, since the preaching was addressed to those who had not yet accepted Christ, and its purpose was their conversion. Consequently, emphasis was laid on the great central themes of the salvation history: Jesus' death, resurrection, exaltation, His sending the Spirit, His glorious return. The Gospels, on the contrary, were written for those who were believers, and they bring into prominence the meaning for man's salvation of Jesus' ministry. That does not necessarily mean that the traditional data concerning the ministry were modified in the gospel record under the influence of the Easter faith. Each text in which such modification can be suspected must be examined carefully before a decision is reached. But if the examination bears out the suspicion, it would be foolish to deny such modification because of an aprioristic conviction that it would have been impossible.[8]

There are other influences, related to the paschal faith, which must be allowed as possible sources of modification. The life-giving words of Jesus were seen as addressed not merely to those who first heard them, but to all who had come to believe in Him after He had risen from the dead. In many instances, nothing had to be changed to make them pertinent to Christians of whatever generation; in others, they originally had a meaning which was directly applicable only to those to whom they had been spoken during Jesus' public life. It would not be impossible that the early

Christians, or the evangelists, conscious of possessing the Holy Spirit who would lead them into all truth (John 16:13), might, under the influence of the Spirit, have introduced changes into those words, or have added to them, in order to apply them to their own situations.[9] The life of the Savior, and particularly the redemptive act, was seen as the fulfillment of the Old Testament, foreshadowed and prepared for by the events of the sacred history of Israel, the words of the prophets, and the inspired prayers of the ancient people of God. It can hardly be thought that this interpretation was a creation of the Christian community; it seems, rather, that it goes back to Jesus Himself. But it is not surprising that in the gospel record, and especially in the Passion accounts, there are some details which seem to have been composed in order to emphasize the Old Testament fulfillment.[10] Again, whether that was actually done is a question which can be answered only after a careful examination of the texts.

FORM CRITICISM

Here it will be appropriate to make some mention of Form Criticism (*Formgeschichte*), which has made important contributions to our understanding of the synoptic Gospels, even though much of the work of its proponents, especially that of Rudolf Bultmann, has been destructive of the historical value of the Gospels and is marked by presuppositions which are unacceptable. Form Criticism was a product of German scholarship; the works in which it was proposed appeared in 1919 and the early 1920's. The two most important are Martin Dibelius' *Die Formgeschichte des Evangeliums*,[11] and Bultmann's *Die Geschichte der synoptischen Tradition*.[12]

The position of the form critics is, in the first place, that the chronological and topographic framework of the synoptics is almost entirely artificial. They point out, further, that those Gospels are not compositions of three individuals who can be called authors in the now accepted sense of that term; they are, rather, compilations of little units which were originally independent, which had originated in and circulated in the oral tradition of the Christian community and had developed according to the laws of popular literature. Only the Passion account seems to have been,

from the beginning, a continuous narrative.[13] The two most obvious classifications of the Gospel material are the sayings and the
narratives. In the latter, two types can be discerned, which
Dibelius called "Paradigms" and *Novellen* respectively. The
paradigms are accounts which lead up to some memorable statement of Jesus (e.g., the account of the disciples' plucking the ears
of grain on the Sabbath, Mark 2:23–28); the *Novellen* are accounts which normally tell of a miracle of Jesus. Bultmann calls
the latter "miracle stories" and the former "apophthegms," and
since the statement of Jesus is the important point in the apophthegms, he classifies them under the sayings-material rather than
under the narratives.

The rest of the narrative material is difficult to classify according to form. Dibelius includes the majority of it under the designation "Legend." Since we are inclined to equate "legendary" with
"fictitious," it must be emphasized that that is not the meaning of
Dibelius' terminology. For him, "legend" is a neutral term so far
as the historical value of a narrative is concerned: "The legend-
form as such furnishes no decisive argument against the historicity
of the hero or of an event—nor, on the other hand, does it give
any guarantee that the account corresponds to reality."[14] He
compares the Gospel legends to the medieval legends of the saints,
pious stories about the life and death of a holy person. The Passion account is an etiological cult legend, the purpose of which is
so to present the condemnation and execution of Jesus that the
hearer or reader may see in them the expression of God's will.[15]
Personal legends, which tell of the holiness, wisdom, or piety of
their chief character are relatively few in the Gospels; the clearest
example of one about Jesus is Luke's account of Him in the temple
at the age of twelve (Luke 2:41–50). Finally, the Christ myth
according to which Jesus is the divine Son of God who came into
the world from heaven is clearly present in the accounts of Jesus'
baptism, temptations, and transfiguration; it has influenced some
of the *Novellen* such as Mark 6:47–52 and some of the sayings
such as Matthew 11:25–30.

For Bultmann, the narrative material exclusive of the miracle
stories is "Legend and Historical Narrative (*Geschichtserzäh-
lung*)." The legend may have an historical basis, but it shows no
particular interest in the historical as such; it has a religious and

edifying rather than an historical character.[16] For practical purposes, the distinction between legend and historical narrative is as good as nonexistent: "a separation of legend and historical narrative seems impossible," because ". . . historical narrative is so completely dominated by legend that it can only be treated together with the treatment of legend."[17] In their final form, the gospels show the considerable influence which the Christ myth exercised; this is especially true of Mark among the synoptics, and of John.[18]

It is not our purpose here to attempt a criticism of this system.[19] Let it suffice to say that there is no doubt that in trying to trace the various elements of the Gospels to their "situation in life" (*Sitz im Leben*), that is, the circumstances in the early Christian communities which led to the formation of the material, both Dibelius and Bultmann assigned an unwarranted role to the creative power of the community, and arrived at excessively negative judgments about the historical value of the Gospel record. In that respect, Bultmann was the more radical of the two. Little place was allowed for the activity of those who had been eyewitnesses of the events; supposedly, those who were in a position to give information about Jesus' words and deeds had little or no interest in doing so. But the form critics give no satisfactory basis for that extraordinary hypothesis.

On the credit side, however, it must be said that the methods employed by the form critics can be useful tools in the hands of the Catholic scholar, provided they are used with discrimination,[20] and that the form critics have arrived at some conclusions about the Gospels which deserve acceptance.

It is clear, in the first place, that what they maintain about the chronological framework of the Gospels is in large part true. Probably there are few careful readers of the Gospels who had not recognized, before they ever heard of Form Criticism, that in the majority of cases it is impossible to determine the time order of the particular events of Jesus' ministry. But some scholars still hesitate to apply that principle consistently. Faced with the fact that the Johannine account of Jesus' cleansing of the temple (John 2:13–22) puts it at the beginning of the ministry, while the synoptics (Mark 11:15–18 and parallels) put it at the end, they take what T. W. Manson has called "the desperate solution of two cleansings,"[21] a solution which, as has been remarked, by duplicating the event lessens its significance.[22]

Secondly, there are instances in which the same event is related differently in different Gospels. Some of these accounts vary only by insignificant differences of detail. An example of that would be Mark 10:46–52 and parallels. What judgment should one pass upon the fact that according to Mark's account Jesus cures one blind man, named Bartimaeus, when leaving Jericho; in Matthew, He cures two blind men when leaving; in Luke, He cures one blind man when approaching the city? No other than that the differences are simply the consequence of oral transmission of the same story by different groups.[23] There is surely no reason to try to reconcile them by improbable harmonizations, a technique which was often used by Catholic scholars in the past, and can still be found in so comparatively recent a work as Guiseppe Ricciotti's *Life of Christ,* in spite of the avowed intention of the author to write "a critical work,"[24] and in the even later *Life of Christ* by Andrés Fernández.[25] The accounts of the cure of the centurion's servant in Matthew 8:5–13 and Luke 7:1–10 may be taken as another case where oral tradition has produced two different versions of the same story. And it is at least probable that the Johannine account of the cure of the royal official's son (John 5:46–53) is simply another version of that story.

In cases such as these the differences are not particularly important. But if we compare the Marcan and Matthean accounts of the call of the disciples with the Lucan (Mark 1:16–20; Matt. 4:18–22; Luke 5:1–11) we find that the difference goes far beyond some insignificant variants; in Luke, a miraculous catch of fish is connected with the call. One cannot avoid remarking the similarity between that element of the Lucan story and the post-Resurrection miracle in John 21:1–14. Did Luke himself put into his vocation account the miracle narrated in the Johannine tradition? Or had that already been done before the evangelist began his work on the material which he had received? Does the Lucan version of the call of the disciples depend on the Johannine tradition at all? These are difficult questions and for our purposes we need not attempt to answer them. It is sufficient to note that in Luke's gospel there is a very different version of the call of the disciples from that found in Matthew and Mark. Unlike Bultmann, we do not question the historicity of the miracle, but we may well doubt that its association in Luke with the call of the disciples gives us an historically exact picture of what happened on that occasion.

PETER'S CONFESSION; THE BEATITUDES

We shall now consider two important passages in which it seems that the original data were deliberately modified: the confession of Peter in Matthew 16:16 and the Matthean and Lucan versions of the beatitudes (Matt. 5:3–12; Luke 6:20–23).

In these instances it seems probable that the modifications were made by the evangelists themselves, rather than in the course of the transmission of the data. One of the weaknesses of Form Criticism was that it attributed too little to the initiative of the evangelists and reduced them practically to mere compilers of pre-existing material. Within the past decade or so, a needful reaction to that viewpoint has set in, *Redaktionsgeschichte* ("history of redaction"), which is concerned with the theological preoccupations of the evangelists and the influence of those preoccupations upon the way in which they dealt with their material. As R. H. Fuller expresses it:

Recent study of the Gospels has tended toward a greater appreciation of the evangelists as creative theologians in their own right; each offers his distinctive interpretation of the traditions with which he worked. . . . If we are to study the work of the evangelists themselves, we must pay very close attention to their editorial redactions—the connecting links they forge between the pericopes, their arrangement of the pericopes, the alterations which they make to their sources where we have them.[26]

Yet *Formgeschichte* and *Redaktionsgeschichte* are complementary rather than fundamentally opposed; Bultmann himself has acknowledged the value and legitimacy of the latter.[27]

In treating Matthew 16:16, I should like to present the interpretation of Father Pierre Benoit of the Dominican École Biblique in Jerusalem, a scholar who is recognized as one of the leading scripturists of our day. Benoit dealt with the text in an article on the divinity of Jesus in the synoptic Gospels which appeared in 1953.[28] He developed there a view which he had already expressed in a footnote in his translation of Matthew in the *Bible de Jérusalem*.[29] The following year, Father David M. Stanley took up Benoit's exegesis and added certain considerations which make it, I think, even more convincing.[30]

Peter's confession, "Thou art the Christ, the Son of the living God," is taken by most Catholic exegetes as a confession to the divinity of Jesus. They see in the affirmation that He is "the Son of the living God" a statement of belief that He is Son of God in the fullest meaning of the term; the text, therefore, contains much more than a confession that Jesus is the Messiah, "the Christ."[31] Admittedly, the title "Son of God" does not, of itself, provide any argument for that position. There are Old Testament texts which show that angels (Job 1:6), the nation Israel (Ex. 4:22f.), the people of Israel (Deut. 14:1), the Davidic king (2 Sam. 7:14), and the just man (Wisd. 2:18) were called the son(s) of God. The fact that the king was considered the son of God would make the title peculiarly applicable to the Messiah-King. Strangely enough, it is at least doubtful that it ever was applied to him either in the Old Testament or in the Jewish apocryphal literature;[32] but there is some evidence that the title was used with only messianic meaning by the Christians, as, for example, in the accounts of Jesus' baptism where the words spoken by the voice from heaven (Matt. 3:17; Mark 1:11; Luke 3:22) re-echo, in part, Psalm 2:7.[33] Is Matthew 16:16 a similar case? A comparison of the Matthean version of Peter's confession with the Marcan (Mark 8:27–30) and the Lucan (Luke 9:18–22) suggests that it is not. In the latter two, Peter expresses belief simply in Jesus as Messiah. But there are two significant differences in Matthew. First, the use of the title, "the Son of the living God"; second, and more important since that title might be merely a messianic one, the difference in the question which Jesus puts to the disciples. In Mark and Luke He asks: "Who do men (or "the crowds") say that I am?" In Matthew, "Who do men say that the *Son of Man* is?" Most probably, "Son of Man" here is an allusion to the vision of Daniel 7:13f., where one "like a son of man" advances to the "Venerable One" (God) and receives from Him "dominion, and glory, and kingly power," a universal and everlasting kingdom. This Son of Man is certainly a more exalted figure than the traditional Messiah of Israel. In identifying Himself with this heavenly, pre-existing being in His response to the high priest at His trial (Mark 14:61f. and parallels), in answer to the question whether He was the Messiah, the Son of the Blessed One (God), Jesus indicated that He was more than the Messiah whom Israel was expecting.[34] He asserted His heavenly origin and, for Benoit, His divinity: "In assimilating himself to 'the Son of Man' of Daniel, he (Jesus) gave the title 'Son of God' a meaning which was not metaphorical but proper and transcendent. . . ."[35] That union of titles, found in the trial scene, is also present in Matthew's account of Peter's confession, and if Benoit's opinion of the union is right, "Son of God" has the same meaning of divinity in the fullest sense in Matthew 16:16 as in the texts dealing with the trial.

I think that we may pass over an examination of the reason which Benoit gives for taking the title as a strictly divine one in these texts. As we have already mentioned, his interpretation of the title is the same as that held by the majority of Catholic exegetes even though they may not have arrived at it by the same argument as he has. And it is the interpretation and the conse-quences of it for our understanding of the formation of the Mat-thean account of Peter's confession which are of primary impor-tance.

If Matthew 16:16 contains a confession to Jesus' divinity, how is it possible that the synoptic parallels have nothing of the sort? The suggestion that Matthew's version represents what Peter really said at Caesarea Philippi, and that Mark and Luke omitted "the son of the living God" is entirely improbable. It is, besides, most difficult to think that Peter or any of the disciples had come to explicit belief in Jesus' divinity during His public life. Benoit points out that the too human conceptions which they had of even the messianic role of Jesus, their lack of understanding for which Jesus often reproached them, and their attitude and conduct at the time of the Passion make it impossible to think that they clearly perceived His divinity before the Resurrection.[36] Of all these indi-cations the plainest, I think, is Peter's rebuke of Jesus after the first prediction of the Passion (Matt. 16:22; Mark 8:32), a pre-diction which in all the synoptics follows the accounts of Peter's confession. Consequently, however sure it may be that Matthew 16:16 contains a confession to Jesus' divinity, it seems certain that one cannot suppose that such a confession was made at Caesarea

Philippi. Benoit suggests that it was the author of Greek Matthew (that is, the author of our canonical gospel of Matthew), a gospel which is certainly later than that of Mark, who added "the son of the living God" in the light of the fully developed Paschal faith.[37] But the belief which is expressed by that addition was no creation of the Christian community. The situation was, rather, that through the Resurrection and the sending of the Holy Spirit the disciples came to an understanding of what had been implied in the way in which Jesus had spoken of Himself in relation to the Father (e.g., Matt. 11:27; Mark 13:32), a way which was necessarily obscure but sufficient for laying the foundations of that faith which would gradually come to fullness after the Resurrection.[38]

For Benoit, then, if we wish to know what Peter said at Caesarea Philippi we must go to the accounts of Mark and Luke. Matthew's account is a clear case of theological interpretation of the original data and it cannot, therefore, be taken as a record of what actually happened. A similar view is proposed by other Catholic exegetes. Joseph Schmid says that the words "the Son of the living God" are an addition which raises the confession above the level of Jewish Messianism (on which it remains in Mark) to that of the early Christian kerygma.[39] In his important article on Matthew 16:13–23, Anton Vögtle states that "the proclamation of the early Church's belief in Christ was more important to the evangelist than the long since surpassed, inadequate Messianic confession of Caesarea Philippi . . . by means of the confession to Christ which has been specified and elevated by the addition 'the Son of the living God' he (the evangelist) allows Simon to express who Jesus, the Son of Man, is."[40]

David Stanley's observations on the evolution of the disciples' faith in Jesus are an important complement to Benoit's study, since they deal more fully with what is implied by the evangelist's procedure. His placing a statement of fully developed post-Resurrection faith back into the public ministry indicates the continuity and homogeneity of the progress of the disciples' belief. From the beginning, they had adhered totally to the person of Jesus. But at first they saw in Him only their beloved Master; then, they knew Him as the Messiah of Israel; finally, in the light of the Paschal experience and the coming of the Spirit, they recognized that He was truly divine, the Son of God. In the course of this development there were privileged moments. The event at Caesarea Philippi was one of those, and its importance is shown by Matthew's interpreting Peter's confession to Jesus' messiahship as a confession also to His divinity, although the latter was a truth which Peter and the other disciples grasped consciously only at the end of the process which had begun when they gave themselves totally to Jesus.[41]

Let us now consider the second example of deliberate modification which we have chosen, in this case a modification of the words of Jesus, the beatitudes. Here I should like to present the view of Dom Jacques Dupont, a Belgian monk whose scriptural work has won for him a place in the first rank of modern Catholic scholarship. His study of the beatitudes appeared first in 1954;[42] a second, thoroughly revised and much expanded edition is now in process, and the first volume of it was published in 1958.[43]

The problem presented by a comparison of the Matthean and Lucan versions of the beatitudes is well known. Matthew has nine (Matt. 5:3–12), Luke four (Luke 6:20–23). Besides that, there are significant differences in those beatitudes which are common to both; for example, in Matthew 5:3 the "poor in spirit" are declared blessed, but in Luke 6:20 simply the "poor"; in Matthew 5:6 the beatitude speaks of those who "hunger and thirst after justice," whereas in Luke 6:21 the reference is to "you who are hungry now." Moreover, Luke's beatitudes are followed by a series of "woes" (Luke 6:24–26) which predict misfortune for those who are in the states opposite to those mentioned in the beatitudes, and there is no parallel in Matthew to these "woes."

The conclusions which Dupont has reached after a minute analysis of the texts are presented by him as tentative and of varying degrees of probability. To suggest that they are certain would be to go far beyond the claims of their author. Yet the method by which he conducts his study is the one which the majority of his colleagues agree is the only valid one. Max Zerwick, S.J., professor at the Pontifical Biblical Institute, has called it "the method which Catholic exegesis must necessarily use in the study of the Gospels."[44] It presupposes that at least in theory three levels of meaning can be distinguished in any gospel text which records the words of Jesus: (1) the meaning which the words had when Jesus spoke them; (2) their meaning in the apostolic tradition, that is, when they were being passed down both in

oral tradition and in writing before the final composition of the
Gospels; (3) the meaning given them by the inspired evangelists.[45] Dupont points out that this distinction is a theoretical one,
for it is not impossible that in certain instances various levels of
meaning may coincide. And in fact he believes that in the form in
which Matthew (that is, the author of Greek Matthew) and Luke
received the beatitudes, their meaning was the same as that which
they had when Jesus spoke them: "This form which the beatitudes
had received before they were redacted by the evangelists depends
on the apostolic tradition . . . but it does not seem that it can be
distinguished from a primitive form which corresponds to the intentions of the Master and to the situations of his public ministry."[46] And again, the text which was the basis on which the
evangelists worked "can very well represent the initial form of the
teaching of Jesus."[47] It is a different matter, however, when we
come to the meaning of the beatitudes in the versions of Matthew
and Luke. For Dupont, neither version retains the original meaning of those beatitudes (the four common ones) which, in substance, go back to Jesus Himself. Besides this, each of the two
versions differs in meaning from the other.

The similarities between the four beatitudes common to both
versions are such that one may conclude that they have been
derived from a common source, a document written in Greek.[48]
By eliminating those elements which seem to be due to the literary
activity of the evangelists, one can arrive at the form which the
beatitudes had in that basic document, and it was probably the
following:

Blessed are the poor, for theirs is the kingdom of heaven.
Blessed are the afflicted, for they shall be comforted.
Blessed are those who hunger (and thirst), for they shall be satisfied.
Blessed will you be when men hate you and exclude you and insult
you and utter a bad name against you (i.e., defame you) because
of the Son of Man. Rejoice and be glad, for your reward in heaven
is great; for it was in that way that they persecuted the prophets,
your predecessors.[49]

In determining the meaning of these beatitudes in the basic document, Dupont makes a distinction between the first three and the
fourth. The former are related to the prophecies of Isaiah 49:8—

13, 61:13, in which the benefits of the messianic kingdom are promised to the poor, the afflicted, those who hunger and thirst. By announcing the good fortune, the blessedness, of those who are in that lowly situation in which they count for nothing so far as purely human judgment is concerned, Jesus proclaims that in His person and mission the promised kingdom has come or is on the point of being inaugurated. "If the poor are blessed, it is because Jesus claims for himself the specific task which marks the Messiah whom Isaiah prophesied. That task is defined in relation to the disinherited of this world. In announcing to them that it is going to be accomplished, in fact that it is already beginning to be accomplished, Jesus presents himself as the Messiah of the poor who is described in the oracles of the great prophet."[50] The beginning of Jesus' ministry is the time which suits perfectly this joyous proclamation of the coming of the kingdom.

The fourth beatitude is quite different. It speaks of the recompense which those who have suffered persecution for Jesus, the Son of Man, will receive at the time of the last judgment. The attitude which they have taken in regard to Jesus the Messiah has been the cause of their suffering and it will be the reason for their reward. "If one is blessed in suffering for Jesus, it is because Jesus is the Messiah, the Son of Man, he who will preside at the last judgment. The christological import of the beatitude is inseparable from its eschatological significance."[51] The situation in Jesus' ministry which suits this beatitude is the last period, when the hostility of His adversaries was apparent and growing. It was then that He foretold that His disciples would have to bear the same kind of persecution as He, and encouraged them by the thought of the reward which they would receive from His own hands.[52]

It is clear, particularly in the case of the first three of these common beatitudes, that their original meaning could have pertinence only at the time of Jesus' ministry. A proclamation of the coming of the kingdom would have nothing but historical interest for those who recognized that it had come, and that they were members of it. Yet the precious words of Jesus were there, susceptible of new meaning which would make them applicable to Christian communities of the post-Resurrection time. And under the inspiration of the Holy Spirit, Matthew and Luke reinterpreted them; but each did so in a different way. By his additions to the original beatitudes (poor *in spirit;* hunger and thirst *after justice*

[Matthew 5:3, 6]), and by his incorporation of new ones (5:7, 8, 9), Matthew has given a moral tone to what was originally a joyous proclamation of the kingdom. In his version the beatitudes represent an ideal of perfection, the justice which is demanded of those who are in the kingdom, and they promise reward to those who strive to fulfill that demand. This justice is the principal theme of the Matthean Sermon on the Mount; the beatitudes are a fitting prologue to the sermon and together with it constitute a perfect unit.

Luke has reinterpreted the beatitudes in a quite different manner. Leaving the original text of the basic document much as he found it, he has added the corresponding "woes," which quite clearly refer to social status. Consequently, since those to whom the woes refer are contrasted with those who are declared blessed, the meaning of the beatitudes is changed. They now declare that the poor and afflicted of this world are blessed because they do not live for this world, and their fortunes will be reversed in the life after death.

The situation-in-life which is revealed by Luke's version is that of the early Church, composed in major part of the poor. Naturally it is not poverty as such which is their guarantee of happiness and reward in heaven; right moral dispositions are presupposed. But emphasis is not laid on those dispositions, as it is in Matthew's version. And Dupont thinks it probable that the "woes" were not only added to the beatitudes by Luke, but composed by him under the inspiration of the Spirit in order to give the beatitudes the meaning which they have in his version.[53]

Although both evangelists have modified the original meaning, they have done so by drawing out virtualities contained in the beatitudes as Jesus pronounced them, in order to make them pertinent to the Church of their time. In doing this, they were entirely faithful to the teaching of Jesus, for the meaning found in each version corresponds to teaching which the Lord Himself had given, not, indeed, when He spoke the beatitudes, but at other times during His ministry. The moral perfection demanded in Matthew's version was surely the demand of Jesus as the sayings of the Sermon on the Mount attest; the contrasting fate of the poor and the rich in the next life, taught in Luke's version, with the high estimate of actual poverty and the awareness of the spiritual danger of riches which that teaching involves—all that is an echo of

Christ's doctrine as we find it in the parable of Dives and Lazarus (Luke 16:19–31) and in that of the rich fool (Luke 12:16–21). By making the beatitudes a vehicle for conveying to the early Church a message which was as pertinent to it as a proclamation of the coming of the kingdom would have been anachronistic, the evangelists showed their awareness that the words of Jesus were indeed words of life.[54]

The few examples which we have touched on may be fairly taken as representative of the type of Gospel interpretation now prevalent among Catholic scripturists. Far from weakening or destroying the historical value of the sacred books, it has disposed of many a pseudo-problem and has given insights into texts whose richness had previously hardly been suspected. The early Christians passed down the narratives and the sayings which had been given them by the eyewitnesses of Jesus' ministry, yet they realized that they actually had a better understanding of them than it was possible to have at the time when the deeds were done and the words spoken. The evangelists who put the traditional material into final form, each in his distinctive way, were particularly men guided by the Spirit in their interpretation of the sacred history. It was the intention of those who contributed to the formation of the gospels that the readers should know the full meaning of what Jesus said and did, that they should see that the heavenly Lord of the Church was none other than the historical Jesus of Nazareth and that there was true continuity between His earthly ministry and His present guidance of the Church. Insofar as the community or the evangelists deliberately modified the original data they did so the better to carry out that intention. And the fact that what the eyewitnesses recounted, what the community retold, what the evangelists wrote, was recounted, retold, and written down by men of the Church, for the Church—this fact points to the central role of ecclesiastical tradition in the formation of the Gospels, and shows how foreign to primitive Christian thought is any imagined opposition between Bible and Church.

NOTES

1. Cf. J. A. Fitzmyer's excellent survey, "A Recent Roman Scriptural Controversy," *Theological Studies*, 22 (1961), 426–444.
2. On this, cf. F. McCool, "Revival of Synoptic Source Criticism," *Theo-*

logical Studies, 17 (1956), 459–493, especially 484–486; V. T. O'Keefe, "Towards Understanding the Gospels," *Catholic Biblical Quarterly*, 21 (1959), 171–189, especially 173–176.

3. Cf. on the last point R. E. Brown, "Incidents that are Units in the Synoptic Gospels but dispersed in St. John," *Catholic Biblical Quarterly*, 23 (1961), 143–160.

For a good statement of the understanding of the gospels in recent Catholic exegesis, cf., in addition to the article of V. T. O'Keefe cited above, D. M. Stanley, "The Conception of our Gospels as Salvation-History," *Theological Studies*, 20 (1959), 561–589.

4. H. W. V. Temperley, *Research and Modern History*, quoted in A. Richardson, *Christian Apologetics* (London, 1960), 94, n. 1; cf. also M. C. D'Arcy, *The Meaning and Matter of History* (New York, 1959), espec. 13–62.

5. *History and the Gospel* (London, 1938), 27.

6. "Some Presuppositions of Gospel Historical Criticism," *Studia Evangelica*, ed. K. Aland *et al.* (Berlin, 1959), 69.

7. Cf. C. H. Dodd, *The Apostolic Preaching and its Developments* (London, 1936).

8. C. P. Ceroke's "Is Mark 2, 10 a Saying of Jesus?", *Catholic Biblical Quarterly*, 22 (1960), 369–390, is an example of the type of examination we mean. As a result of his thoroughly scientific study, Ceroke concludes that the question posed in the title must be answered in the negative: "Son of Man in Mark 2, 10 envisions Jesus, not in his earthly public ministry, but as resurrected and ascended. As Head of the messianic community, He exercises the function of the forgiveness of sins on earth" (387).

9. For an interesting study in support of the view that the *interpretation* of the parable of the Sower (Matt. 13:19–23 and parallels) is an example of an addition made to the words of Jesus, "a traditional interpretation which was in accord with the intentions of the Lord and yet pointed His message so that it applied to the conditions of their (the evangelists') own, very different age," cf. F. J. McCool, "The Preacher and the Historical Witness of the Gospels," *Theological Studies*, 21 (1960), 517–543.

10. A classic example of this is Matthew's account of Jesus' entrance into Jerusalem (21:1–11) according to which two animals, an ass and a colt, are brought to Jesus who seats himself upon *them* (!). In the synoptic parallels and in John 12:12–19 there is mention of only one animal. In Zechariah 9:9, which Matthew sees fulfilled in Jesus' entry, an ass and a colt are spoken of, but that is clearly a case of poetic parallelism. In order to emphasize the fulfillment, Matthew holds to the *letter* of the Old Testament prophecy and speaks of two animals; cf. J. Schmid, *Das Evangelium nach Matthäus* (3rd. ed.; Regensburg, 1956), 229. For a discussion of this procedure in the Passion accounts, cf. Schmid, "Die Erfüllung der Schrift in der Passion Jesu," *Das Evangelium nach Markus* (4th. ed., Regensburg, 1958), 304–308.

11. 3rd. ed. Tübingen, 1959. All our references are to the second edition (1933), of which the third is an exact reproduction with the exception of some minor additions to the footnotes, and a supplement by G. Bornkamm.

12. 4th. ed., Göttingen, 1958.

13. Dibelius, *op. cit.*, 178.

14. *Ibid.*, 106.

15. *Ibid.*, 101 f.

16. *Op. cit.*, 260.

17. *Ibid.*, 261.

18. *Ibid.*, 334.

19. Good evaluations of it have been made by P. Benoit, "Réflexions sur la 'Formgeschichtliche Methode'," *Revue Biblique*, 53 (1946), 481–512, and by A. Wikenhauser, *New Testament Introduction*, tr. J. Cunningham (New York, 1958), 253–277. The Benoit article has been reprinted in a collection of his studies and critical reviews, *Exégèse et Théologie*, 2 vols. (Paris, 1961), Vol. I, 25–61.

20. Cf. R. Aubert, *La Théologie Catholique au milieu du XXᵉ Siècle* (Paris, 1954), 18 f.: "Some Catholic exegetes do not hesitate to make their own a number of conclusions of the *Formgeschichtliche Schule*. . . . Monsignor Cerfaux has not hesitated to use (this method) for the study of the New Testament, and in so doing has transformed a method which seemed at first destined to pulverize the historical worth of the Gospels into a very fruitful instrument for penetrating into the first Christian catechesis, permitting one to find there certain primitive aspects, and certain hitherto neglected nuances."

21. *Studies in the Gospels and Epistles* (Manchester, 1962), 118.

22. J. Schmid, *Das Evangelium nach Markus*, 210.

23. This seems certain at least so far as the number of men is concerned; cf. P. Benoit, *Exégèse et Théologie*, I, 42 f. There are some, however, who think that the Lucan location is due to the literary activity of the evangelist himself; cf. E. Osty, *L'Évangile selon Saint Luc* (2nd. ed., Paris, 1953), 16 f.

24. *Op. cit.*, tr. A. Zizzamia (Milwaukee, 1947), vi.; 509.

25. Tr. P. Barrett (Westminster, Maryland, 1958), 559–561. Fernández' harmonizing, however, is confined, to the number; he thinks that Luke has displaced the miracle.

26. *The New Testament in Current Study* (New York, 1962), 72.

27. Cf. *Die Erforschung der synoptischen Evangelien* (4th ed., Berlin, 1961), 53.

28. "La divinité de Jésus dans les évangiles synoptiques," *Lumière et Vie*, 9 (April, 1963), 43–74. This was reprinted in *Exégèse et Théologie*, I, 117–142. Our references will be to the latter, since it is probably more accessible to our readers.

29. *L'Evangile selon Saint Matthieu* (1st ed., Paris, 1950), 103: "To the confession of Jesus' messiahship, reported by Mark and Luke, Matthew adds the formal profession of his divine origin."

30. "Etudes matthéennes: La Confession de Pierre à Césarée," *Sciences Ecclésiastiques*, 6 (1954), 51–61.

31. For an indication of some who think that in this text "Son of God" has only a messianic meaning, cf. D. J. Saunders, "The Confession of Peter," *Theological Studies*, 10 (1949), 522.

32. Cf. S. Mowinckel, *He that Cometh*, tr. G. Anderson (New York-Nashville, n. d.), 293: "It is, however, most improbable that the Jews ever called the Messiah the 'son of God,' although a Messianic interpretation of Ps. ii might have suggested such a title." J. Schmid expresses himself even more positively against the existence of the usage; cf. *Das Evangelium nach Markus*, 17 f.

33. This seems to be the case also in the closely related Temptation accounts; cf. Benoit, *Exégèse et Théologie*, I, 129.

34. It is widely accepted that Jesus' designation of Himself as "Son of Man" is derived from Daniel 7. There is disagreement whether, in addition to that, the late-Jewish Book of Enoch also influenced Jesus in His choice of the

title. In Enoch, as in the gospels, the term is applied to an individual, whereas in Daniel the collective meaning is prominent: the "one like a son of man" (7, 13) is a personification of the Jewish people. However, those who think that there is no need to suppose the influence of Enoch point out that in Hebrew thought the individual and the collectivity may be complementary rather than mutually exclusive, *viz.*, the collectivity (in this case, Israel) is embodied in an individual who is its perfect representative. They feel that Jesus individualized the title in the sense that in Him the true Israel achieves concrete reality; cf. R. H. Fuller, *The Mission and Achievement of Jesus* (London, 1954), 102. However, if one explains Jesus' use of the title solely in terms of Daniel 7, it is difficult to see in it the notion of "heavenly origin" on which Benoit lays much stress. It is not said in Daniel that the "Son of Man" is of heavenly *origin*, whereas he is clearly so in Enoch.

35. *Op. cit.*, 141.
36. *Ibid.*, 129.
37. *Ibid.*, 130.
38. *Ibid.*
39. *Das Evangelium nach Matthäus*, 247. One might point out that the character of the excellent and much praised series to which Schmid's commentary belongs is such that one cannot say that his view is an hypothesis which a professional exegete might present for the consideration of fellow specialists, but which has no place in works intended for the formation of theological students or for the instruction of educated laymen.
40. "Messiasbekenntnis und Petrusverheissung," 2 Teil, *Biblische Zeitschrift*, 2 (1958), 96.
41. *Art. cit.*, 60 f.
42. *Les Béatitudes: Le problème littéraire, Le message doctrinal* (Bruges-Louvain, 1954).
43. *Les Béatitudes: Le problème littéraire* (Bruges-Louvain, 1958).
44. Cf. his review of the first edition in *Verbum Domini*, 33 (1955), 299.
45. *Op. cit.*, 2nd ed., 10–16; cf. also R. Schnackenburg, *La Théologie du Nouveau Testament* (Bruges, 1961), 47.
46. *Op. cit.*, 15.
47. *Ibid.*, 16.
48. *Ibid.*, 35 f.
49. *Ibid.*, 343.
50. *Op. cit.*, 1st ed., 176.
51. *Ibid.*, 136.
52. *Ibid.*, 178.
53. *Op. cit.*, 2nd ed. 305 f.; 342.
54. The important work of Birger Gerhardsson, *Memory and Manuscript* (Uppsala, 1962), should serve as a deterrent from hasty conclusions about the modification of the sayings and deeds of Jesus in the process of transmission. On the other hand, while Gerhardsson recognizes that one of the reasons for differences between parallel gospel texts is "the principles of redaction used by the different Evangelists" (335), he seems not to take sufficient account of the evangelists' redactional work.

4 Miracles and Contemporary Theology

ROBERT W. GLEASON

Today's idea of a miracle is a return to the biblical notion of a message from one Person to another in the encounter of faith.

IN THEOLOGICAL WRITINGS about miracles today there is somewhat less uniformity of opinion than obtained in the eighteenth and most of the nineteenth century. The definition of miracle, its relation to natural laws, and its knowability have been widely discussed. Since miracles are so intimately bound up with the Christian faith, it is perhaps worthwhile to outline somewhat briefly the controverted positions and to see their development in the Scriptures and tradition.

Sacred Scripture presents us with the description of prodigies that manifest God's goodness and power and point to the existence of a world beyond the visible. The Old Testament has as one of its central themes the marvelous deeds worked by God for His chosen people and His command over nature and history. Jahweh is great and incomprehensible; His deeds are causes for wonderment. They are strange, manifesting the presence of a holy and terrible God whose sovereignty extends over all creation.[1]

The Old Testament understands the miracle not only as a physical prodigy but as a sign given to confirm the faith of a people who constantly demonstrated their need for confirmation. Hence Jahweh's miracles are most conspicuous at the time of the Exodus and again at those periods when His power had to be clearly upheld in opposition to that of the Baals of Israel's neighbors. Creation itself is ordered to the covenant and all reality proclaims the greatness of God whose power is unlimited. Nothing is impossible to Him; He can give victory as He chooses. The history of Israel is itself viewed as a prodigious ordering of secular history by God to Israel's salvation. History is not simply an orderly succession of events but a divine, continuous creation.

The physical prodigy is a concrete and concentrated manifestation of God's powerful protection of Israel. Having always the function of a sign, it leads men to acknowledge the transcendent hidden God whose wonderful deeds arouse awe and faith.

Moses is granted the power to produce miracles, as an instrument of God, because he has the task of confirming the faith of His people. Isaiah is aware that he can produce whatever sign Achaz may ask, for the faith of the king is at stake. But the great miracle of the Old Testament remains Israel herself, experiencing continually in her history the active intervention of God.[2] The crossing of the Red Sea is the prototype of God's wonderful actions in Israel's behalf: Moses is present to fit this event into a religious context and to interpret its value as a sign of God's faithful intentions.

For the Israelite the concept of miracle is never divorced from that of sign: a miracle takes place at a particular time, in a particular arrangement of circumstances which sets in evidence God's marvelous intervention in behalf of His covenanted people. "Here, then," said the Lord, "is the covenant I will make. Before the eyes of all your people I will work such marvels as have never been wrought in any nation anywhere on earth, so that this people among whom you live may see how awe-inspiring are the deeds which I, the Lord, will do at your side" (Ex. 34:10). According to the Old Testament, the deepest meaning of the miracle lies in this connection of the prodigy performed and the invitation to faith that it contains. Hence at the beginning of the prophetic age when faith in God had to be sustained against the encroachment of syncretism, miracles will be frequent. During the exile they will also be needed to reassure a defeated people as they encounter a powerful civilization and its false gods. Each period of crisis calls for a new demonstration of Jahweh's power and invites anew to faith.[3]

The interpreter of the miracle is normally present in the person of a prophet who judges history and events and reads the sign to the people. The people have the role of witnesses to God's superiority over the gods of the nations and the miracle is given to testify to this superiority. Israel is to see that in contrast to Egypt's limited powers, Jahweh is supremely powerful. The Israelites are to realize that the dominion of Jahweh extends also over the Assyrians. He can use foreigners to chastise Israel because they too fall under His marvelous dominion. Jahweh alone is the controlling force of history, its directing will. His free choice of Israel over other nations indicates that His power is universal. He can lead the Philistines where He will; he can use Assyria as a rod because history and creation are utterly subject to Him who is subject to no one. Nothing is too wonderful for His power. "The Lord said to Abraham, "Why did Sarah laugh, saying, 'Shall I indeed bear a child, although I am old?' Is anything too wonderful for the Lord?" (Gen. 18:13-14).

The wonderful deeds of Jahweh invite to faith; they also point to the future, to the last times, when the final kingdom of God will be established. The new earth and new heavens of Isaiah are foretold by the miracle with its demonstration of the submission of earthly reality to the will of Jahweh. When He comes to dwell among His people His coming will have been announced ahead of time by His prodigious deeds for the people of the covenant. Israel's miraculous history will then find its fulfillment.

The classic type of miracle—the crossing of the Red Sea—demonstrates the pattern of the Old Testament miracle. The miracle consists in this, that at a particular time and with a particular meaning a crossing was made possible by Jahweh as a sign of His presence in Israel's midst. The elements involved are a physical prodigy, the presence of an interpreter, and a meaning attached, pointing to the future of Israel. To Israel this passing of the Red Sea was no unaccountable freak of nature, but the response of nature to the summons of nature's maker.[4] Miriam's song celebrated it with the words: "Sing to the Lord for he is gloriously triumphant: horse and chariot he has cast into the sea." (Ex. 15,21).

Israel's concept of a miracle was not precisely that of "an exception to a natural law." When Israel reflected upon a universe governed by stable laws she wondered at their constancy and stability, taking them as occasions to glorify Jahweh who so established the world in harmony. But she did not possess the idea of a self-sustaining universe, an independent realm of laws from which

God is absent. He sustains His creation and it submits to His will. Simple natural events and great prodigies as well are all expressions of this will. God is constantly active in history, molding history and events and the universe for the purposes He has in mind for His covenanted people. The regular turn of the seasons, the fall of rain, the growth of crops express God's will. He is not withdrawn from his creation; at moments of crisis, He makes His presence felt in a special manner in His wonderful deeds. After all, His very name is wonderful. It is to be expected that "signs" and "wonders" should fall from His guiding hand. An extraordinary event, or an extraordinary concursus of events, assumes the importance of a sign because, to the Israelite, God is not aloof from the world but immediately present. To Him, in the ultimate analysis, must be ascribed both the regular course of human life and its extraordinary moments. When His presence is pointed out in a special way, when a national prodigy summons the people again to a belief in His active presence in their midst, they would speak of a miracle. It was an event of profound significance because it spoke to them of God's activity in their favor. The Israelites did not attempt a rational, philosophic analysis of nature and her limits. The entire world is a miracle of God and the idea of miracle is implied in God's creative activity. Nature, which in awe-inspiring phenomenon reveals God's presence, is viewed as the immediate and mysterious work of God. To Israel, nature has not the hostile and terrifying aspects it could assume in other religions because it is totally submissive to Him.[5]

God's work in history is accompanied by revelation and this concept of the close connection between miracle and prophetic revelation dates from the beginning of Israel's religious convictions. Belief in God is firmly based upon the fact of His activity in history and history is the background against which Israel's faith stands out. Having intervened in behalf of this oppressed people, He called her into being as a people, a fact to which the prophets constantly point. By His activity for the salvation of His people He reveals Himself as the living and present God, faithful, holy and just. Israel's destiny is controlled by God who intervenes to judge and to save: His interventions are awe-inspiring and majestic but they lead to faith and love. The great event, fixed forever in Israel's national consciousness, was the crossing of the Red Sea.[6]

It would be quite futile to interrogate the Old Testament concerning a "scientific" concept of miracle. The whole burden of Israel's faith is that Jahweh is the transcendent Lord of nature which He submits to His saving will. The people survived every crisis on the basis of this faith. To examine the natural laws which provided the framework for God's rescue did not interest the Hebrew. The fact was clear: over and over again God bent natural forces to His desire to save a helpless people. To seek to explain the wonder of the Exodus on purely natural grounds would have seemed futile and absurd to the Hebrew. Jahweh can and did work wonders in delivering His people. The Hebrew did not debate whether these were done by an exception to natural laws or not. Nature and the constant operations of nature are subject to a personality outside of nature: Jahweh. The operations of nature are themselves a wonder: Jahweh's control of nature and history for Israel's salvation is a wonder. At the heart of the Exodus story is the historical fact that God intervened in a marvelous fashion to shape history and submit nature to His plans. Israel's faith was based upon actual events in which it perceived the hand of God.

In sum we might say of Israel that her faith was based upon miracles: that miracles, while not scientifically examined, were understood as Jahweh's direct and wonderful interventions in history and nature to stand as signs inviting to faith and pointing to the last days when His kingdom would be fulfilled.

As the Old Testament had seen miracles to be a proof of God's intervention in favor of His people, so the New Testament presented Christ's miracles as a proof of His divine mission. In His public life Christ Himself had pointed to His works as confirmation of His divine mission.[7] Throughout the first centuries following His death the Church again referred to Christ's miracles to establish the rational grounds for belief, His deeds being sufficient indication of His divinity. But there was as yet little scientific speculation concerning the precise nature of a miracle or its relation to faith. The word "miracle," as late as the fourth century, had many varied meanings in Christian writings. For Augustine a miracle may mean an extraordinary and marvelous event which is the product of angelic or diabolic power, the prodigies performed by pagan gods, or that which is prodigious, unexpected, and contrary to what we know of the course of nature. Later, Augustinians were

to interpret Augustine as having understood by a miracle that
which transcends the operation of natural causes and requires the
intervention of God. Augustine also believed that God, the author
of nature, had implanted certain virtualities in creatures which
could respond to His activity and thus allow them to produce the
miraculous occurrence when God so willed.[8]

Further speculation on the nature of a miraculous event was
indulged in by the successors of Augustine who stressed the revealing character of a prodigy, that is, as indicating the presence of the
divine power, and pointing to an order above nature and produced
outside of or contrary to the customary order of natural causes. St.
Thomas made the next and decisive step when he defined a miracle
as that which is contrary to the usual course of nature. Hence the
element of the startling, the unexpected, the prodigious is played
down since, as St. Thomas remarks, "even though a thing took
place every day, it would be a miracle if it were beyond the order of
all created nature" (*Summa Theologica* I., q. 110, a. 4). In addition, St. Thomas recognizes as a strict miracle only that which the
angels or devils could not do of their own power but which requires the action of God.[9]

Benedict XIV in his classic work *De servorum Dei beatifica-
tione et beatorum canonizatione* modifies St. Thomas' position
somewhat in conceding that an effect produced by angelic forces,
acting by their own power, with divine approbation, may be called
a miracle. It would, however, be called only a minor miracle, the
term "major" being reserved for those miracles which surpass the
forces of *all* created nature, including the angelic, and demand
God for their author. Benedict also stressed that in evaluating the
phenomena we must look to the religious *purpose* of the event. A
true miracle has a clearly religious purpose and is directed to the
confirmation of truth or of personal sanctity. This line of thinking
was further developed by many Catholic theologians of the nineteenth century. Confronted with phenomena in the religions of
pagan Greece, India, China, and Rome which bore some external
resemblance to the wonders of the Old and the New Testament,
these theologians distinguished the true miracle as one produced
by God and His benevolent angels, while admitting that God might
permit diabolic agencies to bring about externally similar phenomena through their native powers. The character of the event, the

purpose, the *method,* the *circumstances* and the *moral effects* will indicate whether the agent is Divine, angelic, or diabolical.[10] Not all theologians agreed with this position, some preferring to restrict the term "miracle" to those events which transcend the powers of all created natures, including those of the angels and devils. However, by the beginning of the twentieth century the distinction between major and minor miracles had gained ground and today is more commonly admitted. The fact that an event surpasses the visible and corporeal forces of nature is sufficient to establish it as a miracle, if its character manifests that its author is either God or an angel. The event transcends human forces and this marks it as miraculous, granted that the purpose, method, circumstances, and moral effects all point to God or an angel as its author.[11]

Catholic theologians in the twentieth century have often stressed the *sign aspect* of a miracle, something which had been somewhat less emphasized as long as the aspect of transcendence was being debated. They are by no means, however, unanimously in agreement as to the definition of a miracle, but there is evident a general tendency to insist upon its religious context and its value as a divine sign. Many insist also upon the fact that a miracle is a fact perceptible by the senses. Some Thomists, such as Garrigou-Lagrange, adhere very closely to the position of St. Thomas, refusing even to extend the term "miracle" in a strict sense to cover prodigious events accomplished by angelic forces with the approbation of God. They prefer to denominate such events as relative miracles, miracles *secundum quid,* that is, events verifying the definition of miracle only analogously. Others who also insist that a miracle must be perceptible by the senses do not consider suprasensible events such as the virginal conception of Christ as miracles, perferring to call them "miraculous facts." Marcozzi suggests that their principal preoccupation is to tailor the definition of miracles to the statement of the Vatican Council (Denzinger, 1790) that miracles are "most certain signs" of divine revelation.

Those theologians who stress the note of sign in miracles are clearly turning back to Augustine, for whom the preternatural aspect of miracles was less important than that of sign. For Augustine all events were signs of God's power and His love for humanity; the change of water into wine at Cana is astounding, but the appearance of wine-grapes each year is also marvelous. God works miracles to astonish us when we become too accustomed to the daily exercise of His forces in nature and need more striking signs. In the face of ordinary routine life we tend to become blinded to God's presence, so He arouses us by a prodigious sign of His divine power and goodness. Miracles are not just prodigies, they are religious prodigies in a definite context and are a communication from God to man. Christ's healings in the Gospel stress the goodness and mercy of God; they manifest His omnipotence and bounty, and the context in which they take place invites us to faith and gratitude. They are the specific signs of a whole new order established in the world by Christ Jesus who has been sent for the redemption of the world.[12] Outside of this religious context the physical prodigy would be unintelligible. E. Dhanis remarks that the extraordinary event assumes in its context the character of a reply or a sign from God; it is a testimony of God's good will, of warning, of teaching, a seal of approval on doctrines and persons. The extraordinary event in question is so closely linked to a particular religious context that we are able to perceive it as a divine intervention.[13]

Other authors stress the notion of context and sign to such an extent as to find quite incomplete the definition of miracle as an event that surpasses the laws of nature. In their eyes certain Scholastic authors have viewed miracles too exclusively from the viewpoint of efficient cause and not sufficiently from the aspect of final causes.[14] As a result it often seemed that one had only to consider the preternatural aspect of the event to decide whether or not it was miraculous. With some authors today the pendulum has swung completely in the opposite direction. For them the transcendence of a miracle is not disclosed to us in the fact that it surpasses the capacities of nature, but the religious context makes evident that this extraordinary, baffling, beneficial event, a sign of God's message to us, is not produced by natural agencies. Seen in its total context it is clear that the author of the event can only be God, and not a natural agency. Hence the miracle has a double element, an observable fact and the religious meaning *inherent* in this fact. The physical event in all its extraordinariness is a necessary part of the miracle, but it remains secondary in its importance, its full significance comprehensible only in the light of its context, its doctrinal signification, its role as part of a dialogue between God and men.[15]

Consequently some think that the surpassing of nature's capacities should not be stressed as the essential element in a miracle; they point out that to define a miracle in this way is of little practical value since one can never establish with certainty that a given fact is a violation of nature.

Guy de Broglie has commented at length on these two conceptions and on the apologetic value of miracles. His major objection to too great a divorce between the physical event and the doctrine it confirms is that in the concrete it is very difficult to prove scientifically that an event is attributable to God alone, if one divorces it from the context of the doctrine it confirms.[16] And he remarks that it is more difficult than appears at first sight to establish that a certain physical operation is exclusively proper to God. Creation *ex nihilo* is certainly an instance, but the cases are perhaps limited where one can prove by strictly metaphysical arguments that only God could have produced this effect. Could we demonstrate metaphysically that only God can calm a tempest, change water into wine, give sight to the blind? An apologetic of miracles which claims to establish scientifically the divine origin of prodigies from considerations of a purely physical and metaphysical nature inevitably ends up enmeshed in inextricable difficulties. It is quite difficult to prove scientifically the concrete realization of those rare actions whose very nature permits us to reserve them to God alone. How can we establish with scientific exactitude that in the case of a particular raising of a dead man the soul actually had left the body? De Broglie believes that the more sane approach to an apologetic of miracles is to place the physical event fully in its religious context. Christian miracles are complementary signs and cannot be separated from the other fundamental signs that testify to the Christian message, that is, *the excellence of the doctrine* of Christ and the divine *transcendence* of the virtues he displayed. They must be considered in their concrete liaison with the doctrine of the Gospels themselves. The divine transcendence of Christ's doctrine pleads effectively for the truth of the doctrine and the concrete manifestation of divine life pleads effectively for the divine authority of Christ and the Church. Miracles are complementary signs, subsidiary and accidental, linked to the more fundamental signs. They have their full normal value only in conjunction with doctrine and sanctity.[17]

Maurice Blondel had long ago objected to what he considered

an unnatural separation of the physical event of a miracle from its context and doctrinal meaning.[18] His viewpoint was that a miracle was not strictly speaking an exception to the laws of nature since nature does not have such fixed laws. In a miracle we have an extraordinary event, unexplainable, baffling, unparalleled, in sharp contrast to the ordinary course of events—a physical *prodigy*. This prodigy is intrinsically linked with doctrine so that the doctrine illuminates the event and the event confirms the doctrine. Possibly the brute fact is explainable by natural laws, but in the situation God provides adequate proof of His intervention.

It is useless to attempt a proof, *more geometrico,* of a miracle by applying deductive philosophical principles or experimental methods. One must interpret the event by its religious significance which is as form to the matter of the prodigy. This is an event for the benefit of mankind, which points to the supernatural world, completely woven into a doctrinal and religious context and unexplainable and unintelligible without that context. Because it can be grasped only as what it is, in a particular religious context, it definitely bears the stamp of divine intervention, bearing a message to man from God. The circumstances in which it occurs are the ultimate reason that it can be seen as "transcending" the law of nature. But the attempt first to discover the laws of nature and all their possibilities is useless.

Without endorsing Blondel's position and in fact while rejecting his particular understanding of the transcendence of nature, recent writers have tried to bring to the fore again those elements in tradition which Blondel had emphasized. François Taymans notes that when the Vatican Council declared that miracles are most certain signs of revelation which manifest God's power and goodness, it harmonized two aspects of tradition: the fact that a miraculous event has an exceptional character, which the ordinary and normal course of nature does not explain, and the fact that it occurs in a religious context.[19] If Anselm neglected the sign aspect of miracle, St. Thomas did not (*Summa Theologica* III, q. 43, a. 4). But the emphasis of St. Thomas' writings, as with those Scholastics who followed him, was primarily fixed upon the efficient cause. Non-Catholic authors often deduce from popular theology manuals that the Church decided whether or not an event was a miracle by an appeal to its transcendence of natural causes, without any consideration of its context. Moreover, the objections raised against the possibility of miracles often reveal the inadequacy of the concept, as though the fact isolated from its context were intelligible in itself. Taymans insists that a miracle is a sign and that one cannot understand it separated from the reality it signifies. As a sign of Revelation it is a sign of a specific new order, the supernatural order. Precisely because it is a sign of an order superior to nature, it must in itself be recognizable as superior to the order of natural causality. A miracle is therefore a sensible sign which the habitual course of nature does not explain but which God produces in a religious context as a sign of the supernatural.

It is interesting to note that Taymans does not insist upon the note "constituting an exception to natural laws." A miracle certainly contradicts the common and stable observations of mankind, but not necessarily natural laws understood as principles founded critically and scientifically. Were it a miracle only if it did so, the miracle would lose its value as sign for the ordinary man; and the witnesses of the miracles of the Old and New Testaments were not ordinarily scientists. A scientist can have certitude concerning a miracle, but so can a prudent yet unscientific intelligence. This certitude is certainly prescientific, but it is none the less real and sufficient to justify prudent assent. Taymans notes also that Christian tradition has included in the number of Christ's miracles a number of events which the ordinary course of nature does not easily explain and yet which *could* be produced by natural causes. In the concrete religious context in which they were produced, one becomes aware that, although nature might be their author, absolutely speaking, in the context, God is the author. That Christ should order the apostles to let down their nets at a particular spot and time after a fruitless night to catch a great draft of fishes makes it evident that He has intervened. The concept of "exception to the laws of nature" must be sufficiently fluid to allow for such events.

Part of the context of a miracle is precisely the appeal made to God; men pray, wait, hope, and God responds.

In a particularly judicious article on the subject, E. Dhanis notes that certain Catholic philosophers and theologians today have a tendency to abstract from the idea of an "exception to natural laws."[20] He is careful to explain that this formula "exception to natural laws" does not imply that natural laws do not operate in the miracle situation and that natural forces, elevated by a superior power, cannot contribute to the miraculous effect. A transcendent intervention may make use of the proper powers of nature. God may, for example, accelerate the natural healing processes, so that an instantaneous cure takes place, but which follows certain natural laws. *Some* miracles can be so explained. Dhanis admits too that a lively faith in God may merit God's action: and it may also adopt the subject of the miraculous cure to be the earthly point of insertion for God's miraculous action.

Dhanis concedes also that many cannot accept the notion of a miracle as an exception to natural laws; for they think that this would be to deprive the universe of order. But various orders exist in the universe, hierarchically organized, and the orders of ethical and religious realities, and of grace, are superior to the order of nature. An exception to the inferior order is still a part of the total order.

One of the reasons frequently alleged for passing over in silence the notion of an exception to the laws of nature is the difficulty of knowing them fully. Dhanis argues that *in certain circumstances* we can know them sufficiently to make a judgment concerning an exception. If the prodigy is exceptional, contrary to the usual course of nature observed in many and varied situations, if it is free from weird or artificial elements engendering the suspicion that new and artificial factors are at work, and if one is aware of no other such phenomena in secular circumstances, then one may know that he is face to face with an exception to natural laws.[21]

Dhanis believes that the number and variety of circumstances in which an extraordinary event is realized and the normal environment in which it takes place tend to exclude the possibility that it is attributable to the operation of some *unknown* natural factor. The fact that we do not know of similar prodigies in secular or pagan situations persuades us that the event is not simply a case of an exceptional collaboration of known laws of nature. The exceptions to the known laws of nature will not surpass certain limits; they will not fulfill the above-mentioned three conditions.

Dhanis doubts that one can sacrifice the physical transcendence of a miracle—its exception to natural laws—without weakening the certitude derived from miracles. Such a precision from physical transcendence would also, in his opinion, be less consonant with tradition. The Vatican Council, for example, had distinguished miracles and prophecies, one of which reveals the omnipotence of God and the other the divine knowledge; both of these, miracles and prophecy, are most certain signs of divine revelation. But if one takes the approach of certain authors, both miracles and prophecy would be recognizable because of their transcendence *as signs,* authentic signs from God in a providentially arranged religious context. This, however, would not result in two *distinct* types of divine intervention: of power and of knowledge; but would rather manifest one object: God intervening by prudence to arrange the meeting of extraordinary events with religious circumstances and context. It appears that the Vatican Council implied more than that in distinguishing the effects of God's omnipotence and His omniscience.[22]

Dhanis admits, however, that the Vatican Council did not intend to propose the physical transcendence of a miracle as an object of *faith.* It appears to him, however, that the mind of the Council demonstrates that the sign value of a miracle is at least highly guaranteed by its physical transcendence, although the Council does not necessarily imply that one can *only* discern a miracle as such if one takes this transcendence into account. It seems to us that Dhanis' case rests primarily upon his rational arguments to establish that one who prescinds from the physical transcendence of a miracle has no certain basis left for recognizing a miracle as such. If one admits physical transcendence, one has a certain norm for stating that this particular prodigy in this religious context is a sign from God. If one does not admit such transcendence, how can one be sure?

In 1906 Abbé Bros, supporting and developing the ideas of Blondel, had proposed a method for discerning a miracle without appeal to physical transcendence. Like Blondel, Bros did not believe that a miracle could be defined simply by its transcendence of natural laws.[23] The reason for his position was the classic objection: we can never be sure when a fact does transcend natural laws since we do not know everything about natural laws. Moreover, a miracle may well take place when the event *is naturally achievable,* but the context and sign value point to God's intervention. Bros suggested as a norm for recognition of a miracle the theory of "constant coincidents." The extraordinary, baffling and wonderful events all take place in such a context that we can with safety declare that God has intervened. These events bear the mark of the supernatural; their religious characteristics, the circumstances in which they occur, manifest God as the common antecedent. The constant factor is the evident religious connection pointing to God. Seeing the event in its totality we can only conclude that the author of the event is God. Scientific apologetics can then identify a miracle by applying the method of constant coincidents. Through elimination of all the variable and accidental circumstances it discovers one that is constant.

There are, moreover, necessary dispositions of a moral order before one can read aright the sign that is a miracle. An interior spiritual preparation is needed—not faith, for that would be a vicious circle—but at least a receptivity to religious matters, a willingness to believe, if it appears rational and prudent, and an openness to the truth.

Dhanis criticizes this method by pointing out that in the ultimate analysis, if it is to give certitude, it must depend upon a recognition of that physical transcendence which its authors reject or consider useless. He submits that a coincidence of context and prodigy, if found in only one instance, would be of little significance. Here we disagree with him. Even one instance, given the proper dispositions in the viewer and a fortunate set of circumstances, should awaken more than the suspicion that the event is owing to chance.[24]

One should really, he continues, consider several or many prodigies of different types. But even this would not suffice, for if one could discover similar cases, even imperfectly similar, in secular surroundings, the argument would prove nothing. One would be reduced to those miracles which verify the note of transcendence of natural laws and *it is this* which lies at the basis of the theory of constant coincidents.

The theory of constant coincidents should be valid for the future, if it is so for the present and past. But it cannot prove that Providence must in the future assure that at no point in history can there be similar prodigies in secular situations. The only firm basis of such a proof, Dhanis believes, would be the irreducibility of such prodigies to the laws of nature.[25] This argument seems to us weak. In the classic theory Providence assures us that a physically transcendent miracle will not be worked in confirmation of a false doctrine or religion. Why not invoke it also to assure that prodigies will not take place in profane circumstances? If the theorists of context coincidents cannot appeal to Providence to ensure that prodigies do not occur in a profane context, why should the classical theorists appeal to God's wisdom and goodness not to lead man into error through confirming by a miracle a false religion? Moreover, the question of a profane context is not precisely what is at issue. If the constant-coincidents theory is correct, prodigies in a secular context would not even be examined for miraculous properties. The religious nature of the context is intrinsic to the prodigy, whether the religion be false or true. Once you demand a religious context it appears to us that Providence can be legitimately appealed to.

There is perhaps a certain obscurity which prevents our understanding of the relationship between physical miracles and physical laws. In order to throw light on the matter, W. H. Nicholls wrote his article "Physical Laws and Physical Miracles."[26] Nicholls claims that our confusion results chiefly from an overemphasis on the aspect of a miracle as an exception to physical law. Theologians claim that the principle of sufficient reason demands the positive intervention of God as the only possible explanation for the miraculous physical event. In his article Nicholls shows that that is not necessarily the case.

A physical law is defined as intelligibility immanent in the uniform activity of bodies. Denial of the fact that physical laws do exist outside the mind and outside the senses inevitably leads to sheer skepticism. That some physical laws are certain, is obvious, as for example, "A grown man *generally* cannot walk on an unfrozen lake." There are, of course, various types of physical laws— determinate and statistical, unverifiable and empirically verifiable.

A determinate law describes single events which are assigned a probability of one or zero and which can be recognized by words such as "always" or "never." For example: at ordinary pressure, water always expands upon freezing.[27]

A statistical law describes events or a number of sets of events by assigning to them fractional probabilities, using the words *"generally," "rarely."* For example: according to statistical mechanics, under stated conditions of temperature and pressure the probability that a man can walk on a lake for ten seconds is one in $10^{10,000,000,000}$.

Now a physical miracle is defined as a physical, extraordinary observable event of Divine authorship. To be recognized as such it must occur in a religious context and be so extraordinary that God's intervention is certain.

A religious context is had when there is a positive absence of the devil's work and a positive reference to God. An example would be the raising of Lazarus, an act which the principle of sufficient reason moves our mind to accept as miraculous.

The raising of Lazarus is also a physically extraordinary event, having reference to a verifiable physical law which is statistical, objective, and certain. People who have apparently died and have been buried for three days have a *vanishingly small probability* of returning to life. As long as this law speaks of "vanishingly small" probability rather than of a probability, the event is an *exception*, not a violation of a physical law.

A miracle, however, such as that of Peter walking on the water, does not seem to be an exception to any verifiable physical law. Without a religious context this event is inexplicable except in terms of an exceedingly improbable statistical freak within the laws of statistical mechanics (one in $10^{10,000,000,000}$). This might seem merely a chance event within the laws of nature but the religious context is the clue needed to explain the miracle satisfactorily. The human mind could never be satisfied with a mere scientific explanation of the infinitesimal, nonzero probability of someone saying, "Come," and Peter's action of walking on the water. The religious context, not the existential skeleton of the incident, frees the mind of doubt and gives certitude to the intellect. It is a case of common sense, not modern science, and of a religious context intimately joined with a physical event.[28]

The certain recognition of the miraculous, then, does not depend on our knowledge of physical laws, or even on the recognition of a strict exception to any verifiable physical law. These are not necessary, for a highly improbable case within a statistical framework can *under suitable circumstances* be recognized as a miracle. Such, at least, is the opinion of Father Nicholls, who points out that to claim that we can prove that a given event

In Loving Memory of

MARGARET KEYES
Passed Away
January 21, 1991

Mass of the Resurrection
Holy Cross R. C. Church
Saturday,
February 2, 1991 - 10:30 AM

Interment
St. John's Cemetery

———

Prayer Of
St. Francis Of Assisi

Lord make me an instrument of
your peace, where there is hatred
let me sow love; where there is injury,
pardon; where there is doubt, faith;
where there is despair, hope; where
there is darkness, light and where
there is sadness, joy.

Grant that I may not
so much seek to be consoled as to
console; to be understood as to under
stand; to be loved as to love; for it is
in giving that we receive; it is in
pardoning that we are pardoned and in
dying that we are born to eternal life

contradicts the laws of nature would seem nonsense to a scientist. Our knowledge of nature is too meager. A scientist would admit that Peter's walking on the waters was extraordinary, but would add that modern science does not exclude the possibility but merely reduces the probability to the vanishing point. The fact that a grown man cannot walk on an unfrozen lake is only statistical law, but it is certainly true, it can be empirically checked, it is verifiable. However, even if *all* physical laws were of this variety we could recognize a miracle when the vanishingly small probability occurs, *if the religious context and sign value were to be taken into consideration.* The raising of Lazarus demonstrates the same point. It cannot be simply an improbable statistical freak in the precise *context* in which it occurs. In other words, it is not necessary to verify the presence of an *exception* to some certainly known physical law in order to recognize a miracle. Nicholls believes that miracles do confront us with the evidence of a special divine causality expressing itself as a violation of some, perhaps *unverifiable,* physical law, but that it is not necessary to recognize a violation of a *certainly* known physical law to declare that a miracle is present.

Modern science seems generally to accept the fact that all scientific laws are not sufficiently known to establish with certainty what is beyond the powers of nature. The scientific investigation of miracles has been made more difficult by the transition from a deterministic viewpoint of the universe to one which looks on the laws of nature as statistical. One type of statistical theory prevalent today deals with large numbers of observable events, and furnishes a difficulty to the theory of miracles in that it allows for the concept of fluctuations. Fluctuations are improbable, but *possible;* no deviation from the law is outside the scope of theory. The laws of probability simply make exceptions unlikely. Hence the scientist, when confronted with a baffling event, does not see this as an *exception* to the law, but as one included, with a very slight degree of probability, in the law itself. He is aware that his knowledge of the laws of nature is incomplete and hence his reaction is not likely to be that the startling event is impossible.

A second type of statistical theory in vogue today is that of quantum mechanics, a highly intricate mathematical formalism developed largely in the third decade of this century. While the first type of statistical theory deals with the behavior of systems composed of large numbers of particles, quantum mechanics deals with the behavior of individual microscopic particles. It is basic to this theory that a statement made about an individual particle or event must be stated in the language of probability. A quantum-mechanics law can tell us only what will probably happen in any given case. This gives added strength to the objection to miracles taken from statistical theories; how can we state that something is contrary to the laws of nature if the laws of nature give us only probabilities?[29]

In conclusion, we may attempt to summarize the varying positions of Catholic theologians today on the subject of miracles. Certain theologians believe that a miracle is physically transcendent, that it can be known as such with certainty and *without* appeal to its seismological transcendence. Others believe that it is hardly ever possible to *prove* physical transcendence and that this element is not needed in the definition; thus the question as to whether or not a miracle is *de facto* physically transcendent is relatively unimportant. Others believe that a miracle is physically transcendent and should be so defined but that this transcendence cannot be known aside from the seismological transcendence. Hence, as regards the knowability of a miracle, the element of physical transcendence can and should be underplayed. It is sufficient to establish the existence of a divine sign without entering into the question as to whether the event is caused by a direct intervention of God or by His providential arranging of the joining of context and prodigy. Finally, some have suggested that God might have from the beginning foreseen and planned a statistical fluctuation to take place in a definite context and that this fluctuation, *in accordance with* natural statistical law, is sufficient for a miracle.

It should be obvious that recent insistence upon the total context and sign value of a miracle is an improvement over the more rationalistic position which had become generally accepted in manuals of theology. Almost all writers on the subject of miracles agree on this. Dhanis, who does not believe that the sign value is necessary to discern physical transcendence, has nevertheless provided one of the most illuminating analyses of miracle as sign. A considerable time will probably have to elapse before a final judgment can be given on these various theories. The area of disagreement is not so large as it may appear at first glance, and in some cases what appears new is a return to a position which is highly biblical and traditional. Augustine had emphasized the biblical concept of miracle as a divine sign. He would no doubt have appreciated the contributions of Pascal, Newman, and Scheler to an analysis of the subjective attitudes required for a real understanding of miracle. Those writers who stress the total context of a miracle are certainly close to the biblical notion of a miracle as an invitation on the part of God, a message addressed from one Person to another in the encounter of faith. The reintegration of the notions of context, sign value, and spiritual preparedness in the discussion of miracle makes it evident that Catholic theology is gaining balance and completeness in its treatment of miracles. The present-day treatment is thoroughly biblical. There did exist at one time the danger of one-sidedness in an approach to miracles simply as physically transcendent, when controversy with determinists and deists urged theologians to devote most of their attention to this aspect.

In the opinion of this author, dogmatic tradition persuades to the view that a miracle *is* physically transcendent, without imposing such a position as a matter of faith. However, the arguments used to prove that one can establish this physical transcendence independently of the religious context do not appear to me convincing. It seems that a prodigy which is an exception to physical laws from the statistical if not from the metaphysical viewpoint, and which is an effect of Providence, can be in certain contexts unmistakably recognized as a divine sign, whether or not one calls this a miracle in the strict sense. Again, whether a prodigy is caused by a *direct* intervention of God or by His mediate causality can be left an open question. In practice, as regards the *knowability* of a miracle, it seems to me a well-nigh impossible position to attempt to prove physical transcendence apart from the total context. If one *can* establish physical transcendence it will be only with the assistance lent to us by the total context.

When recent theologians speak of dispositions required for the recognition of a miracle, they are not implying that faith is one of them. But some appreciation of the supernatural quality of the sign seems to be demanded and a recognition that man must have an openness to religious truth together with an initial desire (not exigency) for a closer supernatural relationship with God which will open the mind to a higher order of reality than the natural. Grace can and does arouse in man a longing, howsoever vague, for that supernatural destiny to which man is *de facto* called. We believe that in the ordinary course of events this grace is operative in enabling man to discern in the miracle what it is—a sign of the supernatural world to which God invites him.

Father Liégé has aptly described the complex reality that is signified by a miracle:

As an extraordinary and beneficent event, it reveals the God of grace and of fatherly tenderness; as an act of healing it announces spiritual salvation; as an historical event it manifests the entrance of God into history. In brief, its whole significance bears witness to the coming of the Kingdom, the presence of God who vivifies and saves, who has pity on the human condition: it announces the Gospel.[30]

In the early part of the twentieth century, Modernism and liberal criticism tended to reject miracles as absurd. Today the situation has changed. There is a growing interest in exceptional phenomena which in some cases has progressed so far as to degenerate into irrational desire for the marvelous in religion.[31]

As Catholics we must remember two important points: (1) the traditional Christian view of miracles; (2) the final discerning of miracles is the prerogative of the Church.

The documents on which our Christian faith rest do contain a miraculous element. Deeds are attributed to Christ which are not considered normal. These are called marvels which cause wonder and awe because one meets in them something inexplicable of which God is maintained to be the cause. In these events God appears to work beyond the order of secondary causes, or if secondary causes are used, the effect seems to be beyond their ordinary capacity.

It is impossible to eliminate miracles from the Gospels for the sacred authors are convinced that there exist miraculous events performed by Christ by means of supranormal powers which show His union with the Father. Miracles can be denied only by saying that the Gospels are not historical.

However, the gospel writers do not list miracles for their own sake but rather as signs that point beyond themselves and draw out attention to something else. St. Mark uses them to indicate that God is at work in Christ to support His claim as Messias and Son of God; St. John, to indicate the glory of God present in the salvific work of Christ.

Miracles are acts in which God's salvific purpose is revealed. They are prodigies in which God intervenes directly or makes use of secondary causes to reveal His purpose. They are not *lawless violations* of natural order but rather a sign of a higher order, that of God's freely offered healing and elevating grace.

Miracles must always be recognized for what they really are— signs. The full significance of miraculous events dawns only on the mind that is illuminated by goodwill and drawn by grace. Miracles are objective, but it is only with the power of the Holy Ghost that their *full* meaning as signs can be grasped.

NOTES

1. C. Tresmontant, *Etudes de métaphysique biblique*, Paris, 1955, pp. 223–228.

2. H. Knight, "The Old Testament Concept of Miracle," *Scottish Journal of Theology* (1952), 335.

3. E. Jacob, *Theology of the Old Testament*, New York, 1955, pp. 223–235.

4. A. Lefèvre, "Miracle," *Dictionnaire de la Bible, Supplément*, col. 1301.

5. B. Anderson, *Understanding the Old Testament*, Englewood Cliffs, N. J., 1957, pp. 43–49.

6. H. Robinson, "The Nature Miracles of the Old Testament," *Journal of Theological Studies* (1944), 1.

7. P. Menoud, "Miracle et sacrement dans le Nouveau Testament," *Verbum Caro*, 1952, 142. Cf. J. Benoit, "La divinité de Jésus Christ dans les Evangiles Synoptiques," *Lumière et Vie* (1953), 43–74, and L. Cerfaux, "Temoins du Christ," *Angelicum* (1943), 166–183.

8. W. Carroll, "St. Augustine's Preaching on Miracles," *Homiletic and Pastoral Review* (1948), 755–762. See also: P. De Vooght, "La notion philosophique du miracle selon S. Augustin," *Recherches de théologie ancienne et médiévale* (1938), 317–343, and "La théologie du miracle selon Saint Augustin," *Recherches de théologie ancienne et médiévale* (1939), 197–222.

9. J. Hardon, "The Concept of Miracle from St. Augustine to Modern Apologetics," *Theological Studies* (1954), 229–257, and K. McNamara "The nature and recognition of miracles," *Irish Theological Quarterly* (1960), 301–302.

10. J. Hardon, *art. cit.* 235–245. Cf. A. van Hove, *La doctrine du miracle chez. S. Thomas et son accord avec les principes de la recherche scientifique*, Paris, 1927.

11. J. Hardon, *art. cit.*, 247.

12. L. de Grandmaison, *Jesus-Christ*, Paris, 1928, Vol. II, pp. 225–255. Cf. A. Liégé, "Reflexions théologiques sur le miracle" in *Pensée scientifique et foi chrétienne*, Paris (1953), 206–218; also E. Masure, "Le miracle comme signe," *Revue de sciences philosophiques et théologiques* (1959), 274 ff.; D. Dubarle "L'attitude du savant chrétien en face du fait merveilleux," *Lumière et Vie* (1957), 321–350.

13. E. Dhanis, "Qu'est-ce qu'un miracle?" *Gregorianum* (1959), 201–241.

14. V. Marcozzi, "II Miracolo," in *Problemi e Orientamenti di Teologia Dommatica*, Milan (1957), 108–109.

15. M. de Locht, "Maurice Blondel et sa controverse au sujet du miracle," *Ephemerides theologicae Lovanienses* (1954), 344–390.

16. G. de Broglie, *Pour une théorie rationale de l'acte de foi*, Part II, Paris, 1948, pp. 43–51.

17. *Ibid.*, pp. 51–54.

18. M. Blondel, *L'Action*, Paris, 1893, pp. 392–398. Cf. *Annales de philosophie chrétienne*, 1895–1896, pp. 337–346, 466–482, 599–616, 131–147, 255–267, 338–350; also A. Lalande, *Vocabulaire technique et critique de la philosophie*, Vol. I, pp. 469–471. See also P. De Locht, "Maurice Blondel et sa controverse au sujet du miracle," *Ephemerides theologicae Lovanienses* (1954), 344–390, and B. Welte, "Maurice Blondel," *Theologische Revue* (1955), 5–12.

19. F. Taymans "Le miracle, signe du surnaturel," *Nouvelle revue théologique* (1955), 222–245. For a full discussion of the importance of context see L. Monden, *Le Miracle signe du salut*, Paris, 1959.

20. E. Dhanis, "Qu'est-ce qu'un miracle?" *Gregorianum* (1959), 201–241; See also Dhanis, "Un chaînon de la preuve du miracle," in *Problemi scelti di teologia contemporanea* (Analecta Gregoriana 68) Rome, 1954, 66–70.

21. Dhanis, "Qu'est-ce qu'un miracle?" 213–214.

22. *Ibid.*, 219–224.

23. A. Bros, "Comment constater le miracle?" *Annales de philosophie chrétienne* (1906), 250–267.

24. Dhanis, "Qu'est-ce qu'un miracle?" 225.

25. *Ibid.*, 227.

26. W. Nicholls, "Physical Laws and Physical Miracles," *Irish Theological Quarterly* (1960), 49–56.

27. *Ibid.*

28. *Ibid.*

29. J. Carter, "Theological Recognition of Miracles," *Theological Studies* (1959), 175–197.

30. P. Liégé, "Le miracle dans la théologie catholique," *Lumière et Vie* (1957), 79.
It is of interest to note that the Protestant attitude to miracles has undergone an evolution in this century. See A. Fridrichsen, *Le problème du miracle dans le christianisme primitif*, Strasbourg, 1925; F. Torrance, *Expository Studies in St. John's Miracles*, London, 1938; A. Richardson, *The Miracle Stories of the Gospels*, London, 1941; and G. Marquardt, *Das Wunderproblem in der Deutschen protestantischen Theologie der Gegenwart*, 1933. Protestant theology after the First World War, with some exceptions, tends to approach the Catholic positions on miracles.

31. I. Hislop, "Miracles and the Gospels," *Blackfriars* (1958), 57–60.

5   *How Do We Prove That God Exists?*

J. MACDONALD SMITH

The challenge of contemporary atheism forces a re-evaluation of "proofs" of God's existence and leads to new approaches to the Absolute.

THOSE WHO FIND themselves unable to accept the view that the existence of God is rationally demonstrable fall into two classes. On the one hand there are those who as Christians believe in God, yet are unable to accept the traditional proofs of his existence, while on the other hand there are the antimetaphysicalists who are not even theists, precisely because they can see no reason for asserting the existence of God. For the former group, reason is useless, a broken tool in the hands of a fallen artisan; therefore the statement "God exists" is not significant, because what is really required is a confrontation of the individual with the living, revealing God. A distinction is made between "the God of the philosophers" and "the God of the Christians" and the traditional threefold distinction between believing that God exists, believing God, and believing in God is reduced to at most the twofold distinction between believing God and believing in God, and sometimes even to the single position summed up in the statement "I don't believe God exists; I believe in God." For the second class, philosophical empiricism, the result of the revolution which has overtaken philosophical studies during the last fifty years, has rendered somewhat old-fashioned the attitude that reason is the omnicompetent and infallible guide to truth, substituting for this the view that there is after all no certainty at all; and by demanding sense verification for every meaningful statement it has reduced all theological and metaphysical statements to the level of descriptions of mental states or of proposed modes of living. The statements "God exists" and "God loves men," being theological statements, cannot by their nature be contradicted by any empirical evidence; therefore, says modern philosophy, they cannot be statements of fact, and such meaning as they possess must be related to the individual making them, so that "God exists," for instance, means "I am going to live a certain sort of life." From denying all meaning to theological and metaphysical statements, modern philosophy has at least progressed to the point where it is willing to allow to such statements a certain restricted meaning; but that this is an infinitesimal gain is easily seen by reflecting that in an examination the wrong answer gets very few more marks than no answer at all.

Although Christian thought is stimulated and carried out within the context of revelation, it is still necessary to find common ground between believers and unbelievers. If this common ground does not exist, there can be, humanly speaking, no hope of winning the unbeliever to the Faith. This thought indicates at least a priori the necessity of a natural religion or Christian philosophy; while the fact that unbelievers have been converted to the Faith indicates (empirically) its possibility. This last consideration bypasses the usual empiricist objection to theological utterances which takes the form of asking the question how the statement "God exists" can be a factual statement if no empirical evidence can ever prove it to be untrue. The Christian can, at least to his own satisfaction, meet the empiricist on his own ground here: the empirical evidence for the existence of God, indeed for all theological utterance, the observable fact whose nonoccurrence invalidates all theological statements, is the coming of the Messiah. The Jew, living under the Old Covenant, could answer the empiricist's objections: he could say that the statement "God loves me" will be invalidated by the nonappearance of the Messiah. The Christian, living under the New Covenant, can say that all theological utterance has been validated by the empirical fact of the coming of the Messiah, and that no event whatsoever could disturb his conviction that theological utterances are factual.

For the empiricist, however, this is all rather meaningless; hence the necessity for another approach to empiricist philosophy. There is no question of deserting the universe of Christian thought in order to build up a Christian philosophy, as some appear to think is the case. There is no question of thinking of "unaided reason" as something essentially independent of the Christian revelation; on the contrary, reason, in attempting to build up a Christian philosophy, is very much aided since it sees all things from a point of view which would be impossible without revelation. But, seeing all things from within the context of revelation, Christian reason is still properly called "unaided" insofar as it nowhere makes use of facts of revelation, facts which the unbeliever cannot be presumed to know. The present essay is governed by these terms of reference. It is an attempt at an approach to the problem of the existence of God from within the context of Christian thought, which will use no facts but such as all may be presumed to agree with; it is an attempt to meet the empiricist on his own ground, an attempt to show that the circle of Christian doctrine may be connected up with that of empiricist belief.

Before commencing our task, however, it is worth while emphasizing its character: the attempt will be made to show that the statement "God exists" is demonstrable, and that what is demonstrated is the existence of a Being and not a state of mind or an emotion or a good resolution in the demonstrator. The attempt at the demonstration of the existence of God is not a disguised way of persuading empiricists that perhaps there is another language which it would be worth their while to learn, and in which meaningful statements may be made about an area of reality which is not the object of sense experience. This was the problem which Professor I. T. Ramsey set himself to solve in his book *Religious Language*. Our problem is more fundamental than that one, for the simple reason that no one is going to take the trouble to learn a new language until he is convinced beyond all doubt that the subject of the language really exists. It is essential for a missionary to be sure that there are Hottentots to be evangelized before he learns their language. In the same way it is essential for an empiricist philosopher to be assured of the existence of God before it is possible for him to believe in Him, and certainly before it is possible for him to begin an analysis of the logical status of language used in talk about God. For theological language is based upon theological conviction and experience, and it is just not possible to learn the language and then have the experience and arrive at the conviction (it is, of course, just possible that learning the language may elicit appropriate experience).

To demonstrate the existence of a logically "odd" language be-

fore demonstrating the existence of that of which the language
speaks is, therefore, to put the cart before the horse. Moreover it
just does not help; for it may be replied that there *cannot* be a
logically "odd" language, and therefore the reasoning which leads
up to it must be faulty. And if the statement "there cannot be a
logically 'odd' language" is a fundamental principle or a consequence of a fundamental principle in any philosophical system,
then there is no contact between that system and Christian philosophy. On the other hand, to demonstrate the existence of a logically "odd" language plays straight into the empiricist's hands: he
only has to reply that it is not necessary to prove laboriously that
languages exist which are logically "odd," for he knows this by
observation already; while, further, it has not yet been shown that
this language is about anything, and he simply does not believe
that it is about anything. Unless we prove the existence of God at
the start, in such a way as to demonstrate the necessity for a
logically "odd" language, there is no answer to the modern philosopher. As Dr. Mascall has pertinently observed: "the one thing we
must not do [with the modern philosopher] is to try to prove our
conclusions from his premises" (*Existence and Analogy*, p. 84).
Once the modern philosopher has been led into the Christian universe of discourse through the acceptance of God's existence, his
methods may well be of considerable use both to himself and to
theologians; while on the other hand it may be possible to com-
mend the Faith to him in terms which he is able to comprehend
and which he himself uses. But this is not the same as proving
Christian conclusions from empiricist premises; rather it is the
baptism of a non-Christian system of thought to bring it into the
service of Christ.

Man is born an enigma into an enigma, and this is at the root of
his ability to assert the existence of God. The twin mysteries of his
own nature and of his environment are resolved together in the
assertion of the single mystery of their common Creator. Man finds
that he is by nature completely unable to make a full and complete
act of understanding either of himself or of the universe into which
he is born. Complete explanation is impossible to him, for however
many questions he may answer there are always others, the answers to which elude him; while the laborious way in which he
discovers or invents his answers brings home to him the basic

impossibility of his ever making one complete, all-embracing act of understanding which will include within itself the reason and meaning of everything that there is. When he is careful to distinguish between knowing anything completely and knowing anything with certainty, he realizes that, although he is able to do the latter, the former is forever impossible. And yet his own meager acts of understanding are a witness to the possibility of such an unrestricted act of understanding. Dare he assert that it exists?

There is thus a double polarity about the life of man; at one pole he is a mystery to himself, and at the other his surroundings are equally mysterious. It seems as if man is unique in this respect, for at least there is as yet no evidence (as opposed to speculation) that animals make such a sharp distinction between "myself" and the "rest of the universe"—a distinction which by the use of the word "rest" recognizes "my" fundamental unity with the universe, even if "I" have to make a rather special effort to get outside "myself" in order to recognize this. This polarity, this sharp division which the individual makes between himself and his environment, is therefore closely connected with his self-awareness. It enables him to ascend to the fundamental questions: "Why do I exist?" and "Why does anything else exist?" and from there it is but a step to the question, which prescinds from the polarity just mentioned, "Why does anything exist?" This question immediately raises the further question "Why is it possible for anything to exist?" for, descending the scale, man notices that things come into existence and pass away. It is at about this point that a man may begin to experience the terror and despair which is justifiably experienced by non-Christian existentialists; or he may go on to raise the most fundamental of all questions: "What is existence anyway?", thereby setting his feet on the metaphysical way.

It is in some such way as this that the idea of God arises in the minds of men. Their completest act of understanding is never more than partial, but they know on reflection that a complete act of understanding is not intrinsically impossible, is not self-contradictory. As the Damascene states, *the knowledge of God is naturally implanted in all* inasmuch as a man's nature is such that reflection on it leads to the assertion of God's existence; yet, as St. Thomas replied, the divine existence must be demonstrated. Men, and everything else of which they know anything, exist in a contingent

manner, coming into existence and passing away, yet they can see
that necessary existence is not an impossibility. But to have the
idea of God and to make the judgment that God exists or does not
exist are two very different things. To have in the mind the idea of
a Being than which no greater can be conceived and to assert that
therefore such a Being must exist in reality is to confuse essence
and existence (as will be seen, Anselm did not in fact make this
confusion). To assert God as a sufficient explanation of the phenomena which are so puzzling is not enough; he must also be the
necessary explanation, and this requires justification. But can rational justification be given? There is the notion of God, and it is a
notion which can be analyzed; prescinding from the question of the
divine existence, a great deal may be said about God, for though at
the moment God is but a theory, a hypothesis requiring justification, a hypothecated entity is usually amenable to fairly detailed
analysis. Yet no amount of analysis of a hypothecated entity will
ever justify the statement that it does in fact exist. There is an
approximately parallel case to this in modern physics, for the
neutrino, which like God 'no man hath yet seen,' because it is
chargeless and very nearly weightless, might at first sight be thought
to be an unnecessary complication, a hypothesis put forward by
somebody who was either trying to complicate the issue or make
the scheme of fundamental particles tidy. But the neutrino, for all
its apparent impossibility, has effects, and it is by these effects that
the assertion of its existence is justified. So it is with God; whether
he be thought of initially as an unnecessary complication for
"practical" men, or as an unjustifiable and meaningless metaphysical hypothesis, his existence, suggested as a possible answer to
the questions which beset all men, may be justified with certainty
on the basis of his effects.

In *Summa Theologica* 1, ii, 2, St. Thomas shows that the demonstration of God's existence will be a posteriori through his
effects, and not a priori; thus the logical order of the proof is the
reverse of the ontological order of cause and effect. He also clears
up one or two confusions, perhaps the most dangerous of which is
that which confounds the existence with the attributes of God, for
to the objection that God's existence cannot be demonstrated because the effects are not proportionate to their cause he replies that
we are not interested as yet in the attributes of God as such, but

solely in his existence, and this certainly can be demonstrated from his effects. St. Thomas does not absolutely deny the Damascene's statement that *the knowledge of God is naturally implanted in all,* but contents himself with saying in effect that man does not know this immediately, for he must meditate on the works of God in human nature and the universe to make explicit his knowledge of the divine existence. The Five Ways are therefore not so much proofs as arguments designed to make explicit what is already implicit by directing the attention to certain aspects of the universe which most clearly witness to the divine existence. They are not designed to lead a man from something he does know to something he does not and could not otherwise know, but rather to lead him into a moment of insight, in which he is enabled to say "Whereas I was blind, now I see; I knew it all along, but only now has it be become clear to me." We do not nowadays expect the Five Ways, administered neat, to convert anyone, but this does not imply that they are necessarily invalid. In fact, we use precisely the same principle, only we point to slightly different divine effects and in a slightly different way; and he is the truer Thomist who is prepared to desert the letter of the *Summa Theologica* in order to retain its spirit.

The question is now appropriately considered whether the divine existence is known as the conclusion of a syllogism, or as the conclusion of an argument which, while it is rational, is not syllogistic. The syllogism to be considered may be cast in several forms, perhaps the most general of which is that given by Lonergan (*Insight,* p. 672): If the real is completely intelligible, God exists. But the real is completely intelligible. Therefore, God exists. It is arguable that it is not possible to accept the major without having first implicitly accepted the conclusion, and that therefore the syllogism is useless; this will be discussed later on in this article. But at the present stage the divine existence is a hypothesis demanding proof of some sort. The position is very much the same as that of the schoolboy taking an examination in mathematics, who is *almost* sure that the sum of the first n natural numbers in n $(n + 1)/2$ and who therefore has to check what is at the moment a hypothesis. When he checks it he finds he was right and attains certainty. Now his check may take one of two forms, for he may be so sure that he has the right answer that he feels it is adequate to check it by two or three substitutions, to apply it to a few special cases, or he may not feel quite so sure of his ground, in which case he will have to work the answer out afresh. In the present example the first of these methods is pragmatic and unrigorous, but for an examinee very nearly certain of his facts it "delivers the goods" in the shortest possible time. It corresponds to the ordinary non-philosopher's method of convincing himself of God's existence in moments of doubt. The alternative for the schoolboy to his first, pragmatic method is to ask himself the question: "What is the sum of the first n natural numbers?" and then to perform the rational process which leads to the correct answer. Is there an analogous approach to the question of God's existence? It is obviously very difficult to formulate the corresponding question, but for the sake of argument let it be supposed that this can be done; it would seem as if the appropriate question would be something like "What explanation can be offered as to the origin of the world?" It has already been pointed out that independently of this question the idea of God may arise in the mind, but in this case one is not allowed to let this idea affect the answer, for, to be strictly honest, while one may have a suspicion that the answer is "God," just as the schoolboy suspects he knows the answer to his question, one must initially ignore that answer altogether. One must start with the question and produce the answer "God," or some other answer, from scratch. It is, surely, obvious that it cannot be done.

It is, therefore, impossible to assert "God" as the answer to a question which does not include the word "God" or one of its equivalents as one of its terms. To take the example given above, anyone who seriously asks this question is at least convinced that the universe has an origin, whatever in this context the word "origin" may be seen to mean. Thus it is just not possible to forget all about God's attributes and deduce his existence, as it were, from nothing. A deadlock is arrived at which is not resolved by a proof that the basic principles of antimetaphysical philosophy are metaphysical. What is required is an invitation to a change of heart on the part of the empiricist; he must be persuaded to admit that his everyday experience leads to rather different conclusions from his philosophy. It may be that then he will be willing to admit that he has overlooked something essential.

If the illustration of the schoolboy taking an examination be valid, it is possible to dismiss any method of arriving at the existence of God which corresponds to the schoolboy's second method of arriving at the answer to his problem. That is, it is possible to see that the existence of God cannot be deduced. This may seem a simple point, and it may be that a lot of paper has been used to make it obvious. But is it in fact so obvious? Are words used by the intelligent educated adult, or even the professional philosopher, with such precision that he always explicitly distinguishes demontration from derivation? Is it always realized that in derivation you start with a question and some data and perhaps a conviction that there is an answer, while in demonstration you start with an answer and enough data? There are two replies to a command which begins "deduce" and one of them is the assertion that the command is meaningless and therefore impossible to carry out, while there is only one approach to the command beginning "Prove that . . . ," even if, in the case of the existence of God, it is possible to word the former without immediately turning it into the latter and thus misusing the word "deduce." Having "deduced" who the criminal is, the detective proceeds to "prove" that X did the murder in a court of law, but no one in modern times has seriously suggested that we ought to choose from among several candidates the originator of the universe; it is all along a question of proof, and the only line of retreat open to the opposition is that of claiming that the question "Who did this?" is, in this case, meaningless. We do not, therefore, deduce the existence of God; we prove that our conviction that he exists is the truth. This is why, in the first place, there is no hope of our being able to prove our conclusions from empiricist premises and, in the second place, why the proof of the divine existence does not resolve an issue between Christian thought and "modern" philosophy (for there can strictly speaking be no issue between two groups with literally nothing in common), and why it does resolve the issue between two rival schools within Christian thought.

Serious thought indicates the impossibility of wording a command beginning "deduce . . ." for the existence of God, in which the word "deduce" has precisely the same meaning as it has in the command "deduce the roots of $x^2 + 2x + 3 = 0$"; at each attempt the word's meaning changes, and "prove" becomes the right word to use. Thus, one cannot "deduce" the "cause of the universe" or the "reason for one's own existence," for each of these is a partial synonym for the word "God." This impossibility, which seems to be written into human speech and thought, must surely be more than accidental; Christians are able to explain it, and are justified in asking the empiricist for his explanation of the fact that human beings who are able to make one set of meaningless statements are unaccountable prevented from making another allied set. The Christian, of course, will assert a connection between this truth and God's creative omnipresence; he will say it is entirely congruous with the fact that on looking into himself, as well as out onto the world, he finds God, and in this the mystery of the otherwise inexplicable polarity of himself and the universe is to some extent resolved. This, of course, is quite apart from the obvious fact that the problem of the deduction of the roots of an equation is one of a wide class of problems with rules for their solution. This is not true of the problem of the deduction of the existence of God, which is a unique problem. Now it was pointed out that the schoolboy's first method of obtaining his answer was a practical, unrigorous method, suitable for a problem of which one is very nearly sure of the answer. It would not do, for instance, as the answer to an examination question, but only as a quick check on a formula used in obtaining the answer to a question. Does this mean that any proof of the existence of God must be of the same nature, pragmatic and not really rigorous and logical? By no means, for in this case the schoolboy was not really proving a result but checking an answer of which he was very nearly certain. Now this is what many people do in regard to the existence of God. They are sure he exists, but not being trained philosophers they do not know how to demonstrate his existence with the refinement such a proof requires. They throw out pointers, hints, which help them to ground their conviction in reason, or, to put it another way, they *recognize* the presence of God in the universe, and make their conviction reasonable to themselves by saying, for instance: "Well, if God didn't exist, nothing else would, would it?" Nor are they to be despised for this, though their argument requires formalization and refinement; if the proof of the existence of God were not a refinement of everyday experience and everyday thought we should be in a sad case.

But there is a third approach: the schoolboy could have proved his result by induction. He could have said the following: if the sum of the first n natural numbers is $n(n+1)/2$, then adding $n+1$ to $n(n+1)/2$ ought to give $(n+1)(n+2)/2$ and the formula ought to give the correct result, which I can easily check for, say, $n=3$. This I find to be true. Therefore, the sum of the first n natural numbers is $n(n+1)/2$. This method of proving the result is entirely rigorous and is a refinement of the first mentioned check on the result, which may be regarded as corresponding to the "common sense" method of proving God's existence. It is a refinement because the obvious extrapolation of the first method is to check the result by applying it to every possible case—a manifestly impossible task as it stands, but fundamentally no different from applying the result to two or three cases. The method of induction provides the required refinement; it makes possible the application of the result to every possible case. It corresponds to the philosopher's method of proving God's existence. Indeed, it may be said with some truth that the Five Ways of St. Thomas Aquinas parallel in the philosophical sphere the mathematical proof by induction—they apply the given answer to every possible case in a refined manner.

Now, in the mathematical proof by induction, the answer is given—either by authority, that is, the examiners, or possibly under slightly different circumstances by the individual himself, in the form of a suspicion or even a conviction that this is the correct answer. That is, the answer is given by authority proximately in the first case, and remotely in the second case, for no one can have a suspicion in a matter like this, much less a conviction, unless he has heard the answer before. Thus in the second case the answer comes truly from the individual, yet ultimately from whatever authority it was from which he first learned it. Of course the proximate authority carries more weight than the remote; that is, barring misprints, an answer given to be proved in an examination paper is far more credible than a half-remembered "hunch." If one is unable to prove the former, one expects to lose marks, whereas in the latter case one's inability is put down to a faulty memory or other causes. The parallel in the case of the existence of God is exact: the answer is given and by the same types of authority. The proximate authority is God himself speaking through special and general revelation (the knowledge of God is naturally implanted in all), while the remote authority is, say, all one's early religious instruction backing up a strong suspicion that the assertion "God exists" is correct. But this suspicion or conviction requires justification in reason, and it becomes a certainty when the proof is completed. There is therefore no possibility of proving the divine existence independently of some sort of apprehension of God; one must see, however vaguely, *that* God exists before one is able to see why. To put the same point in another way, the apprehension of God and the rational proof that this apprehension is a true one do not follow on each other so much as develop together. One cannot first prove the existence of God and then begin apprehending him; one apprehends God, perhaps in a very immature way, and at the same time one begins to justify this apprehension so that when the proof is complete one can then see why it is that God must exist, why one's apprehension was a true one. It might almost be said that one does not prove the existence of God, so much as one proves that one's original apprehension was a correct one; this, it seems, is congruous with the approach of St. Thomas.

It is therefore apparent that no amount of syllogizing will ever prove the existence of God. We have already quoted Lonergan; let us now quote him more fully. He says (*Insight,* p. 672):

The existence of God, then, is known as the conclusion to an argument and, while such arguments are many, all of them, I believe, are included in the following general form.

If the real is completely intelligible, God exists. But the real is completely intelligible. Therefore, God exists.

To begin from the minor premise, one argues that being is completely intelligible, that the real is being, and that therefore the real is completely intelligible.

But in fact one does not normally begin from the minor premise; one normally begins from the major. In addition, the hypothetical syllogism usually has to break down a psychological sales resistance due to the use of the word "if." To take an extreme example, in the syllogism: If a man is an ass, he is irrational; a man is an ass; therefore, a man is irrational, while disagreement will center around the minor, the "if" which starts the major will immediately arouse a suspicion that something which is *not* the case will follow it. A man is not an ass, and therefore our syllogism must begin "*If a man is an ass.*"

But, once again, it is customary to start from the major. But what does this major state in the way of fact? If the real is completely intelligible, God exists; if a man is irrational, he is an ass; these say nothing at all about reality, they are not factual. Anyway, a man is not an ass, and, as we have seen, we are tempted to add, the real is not completely intelligible; at least we are now arguing about fact, and, incidentally, about the truth of the minor. It is not just a question of "to begin with the minor" but rather a question of *having* to begin with the minor. In which case why bother with the major at all? Why bother to have a syllogism? If argument will center, as it always does, around the truth or falsehood of the statement which is to be made in the minor, surely the appropriate course is to direct attention to those aspects of the universe which will be stated in the minor; surely the right thing to do is to point to the universe itself, rather than to a hypothetical syllogism about the universe. The universe is intelligible, the universe is contingent, it is created and real and dependent, and in actually seeing it in this way a man sees at the same time that the Creator of the Universe cannot but exist. The proof of the existence of God does reduce to an argument as to the nature of the universe, but one does not need a syllogism to arrive at this conclusion. If a convenient summary of the Five Ways is needed, then one need only point to the minor and conclusion of Lonergan's syllogism: the real is completely intelligible; therefore God exists. Thus, *that* God exists is seen through seeing creation in the right way; then *why* God exists is seen by reflecting on the way in which creation is viewed; the second of these two processes brings with it the conviction that the apprehension of God was no mistake, so that the apprehension (at first tentative and vague, later a fully developed certainty), and the proof develop together; and finally the resulting argument, however refined, is simply a formalization of the ordinary man's assertion that if God didn't exist, nothing else would. Setting up syllogisms is a process which is untrue to the facts, for it implies that *why* God exists is realized prior to the realization *that* he exists. The statement "God exists" will then be a hypothesis because it will always be logically possible to find a better explanation of the facts about creation upon which the syl-

logism is based. But, on the other hand, God, apprehended as the
ground of creation, cannot but be a certainty, while reflection on
the nature of creation provides the justification for this certainty.

To conclude: the schoolboy in the examination knew the answer
to his problem before he started; we know God exists before we
start to prove it. But how do we know? We know as a result of a
moment of insight: *the* Intelligible, God, exists. Then we reflect:
without God the universe would be a meaningless jumble of unin-
telligibility. So we see God as the Cause and Ground of various
attributes of creation, its dependence, finitude and so on. We raise
the question: The world is like this—why? We assert the answer
with certainty, not only because of our original and undeveloped
apprehension of God, but also because *by now* our judgment on
creation is a certainty. Hence our apprehension of God is immediate but rooted in a judgment about the universe—and we cannot
remove the scaffolding after we have built the building. The insight
which leads to the apprehension of God is a consequence of the
fact that we are human beings with a certain definite nature (the
knowledge of God is naturally implanted in all), and the mecha-
nism which goes into action when it occurs goes into action in just
the same way on other occasions too. It went into action in
Archimedes on a famous occasion when he knew the answer to his
problem before justifying it, and knew it because he was aware of
his surroundings in just the right way. There is a real parallel with
physics here, for it is not possible to prove a foundation theorem
of science; it is known to be correct, and its consequences are
worked out after the moment of insight has come. In the same way,
the consequences of the moment of insight in which God's existence
is apprehended are worked out after the event, and the result will be
the Five Ways or something similar. These "Ways" may then be
used to trigger off the same moment of insight in others. But they
will not be compelled by any force of argument; they will not be
put in the position of saying "I suppose it's logical but I still don't
agree"; they will be compelled by the ontological status of creation
itself, by hard fact. Regarded in this light (and we think that St.
Thomas would agree), the Five Ways are rather more apologetic
than philosophical, though it is possible to philosophize about
them, and the present article has been doing this.

It is at this point that we can see a way of reconciling the Five

Ways with the Ontological argument and with the double polarity
which introduces such tension into the life of man. Observing
being in the right way from the outside leads to the assertion of
God's existence, and the Five Ways may be appropriately used in
apologetics. But it is also appropriate to look to the other pole, to
see things within oneself, to revert to self-consciousness. In this
case, God's existence is seen in a somewhat similar way, but the
appropriate argument here is the Ontological. However, unlike the
Five Ways, the real point of the Ontological argument is not to
help us to see why something is true which we already know to be
true, but to assert something about the nature of the Being
whose existence we are already certain of, after looking within
ourselves and experiencing for ourselves what it is really like to be
contingent and dependent. The Ontological argument is not about
God's existence, but about God. Here the double polarity of our
existence as conscious beings is resolved. For Jones, thinking of
Smith as a phenomenon external to himself, the Five Ways is the
appropriate line of argument; but for Smith and Jones, looking
each into his own heart, the Ontological argument is the appropriate argument to adopt, and the double polarity comes together
and is reconciled in the assertion of God's existence together with
the assertion of a truth about him which must be true. A man
knows from his own experience of himself, from knowing what it
is to be, that God cannot not be; he knows from other beings, from
knowing what it looks like to be, that God must be.

6 *Faith: Personal Encounter with God* *

RENÉ LATOURELLE

Modern psychology insists on the interpersonal, dynamic character of all speech. And theology can apply this insight to God's speaking to man, that is, to divine revelatiom. In this sense revelation is more than the uncovering of certain truths; it is God's uncovering of his very personality motivated by an intense love; it calls for a response of faith accompanied by love, for a personal commitment.

R EVELATION IS ONE of the many forms of speech, which St. Thomas and other Scholastics defined as a manifestation of one's thought to another by means of signs. The Scholastics emphasized the fact that speech effects the uncovering and participation of thought, a rather static concept. But De Lugo did not view speech in this light; he was one of the few to emphasize its dynamic nature, to note its essential to-anotherness. Speech does not merely set forth an object of thought; it wants to see the object grasped.

This same approach can be seen in contemporary theology, which takes into account the philosophy and psychology of speech and rightly insists on its interpersonal, existential, dynamic, and offering character. For example, Karl Bühler distinguishes three aspects of speech: (1) It has *content;* it signifies or represents something; (2) it is a *summons* addressed to someone and tending to elicit a response from him; and (3) it is an *uncovering* of the personality, a manifestation of one's interior attitude and dispositions. In brief, speech is an action by which one person addresses another and expresses himself to him in order to communicate.

Speech is a summons, a call for a response. It tends to set up a summons-response circuit which develops into a dialogue, and this is especially prominent when the affective state of the speakers is

* "La révélation comme parole témoignage et rencontre," *Gregorianum,* 43 (1962), 39–54.

aroused. This circuit can take various forms: command-obedience, prayer-concession, promise-trust, explanation-attention, testimony-faith. The purpose of this communication can vary; it can be, for instance, utilitarian, a mere imparting of information; this is the speech of the newspaper and television, of daily family and professional life. In this utilitarian role speech is functioning at its lowest, impersonal level.

On a higher level, speech becomes self-expression, a revelation of the person. This happens when we put ourselves into our speech and truly communicate with another by aiming at him in himself, as a person. For communication and dialogue to become a reciprocal opening up, a mutual revelation, both the speaker and the hearer must respect one another in the mysteriousness of their personalities; there must also be mutual trust, utter availability, and at least the beginning of friendship.

When speech reaches this higher level it is the sign of friendship and love; it is an overflow and expression of the freedom by which one opens himself to another and gives himself to him. Speaker and listener give and are given to each other. And where the word is not equal to the expression of this giving, it is accompanied by a gesture, or even by a life commitment as in conjugal love or in the apostolate.

REVELATION A SUMMONS

In divine revelation God Himself turns to man. He wills to be for man an "I" calling to a "you." This utterance that arises from the transcendent world of the divine life *summons* man, invites him to the obedience of faith with a view to sharing life. God's speech is pregnant with the extraordinary news of salvation; it fulfills the plan of love He has pursued from eternity. For God's speech does not merely speak and inform; it effects what it signifies, changing the status of man.

Moreover, God's speech is an utterance of love. His loving intent is clear first of all in the fact of the speaking itself. Through revelation the uncreated person contacts a simple creature; God overleaps the infinite distance that separates Him from man. The action by which He emerges from His mystery and condescendingly makes Himself present to man can mean for man only salvation and friendship. If God wills to reveal Himself, He can intend nothing else than to establish bonds of love and friendship with man and to share His life with him; and, on the other hand, if God wills to enter into friendship with man and share the divine life with him, He does this to reveal Himself.

We see the intent of love in the divine speaking more clearly when we consider that the creature who is called by God into a relation of friendship is in revolt from God. God approaches a creature that has been an enemy. What is more, God goes so far as to take on the very condition of the creature, making himself one with man by assuming his flesh, in order to bring man to the level of God.

The loving intent of God's speaking appears not only in the *fact* and in the *economy* of revelation but also in its *object*. This object is not only the religious truths of the natural order but also and chiefly the mysteries of the divine life. The mystery of the Trinity is the first of the divine mysteries. By revealing it, God initiates man into the mystery of the divine life, into the heart of His personal subsistence. God can make such a revelation only to one to whom He wishes to unite Himself in friendship. God's revelation of the Trinity, then, begins man's participation in the divine life and constitutes a *giving* of God to man.

God pursued His giving of Himself to man to the utmost limits of love. Christ, after exercising his prophetic ministry by making known the name and the teaching of the Father, completed the gift made by His word by the sacrifice of His life. The word *spoken* became the Word *immolated*. On the cross Christ spoke the love of the Father up to that last strangled cry in which everything was spoken. The word of God exhausted itself into silence. Everything incommunicable in the divine communication was expressed in the outstretched arms, in the body drained of its blood, in the heart pierced by the sword of the centurion. The revelation of the word was completed and confirmed by the revelation-action of Christ's death.

TESTIMONY INVITES FAITH

Revelation is a specific kind of speech, namely *testimony*. It invites a specific kind of response: *faith*. As testimony, revelation is the act of a witness. Scripture describes revelation as a procedure of testimony. In the Old Testament, God singles out privileged persons who bear witness to the truth. These persons speak in the name of God and say, "Here is what God has told me to tell you. You are invited to welcome my word in faith, for my word is His." These persons exercise influence by the authority of their speech, by their deeds of power and mercy, by their patience, and above all by martyrdom. In the New Testament, Christ is the witness beyond comparison. He tells of what He has seen and heard in the bosom of the Father, and we are invited to the obedience of faith. He establishes a body of witnesses, the apostles, who testify to His life and teaching. They call all men to believe what they have seen and heard, what they know by experience of the Word of life. Those who believe are introduced by baptism into a new society, the Church. They participate in the Body and Blood of Christ; they live His life. What the apostles give over to the custody of the Church is *testimony*. This the Church receives, conserves, protects; this the Church explains, interprets, understands ever better.

In the same way that witness binds souls to one another throughout the course of history, it also binds time to eternity. Scripture, in fact, describes the revealing activity of the Trinity under the aspect of mutual testimonies. The Son appears to us as the witness of the Father, and He makes Himself known to the apostles as a witness. The Father, in turn, testifies that Christ is His Son by the attraction He produces in souls, by the works given the Son to do, and especially the resurrection, which is the decisive testimony of the Father in favor of the Son. The Son testifies to the Spirit, for he promises to send the Spirit as a teacher, consoler, and sanctifier. The Spirit comes and testifies to the Son by reminding us of Him, by making Him known, by uncovering the fullness of His words, by making room for Him in our hearts. Thus in the interchanges of the three divine persons with men we see a reciprocity of testimony that aims to set forth revelation and to nourish faith.

Theologians generally define divine revelation as "speech by God that gives testimony to something." To explain testimony they contrast it to teaching: In the language of teaching, one assents to what is said because of arguments whose intrinsic validity he sees; in the language of testimony, one assents because of the authority of him who speaks; he believes *in the word because* of the knowledge and truthfulness of him who speaks. In both instances the human mind is enriched with new truths. The essential difference lies in the motive of assent: In teaching it is the evidence of demonstration; in testimony it is only the authority of the speaker.

HUMAN TESTIMONY

Testimony is essentially an utterance by which one person invites another to accept something as true, relying on the invitation itself as the proximate guarantee of truth and on the authority of the speaker as the remote guarantee. When he gives testimony, he asks the other to trust him, and he binds himself to tell the truth. The testimony therefore engages not only the mind but also the will. To bear witness is not merely to narrate, for testimony "involves" the witness. His utterance must become for the believer a substitute for direct experience. By believing, one in some sense resigns his reason—but legitimately so, because in this case reason relies on the intellectual and moral integrity of the witness.

But the authority of human testimony is not its ultimate guarantee of truth. By nature fallible, human testimony needs objective signs of its validity. This evaluation of the witness and of his reliability is a complicated business like all personal knowledge and is, consequently, exposed to error and deception. But even when, by carefully examining the credentials of the witness, we have all possible guarantees, still we can never rely absolutely on human testimony because human knowledge and truthfulness are always precarious. Only God can give His word an absolute guarantee, because His word has an eternal and absolute identity with Himself. Merely human faith can never be purely and simply a faith in authority.

From one point of view, then, testimony is inferior to evidence. From another point of view it is superior because of the values involved. While demonstration of evidence appeals to the understanding, testimony, because it demands an intensity of confidence that is measured by the values at stake in the act of belief, involves not only the understanding but also, in varying degrees, love and will. The possibility of interchanges among human beings rests on the confidence claimed by the witness and on the promise tacitly made by him not to deceive. We have then the moral commitment of the witness and that confidence of the believer which is already the beginning of love.

Moreover, when there is a question of knowing persons rather than of knowing the natural world, it becomes also a question of testimony rather than of evidence. On the personal, intersubjective level we meet mystery. Persons are not problems that can be capsuled in formulas or resolved into equations. We have access to a person's innermost being only through testimony. And persons give testimony to themselves only under the impulse of love. Testimony affords an inferior kind of knowledge in those instances in which we can have direct and immediate evidence of some kind of reality. But the knowledge it affords is not inferior when the realities in question are persons; in these cases testimony is the only means of uniting with a person and establishing contact with his mysteriousness.

DIVINE TESTIMONY

Divine revelation is a revelation of the mysteriousness of God's personal life. God is innerness beyond compare, the personal and sovereign Being whose mystery can be known only by testimony, that is, by a spontaneous assurance which we are invited to receive through faith. Christianity is a religion of testimony because it is a manifestation of persons. Christ speaks, teaches, and makes laws just as other founders of religions. But what he says, teaches, and communicates is the mystery of His person. The whole Gospel appears to us as a confiding of love in which Christ progressively discloses the mystery of His person, the mystery of the life of the divine persons, and the mystery of our sonship.

God's testimony is unique in that, while he affirms the truth of what He proposes for belief, He at the same time affirms the absolute infallibility of His testimony. When God gives witness of something, He witnesses simultaneously to His own infallibility; for He is the pure, subsisting witness whose act of testimony is one with His being. God is Himself His own security for the truth of His testimony. In Christian revelation signs are to identify the witness, to make known in the human speech of Christ the testimony of the living God and, in the preaching of the apostles, the authentic message of God.

The testimony of God is unique in another way. The invitation to believe has a twofold aspect, external and internal. Through the prophets, Christ, and the apostles, God makes known to men His plan of salvation and invites them to an act of faith, to "repent and believe in the gospel" (Mark 1:15). But the divine testimony is not limited to this external manifestation working through language and signs. Its deepest dimension is a wholly internal action, an act directly on the soul. To describe this action, Scripture speaks of a revelation (Matt. 11:25, 16:17), and illumination (II Cor. 4:4–6, Acts 16:14), and unction (II Cor. 1:21–22), an attraction (John 6:44) an interior witness (John 5:37, John 5:6). As a divine witness God can infuse into human spirit a light by which he draws it to conform its knowledge to the divine knowledge and subordinate itself to the primary truth by doing homage to truth's infinite authority. He draws man to admit the divine testimony because of the unique excellence that makes God the ultimate security of its truth.

FAITH AN ENCOUNTER

Every use of language also involves an encounter. There must be an "I" and a "you"; the "I" seeks to contact the "you" and intends to be heard by him. The use of language becomes real speech only when an encounter takes place; at the minimum some contact must be established, and the true aim is to establish an authentic dialogue, a reciprocal union, a mutual engagement. And it is only in an encounter of love that this reciprocity can be complete; there it is the result of a mutual revealing and giving.

We find such an encounter of love when God's revelation meets a response of faith. God turns to man and communicates to him the Good News of salvation, but there is no real encounter except when man responds with faith, when he welcomes and recognizes God's living word. God invites man to the interchange of friendship; if man answers the call by faith, he opens himself to God, shares in God's thought, allows himself to be absorbed and directed by that thought. Here God and man encounter one another, and this encounter grows in the sharing of life.

Thus revelation and faith are essentially interpersonal. Faith is the encounter with a personal God in His word; it supposes that the believer adheres to the message of God, for if God manifests Himself as a God who speaks, faith must be an assent to what is spoken. Faith begins in a dialogue, an encounter that will be perfected in *vision*. Paul and John often describe faith as an all-embracing attitude of man responding to the advances of God, as a tenacious whole in which knowledge and love function only within the spiritual aspirations of the person. The whole person accepts all of God's truth and gives to God his whole heart and soul.

We must note some of the characteristics of this encounter that is achieved by faith. One is that God always takes the initiative. In the area of revelation and faith, everything comes from the power of grace: God's action unfolding out of His own mysteriousness, the economy of the revealed word, the message of salvation, the capacity to answer the message and to encounter God in faith. It is God who begins in us the movement by which we return to Him; He places in our understanding a tendency, a supernatural impulse that is directed to Him; He creates the ontological basis in virtue of which, while still remaining men, we can make the theological act of faith. But this action of God does not cramp our freedom. We remain free to welcome or not to welcome this other liberty spread out before us.

ALL OR NOTHING

A second characteristic of the encounter with revelation is the importance of the decision that is entreated. The word of God brings into play our sense of personal existence and our sense of the whole of human existence. Here it is not a question of simply modifying our prevailing system of values; it is a question of reorienting our whole being. It is a matter of voting for God or the world, for God's word or man's word. It is all or nothing. Faith is a decision for God, and our whole life ought to pivot on this dramatic decision which involves us even to our innermost aspirations. An involvement of this kind is an uprooting of the human "me" and a rooting in Christ (Eph. 3:17). This death to self cannot be had simply by intellectually contemplating the message of revelation; there must be an attraction of love. God speaks to us His love, and it evokes our assent only because it is a love revealed and manifested to the point of uttermost sacrifice. Revelation as encounter succeeds in becoming welcome, dialogue, and reciprocity only because the love expressed in Christ and achieved by His Spirit transforms the stubborn heart into the heart of a son.

A third characteristic of this encounter is the depth of the communion established between God and man. He who receives the word of Christ and lives by this word passes from the status of slave to that of son and friend; he shares in knowledge and love of the Father, Son, and Holy Spirit. Christ said, "That they may all be one, even as you, Father, in me and I in you, that they also may be one in us . . . , that they may be one even as we are one; I in them and you in me, that they may be perfected in unity" (John 17:21–23). No human encounter, however perfect, can attain the degree of intimacy and union that the encounter of faith initiates through God's love.

Thus, whether looked upon as utterance or witness or encounter, revelation always strikes the same basic note: God is love and his word is a word of love. Faith is not submission to the will of a God who gets some pleasure out of exacting the homage of the human spirit; it is rather man's recognition of God's loving plan and of man's free place in that plan; faith is an opening up to divine love inviting us to share in its own life. Revelation and faith are the work of love.

7   The Preambles of Faith*

GUY DE BROGLIE

Father de Broglie contends that from St. Thomas till the time of Descartes it was universally accepted that the preambles are not prerequisites for the act of faith; rather they form part of the material object of faith. Thus they need not be accepted as true before the act of faith; they can be known for the first time with certainty in the act of supernatural faith itself.

ANY DISCUSSION OF the truly mysterious area of Christian faith is destined from the outset to limited success at best. An acceptable theory of faith must reconcile the action of God's grace with both human freedom and the demands of man's rational nature. Ultimately the act of faith is itself an object of faith. But in addition to this intrinsic difficulty, terminological obscurities have arisen which today further complicate inquiry. For example, "the evidence of credibility" has meant one thing for St. Thomas, another for the Renaissance theologians, and still another for most modern theologians. Likewise the meaning of "preambles of faith" varies according to one's position on other points of theology.

THREE INTERPRETATIONS

At the present time three interpretations of "preambles of faith" may be found in theological writings. The first and by far the most common interpretation defines the preambles as "truths which must be known with certitude before the act of faith in order to formulate a reasonable judgment of credibility." These truths are found in two orders: the metaphysical order: e.g., the existence

* "La vraie notion thomiste des 'preambula fidei,' " *Gregorianum*, 34 (1953), 341–89. This article has been developed at greater length in *Les signes de credibilité de la révélation chrètienne*, collection "Je sais, je crois," Librairie Arthème Fayard, Paris, 1965.

and veracity of God; and the historical order: e.g., the fact of revelation.

Ill at ease in the presence of some texts of St. Thomas, a second group describes the preambles, when strictly considered, as including only the truths of the metaphysical order. Knowledge of these is considered as necessary for the judgment that what faith proposes is credible.

The third and numerically smallest group denies there is any relation between the preambles and the judgment of credibility. According to this group the preambles are truths of faith which can be known with reason also. Certain and prior knowledge of these truths, however, is in no way required as a condition for the judgment of credibility. It is my purpose to show that this is precisely the meaning St. Thomas attaches to the preambles of faith.

A modern student of theology most likely would be astounded at hearing this third position proposed as St. Thomas' teaching. Most of the theological manuals either use Pesch's definition of preambles or one very similar: "The preambles of faith are truths which must be known certainly as a prerequisite for faith." With this as background, the young theologian will think that this same position is contained in such texts of Thomas as: "The unity of God, as it is demonstrated, is not called an article of faith, but is presupposed by the articles" (*De Veritate* 14, 9, ad 8). "That God exists is not an article of faith, but is antecedent to the article" (*Ibid.*, ad 9). In other words the modern student of theology will feel that from the thirteenth century until the present, it has been the common teaching of theologians that the knowledge of God's existence is contained in the preambles of faith and as such is a prerequisite for the judgment of credibility.

APPARENT CONTRADICTION

This might be the end of the discussion if St. Thomas did not explicitly state that the preambles of faith are not required as a prior condition to the act of faith; that in fact the preambles may be known in the act of faith itself.

That God exists . . . is believed by him whose intellect cannot attain to demonstration: because faith, considered in itself, sufficiently embraces all things which accompany, follow, or precede faith (*In III Sent.* d. 24, q. 1, a. 2, sol. 2).

Those things which are able to be demonstratively proved [concerning God] are included among those things to be believed, not because these are simply a matter of faith for all, but because they are required for those things which pertain to faith; and it is necessary that these things at least be supplied by faith for those who have not demonstrated them (II-II, 1, 5, ad 3).

Thus St. Thomas and the modern manuals of fundamental theology seem to teach contradictory views concerning the nature and function of the preambles of faith.

This evident disagreement over the meaning of the "preambles" is rooted in a radically different approach to the evidence of credibility. First of all, it must be noted that all theologians agree that every virtuous act must be preceded (at least with a priority of nature) by a judgment of conscience confirming the moral suitability of the act. The act of faith is not exempt from this principle. Thus every legitimate act of faith must be preceded by evidence which is strictly personal and morally compelling. As St. Augustine has written: "No one believes anything before previously thinking he should believe it" (*De Praedestinatione Sanctorum*, 2, 5, P. L. 44, 962). But if theologians are in agreement regarding the necessity of this evidence of credibility, they have not been equally unanimous in their understanding of the nature of this evidence. From the fourteenth to the middle of the seventeenth century, one explanation was generally accepted. Influenced by the Cartesian approach to knowledge, a new explanation developed after 1650 which reached its highest popularity around 1900 and is still the dominant school. An understanding of these two explanations of credibility is imperative if we are to arrive at St. Thomas' meaning of the preambles.

PRE-CARTESIAN

The pre-Cartesian approach to credibility can be briefly formulated: "Having seen the signs and concrete indications which beckon to me, I am able and I ought to believe (*Je puis et dois croire*) that the doctrine of the Church is revealed by God and is divinely true." Several observations may be made about this for-

mulation of the judgment of credibility. First of all, the fact of
revelation was the first thing to be believed. In no way did the
acceptance of this fact precede the act of faith. The act of faith,
says Capreolus, can be compared to sight which sees light and
color at the same time. True, it is due to the light that one can see
the color; but both are seen at the same time in the same act.
Similarly it is due to the fact that God reveals, that we know, for
example, "God is three Persons in one nature"; but we also know
the fact of God revealing in the very same act that we know "God
is three Persons in one nature."

Secondly, the pre-Cartesian evidence of credibility was not presented in a compelling syllogism. This would have seemed
Pelagian to the theologians of this period. Rather it was the function of the evidence to make possible a virtuous act which was
both prudent and imposed by conscience—a distinction which
later theologians would refine and slightly distort by their concepts
of "credibility" and "credendity." The judgment of credibility,
which is nothing other than the judgment of conscience, pronounced merely on the moral suitability of the free act of faith in
which the fact of revelation would be accepted as certain. Thus
there is question here of a judgment of a rather practical kind. The
person who is open to believe whatever God may reveal judges:
"Such being the signs of revelation which I perceive, I have an
obligation to accept this revelation as divinely inspired." This
judgment is in an entirely different order from the cold speculative
judgment which reasons syllogistically about the fact of revelation.
The difference is much the same as that between the judgment of
an individual face to face with a poor derelict who asks for alms
and the closely reasoned conclusion of a scientific inquiry into the
poverty of a nation.

CARTESIAN INFLUENCE

In 1637 Descartes published *A Discourse on Method*. Two
tendencies can henceforth be seen in discussions about truth. Truth
is to be found only in a judgment which is determined exclusively
by external evidence confronting a totally indifferent intellect.
Thus the practical truth which earlier theologians found in good
inclinations is necessarily excluded as a valid approach to a "ra-

tional" judgment of credibility. Secondly, the Cartesian influence also tended to constrain speculative knowledge itself within the limits of deductive procedures.

In this atmosphere it was only a short time before the fact of revelation ceased being the first thing believed and instead became the last object known before the act of faith. Inevitably also the role of grace was minimized. Instead of providing illumination throughout the whole approach to faith, the post-Cartesian theologians saw grace merely as an external aid in a totally natural and scientific process. Finally, out of Cartesian principles there naturally evolved a great distrust of every absolute dictate of conscience which was not previously confirmed by speculative knowledge.

Disregarding the theological tradition of the previous four centuries, the post-Cartesian theologians required a speculatively known "God revealed" as a prerequisite for the judgment of credibility. Any dictate of conscience which was not based on the following syllogism was branded as dangerous illuminism:

What is revealed by God must be believed as true.
But this particular doctrine is revealed by God.
Therefore this doctrine must be believed as true.

The earlier theologians, faithful to their Aristotelian tradition, had held: "We do not have the evidence of the fact of revelation, but we do have evidence that it is morally possible and even necessary to believe this fact." Out of the new Cartesian philosophical tradition, with its emphasis on "distinct" knowledge, comes a new statement: "The judgment of credibility, if it is to be rational, must be founded on the twofold speculative knowledge of the fact of revelation and the veracity of God."

Admittedly the early promulgators of this teaching, Elizalde, Huet, Gonzalez, did not meet with immediate success. It was not until the nineteenth century that theologians, fearful of the inroads of Kantianism and desirous to establish the faith "rationally," accepted wholeheartedly their newer position. The teaching of the earlier Scholastics had meanwhile been lost. The *Dictionnaire de théologie catholique* testifies to the triumph of the post-Cartesian view. This may be seen in Gardeil's article, "Crédibilité," or Harent's, "Foi." In the latter article, fideism, condemned in the Vatican Council, is defined as the system ". . . which denies that one first proves the preambles of faith by natural reason and is thus conducted by reason to faith." According to this definition, St. Thomas would stand condemned as a fideist!

HUMAN FAITH?

Refinements, however, were developed to meet certain difficulties. For example, it was patent that many people were not capable of speculatively proving the fact of revelation or God's existence. How would these folk approach the act of supernatural faith? An answer was drawn from the texts of St. Thomas, as we have already seen. St. Thomas clearly says that faith supplies knowledge of God's existence for those who cannot know this through *scientia*. But since, according to the principles of the post-Cartesian tradition, this faith could not be supernatural faith, it must be *fides humana*. A child, for example, will be instructed by his parents or the parish priest. By this clever maneuver two difficulties were dispatched. One who does not have the requisite prior knowledge is supplied with it, and this according to some troublesome texts of St. Thomas. Harent, for example, uses this approach in his article, "Foi," in *Dictionnaire de théologie catholique*.

But does the teaching of St. Thomas submit to this meaning of *fides*? A careful reading of the texts usually cited in this connection (*In III Sent*, d. 24, q. 1, a. 2, sol. 2; II-II 1, 5, ad 3) will show that the *fides* referred to is always supernatural faith and never *fides humana*. Furthermore St. Thomas always employs *fides humana* as a comparison with supernatural faith, never as introductory to it. Finally, when St. Thomas speaks of faith supplying knowledge when natural reason is inadequate, he does not limit himself to knowledge of God's existence. To be sure, he does speak of this, but he also refers to other truths which reason can prove such as God's omnipotence and omnipresence. Thus if we understood *fides* to refer to human faith as explained above, it would be necessary to conclude that these other truths would have to be known either by reason or human faith prior to the act of supernatural faith. Since this is obviously absurd, we must conclude that, as used in these texts, *fides* refers to supernatural faith.

BELIEF BEFORE KNOWLEDGE?

In *De Veritate* 14, 9, ad 9, St. Thomas clearly teaches that supernatural faith may supply knowledge of God's existence for those who do not know this by reason. In this question St. Thomas asks: "Can one arrive at knowledge of God's existence by an act of faith if this act is performed in order to please God?" The difficulty posed is obvious: "How can we please someone, and that by believing in him, if we are not certain even of his existence?" But St. Thomas does not hesitate. He says this can be done. As always his phraseology is terse:

Someone can begin to believe what he did not believe before but which he held with some hesitation. Thus it is possible that before believing in God, someone might think that God exists and that it would be pleasing to God to have him believe that He exists. In this way a man can believe that God exists because such a belief pleases God.

In this text St. Thomas psychologically explains a possible genesis of the act of faith. A person first sees signs which establish a more or less firm opinion concerning the divine orgin of revelation and the existence of God the Revealer. Gradually, aided by grace, the person sees that the evidence is credible. This state is a sufficient and necessary (*droit et devoir*) condition for the well disposed person to exercise the act of faith.

To explain how one can learn of the existence and particular thoughts of a person at the same time, Lugo has recourse to the example of a man who hears a shout in the night. When one hears the voice, he knows at the same time that the caller exists and has a message. Similarly in the *De Veritate* text just quoted, St. Thomas says that we can learn of God's existence, the fact of revelation, and a particular truth of revelation in the very same act of faith. If this is true, it is obvious that there is a wide divergence between St. Thomas' meaning of preambles of faith and the preambles of faith of modern theologians. The former "preambles" can be known by the act of faith itself, while the latter are a necessary prerequisite for this act.

Before presenting St. Thomas' doctrine concerning preambles of faith, we shall briefly summarize what we have thus far seen concerning the meaning of "preambles" and the judgment of credibility in the history of theological thought. First, by "preambles" we have seen in general that St. Thomas understood all the truths which are held by faith and are capable of rational demonstration. This would include such knowledge of natural theology as the incorporeality, omnipotence, omnipresence, and providence of God as well as truths referring to creatures as the spirituality and immortality of the human soul (*De Veritate* 14, 9; *In Boet. de Trinitate* 2, 3, c.). Modern theologians, on the contrary, understand by the preambles of faith the knowledge of the existence and veracity of God and the fact of revelation.

The significance of this difference becomes evident when we realize that St. Thomas did not look upon the preambles as leading up to and necessitating the judgment of credibility. Since the preambles are established demonstratively, that is, speculatively, they established *compelling* knowledge. The motive of credibility in St. Thomas, however, concerned necessarily with concrete, contingent circumstances can only result in a judgment of credibility that belief is *reasonable*. Thus for St. Thomas, the preambles are in the speculative order, while the judgment of credibility moves on the level of practical reason. Not so for the post-Cartesians. For these the preambles, although speculative, are requisite, antecedent conditions for the judgment of credibility.

PRECEDE ARTICLES, NOT ACT

If this is so, just why did St. Thomas employ the phrase "preambles of faith?" What precisely is the proper meaning of this phrase in St. Thomas? In what sense do these truths precede faith? This may be answered simply. For St. Thomas, these truths do not precede the *act* of faith, but rather the *articles* of faith. His concern was not with the subjective requisites for an act of faith, but rather with the natural truths, objectively considered, which precede the articles of faith. Several texts will make this manifest.

It is not said that "God is One" is an article of faith, but something presupposed before the articles (*De Veritate* 14, 9, ad 8). Although this [God's existence] is not an article of faith, but preliminary to the article, since it can be proved by demonstration (*Ibid.*, ad 9). They are not articles of faith, but preambles to the articles (I, 2, 2, ad 1).

Since for St. Thomas the act of knowing contains its own justification, his noetic theory always centers around three totally different questions: What is the material object of knowledge? What is the formal object? What are the proper causes of this knowledge? In this scheme the preambles would be considered under the material object of faith. For historic reasons St. Thomas was anxious to show that the content of faith was complex: certain elements were proportional to reason and certain elements transcended reason. This is the precise meaning of the characteristic text: "The knowledge of faith presupposes natural knowledge as grace presupposes nature" (*De Veritate* 14, 9, ad 8; I, 2, 2, ad 1).

Since an understanding of how, for Thomas, faith "builds on" or "presupposes" natural knowledge is crucial in Thomas' explanation of preambles, an expansion of this text will be useful.

Just as the life of grace always presupposes in its subject a reasonable nature and just as supernatural knowledge (considered in general) presupposes in the knowing subject a certain minimum of natural knowledge (also considered in general), so the particular and characteristic objects of our faith presuppose in *themselves* particular objects of natural knowledge (preambles) which are intelligibly contained therein.

If we consider faith as stratified knowledge, the lower level embracing truths knowable by natural reason supports a higher level composed of truths known only by supernatural faith. In this sense the "knowledge of faith presupposes natural knowledge" and the "preambles (or natural knowledge) precede faith (or supernatural knowledge)." We must break out of the Cartesian web of concern for guarantees of knowledge before we can even begin to understand the Thomistic doctrine on the preambles of faith.

Thus according to St. Thomas, the articles of the Creed contain in themselves, as basic elements, revealed truths directly proportioned to natural reason, which are able to be known by reason before the act of faith or, if natural knowledge is lacking, by the act of faith itself. For example, in our belief of the Trinity, we do not always add something by way of a distinct act to a previous natural knowledge we may have of God's unity. Rather in the one assent to "God is three Persons in one nature," we attain a complex object, the unity of God and the Trinity of Persons. There is no necessary succession of acts, only a logical complexity. The one act of faith is entirely capable of grasping the two aspects of its object: the preambles—which may or may not be known by reason alone—and the properly Christian element which God has revealed.

8 The Debate on the Question of the Relationship between Scripture and Tradition from the Viewpoint of Their Material Content

YVES M. J. CONGAR

Christians today seek a re-exploration of the central concept of Tradition, a concept which has often in the past been a source of division.

Begun in 1962, the debate upon the relationship between Scripture and Tradition quite obviously still remains open. Between the first session of Vatican II and the middle of 1964, the public controversy was continued in several valuable studies.[1] They will be summarized here not by way of a scientific report but in a synthetic presentation of the question which can be proposed in the following manner:

All Catholics agree that revelation cannot be known in all its fullness and its purity unless it is sought through the Scriptures *and* through or in Tradition. Such is the essential affirmation of the Council of Trent (Denz. 783), with the exception, and the precision is historically important, that the Council did not really recognize nor did it deal with the problem of Tradition itself, but wished, in opposition to the Reformers, to reaffirm under the name of apostolic traditions the value of venerable practices and beliefs in use in the Church. We shall not enter here into the historic question of the meaning of *traditions* at Trent. The idea upon which all Catholics are in agreement is known as the thesis of the formal insufficiency of Scripture.

The question upon which theologians confront one another is that of the *material* sufficiency or insufficiency of Scripture: Are there revealed truths which can be known *only* through Tradition? In other words: Is Tradition, for the faith of the Church, a source *adequately* distinct from Scripture? "Adequately distinct" signifies "that which does not imply the other reality and exists totally independent of it." In other words again: Does Tradition have a *constitutive* value, and not merely an explicative value?

The expression "constitutive Tradition" seems inappropriate in this context: revelation alone is constitutive; Tradition, like Scripture, is only a way for God, in conquering time and space, to communicate to the ends of the earth something which has been given *once* in a particular historic moment and in clearly defined geographic places. But when we speak of "constitutive Tradition" we mean that a part, at least, of revelation should be transmitted to us, and hence knowable to us, *only* by unwritten tradition.

The champion of the position which responds negatively to the question thus asked is Professor J. R. Geiselmann of Tübingen. His position can be summarized in this way: "In what concerns faith, it must be said: *totum in Sacra Scriptura et iterum totum in Traditione,* all is in Scripture and all is in Tradition." The situation is different in what concerns the *mores et consuetudines* of the Church. Here, Scripture is insufficient and its content has to be completed by Tradition, which in this case is *traditio constitutiva.* It is therefore *á propos* of *mores et consuetudines* that it must be said: *partim in S. Scriptura, partim in sine scripto traditionibus.*[2] J. R. Geiselmann has been attacked principally on two points:

I. His interpretation of the history of the decree of Trent. It is known that the Council had at first written that the truth and the discipline of life of which the Gospel is the source are contained *partim* in the Scriptures, *partim* in unwritten traditions. It replaced *partim . . . partim* which, according to Geiselmann, signified "partly . . . partly" (an interpretation questioned by A. M. Dubarle), by a simple *et* which signifies nothing except that that by which the Church is built and lives is contained *also* in tradition (i.e., in traditions). The final replacement of *partim . . . partim* by *et* is A FACT. Certainly no one denies it. But several scholars— Lennetz and Boyer above all—have contested that this replacement had at Trent the meaning which Geiselmann attributes to it, namely, of yielding all claims to an affirmation of the material insufficiency of Scripture and of permitting its sufficiency to be held: no one at that time would have given such a meaning to it. The doctrine which had been expressed at first in the *partim . . .*

partim would have remained beneath the *et* which replaced it: in this way it would have been understood at the moment of the Council and subsequently.[3]

It is possible that not everything seen by Geiselmann is really contained in the replacement of *partim . . . partim* by *et*. Nevertheless, two facts remain:

A.) This replacement followed the criticisms addressed to *partim, partim* by Bonucci, the General of the Servites, and by the Dominican bishop, Nacchianti, in the name of the old idea of the substantial sufficiency of Scripture. Recent experience has taught us how, in the course of conciliar proceedings, redactors seek to give some satisfaction to a demand, even if they themselves do not espouse the cause.

B.) The text of Trent such as it is offered to impartial reading does not contain *partim . . . partim*, but simply *et*: it authorizes, in itself and in its literalness, Geiselmann's interpretation, even supposing that the latter is contestable on the historical level. The redactors did not write *partim . . . partim*, even if that was what they personally thought.

(If I were asked to answer "Yes" or "No" to the question, "Does the decree of Trent (Denz. 783) intend to affirm that certain truths of faith are contained in Tradition alone and not in Scripture?"[4] I would refuse to answer "Yes" for the following two reasons:

1.) The Council of Trent did not speak about Tradition but about traditions, and it intended by that especially rites, practices, and usages.[5]

2.) Such an affirmation is not in the *text* of the decree. It is not written there that such truths are not *contained* in the Scriptures, but only that they can not *be known* by us through Scriptures *alone*: for that we have need also of Traditions. But that implies nothing more than what is said in holding the thesis of the formal insufficiency of the Scriptures. In this sense, the formula of Balić could be admitted: "dici posse adesse veritates revelatas, quae nonnisi Traditione *clarescunt* et *innotescunt,* ac proinde hoc etiam sub aspectu in Traditione *plus* haberi quam in Scriptura."[6] But I would not admit the implications of the author who really goes much further than that.)

II. The second point on which Geiselmann has been attacked

has been his theological position, namely the thesis "Totum in Scriptura, totum etiam in Traditione." Against this position, two strong arguments can be given:

A. There exist, in fact, truths of faith that cannot be established by way of Scriptures alone. We can cite, for example, the canonicity and the integrity of various writings of the New Testament, the number of the sacraments, the Immaculate Conception and the corporeal Assumption of the Mother of God, etc. The Catholic Church, through the voice of the Fathers, of theologians, and of the magisterium, has always affirmed the existence of such truths, and has justified it by invoking texts of the New Testament proving that the Apostles communicated many things verbally (but which? of what sort?).

It is necessary, however, to make four remarks here:

1. "There exist truths that cannot be justified by means of Scriptures read outside of Tradition." *Concedo.*

"There exist truths that cannot be justified by means of Scriptures read within Tradition." Is that as certain?

And again, "There exist truths that cannot be found as such in Scriptures." *Concedo,* but neither does one find affirmed there as such the divinity of the Holy Spirit nor many other doctrines which are nevertheless considered scriptural by all. . . . That one does not find these truths *in some manner* in the Scriptures would have to be seen in each case. The Middle Ages have given, as an example of unwritten tradition, the *Filioque.* What Catholic would say that it does not have at least some bases in Scripture? Now it could be shown (and has been shown) that, for example, the Immaculate Conception and the Assumption also have bases in Scripture. The first of these dogmas does indeed seem to be contained there formally-implicitly; the second, not so much in particular allusions (like *Apoc.* 12) as in the internal harmony resulting from several very explicitly attested truths whose convergence is disentangled by a reason guided by the sense of faith (what is called the virtually revealed). Pius XII has said that this dogma is based also upon Scripture.

2. Indeed when we examine successively and attentively the examples that are invoked of truths of faith that can only be established by Tradition *alone,* it is noticeable that many—perhaps all—are dogmas like the others, which have a basis in Scripture and have known a more or less considerable development and

elaboration in Tradition. Consider for example the canonicity of the writings of the New Testament. It must be recognized that for such or such a writing, for the list of the Canon as such, we have precise assurance only through Tradition, finally fixed or interpreted by the magisterium (the Muratorian Canon and, for the definitive list, not before the Council of Florence). But the principle of canonicity is a New Testament one, for the New Testament affirms that all which comes from the Apostles or from apostolic men approved by the Apostles is normative, that is, canonical.[7] Basically, the Canon is a dogma like any other. Like all dogmas, it employs as simultaneous cause Scripture, Tradition, and the magisterium.

There is no dogma which the Church holds through Scripture *alone*, none by Tradition *alone*: she holds them all by a conjunction of Scripture, of Tradition and of the magisterium, within which the same Holy Spirit operates differently. And finally, in order that a doctrine be declared as revealed, it requires an actual testimony of God in active Tradition. Journet has shown how many truths which theologians say are not in Scripture are there nonetheless.[8] But to understand fully the content of things to which Scripture is a witness, we must read it within Tradition: such indeed is the position of the Fathers.[9] Dogmatic tradition is principally this complete reading of Scripture joined to the appreciative possession of the realities of which it speaks. Beyond that, we do indeed speak of unwritten traditions. But besides the fact that we do not reduce them to *words* and that many consist in examples or gestures and institutions (for which the liturgy is the sacred framework), when a list of such unwritten traditions is collected from among the old writers, it is noticeable that it is a question, *in recto*, of points of liturgy or of discipline.[10]

3. Evidently, proving certain doctrines by starting from Scripture is difficult, but it is not certain that proving them by Tradition is any easier. We have only to think of the Assumption for example. For this reason some theologians have recourse to an a priori and simple justification by means of the previously established authority of the magisterium. But the thesis held by some which identifies Tradition with the magisterium is contradicted by the magisterium itself, which continually speaks of Tradition as an objective deposit to which the magisterium itself refers and to which it submits in its capacity as custodian of it.[11]

4. Were one to wish to have recourse only, or even principally, to Tradition, the problem of how to conceive of it would still remain. A certain number of formulations seem to conceive of it as the transmission, by word of mouth, of *agrapha,* that is, of *words* of Our Lord or of the Apostles, not retained in the writings of the New Testament. Such a conception does not bear close scrutiny. Besides the fact that the most ancient Fathers (Irenaeus, etc.) repeat that the Apostles transmitted nothing in secret, one must consider as a pure fiction or a myth the idea of a whispering campaign, transmitting items to us in an esoteric and secret fashion. The affirmation of the Assumption was not arrived at in this way. We must have recourse to the idea of a living Tradition, by which the Church progressively recognizes the content of a deposit which is not merely a deposit of ideas, but also of realities. It is by meditating upon these truths and these realities with which it lives, it is by undergoing the experience of them, that the Church realizes what they contain. It is what Maurice Blondel with his lucidly Catholic insight had explained as early as 1904.[12] But rather curiously, the partisans of the two sources, the one focusing on the material insufficiency of Scripture, the other on constitutive Tradition, generally work outside of these perspectives, with a notion of an *oral* Tradition.

B. The second argument which is cited is that their position represents the common teaching of the Fathers, of the great Scholastics, of post-Tridentine theologians and of the ordinary magisterium. This argument is maintained in particular in the large volume published by Balić,[13] but if the conclusion of the editor is such, it is very far from what all the authors think and say. The position is held, however, by H. Schauf, who has done much research on the subject of catechisms, starting with our own day and going back as far as the Council of Trent. Schauf thinks that if Vatican II rejects the thesis of constitutive Tradition, it would contradict the four-fold secular teaching of the ordinary magisterium: then, what would its own teaching be worth? But we know that this hypothesis is useless, for Vatican II is not contradicting this thesis. We wish, in any case, to make several remarks upon this obviously weighty argument which Balić or Schauf, and others, have formulated.

1. The Fathers of the Church sometimes do say, especially beginning with the fourth century, that certain things which the

Church holds or practices have been received through Tradition, not from Scripture (for example, the Trinitarian doxology of St. Basil, the defender of the divinity of the Holy Spirit; the baptism of infants, upheld by Origen and St. Augustine). But they say more often still that the whole teaching of faith comes from Scripture.[14] In reality, they do not oppose Scripture and Tradition from the viewpoint of their content: such is the valuable conclusion of the very penetrating book by Hanson,[15] a conclusion already drawn by previous studies[16] and confirmed by recent detailed studies, such as, for example, those on Tertullian. One of the reasons why J. Beumer, an authority in this matter, wishes to avoid the thesis of two independent sources, is that this thesis is not very easily reconciled with the position of the Fathers and of pre-Tridentine theologians.

Concerning medieval theologians and Scholastics, it can be stated, in effect, that:

a) They had hardly any theology of Tradition since Tradition for them was a reality to be lived rather than a problem to be posed; b) they abundantly affirm the material sufficiency of Scripture, at least for truths necessary for salvation;[17] c) when they had no proof from Scripture for points concerning which the authority or usage of the Church left no room for doubt, they quite naïvely had recourse to the idea of unwritten traditions, thinking of them probably as a transmission of words. Such was the case for the cult of images, the *Filioque,* the addition of some words to those of the New Testament in the Eucharistic consecration ("elevatis oculis," "mysterium fidei"). They thus placed side by side an affirmation of a scriptural principle, from a properly dogmatic viewpoint, and the idea of a complementation by an oral tradition received from the Apostles for secondary points. As for the rest, having scarcely elaborated a notion of dogmatic development, they barely envisaged the *implicit* except in the logical or dialectical sphere, not according to a properly historical process: they did not have the resources which we have at our disposal today to justify several difficult cases.

2. Catechisms and post-Tridentine theologians. For catechisms, consult Schauf;[18] for the theologians, consult the numerous studies in Balić,[19] and several monographs. Having read these different publications attentively, the following must be noted:

a) Catechisms and theologians are far from simply affirming

the thesis of the material insufficiency of Scripture or of the constitutive, autonomous character of Tradition for the faith. The volume edited by Balić presents fine investigations of theologians of different religious orders in the post-Tridentine period. Is it not rather remarkable that, for a certain number of authors thus studied, a paragraph can be found entitled "Quaedam sufficientia Scripturae"?[20] Moreover, Tavard has shown that, even in the post-Tridentine period, theologians, such as Christopher Davenport, could be found who favored the interpretation, "Totum in Scriptura, totum in Traditione."[21] Tavard has also shown that several theologians contemporaneous with the decree of Trent interpreted this decree as does Geiselmann and not in terms of *partim . . . partim.*[22] Things are, therefore, not so simple! Furthermore, the most creative theologians—those who have not been content to follow the inclination of the Counter Reformation but who have, personally and without bias, studied the texts and the Fathers— have notably gone beyond the simplistic and global affirmation of a constitutive Tradition. Among such theologians are Möhler, Scheeben,[23] and to a certain degree Perrone and Franzelin,[24] as well as Newman.

When it comes to the question of catechisms, we must no longer simplify things. Many catechisms base their affirmation upon this: the faith of the Church must be nourished, not only by Scripture, but by a deposit or by an unwritten heritage (in Germany, it was fashionable beginning with the eighteenth century, to speak of "Erblehre"). It is with this significance that they speak (enough but not very often) of the "two sources": sources of our faith or of our knowledge (Catechism of Deharbe), or again of two "rules" (as in our Imperial Catechism). The essential affirmation is then that the Apostles have not written everything, that the Catholic teaching is not justifiable from Scripture *alone.* But what does "have not written *everything*" cover? Such elementary manuals as catechisms make no distinction. They wish to inculcate a global and total confidence in the teaching and the practices of the Church. They often cite John 20:30-31, but did not St. John think that he had written what was essential concerning the faith? Concerning *revealed truths* a certain catechism says that the Bible contains "the greatest part" of these truths.[25] But is not this "the greatest part" a little ridiculous? Sometimes a list of some particularly convincing examples is given of truths of faith not contained in Scripture. Those contained in the text of Schauf on pages 50, 70, 134, 145-46, 155, 156, 159-160, 162 are all concerned either with some point of discipline (the baptism of infants, the sanctification of Sundays), or of the most ordinary dogmatic development (setting the number of sacraments at seven, the existence of three Persons in God). We have seen *none* which demands the massive affirmation of a dogmatically constitutive Tradition in the strict sense.

b) The texts invoked by theologians and in catechisms give evidence of the climate of a well-defined historical moment, that of the Counter Reformation, in the formal sense of that expression. When, after having spent some time in reading pre-Reformation authors, we pass to post-Tridentine texts (with few exceptions), we really experience the feeling of having crossed a border and of having entered into another world, a situation attributable to the influence of the Reformation. With some few exceptions, these texts remain in the tradition of anti-Protestantism.

But we are now emerging from that state, and the current question is precisely that of emerging from it without betraying anything of perennial Catholic dogma. Sanctioned by the conciliar vote of November 20, 1962, this emergence from a Catholicism of anti-Protestantism is bound up with several movements of the most profound ideas of our time, namely: 1) the discovery of the notion of development, which has placed the theology of ecclesiastical Tradition in better continuity with Scripture, as is evident in the works of Möhler and Newman. Today we are better able to render an account of facts for which recourse was formerly made, a little too quickly and a little too simply, to the idea of oral tradition; 2) the biblical movement and the liturgical movement with the return to sources which they involve. What was the biblical training, the biblical preoccupation, what were the resources for biblical work of those "catechism eras" to which some people wish to link us? Can we speak today as if we were in a period when the faithful often believed that the reading of Scripture was forbidden, when indeed such a statement was often made to them? Ought we not rather to reformulate the question of the relationship between Scripture and Tradition in a manner consonant with the Biblical renewal with which God has blessed us? Certainly, all must be done in continuity with Catholic Tradition; but it is precisely here that, in order to accomplish this, we have only to take up again the positions held by the Fathers and by the theologians of the Middle Ages prior to the Reformation and to the Counter Reformation. It is here also that the return to sources is, insofar as it is in the same movement, a recentering upon the Christian mystery: a recentering which develops its beneficial applications in preaching, in catechesis, in the training of the clergy and of the laity, in the drawing up of theology manuals. Is not the manual published in monographs by Desclée entitled "Le Mystère chrétien"? This point is absolutely decisive. On the one hand, in effect, when we consider principally the center of all revelation, the Christian mystery, and the relationship of particular truths with that center, we are led to recognize that there is no Christian truth which is not connected with Scripture and whose principle is not expressed in Scripture.[26] On the contrary, if we consider the Catholic Faith as a series of fragmented propositions without organic connection with the center, we are inclined to ask that each one, taken separately, be based upon a reference and to look for, in an oral constitutive Tradition, the reference that cannot be found in Scripture. It would be easy to apply that to dogmas dealing with Mariology. But, on the other hand, there is no need to probe too deeply into the question in order to see that the oppositions manifested in recent discussions indicate a cleavage between those for whom "doctrine" was above all a list of sharply defined propositions and those for whom it was from the beginning the preaching of the Christian mystery. These differences have been well analyzed by R. Laurentin,[27] by Philips and by Dupont,[28] who show, at the root of these divergences, different conceptions of the Word of God and of revelation.

If we are emerging from a Counter-Reformation Catholicism, Protestants are beginning to emerge from a Protestantism of anti-Catholicism. While the reformers of the sixteenth century did not really know the whole problem of Tradition and were satisfied to break out polemically against traditions (hence the reaction of Trent), numerous Protestants and the ecumenical movement are setting about to approach the problem positively.[29] The debate between the Reform and ourselves is far from being settled: it is too serious and too vast. We have, however, drawn closer to one another, not by mutual concessions, but by a return, on both sides,

to a more profound tradition and truth, beyond polemical oppositions. For my part, I would willingly characterize my personal
efforts as a passage from fundamental theology to theology pure
and simple, and even to ecclesiology.[30] Or again as an attempt to
study Tradition in itself: no longer simply as a last resort when
Scripture fails, but as an original mode of transmission which retains all its value even when Scripture speaks. It seems that the
Council capable of producing *De Sacra Liturgia,* with the place
which it has given to Scripture,—the Council of ecumenical openness—requires something other than a chapter of controversies.

C. This very long but necessary exposé was undertaken by
noting the accord realized prior to any discussion among Catholics. To conclude, suggestions are here presented for the accord
upon which the confrontations and discussions envisaged here
could be ended. Several authors have already given the broad out-
lines of a possible accord. Barauna, a Brazilian Franciscan, for
example, in the volume published by Balić[31] has written:

Omnes, saltem in praxi, communiter tenere quasdam conclusiones: 1) Traditio aliquo sensu latius patet quam Scriptura,
quippe quae veritates continet—v. gr. canonicatatem et inspirationem librorum sacrorum—, quae ibidem sufficiens testimonium
haud inveniunt.—2) Datur, ergo, Traditio constitutiva, etiam
dogmatica, sensu sub 1 expresso.—3) Praeter inspirationem et
canonicitatem, necnon traditiones sic dictas disciplinares, nulla
hucusque proposita est dogmatica doctrina, quae ex Scriptura de
facto a theologis non inferatur, argumento continentiae sive ex-
plicitae, sive implicitae, sive virtualis vel alio modo inter theologos
noto.—4) Hoc sensu datur aliqua sufficientia Scripturae ad
dignoscendam Dei revelationem in Christo. Haec sufficientia, ergo,
non est formalis, sed materialis, porre, non absoluta, sed relativa.
Nisi hae conclusiones insimul teneantur, vix inter se conciliari
possunt, ut nobis videtur, duae hae doctrinae, uno aliove modo
decursu omnium saeculorum clare assertae: 1. Scriptura omnia
continet quae ad salutem sunt necessaria; 2. Traditio quaedam in
se habet, quae non in Sacris Litteris inveniuntur.

On the other hand, the differing conclusions of Beumer have
already been summarized. According to him, three positions are in
confrontation, which he summarizes and evaluates as follows:[32]

1. Tradition is a fully autonomous source, objectively or mate-
rially complementary to Scripture (the theory of the two sources).

It is difficult to reconcile this position with the statements of the Fathers and of pre-Tridentine theologians. It cannot refer either to the text of the Council of Trent or to the totality of Catholic disputants.

2. Tradition is an interpretation and, as it were, an unfolding of Scripture, which has a radical material sufficiency. But, says Beumer, the authorities invoked in favor of such a position are not so definite; on the other hand, Scripture itself witnesses to its material insufficiency.

3. There exists an identity of content between Scripture and Tradition as to the essence or nucleus of faith; Tradition goes beyond Scripture only in a relative and subordinate manner. Such would be the position of the great classical writers of the nineteenth century: Möhler, Scheeben, and, in a certain measure, Perrone, Newman, Franzelin.

J. P. Mackey directs the conclusion of his excellent study in the same way. He admits[33] that Scripture gives us everything, and that everything is in Tradition under another form, namely as an explication: not uniquely by way of the exegesis of Scripture, but under the form of a *total* teaching of that about which Scripture speaks.

Would Schauf be entirely opposed to such attempts at harmonization? He himself summarizes his position in these terms:[34] There exist truths of faith which are not contained *expressly* in Holy Scripture, that is, which cannot be demonstrated without the aid of the truth contained in oral Tradition, "Ex sola per se Scriptura sufficienter (probari non posse). . . ."

No Catholic could refuse to admit that in a sense Tradition is broader than Scripture: "latius patet," as already stated by Alber Pigge of Louvain.[35] For our part, we would agree, yet we would not want to say it without saying *also* that Scripture on its side "profundior est": something which the champions of constitutive Tradition have never said and still do not say. We admit also that several truths of faith are *known with certitude* only because of Tradition, even if they are contained in a certain way in Scripture. However, on the one hand, it is not certain that this implies anything other than a good theology of living Tradition, and the formal insufficiency of Scripture; on the other hand, expression of it in this way is preferable for the two following reasons:

1. The spirit in which this formula is currently proposed is concretely contrary to what we have said above about a return to sources and a recentering upon the Christian mystery, about ecumenical openness, about the emergence from a Catholicism of anti-Protestantism.

2. The consequences which certain persons would wish to draw from it, as far as we can see, operate within an ecclesiological and Mariological context to which we consider ourselves alien. In fact, sufficient exorcism has still not taken place, on the one hand, regarding certain presentations of Tradition and, on the other hand, regarding a pretention to indefinite and indeed questionable Mariological developments. The presentation of Tradition about which we speak is that whose genesis we have already traced:[36] it begins by introducing the idea of "active Tradition" in the *definition* of Tradition, it continues by enlarging the part of faith or of the sense of the Church and of the magisterium in such a way that it arrives at this formula, borrowed from Dieckmann and from Deneffe: "Ecclesia sibi ipsi est fons. . . ." How then can we avoid Protestant criticisms such as that expressed by Barth: The Catholic Church identifies itself with its norm, it no longer has anything over against itself ("Gegenuber") in relation to which it can situate itself and which judges it; it is no longer in dialogue except with itself. . . .

The value of the idea of Tradition consists in maintaining a reference to a normative objective given and it is clear that Scripture is the principal part of such a given. Not that this given is identified with what is attested by documents, still less with only the critically approved portion attested by documents: the given is lived, and thus progressively understood, by the Church: that is living Tradition. But the given is really *given* and it is essentially Christ-centered.

For this reason I wish that an exposé of the theology *De Revelatione* avoid speaking, in these or equivalent terms, of "constitutive Tradition."

NOTES

1. The following is a partial list of the principal studies which have appeared recently, those at least with which the author is personally familiar.

Roman numerals used here will be referred to in the subsequent notes. Some less recent studies will be mentioned first:

I. J. R. Geiselmann (only works in French and in English are listed), "Un malentendu éclairci. La relation 'Ecriture-Tradition' dans la théologie catholique," in *Istina*, 5 (1958), pp. 197–214; "Scripture, Tradition and the Church: An Ecumenical Problem," in *Christianity Divided*, ed. D. Callahan, Heiko Oberman, Daniel O'Hanlon S. J. (New York: Sheed and Ward, 1961) pp. 39–72.

II. Y. M. J. Congar, *La Tradition et les traditions: I, Essai historique*. Paris: Fayard, 1960.

III. H. Holstein, *La Tradition dans l'Eglise*. Paris: Grasset, 1960

IV. P. Lengsfeld, *Ueberlieferung. Tradition und Schrift in der evangelischen und katholischen Theologie der Gegenwart*. Paderborn: 1960; French trans., Orante, 1964.

V. J. Beumer, *Die mündliche Ueberlieferung als Glabensquelle* (Fasc. 4 of vol. I of *Handbuch der Dogmengeschichte*). Herder: 1962.

VI. W. Kasper, *Die Lehre von der Tradition in der Römischen Schule*. Freiburg: Herder, 1962.

VII. R. P. C. Hanson, *Tradition in the Early Church*. London: SCM Press, 1962. (Book reviewed by J. Daniélou in *Rech. Sc. relig.*, 51 (1963), pp. 550–557; cf. pp. 728–730.

VIII. J. R. Geiselmann, *Die Heilige Schrift und die Tradition*. Freiburg: Herder, 1962 (in response to his critics).

IX. Y. M. J. Congar, *La Tradition et les traditions: II, Essai théologique*. Paris: Fayard, 1963. (see also a non-technical condensation: *La Tradition et la vie de l'Eglise*. Ibid. Coll. "Je sais, je crois.")

X. G. H. Tavard, *Holy Writ or Holy Church*. New York: Harper, 1959.

XI. P. Rusch, Bishop of Innsbruck, "De non definienda illimitata insufficientia materiali Scripturae," in *Zeitschr. kath. Theol.*, 85 (1963), pp. 1–15.

XII. W. J. Burghardt, "The Catholic Concept of Tradition in the Light of Modern Theological Thought," in *Proceedings of the 6th Annual Convention of the Catholic Theological Society of America*, 1951.

XIII. H. Schauf, *Die Lehre der Kirche über Schrift und Tradition in den Katechismen*. Essen: Driewer, 1963; id. "De Traditione Constitutiva ad mentem Catechismorum," in *Seminarium*, 1964/2, 11 pages.

XIV. J. P. Mackey, *The Modern Theology of Tradition*. London: Longman, 1962.

XV. *De Scriptura et Traditione*, ed. C. Balić. Rome: Pontif. Acad. Mariana Internationalis (xii–742 pp.).

XVI. *Schrift und Tradition*, ed. by the Société allemande de Mariologie. Essen: Driewer, 1962.

XVII. J. Ermel, *Les Sources de la Foi. Concile de Trente, Œcuménisme contemporain*. Tournai-Paris: Desclée et Cⁱᵉ, 1963.

XVIII. M. Bévenot, "'Traditions' in the Council of Trent," in *The Heythrop Journal*, 4 (1963), pp. 333–47.

XIX. J. P. Torrell, "Chronique de Théologie fondamentale," in *Rev. thomiste*, 64 (1964), pp. 97–127.

2. J. R. Geiselmann, VIII, p. 282.

3. See H. Lennerz, "Scriptura sola?" (in German) in *Gregorianum*, 40 (1959), pp. 38–53; "Sine scripto traditiones" (in Latin), ibid. pp. 624–635; "Scriptura et Traditio in decreto IV sessionis Concilii Tridentini," ibid., 42

(1961), pp. 517–522; C. Boyer, "Traditions apostoliques non écrites," in *Doctor Communis*, 15 (1962), pp. 5–21. (Other references can be found in my *Tradition*, II, p. 319, n. 126.)

4. What Balić, for example, considers acquired: XV, p. 709.

5. On this point, see my *Tradition, I*, p. 210; P. Smulders, "Het traditie-decreet van het Concilie van Trent," p. 150 in *Werken van Kathol. theologen in Nederland*, 1947-48; J. Beumer, *Der Begriff der "traditiones" auf dem Trienter Konzil im Lichte der mittelalterlichen Kanonistik*, in *Scholastik*, 35 (1960), pp. 359 s.; J. Ermel, XVII, pp. 69 s.

6. C. Balić, XV, p. 697.

7. See my *Tradition*, II, p. 172 s.

8. C. Journet, *Esquisse du développement du dogme marial*, Paris 1954, pp. 36 s.

9. Cf. II, pp. 47 s., 58 s; J. Beumer, V, p. 37.

10. See II, pp. 64–75.

11. Cf. II, pp. 257 s.

12. See my *Tradition*, II, pp. 123 s.

13. See note 1, XV.

14. Cf. II, pp. 139 s; VIII, pp. 222 s; V, p. 35.

15. See note 1, VII.

16. For example II.

17. See II, pp. 143 s.; IX, pp. 255 s. For S. Thomas Aquinas, B. Decker in XVI, pp. 191–221.

18. See note 1, XIII.

19. See note 1, XV.

20. See pp. 388 s and 395–396 for S. Laurent de Brindes, pp. 435; See Scheeben, pp. 668–69.

21. G. Tavard, "Christopher Davenport and the problem of Tradition," in *Theol. Studies*, 24 (1963), pp. 278–290.

22. G. Tavard, "Tradition in Early Post-Tridentine Theology," *Ibid.*, 23 (1962), pp. 377–405.

23. See V, p. 124.

24. See VI.

25. Schauf, XIII, p. 68.

26. Cf. A. M. Dubarle in *Initiation théologique, I*, pp. 80–81; O. Semmel-roth, "Ueberlieferung als Lebensfunktion der Kirche," in *Stimmen der Zeit*, 148 (1951), p. 4.

27. *La Question mariale*, Paris: Seuil, 1963.

28. *Nouv. Rev. théol.* 85 (1963), pp. 225–238 and pp. 458–468.

29. See my *Tradition, II*, p. 223, and P. Lengsfeld, IV, and for the Con-férence de Foi et Constitution à Montreal, in July, 1963, the chronicles of *Istina*.

30. See note 1, IX.

31. XV, p. 84.

32. J. Beumer, V, pp. 133 ff.

33. J. P. Mackey, XIV, pp. 152–158.

34. H. Schauf, XIII, p. 210.

35. Cited by J. Beumer, V, p. 95.

36. In *Tradition*, I.

9 Functional Christology in the New Testament *

LÉOPOLD MALEVEZ, S.J.

Oscar Cullmann asserts that the Word of God is presented in the New Testament purely in terms of His functions, His revealing actions. For Cullmann there is no revelation of the Word's essence or nature; subsequent philosophizing on it is therefore divorced from the New Testament sources. Catholics, following Nicea and Chalcedon, clearly cannot agree to this thesis; but they do take rather interesting positions with respect to it.

THE EXPRESSION "FUNCTIONAL theology" has various meanings among modern theologians. Some use it to describe our subjective religious representations. Most authors, however, apply this term to the object of our representations, God. They say God has manifested Himself to us, not in Himself, but in His exterior functions, especially in the salvific function exercised through Christ. It is in this sense that we will treat of functional theology here.

We are not concerned here, however, with the objective functional theology of Rudolf Bultmann, who says that our faith attains God only as He wishes to relate Himself to us as our judge and liberator. For Bultmann the reality of the Christian salvific event is singularly reduced; for him Christ's person contains no mystery, no divine union. We will concentrate here on that type of functional theology that sees in Christ some real identity with God.

CULLMANN'S CHRISTOLOGY

Oscar Cullmann's functional Christology claims our first attention. According to him the Christology of the first Christian communities is the fruit of reflection on the historical Jesus. Because

---

* "Nouveau Testament et théologie fonctionnelle," *Recherches de Science Religieuse*, 48 (1960), 258–90.

the entire Old Testament referred to Him, Jesus was thought of as having been at work before his earthly life. As the bearer of revelation par excellence, He must have been the very source of revelation. Remembering that in Genesis all was created by the "Word of God," these communities saw that in creation Christ made the first revelation and took the first step in the history of salvation. A parallel to the first chapter of Genesis is seen in the opening of John's Gospel, where the Word, as the mediator of revelation, is again said to "create everything." This early Christian notion of pre-existence demanded a purely dynamic and functional Christ. It is true that He is God in a true sense; but he pre-exists only as principle of things and as source of revelation. Christian documents cannot and do not recognize in Him any reality within God independent of his revealing function. John considers the pre-existence of the Word only in strict connection with His external action; the pre-existence of Jesus is the first step of the history of Jesus.

This exclusively functional notion of the pre-existent Christ is clear from his Christian titles: in the New Testament, the question, "Who is Christ?" does not primarily ask, "What is His nature?" but, "What is His function in the history of salvation?" The Christology in the New Testament is a history. When Christianity came into contact with the Greek world, the Church was forced to ask the question of natures. Simply by allowing it to be asked, she introduced a speculation that was foreign to the New Testament. Let us consider in this connection three of his biblical titles: Lord, Word, and Son of God.

LORD, WORD, SON OF GOD

"Lord" (*Kyrios*) designates the divine sovereignty of Jesus in the present period of salvation history, Cullmann finds; but it is also used of Christ's mediatorship of creation, and so applies to Christ's pre-existent state. In both applications, however, it signifies only that Christ and the Father are one in their sovereignty over the world.

The title "Word" (*Logos*) Cullmann assigns exclusively to Jesus' pre-existence. The remote Old Testament context from which it comes considers the Word of God as an independent entity through whose mediation the creative activity of God is exercised. This Word, considered as God not in Himself but in His communication of Himself to the world, influenced Christianity directly but not via later Judaism. It is true that the Judaism of Sirach, Qumran, and rabbinism, under the influence of pagan Hellenism, considers the Word, or Wisdom, as a "part of God"; but even here the functional character of the Word is not weakened. It exists in the action by which God reveals himself to the world. And it is this aspect of the older biblical view, preserved also in later Judaism, that appears in the *Logos* of John.

John's original contribution is the formerly unheard-of notion of a Word addressed by God to the world, which became incarnate in an earthly life. And this addition to the basic notion actually strengthens the functional concept of the Word. Cullmann does recognize in the Prologue an ascent beyond creation and revelation to the being of the Word with God. But he shows that, although Christ is neither a creature nor an emanation from God, he is different. For God can be conceived apart from His act of revealing; the *Logos* cannot.

In the title "Son of God" John also implicitly touches upon the question of the relation of essence between God and Christ, independently of the Incarnation. John's answer remains, according to Cullmann: Their unity is their oneness in the act of revelation. Though one may speak of the Father without reference to revelation, one may speak of the Son only in reference to it. Subsequent speculation on the "being" of the Son is merely philosophical, Cullmann claims, and goes beyond what is contained in the sources. He even seems to consider a kind of disappearance of the Son when He has finished His salvific work at the end of time.

ASSERTIVE AND EXCLUSIVE

Absolutely speaking, Cullmann could have confined himself to saying that the writings of the New Testament do not speculate on the divine condition of the Son, apart from His external function. (He could have been "assertive but not exclusive.") To this he could then add: When we undertake to reconstruct a specifically *biblical* theology, we should, because of this silence of Scripture, refrain from introducing a consideration of the independent existence of the Word. This position might raise certain questions concerning the methodology of theology, but at least it would not exclude the Nicene theology's legitimate development. Pierre Benoit, O.P., seems to understand Cullmann in this way; otherwise his unreserved approbation of Cullmann's functionalism is inexplicable. But Cullmann's theology is assertive *and* exclusive, and this is the way it was understood by A. Grillmeier, S.J.

If Scripture closes the way to a concept of the Son that goes beyond His creative and revealing action, then the Nicene *homoousios* is condemned in advance; for to say of the Son, in the Nicene sense, that He is "consubstantial with the Father" is to say that He enjoys with respect to the created universe the same independence as the Father. The post-Nicene theoretician may concede that the Son does not exist without freely positing the eternal act of creation in time, and that the act of creation is not really distinct in the Son from the act of existing (the classical doctrine of the divine simplicity). But he cannot say that the Son exhausts His reality in creative activity. He observes that the eternal union of the Son with the creative act does not formally depend on His condition as Son. With respect to union with the free creative act, the Father is in no way different from the Son. Cullmann holds that Scripture attributes to the Son a relation of union and a necessary identification with the creative act, which is verified in Him alone. But if Cullmann were right, Scripture would be calling into question the divinity of the Son.

CATHOLIC REACTIONS

Catholic exegetes consider Chalcedon's Christology a fully legitimate evolution, for the New Testament does not *exclude* the idea of a *Logos* which proceeds in God independently of His revealing function. Some Catholics admit, however, that the New Testament scarcely envisages the Son of God in any other way than in His salvific function. Moreover, the pre-existent Christ owes his title *Logos* to his function as revealer of God to men. Cullmann cites Jacques Dupont, O.S.B., and M.-E. Boismard, O.P., among the Catholic exegetes who accept functionalism, but regrettably neglects to note their differences from his own thinking.

Dupont says that John's theology is not one of essences, but that it is functional. He bases this interpretation of John's *Logos* on its purely Jewish inspiration. He acknowledges no influence of Greek philosophy in John's application of *Logos* to Christ. In I John 1:12, John tells us that he has seen and touched the word of life, the vivifying Word. In Apoc. 19:11-16 he draws on the Old Testament in calling Christ the avenging or exterminating Word, an eschatological function. In the Prologue, John identifies Jesus with the *creative* Word of God, not to tell us the Word is the person of Jesus, but to show the Word's action in the universe. Nevertheless, Dupont does not neglect to recall that according to John this creative Word was at the beginning with God, and was God. That the *Logos* is with God and that He is God means that He is a divine being whose existence and procession in God are independent of His work of creation.

ASSERTIVE, NOT EXCLUSIVE

Dupont sees in "Son of God" a title more expressive of the mission of Jesus than of His divine nature. But he admits that John occasionally goes beyond this manner of seeing Christ and acknowledges a sonship that is independent of Christ's mission; for example, in 1:18 Christ is called the only-begotten God. Dupont's interpretation, therefore, turns out not so exclusively functional as some of his expressions would lead one to think. Unlike Cullmann's, his functionalism is "assertive, not exclusive." It has to do particularly with the concept of the Word: That the Word was generated by intellectual procession, as later theologians will say, is neither asserted in John's Prologue nor excluded by it. Rather, Christ is called the Word because He is the revealer and the creator. Hence, "The Word was made flesh" indicates the antithesis between man's frailty and the Word which lasts forever. "Flesh" does not indicate man's nature but his wretched condition. "Flesh" is opposed, not to the *nature* of the Word, but to the *condition* of the Word—the Word of God. John is not thinking of the Greek theology of the Incarnation—the union of two natures in one person—but of the concrete Christ. Dupont also gives a functional interpretation to the titles Light, Life, and Truth, and to the glory Christ received from His Father.

Boismard agrees up to a point with Dupont's functional interpretation, but for him the exterior function is expressly attached to the interior nature of Christ. His sonship is functional because He makes us sons; but He makes us sons precisely because He is Himself the Son of God. Generalizing from this, Boismard interprets John as saying that the revealing function of Christ is also founded on the essence of Christ as the Word in whom God thought of Himself and expressed Himself independently of any eventual revelation. This interpretation of John is based on the Sapiential books, which speak of Wisdom in God before God's creative work and independently of it. Hence, Boismard can be ranked as a functional theologian only in a very broad sense.

BIBLICAL THEOLOGY FUNCTIONAL?

The instances of functional theology we have just examined are Christological. But according to their authors, the functionalism that applies here applies to the whole biblical doctrine of God. They assert this, but do not prove it. In my opinion, there is no proof that biblical theology is functional; and functionalism is not a characteristic by which Scripture can be distinguished from natural theology. Admittedly Scripture has a way of looking at God that is not that of natural theology. But to consider God not in Himself but in His free activity, as Scripture does, is also the perspective of natural theology, in which God can be known only from the works of His creation, not directly in Himself. So if Scripture is functional, metaphysical theology is also.

One might attempt to distinguish Scripture from natural theology by saying that Scripture stops at God as author of salvation history, whereas metaphysics proceeds from God's causality in the universe to investigate His essential attributes. But this too is inadequate. Scripture develops scantily the essential attributes of God, but what it does say gives them substantially the same sense as natural theology. Scripture mentions:

divine nature—II Pet. 1:4
divinity—Rom. 1:20
eternity—Rom. 16:26, Apoc. 1:4-8, 16:5; Rom 1:20
invisibility—Rom. 1:20, Col. 1:15, I Tim. 1:17, Heb. 11:27
incorruptibility—Rom. 1:23, I Tim. 1:17

blessedness—I Tim 1:11, 6:15
one who cannot be tempted—Jas. 1:13
God is not unjust—Heb. 6:10, Rom 3:5; 9:14
no one is good but only God—Mark 10:18
God alone is wise—Rom. 16:27

None of these expressions refers either explicitly or implicitly to the work of creation. We have reason to believe that they are to be understood in the sense the Greek mind and natural reason would give them. They are judgments of essence, as Karl Rahner remarks, and not of existence. They are not the judgments of purely functional theology; to understand them it is not absolutely necessary to refer to the special history of salvation.

Opposing function to essence, therefore, does not distinguish Scripture from natural theology. The distinction lies rather in this: The God of natural theology is a necessity; the God of Scripture is a mystery. Philosophy asks itself not so much, "What is He?" as, "What is it that He *cannot but be?*" It arrives at his attributes from the principle of noncontradiction. This characteristic of rational necessity is present in natural theology's basic observation that God is *creator,* and freely so, and in the discovery of His attributes.

SCRIPTURAL GOD A SAVIOR

Scripture also shows us the freedom of God's attitude toward man and toward creative activity. But it especially stresses that this free creation is inspired by a loving desire to save, a desire of which natural thought can have no presentiment. Only revelation can show forth the peculiar character of this gratuitous love. It is an absolute initiative, upsetting and surprising, recognizable only in faith.

Scripture does not present the interventions of God in history as illustrations of already known abstract properties. Rather, through God's actions we are introduced to a knowledge of His highest attributes which, accepted in faith, enrich and interpenetrate our natural knowledge on an altogether new plane. Scripture, as we have seen above, is aware of the natural meaning of the divine perfections, but more often the natural meaning is assumed into the revealed meaning.

We borrow Rahner's examples. When Scripture says that God is the just judge, we see, beyond the justice known by reason, the historical condemnation of sin in the flesh of Christ, made sin for us (II Cor. 5:21). The reaction of the all-holy God to sin exceeds our understanding here, as does its converse, God's patient longanimity (Rom. 2:4). Divine omniscience in sacred Scripture does not mean principally God's knowledge of Himself nor that which He exercises in his creative causality, but rather God's look which pierces to the heart of man to judge him and at the same time to be merciful to him through the gratuitous event of the death of His Son (Matt. 6:4-6). Finally, the infinite power of God belongs to that free and suprarational action of God in the history of salvation which could have made of the stones children of Abraham (Matt. 3:9), which is at work in the resurrection of Christ (Acts 2:24) and in the conversion of the rebellious.

The originality of biblical theology is to be defined, then, by the fact that its content does not express a rational necessity. It is not distinguished by its functionalism nor by the absence of determinations of the divine essence. Scripture does not merely call up these ontological determinations in express fashion from time to time; it also, when speaking of God in His supernatural, salvific function, shows something of His being. God's acts in Scripture show that *for us* He is a *mystery* of love, but through this they hint at what He is in Himself. This scriptural knowledge of God's being remains a knowledge through representations of Him borrowed from the world where God deploys His creative actions. But through all these media it is God that we see.

GOD IS THE END

Scripture thus shows us God's being by showing us His saving action, and even positively invites us to seek His essence in His action. The culmination of God's intervention in our history is to be at the end "when all things are made subject to Him; then the Son Himself will also be made subject to Him who subjected all things to Him, that God may be all in all" (I Cor. 15:28). Cullmann's very disputable interpretation of this text is that it denotes the end of the function of the Word and hence, perhaps, of His being. A better interpretation is that beyond Christ and His salutary work is the excellence and grandeur of God, whose instrument

Christ is. Christianity's aspiration is to bring the Christian to a love of God in himself, in his abyss and his darkness. An absolute functional theology would have to hold such a desire suspect and not conformed to Scripture. But it would seem to be the absolute functional theology that is more in danger of being unfaithful to the authentic spirit of the Bible.

LIMITS OF FUNCTIONAL THEOLOGY

The biblical doctrine of God, then, does not appear to be wholly functional. This now gives us a valuable basis for judging a functional theology of Christ or of the Spirit. If Scripture presented God exclusively in a functional perspective, the presumption would be strong in favor of a Trinity not immanent but "economic"—one in which distinction arises because of different functions in different phases of the economy of salvation. But since Scripture does not so present God, the way remains open for an immanent Trinity, and also for a Christology that is not absolutely functional.

We still must determine whether in fact New Testament Christology is rigorously functional. Dupont's exegesis called forth reservations from Boismard, and it suggests some other remarks. Recall first that Dupont never called into question the divine Son as a person independent of His creative and revealing functions. Nevertheless, some aspects of His functionalism seem exaggerated. Although the New Testament formulas that express Christ's divinity are always at least implicitly connected with His messianic action, it remains no less true that at the source of this saving action the fully divine ontological reality is discernible. For John the very thing that makes Christ's mission possible is His communion with the Father in eternal Sonship. Taken in their most natural sense, the texts say that Christ enlightens because He is Himself light, in a plenitude that is received but is equal to that of the Father. He gives life, divinizes, makes us children of God because He is Himself above the condition of creatures: God-Son but God. If this is St. John's thought, he is not "philosophizing" in Greek fashion or any other; and yet he is expressing himself "ontologically," as would any mind attempting to express a power rooted in the inherent essence of its possessor.

Dupont betrays an effort to purify his treatment of John's

thought from all metaphysical contamination. It is true that if metaphysics is a science of the rational necessities of being, these will hardly be found in John or anywhere else in Scripture. But to Dupont metaphysics means any knowledge of "natures." And thus we have exegetes, like cherubs before the Ark, guarding Scripture from the intrusions of ontology. The guard is useless and too late. Ontology is already within the sanctuary, without profaning it. Dupont admits a divine being independent of creation. What more is required to constitute an ontological judgment? Were one to grant, with Cullmann, that John thinks of the Word exclusively as linked with revelation and the Incarnation, one is still saying: God determines Himself for the communication of Himself to the world. And this is an ontological judgment.

FUNCTIONAL AND ONTOLOGICAL

As a matter of fact, neither ontology nor the designation of natures is a peculiar property of the Greek mind. They are the very structure without which the mind cannot express its slightest content. Dupont says that John's "The Word was made flesh" does not establish what will later be the theological concept of the Incarnation; he claims that there is no idea here of the union of two natures, but simply a concrete designation of Jesus. But it seems strange to posit such opposition between John and later theologians. After all, what does Chalcedon say but that the divine person, who is the Word, has taken our human condition without becoming thereby two subjects.

We must finally confront Cullmann's extreme form of functionalism, which sees the divine being of the Word to be merely the result of the warping influence of the Greek mind. To hold with Cullmann that "We cannot say 'Son' except in relation to God's revelation" results in a modalist theology of the Trinity—hence the gravity of the dispute. Does Cullmann think of the Son as a person distinct from the Father? It is probable, but not certain, that he does. But it is certain that for him the New Testament gives the Son divine rank. This seems sufficient to shake his functionalism.

RESPONSE TO CULLMANN

It is the undisputed doctrine of both Testaments that the God of the Bible enjoys a sovereign liberty with respect to creation and the history of salvation. And according to the New Testament, creation has its source in a free, divine predestination in Christ. Is it right to say, then, that Scripture makes sovereign mastery of the universe the privilege of the Father, and gives no indication that it is shared with the Son? After all, John tells us that the Son has received the power to create, since all things were made by Him. The fact that he has *received* this power distinguishes Him from the Father. But having received it, He truly possesses it as fully as does the Father, unlimited and unweakened. If the Son is divine, how can limits be put to His free creative power?

If, as a matter of fact, the Son in John has the attributes of the divinity, as Cullmann admits, He must also possess in John's thought all the liberty of the God of Scripture with respect to creation. In making explicit the liberty of a nature with respect to its activities, later theological development is not under the impulse of Hellenistic tendencies; but, to use Cullmann's phrase, it reacts to the pressure of tendencies native to Christianity: the fully biblical idea of the sovereign liberty of God in the contingent work of salvation. The Nicene and Chalcedonian theology is an altogether natural interpretation of John's thought. Extreme functionalism, on the contrary, does violence to the biblical concept of creation.

Moreover, in evolving a theology of the Son as independent of creation in His meaning and His existence, Christian dogma served precisely the better interests of that salvation history which Cullmann rightly calls the heart of the message. If the Son is not God, if He does not have all the attributes of God, such as liberty with respect to the created world, then He has not divinized us, nor saved us; no history of salvation remains; no salvation remains.

10   *The Gift of Self-Redemption* *

AUGUST BRUNNER

Self-redemption seems to be a contradiction. We need to be re-
deemed because we cannot redeem ourselves. Still in God's plan
a forced salvation is no salvation at all. He so respects our
freedom that in His redeeming grace He gives us the power
to redeem ourselves. It is this gift that only God can give that
Father Brunner brings into focus.

I N   T H E   Old Testament we read how the people of
Israel, hard pressed by their enemies, demanded a king "as
was the custom among other peoples" (I Sam. 8:5). Until this time
God Himself had been the King of Israel and had guided her
through His judges. And so the request of the people betrayed a
mistrust of God and of His guidance. God said to Samuel, "It is
not you that the people have thrown off, but me, so that I should
no longer be their King." Despite the implied mistrust, God
granted the petition. But in granting the petition He arranged that
a new and more difficult test would fall to the lot of Israel, the test
of being ruled by kings.

This incident is typical of the way God deals with His creatures.
He honors their wishes; but even as He honors them, He incorpo-
rates them into a new and more exacting plan of His own. Thus
does God fulfill the wishes of His creatures and yet not fulfill them,
hinder them and yet not hinder them.

Viewed against the background of this characteristic way of
God's dealing with man, original sin appears in a new light. Adam
and Eve distrusted God and His loving designs and denied Him
obedience. They wanted to become perfect without God. They
wanted to fulfill their destiny by themselves, with their own resources. They wanted to be independent. Independent as God is—
like to God, they would be.

* "Geschenkte Selbster lösung," *Stimmen der Zeit,* 159 (1956–57), pp.
348–57.

And what did God do? He granted their wish. They would be without God, at least in their own conscious experience. They would have to perfect themselves even as they had desired. Their special supernatural gifts vanished, their confident dealings with Him ceased. They no longer noticed His presence in their life; the vision of their spirit was dulled and the power of their heart was paralyzed. They were left to themselves. But they were not happy; they were filled with anxiety, and their anxiety grew as they perceived that they were not equal to the task they had asked to perform for themselves.

But despite the feeling of helplessness before the task of self-salvation, despite the frustration, man can never give up trying. He can never give up trying to achieve control over the strife and disunity deep inside him and to be happy in a life of untroubled harmony. He is forever trying to build his tower so high he can seize heaven for himself. But never does he succeed (Gen. 11).

Since man felt unable to achieve his salvation by himself, he looked for help. Not the kind of help that would violate his autonomy, but the kind that would leave him master of his work. For this reason he turned to the powers of this world, powers he could deal with as an independent partner. Man stands before the powers of this world not as before his Creator, but as before great and ineffable forces he can somehow control.

The history of religion and the history of Israel show us what these powers are. They are such as to give man the feeling that his inner conflicts have been resolved, that his being is secure, that he is superior to all that threatens him.

The first power of this world that man seeks is intoxication of any kind. What else takes away the inner strife so much as this? The history of religious enthusiasm in all its forms testifies to the attraction of this substitute for unity.

Man also seeks bodily health and vigor. He looks for numerous off-spring—children to save his activity from oblivion. Thus the widespread fertility cults which at the same time achieve forgetfulness in sexual orgies. Riches, too, are sought as a way to arrive at power.

Finally comes the worship of man. Man's awareness of his own gift of intellect and of his superiority to the material world brings with it a certain security and enrichment of his being. He becomes identified with the spirit of human endeavor and human progress.

Here lies the secret of the various "culture" religions which have found adherents from the very earliest times. Here is the basis for the cults of race, fatherland, humanity.

IMPOSSIBLE TASK

In vain did man look to the powers of this world for fulfillment and salvation. His efforts were forever being thwarted, by death if by nothing else. There is only one Power which always, and in the face of everything, wins out—the will of the true God. Whoever would achieve salvation must always and in every circumstance have this will on his side. But how can man set himself on the side of the divine will?

There is only one way in which man can identify himself with another's will, and this is the way of love. Love brings the persons in love together, allows the lover to take over the will of the other as his own, allows him to judge all things from the other's point of view. If man was to achieve his destiny, he had to come to God in selfless love, admit that His will is always holy, right, and good, and accept it as his own. But it was precisely at this point that man shrank back. Nothing was farther from his thoughts than selfless love. His mind, darkened by the Fall, could awaken no love for God but only fear. God's commands were threats to his independence and happiness. God was an obstacle against which man battered himself as he strove for self-realization. How could he *love* God? How could he take over God's will for his own in love, when he feared that he would lose himself by doing so?

This was the impossible task. Man saw the need of alignment with God in love. Yet from the deepest part of his being he could not surrender himself. This inner core from which self-realization must flow had slipped away from his control. He was estranged from himself; he no longer had himself in hand.

FORCED SALVATION, NO SALVATION

God had taken man at his word and had given him his way. Man was to seek salvation on his own. But should God have done that, knowing that He was saddling man with a task beyond his power? Does God rejoice in another's misfortune, even when that misfortune is deserved? Is God spiteful?

God would seem to be so if it were not for our knowledge of

two facts: first, the great esteem God has for human freedom. He does not force Himself upon anyone. He was serious in giving man the power of self-determination. Even in the face of the revolt of the entire race, God respects the gift of freedom to His creatures. God knows that a forced salvation is no salvation at all.

The second fact is this: God was prepared to grant man's request for self-redemption. This request is in accord with man's worth as a person. Salvation should not be awarded to man as if he were an irrational being, incapable of self-activity. It was only man's desire to win salvation without God, even against God, that was presumptuous and futile.

But is this not a flat contradiction, this "gift of self-redemption"? On the one hand man can find his salvation only in God: It is God from whom he comes, and it is God to whom he goes; only through Him does man stand fast and secure in reality. But on the other hand man should perfect himself since self-perfection is in accord with his worth as a person and since man himself has so wished it.

Here salvation from without and salvation from within confront each other. The one seems to exclude the other. Easier to build that tower high enough to storm heaven than to try to unite the two!

FROM WITHIN HUMAN NATURE

But what is unthinkable for man is a small matter for God. What is a contradiction on the level of things is possible on the level of persons. At least so it is in this case. For God allowed man to wander down self-chosen roads of redemption only that he might better understand that there is only one path that leads to that goal. All other ways to salvation are but as paths in a trackless woods.

And what means did God's wisdom choose to reconcile man's need for self-redemption with man's need for divine salvation? Jesus Christ, Our Lord. As God, Christ possessed totally and perfectly the very roots of His being as a man. And out of the perfect self-possession of His humanity He was able to reach out in unselfish love to unite men with God. This unselfish love made Him a brother to all men, a brother who might take their place and represent them. His love reached down into the very core of their being and took upon Himself man's concerns as His own. And in making man's concerns His own, Christ acted from a depth within human nature that man himself could never sound. Through His love Christ became the perfect representative of man, a Person who could act in absolute possession of His humanity, something a mere man could never do.

FULFILLMENT: DOING GOD'S WILL

In this way Christ undertook man's redemption on man's own terms. True, Christ, even as man, was united to His Father. Nevertheless he took upon Himself all the results of the estrangement of man from God, even the fear of death in the Garden of Olives, even the sense of abandonment by God on the Cross. But in spite of all the hatred and opposition from outside Himself, He never let Himself wander from His chosen path of selflessness in love and dedication to the will of the Father. Never did He avoid the difficult way of obedience nor make use of the power of force. He knew, as no one else could, that in the affair of man's self-redemption a forced success is the greatest failure.

The will of the God-Man was true as the will of other men ought to have been. From the very beginning of His life on earth, Christ's will was in perfect agreement with the will of the Father, not only when confronted by this choice or that, but in its constant fundamental attitude. Here a man brought to fulfillment man's basic task of self-perfection—his inner unity as well as his harmony with the world outside. In Christ was man released from inner chaos; for in Christ, man was at one with himself in the knowledge that he is a creature of God bound to do God's will.

Why this preoccupation with the will of God when it is man who is being perfected? The answer is simple. It is God's will and God's will alone that moves to perfect fulfillment. Only by being aligned with this will can man achieve success in his inner struggle. Only God's will moves to completion and perfection, and God's will is that man be saved.

But just how does it help mankind that one of its members has reached fulfillment by his own power? It would not help mankind at all if men stood to each other as loveless beings, incapable of belonging together. But as an intellectual creature, man is open to things that are other than he; and he can freely incorporate them into his innermost being. He can make what is at first alien so much a part of himself that it seems to have sprung from him in the first place.

In incorporating external things into himself, man must adapt himself to the object he wants to make his own. He can possess physical objects with a minimum of adjustment. He can master the knowledge of nature through adapting his understanding—a more difficult adjustment. But when he strives to make his own something as profound as the wisdom and life-experience of the God-Man, he is faced with a completely different situation. Assimilation here is indeed possible, but it requires the most profound sort of personal commitment.

GRACE IS POWER TO LOVE

For redemption concerns the whole man, even to the inmost core of his being. Nothing may remain outside the sweep of its liberating activity. The personal commitment of man to Christ must be perfect if he is to achieve perfectly the redemption Christ made possible. This perfect commitment is nothing else than selfless love. This is the attitude of Christ to His fellow men, and this must be the attitude of Christ's fellow men to Him if they want to share, as far as they are capable, in the perfect obedience of Christ to the Father.

Through selfless love for Christ, the two conditions that seemed contradictory are fulfilled. Man is saved while saving himself. Love, as long as it is selfless and sincere, is always a gift proper to the one loving. Love can never, strictly speaking, be imposed. It wells up from the inner depths of man. So deep are its sources that they lie even deeper than man's power of freedom, deeper even than the level of conflict he finds within himself. Therefore truly selfless love for Christ can come only if God Himself gives man the power to love. By His grace God places in the innermost part of man this power to love Christ, this possibility of self-redemption.

This gift of grace, this bestowing of the power of self-redemption, is more man's own than if he had been born with it. It opens up for him a range of existence which he does not have by nature because it allows him to act at a depth which God alone controls.

For when we men give gifts, we can communicate fully only the human elements involved—sympathy, kindness, love. But the gifts themselves can never really become our own. No mere creature can bestow them on us completely. And the reason is that between man and man there is always the element of otherness. We cannot get at the deepest part of each other; the human person is, as it were, an obstacle that no other human person can fully overcome.

But it is otherwise with God. He gives us to ourselves. He gives us not only things that are external but also the power to make them fully and entirely our own. The human person is in no sense an obstacle before God. God can fully plumb the depths of any man. This no other man can do, nor any creature. This is a power proper to the Creator alone.

Therefore Christ, because He is God, gives us redemption not merely as a man gives a gift to his fellowmen, but also as God gives a gift to His creatures. He gives the gift and gives also the power to receive the gift, the power to take it and make it our own. In this way redemption is truly a grace and at the same time truly an act proper to self. What God gives to us is more our own than that which we achieve on our own, since the power of identification comes from God.

PUTTING ON CHRIST

Inasmuch as the Creator does not stand over against His creatures as man against man, redemption through the God-Man is not tainted with the otherness involved in all purely human giving. Christ, in His love, is not a stranger to us. He is closer to us than we are ourselves. His grace results in self-redemption in a much truer sense than any self-redemption that man could have achieved naturally. Even if self-redemption were possible through our power alone, it would not be so deeply and interiorly our own as is the redemption wrought by Christ and made our own through love.

Once man has been made capable of self-redemption, he must prolong the saving power of Christ through his Christ-like life. Love for Christ and, through Christ, for God is, as it were, brought within the normal range of human activity; God is now near. Once God has walked with men as a man, man has a perfect pattern to serve as a guide for his life. And whoever walks with Christ in the union of companionship, putting on more and more His way of thinking, is deepening the work of man's self-redemption. But all the while that this deepening is the work of man, it is also the work of God. For just as the power of self-redemption begins with a gift, the gift of baptism, so does it continue with a gift, the continual outpouring of God's grace. The Christian will never be free of the need for this gift. Only with it is his self-redemption possible.

This progressive taking on of the ways of Christ with the help of His grace remains in utter contradiction to the inborn human tendency to self-perfection by one's own power and in one's own way. Obedience towards God in love always seems too humiliating to the natural man. It is a task against which his natural self rebels. Yet it is only by battling this tendency that he can put on Christ.

The journey of the Christian through life resembles the lot of God's people in the Old Testament. Only by surmounting tests and reverses does the Christian reach his goal. His destiny involves an ever-increasing separation from the aspirations of this world, not a separation brought about by an external segregation, but a separation brought about by an interior exodus from the Egypt of his own pagan self-seeking. The mind of Christ must replace this natural commitment (Philip. 2:5). The Christian must become so much Christ that he lives no longer himself, but Christ lives in him (Gal. 2:20). In a matter so all-pervading as redemption, no personal involvement is possible short of love.

MAN SAVES HIMSELF

And so the desire of our first parents—their presumptuous desire—is still worked out. As always when God grants a desire that goes counter to His original plan, the new way is more difficult than the one originally intended. But it is also more glorious. It is a proof of the unfathomable love of God for man. This love affirms completely and unconditionally the worth of the created person. In the Man, Christ, man has saved himself. Through personal union with Christ, through a higher existence in Christ, by the power of God's grace, each and every man is now able to redeem himself. Through Christ we each possess the gift of self-redemption.

11 St. Paul and a Mystical Redemption *

STANISLAS LYONNET

Many are inclined to interpret St. Paul's statements on the redemption in a legalistic way. They see Christ submitting to the penalty men had deserved by their sins, thus freeing men of the obligation. But what men deserved was the eternal death of hell, to which Christ certainly did not submit. Father Lyonnet insists that in St. Paul the redemption has a mystical meaning. After man had separated himself from God by sin, Christ, by the supreme act of obedience and love that was his death and resurrection, reunited all mankind to God.

THE ONLY WAY to discover exactly what St. Paul meant when he spoke of the redemptive work of Christ is to penetrate the full meaning of the words he used, such as savior, redemption, and expiation. All of these words had a definite meaning to the pagans to whom Paul preached, but they may have had a different meaning in the Old Testament, from which he drew them.

Misconceptions of Paul's thought arise when we assign the legalistic, pagan meaning to his use of these terms. Although he was aware of these pagan meanings and alluded to them, the fullest and deepest significance of the words in his redemptive vocabulary is always found in the original biblical setting.

THE ESCHATOLOGICAL SAVIOR

The title "Savior" is one of the most frequently used designations of Christ. The pagans applied it to their healing gods and to the emperors, who were compared to the gods, and many think that St. Paul applied the term in this pagan sense. He was no doubt alluding to this sense, but it was with a polemical intent: To the illusory saviors of paganism he opposed the only real Savior, Jesus Christ. Aside from this allusion, he used the word in its biblical sense.

---

* "Conception Paulinienne de la Rédemption," *Lumière et Vie*, 7 (1958), pp. 35–66.

In the Old Testament the term Savior occurs most frequently in the Psalms and in Deutero-Isaiah. With rare exceptions, it is an exclusive title of Yahweh, the eschatological Savior, who will assure protection and prosperity for the people of God. Use of the word is rare in the gospels and in St. Paul except for the pastoral epistles. In these three epistles where its use is frequent, Paul clearly uses the word in its biblical sense. He applies it most often to God the Father, who has made good the messianic promise contained in the Old Testament (I Tim. 1:1; 2:3). Even when it is applied to the Son it derives its meaning from its application to the Father. He speaks, for instance, of "the preaching committed to my trust by the command of God our Savior," and follows immediately with "grace and peace from God the Father, and from Christ Jesus, our Savior" (Tit. 1:3-4).

St. Paul clearly proclaims Christ the eschatological Savior promised by the prophets. At times he is the one who will come at the parousia: "Our citizenship is in heaven, from which also we eagerly await a Savior, our Lord Jesus Christ" (Phil. 3:20). He is likewise the one who will come on the "day of the Lord," the day of salvation for the faithful of Israel and of wrath for the pagans, who are enemies of Israel and God: "Much more, now that we are justified by his blood, shall we be saved through him from the wrath" (Rom. 5:9).

This text brings out the interesting paradox that justification is already accomplished, but salvation is an event of the future. This is verified by the fact that the thought of this entire Epistle to the Romans is developed in two stages. The first four chapters treat of justification, and chapters five to eleven treat of salvation. For St. Paul, salvation would not be fully achieved except with the resurrection of the body, when Christ would have triumphed over all his enemies, including death, and then would return the kingdom to his Father.

Nevertheless Paul declares also that God *has saved us*. "He saved us by the bath of regeneration and renewal by the Holy Spirit" (Tit. 3:5). This is not in the least contradictory. In fact God through his Christ *saves* us from the judgment to come because he *has saved* us from the servitude of Satan. The state is now acquired, but its full effect will be obtained only at the end of time, in the eschatological judgment. Hence when St. Paul says that Jesus is the Savior he means that He fulfilled the promise of

Yahweh, has justified us, and will save us body and soul; indeed has already saved us from eternal death.

MEANING OF REDEMPTION

To determine the Pauline meaning of the term "redemption" we must again consult both the Old Testament and pagan usage. In pagan history the noun *lutron* concerns the ransom of a prisoner, designating either the price paid in exchange for freedom or the deliverance that is effected. Paul describes the redemption of Christ as a purchase or a repurchasing, and hence seems to imply this pagan meaning. And as the servitude from which Christ has delivered us is the enslavement to Satan through sin, it is logical to assume that the compensation is paid by Christ to the devil in exchange for our freedom.

But such a representation is opposed to everything the New Testament teaches us about Satan, who is never said to have any right over man. It is true that we have become the property of God by a completed contract, so that no burden remains on us (I Cor. 6:20; 7:23). But, as Father Prat remarks, "The metaphor is not carried further, and no one intervenes in order to reclaim or to receive the price." We could certainly not conclude that Paul represents the redemption as a commercial transaction, or as one in which the jailer agrees to free the prisoner merely for a price.

DELIVERANCE-ACQUISITION

The New Testament directs us to a different notion of redemption. St. Luke recalls in two places the redemption promised by the prophets (1:68; 2:38), and he introduces the eschatological discourse of Christ with that promise (21:28). When St. Paul speaks of the redemption, he clarifies the meaning of this concept by indicating its source: "Jesus Christ, who gave himself for us, to *ransom* us from all our guilt, a *people set apart* for himself, ambitious of noble deeds" (Tit. 2:14). The allusion is to the two great events in the history of Israel, the deliverance from servitude in Egypt and the covenant at Sinai.

The Jews loved to bring these two events together because they felt that they were complementary, negative and positive aspects of one unique mystery. "I am the Lord. I will free you from the forced labor of the Egyptians and deliver you from their slavery . . .

I shall take you as my own people, and you shall have me as your God" (Exod. 6:6-7). Jeremiah no longer seems to distinguish between the two events. In announcing the new covenant he says it will not be like the "covenant which I made with their fathers (on Sinai), in the day that I took them by the hand to bring them out of the land of Egypt (the Exodus)" (Jer. 31:32).

In the Old Testament the deliverance from the Egyptian servitude was only the first phase of a salvific event which was achieved with the covenant on Sinai, in which Israel became the people of God. So also the notion of redemption is essentially positive, as is indicated in the Latin term, *emere,* to purchase, to obtain ownership.

LIBERATION-PURCHASE

The New Testament speaks of redemption precisely in this context. In one place Paul speaks of "the redemption of acquisition" (Eph. 1:14). In the Canticle to the Lamb of the Apocalypse the context clearly refers to Exodus 19:6, from which several expressions are quoted: "Thou, Lord, art worthy to take up the book and break the seals that are on it. Thou wast slain in sacrifice; out of every tribe, every language, every people, every nation thou hast ransomed us with thy blood and given us to God" (Apoc. 5:9). So, in the blood of the Lamb, men and nations become the particular possession of God, just as Israel by virtue of the alliance, also sealed in blood, became the particular possession of God.

Besides this positive connotation we must also note the essentially eschatological significance of the redemption. The full meaning of this word is found in the final acquisition which God will make of His people when the Son, having triumphed over his final enemy, death, will render the kingdom to the Father, to the end that God might be all in all (I Cor. 15:23-28). The acquisition has already been made, but it is not yet complete (Eph. 1:14; 4:30; Rom. 8:23).

For St. Paul, then, to say that Christ redeemed us was to say that he liberated us from the slavery of sin and purchased us for God, or delivered us from sin and acquired us for God. This is well expressed in the English term *at-one-ment.*

Besides the notions of salvation and redemption, St. Paul also speaks of "expiation." "God has offered his Son to us so that we could obtain expiation through His blood" (Rom. 3:25). The Greek notion of expiation was that the gods, having become angry due to men's infidelity, were appeased and rendered benevolent by sacrifices. The holy writers used the same metaphor, but they understood that it was a metaphor, which did not imply any real change in God and still less any human power over God's feelings.

In the Old Testament expiation consisted in a removal of the guilt of sin, a purifying of the sinner's soul, and a consequent reunion of the soul with God. The essential element of the ritual of expiation was the blood of the sacrificial animal, as is seen in the rabbinical adage: *There is no expiation without the flowing of blood.*

MEANING OF EXPIATION

Before we analyze fully this notion of expiation, however, we must note the role that blood played in the earlier sacrifices, that of the paschal lamb and of the covenant. We have already seen that the notion of redemption in St. Paul involves an allusion to the two events to which these sacrifices are intimately connected, the deliverance from Egypt and the covenant at Sinai. It is also significant that the New Testament explicitly connects these two sacrifices to that of Christ.

In the ritual of the first Pasch, the blood of the lamb does not have the function of appeasing Yahweh but of marking for the exterminating angel the homes of those who belong to the chosen people. It separated Israel from the pagans. The annual celebration of the Pasch commemorated the day when Yahweh struck the Egyptians to free Israel from their slavery, which would later be seen as a figure of the slavery of sin. The Jews felt that in offering the paschal sacrifice they purified their homes.

In the sacrifice of the covenant, as in that of the Pasch, the immolation is only the preparatory ritual accomplished through the servants (Ex. 24:4). To Moses personally is reserved the essential rite of sacrifice, the pouring of blood on the altar and the aspersion of blood over the people. This twofold aspersion bears a resemblance to that of the pacts of friendship, where the blood which the contractants exchange produces a psychic communion of the two parties. In the covenant, the blood, which is figuratively the source of life, is spread over the altar, which represents

Yahweh, then on the people. Through contact with the same source of life Yahweh and the people of Israel are united into one life.

Christ is referring to the mystical significance of this sacrifice when he says, in instituting the Eucharist, "This is my blood of the new covenant." He clearly meant that this blood would unite all men to God, making them his people, just as the blood of the old covenant had made the Israelites his chosen people.

We can now see the full significance of the sacrifice of expiation. In this annual ritual the sevenfold aspersion of blood over the propitiatory, which was the privilege of the high priest alone, was certainly the principal ritual. The purpose of this aspersion was "to purify the sanctuary from all the faults the sons of Israel have committed, their transgressions, and their uncleanness" (Lev. 16:16). There follows a sevenfold aspersion of the altar to purify and sanctify it.

PURIFICATION AND CONSECRATION

The sense is clear: The sins of Israel have polluted the land of Israel and everything that is considered holiest—the tabernacle, the altar, the sanctuary, the throne of Yahweh "who resides above the cherubim." They have thus driven God from their midst. By the ritual of expiation the tabernacle is purified and God returns to them (Ezek. 10:18; 43:2). The purification of the tabernacle, however, was the symbol of the purification of the people, of their souls. Hence when God returned to their midst he was reunited to a purified people. Purification and reunion are here simultaneous.

The Hebrews attributed to blood the role of purification and consecration because it is the source of life. "It is the blood that animates all living things, and I have destined it to make atonement for your souls upon the altar" (Lev. 17:11). Blood, the carrier of life, is identified with life itself, which is an essentially divine reality in the Bible.

CEREMONY OF THE SCAPEGOAT

One often supposes that among the Israelites the blood of the victim suggested the chastisement of death they had merited for their sins. Finding it impossible to inflict it upon themselves, they inflict it upon a substitute. But there is nothing in Leviticus or in Ezekiel to suggest such an idea.

This error probably arises from the fact that we have compared, sometimes unconsciously, the sacrifice of expiation to the ceremony of the scapegoat. But this custom constitutes an entirely heterogeneous ritual. In it the sins of the people, by virtue of the imposition of hands which followed the confession, were transmitted to the animal who "took them upon himself" and carried them away to the desert (Lev. 16:5-10). The victim was considered essentially impure. Even Aaron, who had it sent away, and the one who led it to the desert had to be purified.

On the contrary, the victim of the sacrifice is always considered as very holy, as well in the sacrifice for sins as in the sacrifice of reparation; that is why it must be eaten or buried only in a holy place (Lev. 6:18-19; 7:6; 4:12). For the same reason, the scapegoat was sent to the desert, the home of demons (Matt. 12:43), while the victim whose blood is spread is said to be "for Yahweh." Only the latter is immolated, and according to the biblical conception of sacrifice this means that it passes on to Yahweh.

Assuredly this would not come about unless the victim were first transformed. Hence in the holocaust it was certainly not destroyed, for God would not be pleased in its destruction; it was changed into an impalpable material and, as it were, spiritualized, made capable of rising to God. We have seen that in the sacrifice of expiation the aspersion of blood expressed in another way the same desire of union with God, more exactly, a reunion with God from whom sin has separated the offerer.

In the eyes of the Jews, sacrifices drew their principal value from the dispositions of the faithful, who through their exterior gestures affirmed their real desire to be united with God, and consequently to renounce that which separated them from him, their sins. "There is no authentic sacrifice without a conversion of heart." But the Jews did not realize that they prefigured the sacrifice of the Son of God offering himself voluntarily, making an act of supreme obedience and love. The disobedience of Adam, the beginning of universal condemnation is opposed to the act of obedience of Christ, through which all are justified (Rom. 5:19).

THE UNIQUE SACRIFICE

The mystery of the cross is a mystery of obedience and of love, of which the glorious resurrection is the outcome rather than the recompense (Phil. 2:5-11). A theme of the entire New Testament is that the death of Christ is an expression of love. It is "the life given as a ransom for the lives of many" (Matt. 20:28). Paul tells us: "Order your lives in charity, upon the model of that charity which Christ showed to us, when he gave himself up on our behalf" (Eph. 5:2).

As the victim of the holocaust, changed into the immaterial smoke, rose towards God, so Christ, by this act of love and obedience in his voluntary death, returns effectively to his Father. For Paul, then, the redemptive mystery is truly a sacrifice. But the sacrifice of Christ is unique in that *he offers himself*. His sacrifice is identical with his return to the Father, and in him we all return to the Father. He gave himself less in place of men than on our behalf, for our sakes; he performed the greatest act of love that man can accomplish, not to dispense us from loving, but to permit us to love. St. Paul's whole doctrine of the redemption can be summed up by saying that he united the idea of Christ's giving himself to free us from sin to that of our reunion with God (Tit. 2:14).

Christ's return to God and humanity's return in Christ cannot be conceived apart from his glorification, which includes both his resurrection and his ascension. It is because Jesus was raised from the dead that "he has delivered us from the wrath to come" (Thes. 1:10). "If Christ has not risen, vain is your faith, for you are still in your sins" (Cor. 15:17). It is through the resurrection that Christ has become "the life-giving spirit," giving life to humanity.

Christ communicates this new life to all who participate in his act of obedience and love through faith and baptism. Through baptism, the configuration to the death and resurrection of Christ, we attain a state of justice. Since it is the work of Christ, this state is final in itself. In it we are united to Christ in his death and in his risen life. If we do not fall again into the grips of sin, we will some day attain life in all its fullness.

FALSE JURIDICAL CONCEPTS

There are a few particularly troublesome texts in St. Paul which have led many to attribute a largely legalistic notion of the redemption to the Apostle. One of these is Romans 8:3, where he declares that God "has condemned sin in the flesh." He does not mean that God the Father condemned Christ, but that Christ condemned Satan inasmuch as he triumphed over him. For so the Jews represented to themselves the final salvation of Israel. God would condemn his enemies and in this way would give victory to his people (Apoc. 12:9).

Another seemingly juridical text is Galatians 3:13. To those Jews who still seek to find in the Mosaic law the source of their justification, Paul replies that it is only a source of curse. And, desiring to remove the fascination which the law possessed for the Jews, he adds that this curse of the law somehow touched Christ in person: "From this curse invoked by the law Christ has ransomed us, by himself becoming, for our sakes, an accursed thing. We read that 'There is a curse on the man who hangs on a gibbet'" (Gal. 3:13).

But St. Paul does not intend to suggest that Christ on the cross was cursed either by the Father, for he was about to reconcile the world to the Father (2 Cor. 5:19), or by the law, except in the eyes of men. He knew perfectly well that the words of Deuteronomy (quoted in Gal. 3:13) did not refer to a person condemned to the penalty of crucifixion, but only to criminals suspended after their death upon a gibbet of infamy and who offered only an exterior, material resemblance to Christ. He means no more here than when he stated that Christ was "born a subject of the law" (Gal. 4:4), or when he said that God "made him sin for our sake, so that we might become the justice of God in him" (II Cor. 5:21). Christ has assumed our nature and our condition of being a prodigal son with all its humiliations in order that in him it would really be our humanity which returns to the Father in his supreme act of obedience and love.

In the Epistle to the Colossians the sin of humanity is called a debt. But it is not certain that Paul considers it a debt in regard to the law. Paul is certainly thinking of the debt which the whole human race by its sins had contracted before God, namely the condemnation to eternal death. But it is not said that Christ has paid this debt. Paul says only that God the Father "has made us live again with his resurrected son; he has pardoned us all our faults, erased the sentence of indebtedness we had incurred from the law, completely taken it away from us, and nailed it to the cross" (Col. 2:14).

MYSTICAL REDEMPTION

He does not state how God has taken away this sentence, but there is nothing obliging us to believe that it was by causing the condemnation to weigh down upon his Son. Mention of the resurrection suggests rather that by his death and resurrection Christ passes from the carnal condition to the spiritual and we along with him.

So writes Cyril of Alexandria: "Christ through his cross triumphs over the evil powers and enemies. Nailing to the wood of the cross the bond written against us, he has uprooted us from the tyranny of Satan and destroyed sin. Opening the gates of hell to the dark spirits, he has destroyed the power of death, in order that, through his own blood, he may acquire the world for his Father." His mention of the idea of acquisition shows that Cyril's explanation, which is common among the fathers, is in perfect accord with the one we have presented. It is not in the least opposed to the traditional theory of vicarious satisfaction, but it is opposed only to one of a purely penal expiation.

An understanding of St. Paul's doctrine involves an awareness of the Old Testament theme of Israel's return to God, which prepared the apostles to understand the redemption in an essentially mystical light, not a juridical one. The same theme is magnificently developed in two complementary parables—that of the prodigal son's return and that of the good shepherd in search of his lost sheep.

12 *Toward a Psychology of Divine Grace*

PIET FRANSEN

Grace, so often presented in an objectivist fashion is here analyzed in terms of man's psychology and personal response.

INTRODUCTION

Our age is partial to totality. We do not like conceptual dissection; sciences in watertight compartments annoy us and prevent us from reaching the moving, living, and integral reality. This passion for the totality of reality ought not to make us forget the acquisitions of past centuries. Each science, in fact, possesses its own method imposed by its subject. And in its turn this subject only attains one very definite aspect of the reality which corresponds strictly to the point of view proper to the science. Medicine was only able to develop when it was freed from Aristotelian philosophy. It is indubitable that the secret of the immense success of modern positive sciences lies in this emancipation and specialization.

This desire for unity which is the note of our period may give rise to the illusory dream of a unique science, which would threaten the integrity and the wealth of our scientific effort. In this connection we may be reminded of the naïve enthusiasm of the first humanists in the fifteenth century. It is fair to admit, however, that it expresses a very profound truth. Reality is one, truth is one, and the man who thinks and seeks is one. But confusion never can breed unity. Every man for himself, and the whole of mankind journeying throughout history has the intellectual, moral and religious task of elaborating a coherent view of the totality of reality. This work, which appeals intensely to the men of any period who have not lost the strength and courage to be human, will only be accomplished in the scrupulous respect of the subject and methods proper to each science.

The unity and integrity of our vision of reality cannot be limited to a special science or faculty, even to our understanding. It is our personal affair; it depends on an existential and personal choice which appropriates to itself and integrates the multiple data of the different sciences. This fundamental option is sovereign, because responsible; it is not however either independent or blind, because at the same time it is an act of humble submission to reality in its amplitude, but also in its depth. For a believer it will end in an act of faith and adoration.

Whatever may be thought in certain quarters, this anxious search for the unity of knowledge affects the believer above all, not of course him for whom the faith is a comfortable excuse dispensing him from thought, but the true believer who, like Jacob, wrestles with his God. It is one of the chief reasons which has led us to seek for the implications of the divine mystery of grace on the human plane.[1]

DIVERSITY OF THEOLOGICAL METHODS

Grace is before all a divine act. This act is not at all foreign to our life; on the contrary! By that very fact grace becomes a very complex reality. We cannot here refer to the theology of the Christian East, a theology of participation, divinization, image, and light. Even in the West many were the ways followed by Christian thought concerning this fact of faith and, what is more, through their different points of view, they do not entirely coincide. One theology can be studied without having to think of the other. But by the very fact of their unique subject they are truly complementary and mutually correct each other.

If we consider the history of Western theology on grace, we first discover a method which is descriptive by means of symbols, images or reasoning, especially attentive to the *psychological* and *moral* fact. Next comes the *scholastic* method, familiar to theologians, a strictly scientific, reflective, objective, and conceptual method. Starting from a revealed truth, this method searches for the necessary and universal a priori conditions of the metaphysical possibility of this subject of faith. Our age regards this method with a certain disfavor, but easily forgets its qualities of clarity, precision, and depth.

It also has its limits. And so we find, starting from the philosophy implied in Holy Scripture, in the great mystical schools of the Middle Ages and down to our times, a third way which today we may call *existential, personalist* and *dialectical.* It is inspired by a great phenomenology of the personality and may develop in the direction of a true metaphysic of Christian existence.[2]

This article will be dealing chiefly with the psychology of grace. But a purely descriptive psychology would, in that case, be very difficult and open to suspicion. I deliberately outline this psychology as a Christian philosopher and a believer. I shall then endeavor to complete it by a philosophy which is chiefly personalist, inspired by the work of Karl Rahner, S.J., Professor at the State University at Innsbruck, and the dialectical and mystical anthropology of the Blessed John Ruusbroec, one of the most remarkable thinkers in Holland.

In the first part of this essay the essential ideas on the nature of man and his liberty will be laid down: a philosophical study with psychological applications. In the second part, a theological description of sin and grace, based on this first philosophical schema will be presented. In the third part the possibilities and limits of a psychology of grace will be described. As this article is the result of discussions with groups of educators and pedagogues, some examples will be found in it connected with the problems of education and child psychology.

Such a study has many advantages. It enriches classic theology and provides a concrete illustration of dogmatic and theological theses formulated in abstract language. It then demonstrates how a correct philosophy of values and a sane psychology of man can really help theological reflection. At the same time, it clearly defines the proper role of this psychology in the theology of grace. This role remains limited by its subject and method.

Unfortunately, it is still useful to recall that psychology differs fundamentally from theology and philosophy owing to the fact that its subject is purely phenomenal. Psychology as science of observation has as its essential task to discover, describe and interpret by increasingly general hypotheses the facts of experience. Its technique and methods do not allow it to penetrate the heart of onto-

logical and dogmatic reality. Too many Christian psychologists are
still giving way to another form of that temptation which has
been mentioned, and consciously through principle, or unconsciously through ignorance of other techniques of thought, raise
their knowledge into a unique and universal science. This danger
of psychologism remains very present among many intellectuals
who with only superficial knowledge of psychology advance theories and, consequently, often involve themselves in inextricable
difficulties in the domain of their faith. Insufficient knowledge of a
science is always dangerous and is the characteristic of primary
mentality. I believe that there is no science more dangerous than
psychology, at least for those who have not the patience to learn
its techniques, to study its methods, and to define its exact subject.

I. Nature and Liberty

The first point of this article introduces the *fundamental consideration of man and his liberty*. For it is with man above all that
we are concerned.

UNITY OF MAN

Man is not a soul lost as though by accident in a vile and
weighty body, a spirit imprisoned in foreign matter, hostile to his
highest aspirations. Those are gnostic, platonic and manichaean
errors which have not yet been entirely exorcized. *Man is intrinsically one:* a spiritualized body, or, more correctly, a corporal
person.

On the other hand, the soul is not the body. Soul and body are
like two poles in a unique magnetic field, in which the lines of
force cross each other and continually interpenetrate one another.
In no way can the actions, states, even the most subtle or the most
material, which belong uniquely and exclusively to the soul or body,
be disassociated. The psychology of man and child leads to this conclusion and it is therefore unnecessary to dwell upon it.

PRIMACY OF THE SPIRIT

It would, however, be an error to imagine that we look upon
body and soul as two opposing forces, practically equivalent,

different, but purely complementary. It is still more important for our viewpoint to perceive that in this profound unity the spirit still keeps an *inalienable initiative*. The image of God which He in His creative action has implanted in my whole being, is most deeply imprinted in this spiritual center of my being, that center of personal density in which I am most myself, and by reason of that, most in God. It is from this center of existential density that these features of the divine image are diffused through all the levels of my existence, always further penetrating into my intellect and my will, my imagination and my sensibility, all my psychism of heredity and behavior, my habits and my daily actions, to bestow even on my body an aura of nobility and beauty.

Here a Christian theology of the creation and the divine image and a sane personalist philosophy should complete, correct and develop what there is of imprecision and indistinctness in the conclusions of psychology, however just they may be.

A DOUBLE LIBERTY

God is love. The image of God in us will therefore also be love, the force of love of God, of others and of myself in God. This fundamental power of love constitutes my person. I am in fact a person because I am spirit. Because I am spirit, I am liberty and therefore love. For liberty is above all a power of spontaneous gift from one person to another, before being choice, election, judgment and free will.

In fact, there is in us as it were a double liberty precisely because we are corporeal spirits, bodies with a depth of life which far exceeds the requirements of our material and even our earthly life. There is naturally the liberty which we all know from experience, what is commonly known as *free will*. There is further down in us a *fundamental liberty of existential and totalizing option*.

This distinction is of captial importance in order to understand human behavior in general, and especially to detect the incidence of divine grace in us.

FUNDAMENTAL LIBERTY

We know by experience what I have called free will—that liberty by means of which man can to a certain degree order his life. He gets up, he eats, he reads a book rather than goes for a walk, he refuses an invitation, he is obstinate, persistent, or accepts an excuse. Even children very early possess this possibility of choice. It is freedom in the usual sense of the word. All the same, it may be asked whether *as such* it merits the name of liberty.

If it is to become truly human, this early form of liberty must be directed by something deeper, more stable, supported and directed by a profound and total commitment, by a fundamental option in which *I express myself wholly* with all that I wish to be in this world and before God. The fragmentary variety of daily options is therefore unthinkable—I might say, inhuman and therefore animal—without a totalizing, profound, stable and spontaneous orientation of my life, of the whole of myself before the totality of the reality which I either accept or refuse.

UNITY OF THESE TWO FORMS OF LIBERTY

Note well: these two forms of liberty *have no separate existence*. This point is not always understood. The fundamental option is not one particular action, more important than others, following or preceding the more specialized choice of some concrete action. It is not a matter of determining in the first instant a "fundamental option," and then freely developing all the concrete implications, as does an architect who first designs the sketch of the house to be built in order finally to carry out the plan in its least details in the course of several months' work.

For this fundamental option, this existential and total engagement is also impossible if it is not *at the same time* actualized in a series of particular actions, forming the visible woof of life. It is not therefore a concrete action; it is an orientation freely imposed on our whole life. It is *implied* in every truly human and free action, for each concrete and determined action insofar as it is truly free is caught in the free and spontaneous movement toward the final goal of my life.

There is therefore continual interaction between the particular, perceptible and conscious actions of every moment and the fundamental option, obscurely conscious, exercised and present in every particular act. In this fundamental option, subjacent, my humble human actions rediscover their interiority and profound unity, their human meaning and nobility. But also in this daily and almost exterior activity, this option becomes real and veracious, and even simply human. The essential option is therefore like the soul of our daily actions and without those acts it does not exist; there are only dreams, vague aspirations. In short, it is in and by and through daily actions that my fundamental option, my essential liberty of person, is expressed, that I realize it in myself, that it becomes clarified, takes form, becomes incarnate.

The story of a vocation provides us with an excellent illustration of this truth. Whether I feel conscious of a vocation to be a politician, or artist, depends at bottom on a fundamental option which has slowly matured during my youth. This maturation has been expressed in concrete actions, in the choice of my reading, in the disposition of my studies, in the friends and models which I have imitated. By these very concrete actions, this option has developed, deepened, has finally arrived at the degree of maturation and evidence which has transformed it for me into an imperious and determining vocation. Once accepted and expressed in my clear consciousness, I shall find that I have been thinking of it for a long time.[3]

PSYCHOLOGICAL APPLICATIONS

These remarks are important for every form of education. We can teach children and young people a series of attitudes and concrete actions, we can "train" them with consummate art; as long as they have not been offered what is commonly called an ideal, a basic orientation, our education will remain unfinished, threatened by formalism, deceit, because it is empty of sense and humanity.

On the other hand, it is absolutely useless to fill the hearts and heads of young people with magnificent ideas, noble and sublime aspirations. If they have not learned to patiently and perseveringly translate these ethereal aspirations into humble acts of devotion, service, daily work, our education will only have left them with a vague and ephemeral and even very dangerous enthusiasm. It is the tragic story of certain movements of Catholic Action, which either exhaust their strength in technical and exterior occupations, or else quickly let a quasi-mystical enthusiasm, empty of any concrete responsibility, evaporate at adult age or even at the crisis of puberty. A good Christian is not so much he who faithfully accomplishes all his duties, nor he who is elevated by a wave of mysticism, but he who manages to unite in his life a great love to a daily fidelity in the most normal actions.

It is here that we find the profound reason for the discouragement, the bitterness full of resentment, the disillusioned melancholy, of certain Christian "activists," priests or laity, who in the multitude of their occupations have lost the profound sense of their life. Others, the "quietists," find themselves in the same sentiment of solitude and anguish because their vague aspirations remain deprived of life and human and Christian tonality.

This truth provides a solution for many modern problems. For instance, the success of marriage does not depend so much on a certain technique, exterior and dehumanized, of sexual life as on that supreme art with which in one life is united a real mutual respect and love, an ideal of life in common with the multiple and monotonous obligations of living together in a certain house, with certain social obligations, in a certain state of health. The English ritual expresses it with singular nobility: "I take thee to be my wedded wife, to have and to hold from this day forward, for better for worse, for richer for poorer, in sickness and in health, to love and to cherish, till death us do part, according to God's holy ordinance; and thereto I plight thee my troth." The soul of this matrimonial union will always be that "troth," that supreme fidelity of one to the other. But this fidelity has no meaning if it does not incarnate itself in the concrete situation of each life. Is it not because *fidelity* is precisely the assurance and foundation of that real love that God Himself in Holy Scripture has not disdained to make of it His most beautiful appanage?

It is in this union of a real basic aspiration and multiple occupations inherent in our human life that the secret of a life resides. Man is thus made and he can only make a success of his life by accepting himself as he is, spirit and matter, living spirit acting in and through the body, the transparent matter of the spirit in the most humble actions of our life.

THE EXERCISE OF THIS LIBERTY

In order clearly to establish the essential we have had to simplify the problem a little. The human situation is rather more delicate, and it is here that the psychologists come in. Man is spirit and person in this temporal and material world. That is to say that my fundamental option cannot emerge to the surface of my daily activity except by a *long process of maturation in time.* Neither can it incarnate itself in a series of precise and concrete actions except by *traversing a thick layer of humanity,* in which spirit and body intimately interpenetrate and in which man is no longer alone in bearing the responsibility of his life.

1. *The Fundamental Option Is Only Expressed in Time.* Liberty is not bestowed upon us like a beautiful Minerva, rising whole out of the head of Jupiter. We have to conquer it freely, to deserve to be free. I am not yet speaking of grace, which according to the ancient councils restores us to our lost liberty. I am speaking of that human condition, situated in time, borne by the flux of history. Every action which is truly free, every good action, fully responding to the truth of what we are and should be, frees us further. Every bad action, that is to say, false and deceitful, freely degrades that same liberty. In a certain sense, *we are not free; we freely become so.* That is our vocation as men, which has to be fulfilled in the totality of each life.

To be a person, to be free, is the task of a whole life. It is true creation—in the artistic sense—irksome, arduous, prolonged. It is a long process of maturation, appertaining to all living things. It is true that man can distort this process of growth, can interrupt it, turn it away from its true end, and empty it of meaning by a kind of spiritual atrophy, freely accepted under the disillusions of life.[4]

2. *Our Fundamental Option Is Psychologically Conditioned by the Influence of Others.* It would here be opportune to glance at a communal philosophy of the person, but it would take us too far and some psychological considerations will suffice for the moment.

By the very fact that the spirit plunges and sends its roots into this psychosomatic humus of humanity, it can no longer be sovereignly alone. Man is linked to others by his body and his whole psychism; he receives as much as he gives. In his youth, he does almost nothing but receive. He receives his body, and with his body many other things which are largely determinant for him: his heredity, his temperament and character to a great extent preformed in his race, his people, his family and national culture, the atmosphere of his native land.

In order to act he has to reason, which implies a certain intelligence received at birth and later formed in a family, school and cultural milieu. He has to will. It is therefore important that he should possess a certain force of character, stability in his intentions, an amount of endurance in difficulties. A spoiled child inherits, from his sentimental and imprudent parents, a softness which will not affect the child in a large family whom his parents have educated with a virile and strong love. All this therefore does not depend only on his liberty.

Man also needs an atmosphere of optimism, confidence, a nervous and affective equilibrium. To express himself in a fundamental option which is rich and integral he must have control of several faculties (intellect, memory, will) and certain spiritual organs with a psychic basis, such as the sense of the beautiful, the real, others, the sense of values, and even the moral sense. He also must be able to count on a sane and stable equilibrium of his instincts. Finally, even the health of his body is of importance in this total exercise of his liberty.

This total liberty is therefore expressed through a dense network of determinisms, influences foreign to my own will. The success of my life will depend on the art with which I learn to use to the fullest extent everything at my disposal, everything which has been given to me. That is the meaning of the parable of the talents, what is nowadays called the *situation* in which I find myself, from the beginning of my life. The object of all education is to render this situation of departure as favorable as possible.

CONCLUSION

Man is therefore placed by God in a determined situation of which the multiple incidences are far beyond his personal initiative. But these determinisms, these foreign influences, good or bad, cannot raise him to the level of a truly human life unless he possesses in the depths of himself a divine source of life, a force of activity, a creative and a dynamic reflection of the word of God. Man created in the image of God is love above all, the reflection of the first Love, as Dante said in the last verse of his work: "L'amor che muove il sole e l'altre stelle!"

In this depth of himself, man reposes in the hands of God and God sustains him in existence. In these depths reposes what the Bible calls the "heart" of man, the center of all his activity. The mystics have called it the "interior flame," or with St. Francis de Sales, "The fine point of the soul." This "metaphysic of depth" owes nothing to the researches of psychoanalysis. It is part of the Christian philosophy, especially experienced by the greatest mystics. The aim in writing these pages is primarily to express in modern language one of the most profound thoughts of the anthropology of Blessed John Ruusbroec.[5]

II. Theology of Grace

FUNDAMENTAL ALTERNATIVES: SIN AND GRACE

Man's situation, as taught us by Christ and Scripture, is still more complicated by the fact of sin. Man is no longer whole. He is born a sinner. What does that mean? I have just described that fundamental and total option of an entire life: the spiritual and spontaneous engagement of a free person, which takes place in those mysterious depths of personal liberty, but which is incarnated and actualized in my daily actions. It is at that level that the problem of sin is most acute.

That option is situated, in fact, before an essential alternative. St. Augustine's lapidary expression is well known: There are only two possible loves for us, the love of God to the forgetfulness of self, or the love of self to the forgetfulness and denial of God. At first sight this alternative might seem simplistic and foreign to the variety and multiplicity of choices offered to man. But on the level of our fundamental option, St. Augustine could not have expressed himself more correctly. On that level there is only one possible alternative: love of God through love of others, for that is our human condition; or else love of self, the voluntary inclusion in oneself under all the forms of vanity, brutal and even sensual egoism, pride, or simply in the form of spiritual atrophy by a drawing into oneself, a slackening of our activity, a kind of flight from reality and others into a minute world of imagination or bourgeois comfort. This self-love is sin, the only definitive evil of man.

THE CORE OF SIN

In respect to this the fact that sin always has a core of pride, or simply egosim, the petty vanity of the bourgeois, must be empha-

sized. There is often to be found among certain educators or
preachers, even among scholarly theologians, an obsession with
sins of the flesh. Obviously, sexual sin is a sin, and even a grave
one, but it is grave because of a spiritual reason. If it is a grave sin
it is because it is, for men, the most absorbing occasion for incar-
nating and actualizing a fundamental egoism and love of pleasure.
From the specific point of view, of passionate or instinctive dis-
order, it is above all a human weakness.

CONSEQUENCES OF ORIGINAL SIN

   This definition enables us to determine more exactly the nature
of that malice which we all have inherited from our parents and
which we call original sin. I have neither the intention nor the
opportunity of expounding here the whole theology of original sin,
above all the nature of the consequences of that state of perdition
and separation from God, called in technical language *concupis-
cence*. It has been stated quite often that the consequences of
original sin are to be found in a disequilibrium between the tendencies of the body and those of the soul. This explanation is
insufficient. There is something deeper and more essential than
that. This seed of iniquity which infects our life possesses, like
everything else in man, *a spiritual root*. Original sin as a sore in
human nature is a latent love of self, a fundamental individualism
which dwells in man and which causes him to make use of everything which comes into his hands for his own petty and immediate
purposes. It is, besides, because my spirit is "curved in on itself"
that my sexual instincts have such a strong hold on my life, are so
often a cause of sin and that there is an unstable balance between
the aspirations of my body and my soul.
   Thus, from the psychological point of view, the task of an edu-
cator will necessarily be the creation of an atmosphere of devotion,
of service, self-forgetfulness, and even, simply, interest in others.
Everything that detaches the child and man from himself, which
opens windows on reality, nature, his fellows, has a real religious
significance. Man has to be saved from himself, gently and adroitly
extracted from that circle in which the hardness and clumsiness of
adults, as well as his own sinful tendencies have enclosed him.

GRACE IS A NEW LOVE

Let us now turn our attention to grace. It is love above all. It is again St. Augustine who gives us this happy definition of grace: "Quia amasti me, fecisti me amabilem." Because you loved me first, Lord, you have made me lovable: in the double sense of "worthy of love" and "capable of love." In these words is summed up the whole mystery of divine grace. In grace, it is God Who begins, God Who works, God Who finishes: this divine primacy of grace is often neglected by our Western semi-Pelagianism.

Grace has been defined as a divine force, a divine movement in me, a divine gift, supernatural wealth, a merit carefully inscribed in the book of life. That is all true. But grace is much more. It is above all the communication of the divine life to me, as the Greek Fathers have said: God became man so that men might become God. But what does that mean? Grace is, fundamentally, the fact that by the divine love of the Father I have become His child; I have become His own Son, not obviously by identity of nature, but an adopted son by divine gift. I truly share through grace, although in a human degree, in that immense reality which is the love of the Son for His Father. I therefore love the Father through grace in a certain way as He is loved by His Son. I also love other men a little bit as the Son Himself loved them and still loves them. And as it was through the strength of the Spirit that Christ on earth— Ruusbroec would add, and also in Heaven—loved His Father above all in the execution of His work of redemption, so our love of the Father, in the image of that of the Son is borne and sustained by that mysterious Force, so gentle in its divine violence, which is the Holy Ghost.

That love which descended into me by baptism is a new "filial" love in the most profound sense. By baptism we became, as Father E. Mersch writes, "filii in Filio"; adopted children in and through the only Son. This love is nothing else than a participation in the love which the Son has for the Father. The Father loved me first from all eternity as His child in and by His only Son. And, by the creative and saving force of this first eternal and personal love, I can in future love the Father with the Son, like the Son, because of the Son and by the Son, all by the strength of the Holy Ghost.

This love, therefore, does not possess its explanation and root in the fact and experience of human love, but in the revealed mystery of the divine love of the Son for His Father. It is important here to note that being essentially a divine reality which by participation descends into our life, this love, as such, cannot be the subject of psychological experiments or studies. It is supernatural, for it raises us to the level of the divine life in the intimacy of the Blessed Trinity. Moreover, it is given us during this life as "seed," a vocation to be realized in the course of our existence on earth. It is only in Heaven that what we are will appear. As such it is the object of faith.

GRACE AS THE CURE FOR OUR EGOISM

We now can understand how grace really destroys sin in us. It is not a juridical affair, as one might think from reading some theological treatises. Grace truly destroys, burns up in us every trace of sin, because it is an appeal to filial love: precisely the opposite to sin. Fundamentally, only grace can deliver us from self-obsession. This is one of its most profound effects, because grace is love, love of others, and by this sacrament of fraternal charity, by love of God. It is true that this warfare against sin in us and around us will last our whole life long. The primordial fact remains that only grace is able to break that magic circle, that solitude of sin.

There is nothing clearer than this vision of our faith. We are born sinners, or more exactly, in a state of loss, distance and solitude, with that self-approbation which is the immediate consequence. We are the more confirmed sinners the more we continue to actualize this fundamental egoism; we settle down more firmly in our pride. Only the grace of Christ can save us from ourselves, and therefore give us back to ourselves. This grace of Christ restores to us that liberty described in the first part of this article.

GRACE AS THE FUNDAMENTAL INVITATION
TO A SUPERNATURAL OPTION

We must consider in what way this divine life operates in us. This life affects us, in fact, chiefly *in the heart of our free being,* where our existence is and continually flows from the creative Hands of God.

This divine love comes to me first as a call from God, an

exigence from above, a creative ascendancy which penetrates into the deepest part of my being and invites me, draws me, attracts me, as St. John says, to the total and loving acceptance of God in faith, hope and charity. Grace is a reality which, while impregnating the very center of my personality, this existential density we spoke of above, gently urges me, *from inside,* to a fundamental option, this time a supernatural one, because divine, struck in the image of the Son by the seal of the Holy Ghost. It is therefore an existential engagement of the Christian, an engagement of grace: inasmuch as I am, in the depths of myself and in my totality, borne and penetrated by the aspiring force of divine love, to the constant realization in the development of my life of this profound and total gift of my "heart."

Grace is therefore united to this fundamental liberty of my person in order that my intellect, will, and sensibility, and even my body metamorphose slowly, but from the interior, in a lengthy maturation and spiritual growth. If these effects of grace are often so little perceptible in our lives, it is precisely because we are so slow to welcome this divine call. Only the saints witness clearly by their lives the earthly triumphs of grace.

Blessed John Ruusbroec has defined in a few words the supernatural process of this growth in grace in his book of Spiritual Marriage. God, he says, acts from the interior to the exterior. Man on the contrary, from the exterior (words, examples, acquired habits, etc.) to the interior. Thus God acts in every man from the interior, the center of his existence, to penetrate him slowly by an extension and an infiltration of His gracious influence to the peripheral regions of his humanity.

III. Psychology of Grace

Let us first consider the question of the possibility of a psychology of grace, for the answer is not an obvious one. It is not even uniform in Catholic theology. We shall then venture to make some general suggestions for the elaboration of a psychology and phenomenology of grace as foundations for a Christian humanism.

IS A PSYCHOLOGY OF GRACE IMPOSSIBLE?

At first sight it appears as though any psychology of grace is an impossibility. There are various theological and philosophical rea-

sons for this. The mystery of grace is a divine mystery. It entirely
transcends the powers of our created and sinful humanity. Grace is
a participation of the divine life in us. God does not allow himself
to be the subject of experiment.

The fundamental option of grace is, moreover, said to be
supernatural both by its source, which is divine, and its object,
which also is God, the revealed God of our salvation. These two
aspects of our supernatural commitment necessarily elude our
psychological experience. Besides, the supernatural influence which
raises this option to the level of participation in the divine life
does not penetrate it from the outside like a foreign body, or a
coercive force which would break and interrupt the spontaneous
evolution of our liberty. In this case it would impose itself upon
our attention, if only in a negative way, by the force of its impact,
leaving a kind of subconscious trauma in the soul.

No one shows more respect for our liberty than God Himself. It
is the very imprint of His eternal Liberty, the image of His Love in
us. That is why we think the dialectical anthropology of Blessed
John Ruusbroec so important on this point. Grace penetrates us in
the depths of our being, the point at which we are continually
proceeding from the creative hands of God. It is therefore truly
"from the inside" that God acts on our liberty, from that connecting point, if one may so call it, where that liberty is continually
engendered by God and rests in His conservative action. So this
divine influx leads us freely "from inside to outside" ourselves, by
the inwardness of our liberty. Starting from this existential and
total center, the divine influx adapts itself perfectly, without check
or break, to the evolution of our free spontaneity. This is the only
possible explanation, the place where Creator and creature meet,
absolute existence and shared existence.

These theological and philosophical considerations are confirmed by the teaching of the Council of Trent, according to which
we can never acquire the absolute certitude of being in a state of
grace. This conciliar doctrine does not deny the eventuality of a
particular, and therefore extraordinary, revelation on this subject,
nor the possibility which several Franciscan theologians upheld at
the Council, of deducing our state of grace from certain truths of
faith, such as the fact of having received the sacrament of penance
in good dispositions. An acute mind—it can be ascertained from

reading the heated discussions in the Council on this question—
will easily discern the elements of uncertainty implied in these two
particular cases: everything rests on the fact that our psychological
state is never fully clear to us.

Our concrete psychology is very complex. "It takes many things
to make a pudding!" as the English say colloquially. And more
correctly, if perhaps with a certain cynicism, "Every man has
many reasons for what he does: the good reasons and the real
one!" People who have any experience of examination of conscience know very well that it is in practice often difficult to discover under the camouflage of the "good reasons" the "real reason" which has urged us to the action. This determining motive,
although part of our moral and responsible life, still remains in the
concrete exercise of our total liberty implied in a collection of
secondary reasons. It is very difficult, if not impossible, to disen-
tangle it all. The only motive which morally and definitely commits
us is that of our fundamental option. But we have seen how that
option, which takes place in the depths of our existential con-
sistence, is never conscious by itself. It slowly appears from the
general direction of a life. It will thus be impossible to recognize
the elements which *directly* belong to our supernatural fundamental option.

Thus, religious psychology would preserve its meaning on the
purely human, earthly, plane, on the moral level of the commandments. The mystery of grace would take place in quite another
spiritual sphere, the divine and supernatural, secret, and intangible
region, open only to our faith. In this case we should have to deal
with a kind of supernatural subconscious, or supraconscious,
which no psychological analysis could discover. There would only
be one exception to this, the passive states at the summit of the
mystical life. There would therefore be between the supernatural
life of grace and the mystical life, not only a qualitative fission, but
a difference of nature in our own activity.

AUTONOMY OF HUMAN SCIENCES

The opinion which was very widespread during the last centuries
in theological treatises on grace cannot in any way be agreed with.
Their objections allow us, however, to make certain important

concessions, which will influence our final reply. Human and Christian experience does in fact appear to support them. Grace does not change anything in physical laws. It changes nothing in the historical laws which rule our human condition, in the social, psychological and biological laws. The fact that I am in a state of grace does not save me from bankruptcy if I am imprudent in business; from being killed in a motor accident; from becoming ill, from letting my mental equilibrium be affected by an unfortunate heredity, or drink, or sorrow, or overwork.

The world is still what it was before the coming of Christ, as before my baptism. We have seen that it is one of the profound meanings of Christ's Redemption. The Messias did not save us by means of a quantity of physical sufferings. Without knowing it, we represent the Father as a sadist if we think that! Excuse the expression, but certain theological theories and certain sermons do really go rather far in this direction! The world, as it is, with its hates, sufferings, death, is historically the result of our sin. Original sin is a state of separation from God which we are always making more complete by our personal sins. Christ descended *on this, our own earth.* He came into this state of perdition. He underwent all the consequences, except sin. "Unto death, the death of the cross" (Phil. 2:8). He did not change our earth, but took away its poison, that solidarity in evil, that taste for sin. In this world of pride and disobedience to God He became voluntarily the "Servant of Yahweh," the *obedient Son,* for us. "He was obedient unto death" ". . . and that is why God has given him a name which is above every name," the name of Lord (Phil. 2:8). He thus merited the grace of saving us, like Him, by Him, in Him. *For us, too, the world remains unchanged.* But in our turn under the sway of His Spirit we must exorcize it, take away from it its seed of sin by our obedience in faith and charity.

This doctrine of the Redemption is very important. It is truly religious because truly scriptural. It is also profoundly realistic. Heaven is not on earth. With Christ we have to win it, merit it for eternity.

It is thus that the world always keeps its own earthly laws open to the human sciences. These laws ensure to human sciences—psychology, sociology and even pedagogy, theoretical and practical —the autonomy to which they have a right, not an absolute autonomy, proper to what would then be a unique science, yet a complete autonomy in their own sphere. This sphere is clearly limited by their subjects and methods.

DISTINCTION BETWEEN THE PSYCHOLOGICAL, MORAL AND SUPERNATURAL ORDERS

There is even more to be said. God remains sovereignly independent in the distribution of His grace. The essential point in every life is fundamental obedience to God, like and with Christ, that is to say, the acceptance of our life, such as it is, concrete, perhaps painful. It would also be a mistake to think that only the normal, balanced, psychically sane and "integral" man, and even that only the man who observes the norms of Christian morality, can be reached by grace. It is true that grace impels a man to live a moral life. Christ Himself, St. John in his Gospel and especially in his first Epistle, with that realism—I would even call it fanaticism —of true mystics, leaves no doubt on this subject: he who loves Me keeps My commandments!

But all Christian behavior is not necessarily imbued by grace, nor is it always a sign of grace. There is the morality of the pharisee, of the man of the world, of the "honest man" as the last century had it, the "gentleman," unmasked by Cardinal Newman in his *Idea of a University,* of the modern and atheist humanist. There is even a certain morality among gangsters. All this demonstrates that, if grace requires a moral life, all moral living is not yet grace. That is why the fact that our liberty is exercised on different levels has been so strongly insisted upon here. Grace works chiefly in the depths of our total and totalizing personality, while moral behavior expresses itself in practice at the level of particular actions.

To go further still with an extreme case: A man can, while suffering from mental debility, even great affective disequilibrium, be called to sanctity. Essential holiness is not indeed anything but the total acceptance, as we have seen in contemplating the mystery of our Redemption, as and with Christ in grace and therefore in "filial" love, of the situation in which Providence wishes me to be at the present time. Providence is above all that mystery of the divine presence which draws me to the loving submission to His

Will in the position in which I actually find myself. It was thus with Christ. We are too ready to believe that Providence is chiefly a privilege of the elect. It was not so with Christ, and it will not be so for us, at least as a normal rule. God, indeed, keeps for Himself the right to intervene in the development of human causalities. This extraordinary intervention has no other meaning than to confirm our faith in His eternal Presence of love in daily life. Such are the miracles, signs of His Presence and His love.

All sanctity is therefore above all this total acceptance of my life as Christ accepted His: "not my will, Lord, but thine." The situation of the mentally afflicted man may be very sad. It may keep him enclosed in complexes and determinisms which upset his apparent morality. As long as that man humbly and lovingly performs all that is still in his power, to accept his life from the hands of God, he is truly tending to sanctity, the only sanctity possible to him in his condition.

I am quite aware that these words of mine may scandalize certain "geometrical" minds, orderly and positive, for whom the Christian life is reduced rather too much to a certain exterior conformism, to an ordered existence without any problems. These minds should make themselves more sympathetic to their brethren who have not so easy a vocation. An inveterate kleptomaniac will find it extremely hard to observe the seventh commandment. He obviously must do all in his power to arrive at it, but he will not always be able to succeed. His holiness will consist in humbly accepting his wretchedness, his shame, which is not voluntary. This hidden, crucified, sanctity may even go very high. Obviously, it can never be a "canonizable" form of holiness, nor a recommendable one. In fact, the process of canonization in the Church tends to the discovery of those chosen souls whom God has prepared for the edification of all.

All this should prevent us from confusing normal and balanced behavior and even exemplary moral conduct with the true sanctity of grace. This complacency and confusion come from a lack of self-knowledge. It is thought that the reality of sin or grace appears immediately on the level of our particular actions. The pride often hidden under this "irreproachable" behavior is not always perceived. That is why the saints were so severe on themselves and so just. Little Thérèse found only this consolation at the end of her life:

to rejoice in her weaknesses and to trust herself entirely, like a poor abandoned toy, to the Divine good pleasure.

It is true, and must be repeated, that grace requires of us an absolute morality. It is useful to insist upon this, for the primary importance of this moral exigence tends to be forgotten nowadays owing to the mistaken behavior of so many young priests and Christian intellectuals, that dangerous dilettantism in psychology, and the imprudence and lack of real Christian sense in certain psychologists, blinded by their scientific specialization. It is not enough to have been ordained "ontologically" a priest of God to become automatically raised to a state of institutional sanctity which would dispense us from all moral and ascetic effort. And certain psychologists are wrong in thinking that the wise preaching of the great truths of our Faith would normally engender complexes. We are entirely in agreement that insistence on the evil of mortal sin, the uncertainty of the moment of our death, the seriousness of hell, is unwise in front of children—too often thus confronted—or before those with scrupulous, worrying minds. But it is high time that a more virile tonality be bestowed upon our education and the training of religious Christians, and young priests: we should free ourselves from that religious sentimentality, and especially from that idiotic phobia of complexes which is by far the greatest phobia of our time!

THEOLOGICAL FOUNDATIONS OF A
PSYCHOLOGY OF GRACE

In these preliminary considerations all those who for theological, philosophical or psychological reasons are opposed to the possibility of a psychology of grace have been left free to speak. Their objections demonstrate that the problem is not a simple one. They free us from any naïveté or undue enthusiasm. What is more, they provide an impetus for delineating certain distinctions, very important in practice.

First of all, the position outlined in this circle is predicated upon an unquestionable preference for the ancient doctrine: the doctrine of the Fathers, especially of St. Augustine, the pre-Scholastics and the great theologians of the thirteenth century. After an eclipse of several centuries, this doctrine has in our time acquired a preponderant position in Catholic theology. We therefore accept without hesitation the thesis called Thomist, according to which there really exists a psychology of grace. The reasons are given above. The strong conviction in this doctrine has led to the belief that a philosophy of man, even if pretending to be a philosophy of pure nature—of man without grace and delivered over to himself alone—even if it is an atheistic philosophy, will be influenced and conditioned, often unconsciously, by this primordial reality of our existence.

All philosophy, even objective, as it is called now, and conceptual, must inevitably start from man's concrete experience, the experience of departure, also controlled experience. This experience cannot but be influenced by this primordial reality: *the fact that God calls every man to a supernatural intimacy with the Blessed Trinity.* It is true that only believers possess a definite consciousness of this, received through Revelation. That does not alter the fact that since the Promise on the threshold of our history, mankind has lived in what is called in theology the "status hominis lapso et raparati"; every man lives under *the concrete and creative will of* God, Who wills to save us in Christ. This Divine will *has radically changed the very basis* of our existential and concrete dynamism. Karl Rahner has called this obscure aspiration of every man toward the God of Salvation a supernatural "existential," that is to say an a priori constituent of our historical and concrete existence.

If every man is fundamentally orientated towards God from birth, what of the man who freely lets himself be urged by this supernatural impulse, and accepts by fundamental option this interior vocation of divine grace? What was at first only an obscure urge, an implicit tendency, a fundamental orientation—"offered grace," as Karl Rahner says—becomes under divine influence "grace accepted existentially." We thereafter act under the impulse of a fundamental option of grace, supernatural; we are really in a state of grace, really justified and sanctified. We have already dealt at length with this state of grace under the divine influence and in the fundamental consent of our liberty.

There is another aspect which is not sufficiently taken into account in the Western theology of grace, which is often somewhat Manichaean. Grace can in a certain measure, as we see in the life of

St. Teresa of Avila, become a *force of spiritual and psychic health.* Grace, in fact, tends to heal us completely, certainly after this life, but to a certain extent already on earth. It depends among other things on the will of God and also on the fullness of our submission to the call of grace. This theology is to be found among the Greek Fathers, who often describe grace by its *corporeal* aspect as the seed of incorruptibility and immortality. Grace possesses already and now a real sway over the whole of our humanity. It thus remains a fact that for most men a defective psychism may continue, as we have seen, to hinder to a large degree and to inhibit the development of their moral personality, even with grace. Grace is not yet Heaven. But it effectively guides us to Heaven and because of that, as the seed of eternity, prepares us and predisposes us to the resurrection and eternal beatitude.

REPLY TO THE CHIEF OBJECTION (THE RATIONALISTIC)

On the plane of clear and distinct concepts, the Suarezians are perfectly right. Vital commitment cannot be immediately and completely brought to light. But man also possesses more essential, because deeper, certitudes, than those which can be expressed by abstract concepts. These certitudes, or rather their essential structures, only become visible to our reasoning minds after long deduction, for instance, in a transcendent or existential analysis. But they are all the more real because *lived and exercised* in our existential activity, obscurely perceived in the very response of our love.

There will always be, therefore, a certain chasm between the actual apprehension of God as the supernatural and total aim of my life, and my precise consciousness of it. This phenomenon of a gap between a profound and existential conviction and the conscious motives, which can be expressed in clear language is an entirely normal phenomenon. It is only an inveterate rationalism, instilled into our youth by a mistaken and purely conceptual apologetic, which gives us an uneasy conscience as soon as we approach the problems of our Faith. Any manifestation of the inner mystery of one person to another is a revelation, and any definite commitment with regard to a person involves an act of faith, naturally a human act. Parents exercise it with regard to their children, children with regard to their fathers and mothers. Any friendship, any total gift of oneself in love implies an act of faith, a risk and a commitment, the content and spiritual significance of which is superior to all the reasonable motives which we could formulate. The notional certitude is sufficient as long as I look at others from the outside, as useful or dangerous "things." It may in this way *prepare* for the loving knowledge which is the gift of self by a primary motivation, necessarily rudimentary. But as soon as I rise to the personal plane, as soon as "I" meet "Thou," this primary order of objective certitude, this colorless precision, must be transcended in order to penetrate into the sphere of faith and love, intuition lived in the loving ardor directed to the beloved.

In grace, it is God Himself Who comes to meet me, the Divine "I" says "Thou" to me in the Son. The Father indeed meets me in the incarnate Son, by means of the visible Church, my brethren, the Sacraments. The human structure of the personal encounter remains unchanged. Inwardly it is immensely intensified, raised by participation to the mysterious heights of the eternal encounter of the Father and the Son in the love of the Holy Ghost.

The supernatural, "filial," motivation is really present in the development of our Christian psychological life, but in an obscure manner—as regards the mind—and exercised and lived in the acts of our life. That is why concrete actions are so important, and, according to St. John, fraternal charity is the proof, the assurance and the sacrament of my love for God.

This motivation remains on the one hand at the side of the motley, fluid and changing, always slightly deceptive, image which my reason, my imagination, my acquired representations, ¯my confused sentiments, form of my actions. It rests in fact in the most intimate part of my heart. On the other hand, by its wealth of conviction, its totalizing sway, its stability and its loving urge, it tends beyond this same image. Monsignor Guardini expresses it in this short formula: "Glauben heisst sehen und er es damit wagen!" (To believe is to see and then risk all!)

WAYS OF A PSYCHOLOGY OF GRACE

If what we have stated so far is true, grace and the life of grace are of paramount interest to the psychologist. There is only one condition for success. He must at least accept as a real possibility the existence of a personal God of love Who interests Himself in man. It is obvious that faith and charity will greatly sharpen his spiritual sense. One can only understand a life by living it oneself. That is the meaning of the words of that great psychologist of grace, Augustine, so often repeated by the mystics:

Give me one who loves and he will understand what I say; give me one who desires, who is hungry, who feels the nostalgia of solitude in this exile, and who is thirsty and sighs after the living waters of the eternal fatherland; give me such a one, and he understands what I say. But if I must explain myself to a frosty indifference, he will not understand.

This psychology remains a closed book to the man who has chosen an atheistic or vaguely pantheist materialism.

Here follows a quotation from a man who is not a Christian but a spiritualist and who has written a whole book in order to free himself from the specter of materialistic psychoanalysis.

As a child I had a curious plaything. It was a paper covered with an intricacy of very fine blue and red lines. Nothing could be distinguished. But by covering it with a paper of red silk, the red lines of the design vanished and the blue lines formed a picture. It was a clown in a circus, holding a ring, with a little dog which was jumping through it. And if one covered the same design with a blue transparency, a roaring lion appeared chasing the clown around the arena. *This can be done with anyone, living or dead.* He can be looked at through the Sonia transparency (the psychoanalyst) and a biography of Napoleon can be written from the angle of his pituitary gland, which has been done; that he, incidentally, conquered Europe will only appear as a derivative symptom of the activity of those two minute lobes of the size of peas ... the image obtained through the blue transparency will be *no less true and no less complete.*[6]

It will even be more complete, because exposed to the *totality of the real.*

A PSYCHOLOGY OF GRACE

Psychology is mainly a science of observation. It must observe, consider and describe individual or collective religious experience.

Here there is an immense field of study open to the psychology of grace.

The Christian psychologist will however feel specially drawn to certain experiences, the freshness, authenticity and inner intensity of which attract his attention. The difficulties of which we have spoken above, which make it so hard to discern the fundamental inspiration of a concrete life, inevitably bring out favorable examples. The testimony of converts, or the long story of eternal pilgrims like Péguy or Simone Weil come to mind. Their youth and their intellectual, sentimental and spiritual formation has often been deprived of typically religious or theological influences. They do not know the religious clichés, the pious reflexes, the "suitable words," which so often disguise the sincerity or real fervor of the believer coming from old Christian stock. The conventional language of certain nuns is of little use in these psychological studies! Take for example the discussions concerning the manuscript of the "Story of a Soul" of little St. Thérèse!

There are also moments of intense or prolonged religious life which force us to a greater nudity in our gestures, attitudes and words. They recur at times of bitter trial or great joy, in the story of a vocation or a great love. All true love purifies, in marriage as well.

These different advantages are all to be found in the lives of the great mystics. They have all been the privileged subjects of religious and Christian psychology. We are still too easily distracted by the study of the extraordinary phenomena which belong to psychopathology or parapsychology. These studies have their own importance but the inner life must exert an irresistible attraction for any psychologist who is really fascinated by the problem of man and his destiny. In the mystics we shall discover that only the true act of virtue is really free, the secret and the originality of true liberty. There is nothing more fascinating than this infinite originality of the saints, compared with the monotony of sin, the mechanical and empty automatism of evil.

To these central themes could be added tributary subjects for study, which may be of great utility when treated with prudence and discernment. First, there is artistic religious expression. The artist who treats a religious subject is not always a believer. Aestheticism, as we know, floats in the space between dream and reality. On the other hand, true artists have a power of introspection and of specially suggestive expression which not all the saints possess.

There is also the comparative study of other religions. And in this connection, it is not primarily a matter of demonstrating what they lack. According to our faith every man is called by God and every sincere man will find God in the intimacy of his heart and by means of the traditions, doctrines and authentically religious actions of his beliefs. We can therefore discern in these other religions those fundamental attitudes which already foreshadow the actions of the Christian. For instance, it is remarkable to note how the great Chinese convert, John Wu, distinguished jurist and politician and former Chinese ambassador to the Holy See confesses that he rediscovered, enriched and unified in Catholicism, the noblest aspirations that he had nourished in Confucianism, Taoism and Buddhism.

I have always been struck by the difference between the "great converts" and those whose sincere conversion leaves something to be desired on the human and religious plane. The former have perhaps struggled and suffered much before taking the decisive step, but after having found peace they never refuse to witness to their profound gratitude for the most authentic teachings of their ancient beliefs. The converts whom I may shortly describe as poor and pitiful can never rid themselves of a certain "renegade" complex. They have a quite useless desire to attack and deride their former coreligionists, showing thereby that their conversion is not yet complete, but remains impure, stained by an agressiveness which is not religion.

Finally, collective religious phenomena cannot be set aside. There is naturally the folklore and religious symbolism to which Jung has drawn attention, and which so easily deteriorates by the weight of the human masses into superstitions and magical practices. But there is more than that. It is false to think that people as a whole are exclusively inclined to materialize religious sentiment. In this connection it would be well to provide a special place for the study of prayer, its fundamental attitudes, its universal structures, its privileged positions, its great themes and its communal expression in liturgy. Those who have followed closely the revival of the celebration of the Paschal Vigil know that people are capable of an authentic religious life if they are initiated into religious mysteries by an enlightened preparation and a liturgical symbolism which touches their own lives. It is true that sentimentality is the poetry of the masses, but they are able to go beyond it when invited to an active and intelligent participation.

PSYCHOLOGY AND PHENOMENOLOGY

The psychologist has not only to observe, but must try to understand. Every science of observation understands by unifying, discovering under the multiplicity of phenomena what is their deeplying meaning, their identical structure. It is here that psychology can develop into phenomenology.

There are many definitions of phenomenology. There is Husserl's (which he explains in a masterly way in the *Encyclopaedia Britannica*); there is that of his many pupils, of Heidegger, of Monsignor Guardini. We might also call the "dialogue" religious philosophy of Martin Buber and Abraham Heschel a phenomenology of the Jewish religion, placed between Jewish Western liberalism and Oriental mysticism—Chassidism. Phenomenology touches on the one hand existential and personal metaphysics and on the other hand the simple suggestive description of the essential psychological attitudes—of the "ethos" of a person, a life, a religion. In this sense, Cardinal Newman is much more a phenomenologist than a philosopher.

As was said at the beginning of this article, it is not necessary to linger on questions of technical methodology. It is enough to describe it in these terms. We here mean by *phenomenology* any psychological description of the fundamental and concrete attitudes of man in a particular experiment aiming at the discovery of those structures and forms which by their uniformity, intensity and depth give a meaning to and explain the foregoing experiment. Religious phenomenology will therefore attempt to discover by successive reductions the concrete, existential and personalist structure of religious experience, that is, fundamental experience in its pure state.

We are here confronted by an extensive and little-explored region. This article has chiefly been speaking of grace; I now propose to suggest some chapters for a phenomenology of grace. This example will go further than the description to explain what we mean by these words.

The life of grace, especially if it is intense, always implies a *feeling of the divine presence* from the objective point of view. I find myself entirely absorbed by an invisible personal mystery. It is a total, living presence, a divine activity, more real than my surroundings. Visible things both hide and display it. This divine mystery is in things and beyond them. It is silent and speaks to me, beckons to me through this created world which separates me from and unites me to my Lord.

It is moreover a *holy* presence. It fills me with fear, with an immense respect, a religious terror. At the same time I feel drawn to it, warmed, followed by a loving gaze, an intimate union with this mystery which surrounds and penetrates me.

When I now turn my attention to the subjective aspects of this experience as far as it seems to appear at the surface from the depths of my consciousness, I am aware of a deep tearing away, an inner suffering, an inexpressible *solitude*. I feel myself alone before my God, misunderstood by others, but also far from God Himself, because totally unworthy of His Presence. The better I know myself, the more the distance between the divine sanctity and my unworthiness increases, like an unbridgeable chasm. The more I allow myself to be penetrated by the sanctity of His Presence, the further I descend, the further I am from my Love. It is the night of the mystics, the wounding of the soul experienced by every man who has to lose himself to find himself by finding God. It is also the anguish of risking all, of the leap into the invisible. One perceives with ever-increasing clarity that one must truly leave all to find all, to lose everything which supports my human certainty.

And yet this suffering is accompanied by a profound *joy,* an ineffable accomplishment. Even in physical sufferings, in the sorrows of life, this peace and intimate sweetness never leaves me. It is such a sweet joy, which seems hardly perceptible, and yet I feel it in me strong and unbreakable, able to change me entirely, to carry me along above the worst trials. It is known that this joy can sometimes become so intense that it has to express itself by gestures, song, cries and tears of joy. It is a sweetness which brings us also *near to others:* we can no longer keep it jealously for ourselves. Others also, our brethren, must know and share it.

It might be thought that an experience such as this appears to be disconnected, unbalanced and torn by contrary sentiments. But the contrary is true. If there is anything certain it is that this religious experience exerts a wonderful power of interiorization. It is supremely unifying, totalizing. A man may lead a life torn by multiple responsibilities, destroyed by terrible trials; nothing escapes this aspiring power of spiritual integration which arises from his heart. Nothing surprises him, nothing dismays him, nothing discourages him. Everything takes on a meaning and becomes possible, for he is possessed by love. It was noted above that this unifying presence can also attain to the integration of physical forces and even cure a mental lack of balance from the inside.

We have attempted to describe the chief themes of the experience of grace, as living presence before God. This analysis could be continued by passing to the study of the *fundamental religious option*, how this option is expressed in faith, hope and charity and is incarnated in a *vocation*. The reader is referred to the many modern books which deal with these matters. For faith, A. Mouroux and A. Brunner; for hope, Ch. Péguy and especially Marcel; for charity, Kierkegaard, A. Nygren (with certain reserves), M. Scheler, D. von Hildebrand, M. d'Arcy, M. Nédoncelle, J. Guitton and J. H. Newman.

The most remarkable author from this viewpoint seems to me to be Romano Guardini. He has for a long time explored the central problem which he himself calls "Unterscheidung des Christlichen": the perception of the "ethos" proper to the Christian, the Gospel, the life of the Lord. I would not say that he is a psychologist, but his scriptural, philosophical and theological analyses retain a very close contact with the experience of Christian life, minutely observed and described with subtle art.

DEFENSE OF SPIRITUAL HYGIENE AND HEALTH

We have made a few suggestions for a psychology and phenomenology of grace. The importance of such studies will be realized by all. They save the theologian from his abstractions, present the philosopher with the description of a vital, concrete and rich experience which is able to control his systematic analyses. For the psychologist by nature and vocation they seem to me to be of most superior and absorbing interest.

I would like to end this article by drawing attention to the practical utility of these studies for a sane and normal religious life. The psychologist indeed is almost the only one, if he remains truly faithful to his Christian sense, to be able to unmask with authority all the manifestations of a sickly and false religiosity. There is nothing more harmful to the life of grace than that hysteria or paranoia which apes religion. On the other hand, nothing so attracts unhealthy minds as the mysteries of our Faith. It happens that priests, and often even religious or ecclesiastical superiors are easily deceived. An eminent superior of a religious Order confessed one day that it had taken him ten years of experience to realize that most of his subjects who had laid before him vast plans of reforms or activities were psychically unstable. This hidden disease, which is moreover terribly infectious, is a real menace to any life of grace. It distorts that maturation in grace which has been spoken of, and also creates unhealthy and fallacious illusions which spoil many lives. Vanity and pride soon take their part in it, for these forms of unhealthy religiosity are so much easier, so much more alluring, because more obvious and exciting. With a defective theology of the supernatural and a propensity for the extraordinary, one soon arrives at despising the humble work of every day and exalting all forms of activity or apostleship which are in any way out of the ordinary. An incessant disquiet urges these injurious minds to continual reforms which, scarcely outlined, give way to other manifestations, each more striking and unexpected than the last. This disease is a threat to religious orders, schools of spirituality, youth movements, and many other institutions in the Church which could be so useful without it.

It is the task of the Christian psychologist to educate his contemporaries and demonstrate to them the ways of a real mental hygiene and frankly to draw their attention to the many dangers of deviation.

THE PSYCHOLOGIST AS CHRISTIAN HUMANIST

Humanism and Christian humanism is much talked about. The Greco-Roman humanism has exhausted its resources. Confronted by this new world opening before us, with its technology, its totalitarian spirit, its mixture of races and civilizations, we need a humanism more conscious of itself, more conscious also of its possibilities and its limits. The Christian psychologist has a very special vocation in the world of today. He is able to collaborate in the evolution of a true Christian humanism, wiser because more universal in depth as in breadth. Humanism is not of course grace. But the Church has very rightly always believed that it was indispensable for the normal development of the interior and divine life in this earthly society, the rough draft of the Future City.

NOTES

1. I was also encouraged in this study by the interest of Christian psychologists and pedagogues in this eminently practical subject. The substance of this address was given for the first time on March 23, 1954 at Antwerp before the Institute pour la Connaissance de L'homme, founded and presided over by Dr. R. Dellaert, Professor of Psychology at Louvain University. I had the honor of presenting the same ideas before the Commission Internationale du Plein Air on June 26th, 1955, at Fribourg in Brisgau and on March 9th, 1956, during the Study Days of the Commission Catholique des Colonies de Vacances at Paris, under the chairmanship of His Excellency Monseigneur Piérard. I owe special thanks to Canon H. Misonne of Brussels for his help in defining some of the points in our article.

2. I do not want to multiply notes. Those who want to go further into these questions of theological methodology, will find a basic article, too little noticed, by the eminent historian of the theology of grace, Professor Dr. J. Auer of Bonn: "Um den Begriff der Gnade" in ZKTh 70 (1948), pp. 341–368. This point of view has been confirmed more and more by different studies in positive theology, such as those of Msgr. A. M. Landgraf, *Dogmengeschichte der Frühscholastik*, Regensburg, I/1 and I/2 (1952–1953): *Die Lehre von der Gnade; H. Bouillard, Conversion et grâce chez saint Thomas d'Aquin*, Paris, 1944; W. Dettloff, *Die Lehre von der "Acceptatio divina" bei Johannes Duns Scotus*, Werl, 1954; and recently the study of the dean of theology at the Gregorian University at Rome, the Rev. Z. Alszeghy, *Nova Creatura*, Rome, 1956. J. Maréchal, doctor in sciences and a remarkable metaphysician, in 1924 in his *Études sur la Psychologie des Mystiques*, Vol. I (Bruges), had already established the chief laws of a "Psychologie religieuse comme science empirique" or of a "Phénoménolgie générale de la vie mystique," at the same time distinguishing them from the ontology and theology of Christian mysticism. He remarks: ". . . We shoud have liked to limit our task to the disengaging of the simply descriptive characteristics or, if you will, the special 'phenomenology' of the mystical states, if this phenomenology had not, at a certain moment, led to an eminently ontological option in order to perfect it" (*op. cit.*, p. 184).

3. On this subject an interesting psychological article by Reverend Father Ernst, S.J., may be consulted: "L'option vitale: Contribution à une psychologie ascétique de la vocation," *Nouvelle Revue Théologique*, 69 (1947), 731–742 and 1065–1084. The conclusion is of special interest: "There exists an option which is deeper, more essential, which presents itself as a more affec-

tive tendency towards a connatural end. This vital dynamism is primary. The conscious and rational elements are subsidiary but the affective urge supports and totalizes them." *Art cit.*, 1084.

4. This spiritual atrophy may find its source in certain forms of illness or senility. It is then involuntary and pathological. But it may also be freely willed as a form of personal suicide. See on this subject the remarkable article by J. de Guibert, "La médiocrité spirituelle," *Revue d'ascétique et de mystique*, 16 (1926), 113–131.

5. The best introduction I know of to the anthropology and theology of Ruusbroec is that by the Rev. P. Henry, "La mystique trinitaire du Bienheureux Jean Ruusbroec," in *Recherches de Science religieuse*, 40 (1951–1952), pp. 335–368 and 41 (1953), pp. 51–75.

6. Koestler, *Croisade sans croix*, Paris, 1947, pp. 238–239.

13 Modern Theories of
the Atonement

GEOFFREY GRAYSTONE

*The work of Christ in his paschal mysteries is re-examined in
the light of contemporary reflections on the Redemption.*

D URING THE PAST thirty years or so, there has been
remarkable activity among English non-Catholic writers on
the subject of the "Atonement" or, more accurately, the atoning
value of the Death of Jesus Christ. Some fifty volumes can be
counted, and this is not to speak of the innumerable articles and
essays consecrated to the subject, or the abundant incidental
treatment of the same theme to be found in works dealing with the
Gospels, the life and teaching of Christ, the Pauline Epistles, etc.
So far as I am aware, there is no up-to-date Catholic treatment of
this interesting, if at times perplexing, theme of contemporary
theology. The most recent Catholic appreciations in English are
those of the American, Dr. Rudolph G. Bandas, writing in 1925,[1]
and of the late Dr. Bernard Grimley, in a paper read at the Cambridge Summer School of Catholic Studies in 1926.[2] In endeavor-
ing to supplement their work, I do not propose to furnish a full
explanation or justification of Catholic teaching and Catholic theology on the Redemption—that has already been done, and ably
done, by the late Abbé J. Rivière and many others;[3] nor do I mean
to criticize the various theories from a strictly philosophical and
theological point of view, as was done by the two scholars mentioned above. My purpose is a humble, though, I trust, nonetheless
useful, one, namely, to outline the theories or trends in the periods
stated and briefly to examine them in the light of the mind and
teaching of Jesus Christ himself on the subject of His Death, as

revealed to us in the Gospels, more especially in the three earlier or "Synoptic" Gospels.[4] As a matter of fact, many modern writers on the Atonement do take the Synoptic Gospels as the foundation, or at least the starting-point of their investigations; on the other hand, those who prefer a broader basis for their theories, or whose principal appeal is rather to Christian "experience," will I am sure, agree that their opinions are wanting in solid foundations if they fail to take into account the express teaching of Him who actually accomplished the Atonement by His Death on Calvary.

THE PROBLEM OF TERMINOLOGY

It is usual to classify theories of the Atonement according as they are *objective* or *subjective*. Broadly speaking, in the "objective" theories the Death of Christ possesses a certain redemptive value in itself, quite apart from the reaction that may be produced in the believer who reflects upon it; contrariwise, in the "subjective" theory, the atoning value of Christ's death consists essentially in the fact that, as a theme for mediation, it is peculiarly apt for producing salutary effects in the heart of the penitent believer. However, the use of this terminology has produced protests, and indignant protests, on the part of those whose theories have been summarily labeled "subjective." Dr. C. J. Cadoux, the well-known Congregationalist scholar, writes as follows:

By recognizing in the forth-going love of God the root cause whereby the sinner is moved to repentance, we are clearly not advancing (as is so often and so perversely suggested) a purely subjective theory, but are positing an objective basis of redemption, namely, the willingness of God to meet out of his own resources the cost of the damage wrought by human sin.[5]

His co-religionist, Dr. R. S. Franks, speaks in the same strain about his own theory:

It is in truth fundamentally objective, inasmuch as God, Christ, His Cross and His divine love are all objects of human trust and responsive love. It would be more correct to speak of the "experiential" theory.[6]

Clearly then, the terms "objective" and "subjective" are ambiguous and misleading in the present connection. The alternative proposed by Dr. Franks, "experiential," is, I think, equally open to the danger of ambiguity;[7] other terms proposed as substitutes for "subjective"—"moral influence," "ethical," "exemplarist" and "revelatory"—are useful, but perhaps a little too vague, and they all suffer from the drawback of leaving intact at the other side of the scales the label "objective," to which exception has also been taken. In an effort to cut the "Gordian knot," I propose to adopt for the purposes of this essay the distinctions, *God-ward* and *man-ward* theories of the Atonement.[8] The terms may be defined as follows. A *God-ward* theory is an explanation of the Atonement in which Christ in His Passion and Death is visualized as performing, on behalf of man, as his representative or substitute, some work that has value before God for the procuring of man's salvation— be it the oblation to God of a sacrifice of reparation, or the vicarious enduring of the punishment or penalty of sin, or the offering of vicarious or representative penitence for sin. More briefly, Christ's atoning work is concerned in the first place with God. On the contrary, a *man-ward* theory, as the name suggests, is an explanation of the Atonement that envisages the work of the suffering and dying Savior as essentially concerned with and directed towards man—taking the form of an inspiring revelation (whether of the attributes of God, or of the malice of sin), whereby the sinner is moved to turn to God in penitence and love, and receive the free forgiveness of his offenses. In this theory, then, Christ's work, insofar as its effects are concerned, touches God only indirectly, i.e., by removing the obstacles on the part of sinful man, it enables His forgiving love to have free rein.

No doubt, by adopting these categories and definitions, I lay myself open to the charges of oversimplification and overschematization. In reply, I can but plead the exigencies of practical convenience in an eassy of this kind, and at the same time crave pardon in advance of any author whose views I may misplace, or—*quod Deus avertat!*—misinterpret.

I. MAN-WARD THEORIES OF THE ATONEMENT

Reduced to its simplest form, the "man-ward" explanation of the Atonement is that the Death of Jesus moves sinful man to repentance (the one and only condition necessary for forgiveness) because it reveals and exemplifies[9] the love of God for him. "Their value," writes Dr. R. S. Franks, speaking of the sufferings of Christ, "is not purificatory, or expiatory, or satisfactory: it is revelatory."[10] "From first to last," remarks Canon V. F. Storr, "the Cross of Christ is an exhibition of divine love."[11] In its essentials, this theory may be traced back to the Socinians and to Abelard; during the eighteenth and nineteenth centuries it was developed by Schleiermacher, Ritschl, Harnack and Sabatier; and during the period under consideration, it has found adherents and exponents among writers of various creeds and denominations.[12] Moreover, the simple lines of the theory, as traced above, have been amplified, adorned and embellished with a variety of new considerations and a wealth of fresh terminology, all of which, however, leaves unchanged the essential "man-ward" aspect of the system. Thus, for example, Christ is spoken of as "challenging" sin, "bearing" sin, "overcoming," "revealing" and "condemning" sin, of "saving men from the power of sin." We read, too, of God "going out in Christ to redeem the world," "meeting the cost of redemption and forgiveness out of His own resources," "bearing sins on His heart," "transforming sin into grace" and so on; His "holy, forgiving, atoning, suffering" love—call it what you will— "breaks in" on the sinner," "deals with" sin and removes guilt. Sometimes there is a question of "spiritual forces," of a "new dynamic" being "created" or "released" by the Death of Christ, and of "cosmic victory" being attained; occasionally, even the term "sacrifice" is employed.[13] Interpreted in their context, all these new expressions are, I believe, just so many different ways of setting forth the central theme, namely, that the Death of Christ is possessed of a powerful, inspiring and effective revelatory influence, by means of which man is more surely moved to repent, more readily assured of divine forgiveness, and more effectively consoled and encouraged, so as to overcome sin for the future. "Our will must be won, and that is the essence of atonement," writes Dr. E. Grubb, the Quaker scholar.[14] "The difficulty," says R. S. Franks, "is not how to make sin forgivable but how to make the sinner forgivable."[15]

In order to avoid needless repetition, I shall forego the separate examination of the theories of each individual exponent of the "man-ward" system, and content myself instead with tracing, or shall I say disentangling, what seem to be the principal trends or developments of the system as a whole, making special mention of those authors who have introduced new elements, or suggested fresh considerations of any importance. It must be understood that these "trends" do not represent any well-defined "schools" of thought—in fact it is rarely possible to confine any one individual within the limits of a particular "trend."

SIMPLE PRESENTATION OF THE THEORY:
THE CROSS AS REVELATION OF GOD'S LOVE

The simple presentation of the "man-ward" theory in 1919 by Dean Hastings Rashdall marks a convenient *terminus a quo* for this survey. He held that Christ's Death—a "piece of self-sacrifice" for His people—set the seal upon His life and teaching by manifesting in supreme fashion His own love, and hence God's love too, for sinful men; they are thereby moved to repentance, and so obtain forgiveness.[16] This unadorned version of the "moral influence" theory was soon criticized, even by those who took up fundamentally the same position,[17] on the grounds that it offered no reason, or very little reason, why the Death of Christ—any more, let us say, than the death of any just man, or even prophet or saint—should move us to repentance. What relation was there between His sufferings as such and our penitent reaction? Why should His Passion, however nobly endured, prove supremely His love for us men?[18]

"HISTORICAL NECESSITY" FOR THE DEATH OF JESUS

To meet the obvious difficulty urged above, there arose what has not inappropriately been dubbed the "clothes and peg" theory of the Atonement.[19] The connection between the Death of Christ and man's repentance and salvation, it was now proposed, lay in the fact that there existed, in the concrete circumstances of His ministry in Palestine, a "historical necessity" for Him to suffer and die, if He were to be true to His mission of revealing God's "all-inclusive love" to men. W. E. Wilson writes: "In the process of winning men to God by exhibiting Him as love, Jesus had to face a fight to the death with those who opposed this message"[20] (i.e. the "historical necessity" arose out of the hatred and unbelief of the leaders of the Jews). This is the historical "peg," and on it have been hung the "clothes" of various shades of "man-ward" theories.[21]

Such a purely historical explanation of the necessity of the Death of Jesus is, I think, at variance with the records of the Synoptic Gospels. It fails to do justice to Our Lord's repeated predictions of His Passion and Death, even down to details, as something He "must" undergo,[22] or rather, a work He must perform, a "consummation,"[23] a "baptism wherewith He must needs be baptized"[24]—necessary because it was foretold by the prophets[25] because it pertained in vital fashion to "the things of God."[26] Did He not say that He *had come*, i.e. that it was His God-given mission, "to give His life a ransom for many"?[27] Careful reading of the narrative of the events of Holy Week will show that Jesus was in complete control of the situation right up to the time that He freely submitted to being arrested in the Garden; is it true to say, then, that His death was, historically speaking, the "inevitable consequences of His life"?[28] Moreover, it seems clear that the rulers condemned Jesus to death, not for what He taught or revealed, but because He claimed Messianic, nay, even divine dignity and authority.

Other attempts have been made to relate the historical Death of Jesus in some way to our spiritual needs (for everyone who holds to the merely "man-ward" theory of the Atonement must face this problem); for example, that it was "representative" human sins and tendencies, rather than the actual crime of the Jewish leaders, that led to the Death of Jesus;[29] or that Jesus "challenged," "overcame" or "bore" sin *as such*—generic sin—through entering somehow into the sinner's experience. The latter theory I will return to presently. As to the former, it runs counter to the Gospel story as it stands; for there we find, as regards the historical sequence of events, that the grave responsibility for the unjust condemnation and execution of Jesus is laid squarely at the door of the religious leaders of the Jews. Suffice it to recall the facts briefly. Jesus Himself, both openly and in parables, and in the strongest language, denounced those leaders and made clear their guilt in rejecting and condemning Him, a crime which would be visited with the direst punishment.[30] The narrative of the Trial and Passion of Jesus gives a vivid picture of the hatred and malice of the

Jewish authorities against Him, a hatred which would stop at nothing till its fury was fully sated: justice is travestied—false witness is sought against Jesus by His very judges and jury, the witnesses are heard together, instead of separately, and, when this does not suffice, the Accused is forced to pronounce His own condemnation; trumped-up charges are laid before Pilate, the Roman governor, and no stone is left unturned to force his hand—scourging is not enough, Jesus must be crucified, and even a murderer and a robber are preferred before Him; finally, when the deed is done, the Jewish priests and scribes and Pharisees come to gloat over their Victim as He hangs in agony. Pontius Pilate did strive to release Jesus, or certainly to shirk responsibility for His condemnation; the Jewish leaders, on the other hand, publicly assume that responsibility, crying out through the mouths of the mob they had stirred up, "His blood be upon us and upon our children."[31] Whatever, then, about the theoretical question as to what we might have done had we been in their place, there can be little doubt that it was the grave crimes of the responsible Jewish leaders that led, historically speaking, to the Death of Jesus.

THE CROSS AS REVELATION OF THE TRUE NATURE OF SIN

So far, the atoning value of the Death of Christ has consisted chiefly in a supreme manifestation of God's love for the sinner. Yet, is this sufficient? Does this conception of the Atonement, it is asked, adequately safeguard the holiness of God? Does it not, rather, tend to make little of sin? How, then, can it be of any real value in securing deep and lasting repentance on the part of the sinner? Effective atonement, it is pointed out, must also include a full revelation of the true nature of sin and of God's radical opposition to it. Christ's redeeming work must show forth God's holy and righteous love as judging and condemning sin, even whilst it forgives the sinner. This new approach to Christ's redeeming work —which is given no small emphasis in most recent literature on the Atonement—is then formulated somewhat as follows. Precisely because "sin" (i.e. sin in general)) crucified the Son of God—or, at all events, one in whom God was "fully revealed" to man—it is fully and finally exposed in all its real malice. "Sin in all its exceeding sinfulness was placarded there," writes R. Glanville;[32] and

Dean C. Alington states in the following words what he considers the basic truth of the Atonement: "The Cross is a revelation in time of an eternal fact, or rather of two eternal facts, the hatefulness of human sin and the divine reaction to it."[33]

This new aspect of the "man-ward" theory lies open to the same criticism as has been urged above: namely, in the absence of any "God-ward" expiation of human sin by Christ, it fails to establish any real connection between the sins of mankind in general and the Death of the Savior. It was not, I repeat, sin as such, generic sin, representative sin—call it what you please—that crucified Jesus, that was historically responsible for His Death, but the actual specific sins of His contemporaries, notably the Scribes, Pharisees and Chief Priests.

THE CROSS AS REVELATION OF A "SUFFERING GOD"— DIVINE ATONEMENT

The question of the revelation in Christ of the malice of sin and of God's opposition to it is now carried a step further in an endeavour to build up a valid and effective connection between the atoning work of the Savior and human sin in general (they speak, of course, of what we call "actual sin"; "original sin" does not, and for obvious reasons *cannot,* find a place in the "man-ward" theory of Atonement). This brings us to one of the most remarkable, and yet most characteristic and logical developments of the "man-ward" system: the revelation in Christ of a God who has always suffered at the sins of His creatures. Christ's reaction to "sin," as exemplified in the conduct of His enemies during His life and particularly at His Passion, was to meet it by love, to "bear" it and endure its consequences; and this, they say, is a perfect reflection of the eternal reaction of God Himself to human sin. In other words, God endures real suffering at the sight of our sins; sin has always caused Him pain, so that—to borrow a favorite expression of our contemporaries—the Cross on Calvary was but a manifestation in time of an eternal Cross in the Heart of God Himself. Where is the sinful heart so hardened that it would not be touched at this thought?

Belief in a "Suffering God" forms an integral part of the theories of the Methodist, Principal H. M. Hughes (1924),[34] of the Angli-

can, Canon V. F. Storr (1924),[35] of the Congregationalist, Dr. A.
T. Cadoux (1922 and 1940),[36] and of the late Professor H.
Wheeler Robinson, the Baptist scholar (1942).[37] It is adopted
almost as an established doctrine by many other writers on the
Atonement, even by some who propose "God-ward" theories.[38]
In fact, apart altogether from the question of the Atonement, belief
in a "passible God" is widespread among contemporary non-
Catholic theologians, in such wise that it has been described as
"one of the most characteristic trends that run through the post-
war period in English theology," which "gives a distinctive color to
the contemporary period."[39] It is given sympathetic mention in
the Report of the Anglican Commission on Doctrine in 1938;[40]
and, in fact, the basic principle of the belief—the idea that God
voluntarily limited Himself by the very fact of Creation—is defended by many leading Anglican and other theologians.[41]

To return to the question of the Atonement, the most developed
form of the "Suffering God" motif is that of *Divine Redemption,*
i.e., that it is God Himself that eternally makes atonement for
man's sin (while Jesus Christ reveals this fact to us). Man's sin, so
the theory runs, has always wounded, pained and grieved the
Heart of God, but He endures the pain, "bears" the sin, His
reaction is not one of punitive wrath, but of "suffering love," for
such is His nature. Sin is "God's greatest travail," for, by "bearing" it, He "transforms" it into grace or mercy, and thus "begets"
forgiveness—a process which Dr. Wheeler Robinson calls "spiritual alchemy."[42] The Cross of Christ manifests in time this eternal travail of God, reveals the fact that God Himself is bearing the
cost of Atonement, meeting it out of His own resources. "God
Himself suffering both in His Son and beyond the historical suffering of His Son, is the ultimate Redeemer"—so Dr. Wheeler Robinson sums up his theory.[43] The practical advantage of this theory,
according to Canon Storr, is that "by setting sin in relation to
God's heart of love and emphasizing the cost of divine forgiveness,
it brings out the true nature of sin in all its baseness and gravity."[44] Perfect "atonement" is thus made for sin; all that remains
for man to do is to let himself be moved by contemplation of so
touching a reality, turn to God in penitent love, and accept the
forgiveness which He offers. This theory, it is urged in conclusion,
has the advantage of showing the real relationship between the
work of Christ (revealing the eternal atonement of God) and the

forgiveness of all human sins, including those committed before the Savior came on earth, and those of the pagans who have never heard of Him.

Just how, we may well ask, do the human sufferings and feelings of Christ reveal the nature of God as a "suffering," nay, even an atoning" God? The fact is that the idea of a "passible God" is derived not so much from the Gospels, as from a series of what we might call *rationes convenientiae,* in the hypothesis that the essence of God is love,[45] and that the perfection of love is to be gauged by human standards. If God be truly love, they say, He must be capable of suffering and self-sacrifice, for "it is love's nature to suffer,"[46] in fact love can really prove itself only by suffering. God would be unspeakably "selfish" were He to remain unmoved by the manifold evils, spiritual and temporal, that afflict His children; He would not be a "Christ-like God."[47] If self-sacrifice be the highest form of attainment, how can we deny such experience to God?[48] After all, if God freely "limited" Himself by endowing man with free-will at the Creation—for man, by abuse of that free will, can "frustrate" His plans—He *must* suffer constantly from the rebellions of His rational creatures.[49] From this, furthermore, it is but a short step to conclude that, of His very nature, God *needs must* redeem fallen man. "The Atonement was necessary not merely in order that man might be truly man, but that God might be God. We dare to make the assertion that God could not but redeem mankind"—so writes the Congregationalist, R. Mackintosh.[50] The same necessity bore on the actual crucifixion of Jesus: "The Cross is the price God must pay to get to us in spite of our sins";[51] it is "not the price the devil demanded, not the price God demanded, but the price I demanded. For no less a price would have won me."[52]

Is this the picture of God that the Gospels paint for us, is this the nature of God as Jesus reveals Him to us? Undoubtedly the God of Jesus is a God of Love, a merciful Father who will welcome the truly penitent prodigal—but is this the complete picture? Is the God of Jesus distinct from Yahweh, God of the Old Testament, one, transcendent, unchanging and hence impassible, sovereign and mighty, whose purposes none may thwart, who is glorified as well in the punishment of the rebellious and evil-doer as in the blessings of the righteous and faithful? Assuredly, there is no such distinction; in fact this other side of the picture is stressed in

Our Lord's teaching, too, although, alas, it is frequently neglected, explained away, or even discarded as non-authentic, or at least as "tendentious" and "highly-colored," by many of the scholars whose views we are discussing. Let us recall briefly a few salient texts—the frequent references in the Sermon on the Mount and elsewhere to the stern judgment of God on the unrepentant sinner, and the punishment he must undergo till "the last farthing" is paid;[53] the parables of the Great Supper, the Unjust Steward and of Dives and Lazarus in St. Luke's Gospel, and of the Wheat and Cockle in St. Matthew's;[54] the rejection by God of His own Chosen People, and their dire chastisement for their unbelief, coupled with the stern and salutary teaching on the End of the World, the Last Judgment, eternal reward of the just and eternal punishment of the wicked in hell fire—teaching that occupies a prominent position in the last and most solemn discourses of Jesus before His Passion.[55] Is this the God whose power is "limited" by man's free will, whose purposes are "frustrated" by his sin? Is this the God who "pursues" the sinner with His "suffering love," no matter how often it be rejected, till his obstinacy be overcome? Is this the God whose very essence is "holy Father-love" for man, so that He *must* redeem him, *must* save him at whatever the cost—as if man were God's last end, instead of God being man's? The conduct of Jesus, they say, His reaction to man's sins, fully "reveals and exemplifies" the eternal nature and activity of God. If that be so, then let us bear in mind not only His mercy to the repentant sinner, but His prophetic "woes" against the unrepentant cities,[56] and against the Scribes and Pharisees who were obstinate in unbelief;[57] let us recall how He stigmatized the crimes of His own generation, especially the religious leaders—a "sinful, adulterous, unbelieving and perverse generation . . . generation of vipers" deserving the "judgment of hell";[58] finally, let us not forget how He drove the traders out of the Temple in His righteous anger and zeal.[59] If it must be "a Christ-like God or nothing," then let us bear these points in mind, too.

THE CROSS A SOURCE OR REVELATION OF "NEW SPIRITUAL ENERGIES"

So much for the Cross as revelation of God's nature as holy, suffering and sacrificial love, and as the supreme manifestation of the malice of sin. Yet, in order truly to repent, "we need something more besides knowledge and light, we need power"; so declares W. Fearon Halliday, and he goes on to say, "here all merely moral theories break down."[60] It is to meet this need that a number of writers have incorporated into their theories of the Atonement such new features as the following: through the Death of Christ, new spiritual energies, new creative and healing forces are released;[61] a new power for good, a new "dynamic" is generated[62] by means of which man is enabled both to repent, and afterwards, casting off the shackles of his old evil habits, to lead a new moral life. What exactly is meant by these statements? Is it a question of something really objective, something in the nature of grace or spiritual strength merited by Christ, which has existence and value apart from the reflections of the believer? I do not think so. It is simply a question, I think, of a peculiarly compelling or constraining kind of revelatory influence, viz., the manifestation of the inspiring, "irresistible" appeal of God's "sacrificial love" in the person and work of Jesus. In such wise, Dr. R. S. Franks speaks of the influence of Christ as "a mighty, constraining power over the minds, hearts and conscience of men," and of the power of the Cross, as "the power of the love that died," which "brought to a focus the whole energy of love," and which "concentrates the Divine love for sinners into one single burning point."[63] Similarly, Dr. C. E. Raven says of the "sin-bearing" love of Jesus: "the power of that appeal is irresistible to all normal persons."[64] These new features, then, add nothing worthy of special consideration to what has gone before.

THE CROSS AS REASSURANCE AND PLEDGE TO THE SINNER-CHRISTS' PSYCHOLOGICAL "SIN-BEARING"

There is still something further, we are told, that is needed to constitute perfect atonement: in the work of Christ, the sinner—discouraged as he is—must be able to discern some heartening assurance that God really has forgiven him, and that He will most certainly save him in the future both from sin and from the consequences of sin; some powerful pledge that the "hostile forces of evil" have been overcome and will be kept in check for the time to come. Such assurance some would find in the "suffering God" or "Eternal Cross" theories described above: viz., that the Cross is a revelation of God's love as forgiving and compassionate, a love that has borne the sin and condoned it, that has thus completely "overcome" it.[65] Others think to discern a more potent assurance of divine forgiveness and salvation in what may be described in general terms as the "sin-bearing" of Christ, that is, His entering completely into the sinner's "experience" in order to save him. This theory is found under many forms or degrees of development.

In its more general form, the theory runs somewhat as follows. Our greatest assurance of forgiveness and salvation lies in the fact that, during all His life, but especially at His Passion, Jesus freely "bore" the sins of men through sympathetic self-identification with the sinner; He entered into the sinner's experience (whilst remaining personally sinless), enduring the consequences of sin, particularly the sense of alienation from God, and patiently suffering the effects of men's sin, i.e., persecution by His enemies.[66] Like previous theories, this new hypothesis also aims at building up a real objective connection between the Death of Jesus and our salvation—a connection which the Presbyterian scholar, Dr. A. B. Macaulay, calls the "historical and experimental necessity" for the Passion of Christ, i.e., His Death was necessary, not simply that He might be true to His mission, but also that He might experience to the limit the sinner's lot. He explains himself thus:

> From a perfected personal experience of the enmity of the carnal mind to God, the bearer of divine forgiveness might hold out an offer of reconciliation and peace which would satisfy every awakened conscience and conquer every tortured heart despairing of mercy.[67]

The question of Christ's "sin-bearing" will be considered more fully presently; for the present, it may be noted that the authors we are dealing with do not think of this experience of Christ as "penal" in character (i.e. that Christ endures the divinely-apportioned punishment of our sins, as our substitute before God), so that their theories remain essentially "man-ward."

A more developed form of this general type of theory is that of the Methodist, W. R. Maltby, whose views are shared, to a large extent, by his co-religionist, Leslie D. Weatherhead. The redemptive virtue of the Death of Christ, he claims, is in the nature of a *pledge* to the whole human race, and to every individual member of it, of His dedication to the work of man's salvation. Having "burdened Himself with the whole situation which our sin has created," Jesus "dedicated Himself without reserve, in the face of all that sin could make of us, to the task of our recovery to God and to holiness."[68] Moreover, after the "strain" of a ministry of "sin-bearing," Jesus is "set free" by His Passion and Resurrection, to pursue His saving activity with unimpeded vigour.[69] The author claims a high degree of "objectivity" for his theory, though, personally, I cannot see in it anything but another form of the "man-ward" system: the redemptive work of Christ, characterized by His entering fully into the sinner's experience, possesses only revelatory or "inspiratory" efficacy; it moves us, not primarily to love and repentance, but to complete confidence in Christ's will and power to save us. The whole theory, like several of the preceding, fails to distinguish adequately the work of redemption and that of salvation, in fact they are bracketed together, for all practical purposes. Salvation, Maltby writes, "is not in His Death, nor in his Rising, but in Himself who died and rose again and abides with all who believe in Him."[70] Like the "Eternal Cross" theories, this theory, too, misrepresents God's dealings with the sinner—He is said to follow him ceaselessly with His love, knowing that his consent may be indefinitely withheld.

Another form of the "sin-bearing" theory is that which takes the Atonement as concerned, not primarily with sin, but with saving men from the consequences of sin, the natural consequences of their own sinful deeds. This is the theory of E. W. Johnson[71] and W. Fearon Halliday,[72] who work on the principle—accepted by many others too—that there exists, as it were, an autonomous moral order, with its inexorable system of "natural consequences," quite distinct from God and His Providence. Hence, we may not speak of divinely-inflicted or divinely-willed punishment for sin, or even of "punishment" at all, in the strict sense of the word—it is simply a case of the natural result of wrongdoing, the reaction of man's own constitution and of the world around him to his evil action, the harm done to his own health and moral character, the deepening of the evil habit and hence a growing separation from God. Thus, "sin is its own punishment."[73] By entering fully into the sinner's experience, by tasting to the full these "natural consequences" of wrong-doing, Christ is fitted to rescue sinful man from their clutches. Substantially the same, though more restricted in scope, is the theory of the Anglican, C. Ryder Smith, which might be called the *psychological* theory of the Atonement (though he himself prefers the term "societary")—by entering into the sinner's experience, by psychologically identifying Himself with him (remaining truly innocent Himself), Christ is able to save him from that degradation of character which is sin's inevitable outcome, and may, in fact, be called "sin."[74] Of this theory and the preceding, it may be said that they are more taken up with a process of salvation rather than with the value of the Death of Christ. How, exactly, one may ask furthermore, does Christ's sharing of the sinner's experience enable Him to rescue the guilty one from the consequences of his wrong doing? Once more, it is simply a case of a "revelatory" power, viz., the inspiring influence on the minds and hearts of men of what Christ endured for them on earth. Johnson writes:

When it (i.e. love) willingly bears the suffering of sin for love's sake, for the sake of the person loved and for the sake of the love of goodness (for holy love's sake) it has the greatest moral worth, and when understood, has power that nothing else has to move purify and redeem the hearts of men from the love and power of sin.[75]

Human analogies, such as the good influence of a sympathetic parent or friend on the wayward miscreant, are freely cited.

Yet another form of this "psychological" theory worked out along more technical lines, is that of F. H. Stead.[76] According to Stead, there are two determinative laws regulating human conduct, both individual and social—the "law of succession" and the "law of reciprocity." The "law of succession" concerns the deepening and strengthening of habits, whether good or bad, individual or social, by means of successive acts. When an evil social habit, under this law, becomes strongly entrenched, tremendous willpower is necessary on the part of him who wishes to react against it, and, by his inspiring leadership, to break its hold, its "spell" over others. The example of the first pioneers of total abstinence is quoted![77] The "law of reciprocity" concerns human conduct in "coexistence"; under the working of this law, the evil effects of the sins of the wicked in human society fall, not upon themselves primarily, but upon the just and innocent; however, the spectacle of the suffering of the innocent oftentimes has power to provoke a general change of heart and reaction for good, so that society is transformed.[78] Jesus, entering into the conditions of human existence, came firstly under the "law of succession"; He it was that, in His holy life and heroic death, gave the inspiring lead in opposing and breaking sinful social habits, bearing in the process the full shock or reaction of these ingrained evil tendencies and so, by His example and personal influence, He broke the "spell" and set men free to follow in His footsteps. Coming, in the second place, under the "law of reciprocity," Jesus, as the supremely just man, suffered exceedingly, even unto death, from the evil doings of the wicked; His sufferings provoke a general penitent reaction, which, like a new creative power, works a transformation in the moral character of society. Many criticisms might be made of this theory. It fails, in the first place, to assign any special significance or value to the Death of Jesus. Where, we might ask, did this "breaking of the spell" this transformation of society take effect in the case of the mass of the Jewish people to whom Our Lord's ministry was directed in the first instance? Any attempt, moreover, to bring Our Lord's life under the play of blind determinative laws lies open in still greater measure to the criticism of the hypothesis of purely "historical necessity" for His Death: it runs counter to the Gospel evidence of His complete freedom and mastery of events, coupled with His voluntary obedience to a personal decree of His Father's respecting His Passion and Death. Nowhere, as we pointed out above, is Our Lord's freedom and mastery over events seen in such strong light as during the last days of His mortal life, when neither the hatred of the Scribes and Pharisees and the snares they laid for Him, nor the machinations of the Sanhedrin and the Temple authorities, nor the treachery of Judas could harm Him, till He freely placed himself in the hands of His enemies in the Garden. Assuredly, Our Lord's life, and His Death even more so, was regulated, not by blind natural laws, but by the will of His Father, whose Providence, He taught, extended to the birds of the air, the lilies of the fields, even to the very hairs on man's head.[79] "Thy will be done, on earth as it is in heaven" "Not my will, but thine be done"—such was the law Our Lord freely submitted to; and when

He says that He *must* suffer and die, even so that the Scriptures may be fulfilled, that His Passion, Death and Resurrection are the "things of God," that He has "a Baptism wherewith He is to be baptized," that He has come "to give His life a ransom for many," that His Blood will be "shed for many unto the remission of sins,"[80] what has He in mind but the known will of His Father, for whose honour His life is consumed?

To conclude, in what way do the Gospels speak of Christ's "sin-bearing"? Do they tell us that He entered "psychologically" into the whole experience of the sinner, so that—by the resultant "moral influence" He might exercise over him—He might save him from sin and the consequences of sin? I do not think so.[81] If Christ "bore our sins," it was by way of a truly "God-ward" expiation, by the sacrifice of Calvary offered in satisfaction to His Father. Such, indeed, was the character of the "sin-bearing" of the prophesied "Servant" of Isaias 53,[82] with whom it seems reasonably clear that Jesus identified Himself;[83] such was the "sin-bearing" implied in the words, "The Son of Man is come . . . to give His life a ransom for many" and "This is my Blood of the Covenant, which shall be shed for many unto the remission of sin."[84] In such wise did Our Saviour meet and conquer sin, in such wise did He merit for men strength to overcome it and its evil consequences.

THE CROSS A REVELATION OF VICTORY OVER EVIL

It might seem that the tally of variations on the "man-ward" theme is complete—but there remains one more "deficiency" to be supplied, viz., that, so far, the various theories have been largely concerned with the needs of the individual sinner, and have not attached sufficient importance to the *cosmic* aspect of the Saviour's work, its power to overcome cosmic evil and re-create the moral universe. "It is not an individual salvation only that we need, but an assurance of God's victory over corporate evil," as one writer puts it.[85] In a word, Christ's atoning work must be a *victory*. This expression, applied to the Redemption, was very popular with the Fathers of the Church, and, even still, figures prominently in the liturgy. There is certainly an "objective" ring about it; yet I believe that, in its modern usage at all events, it represents but one more facet of the many-sided "man-ward" revelation inherent in the salvific work of Jesus. In recent years the idea is especially associated with the name of the Swedish scholar, now bishop of Strangnas, Gustav Aulén, whose work, *Christus Victor*, has been translated into English and has exercised no little influence on contemporary thought. "Christ—Christus Victor," he writes, "fights against and triumphs over the evil powers of the world, the tyrants under which mankind is in bondage and suffering, and in Him God reconciles the world to Himself."[86] This theory he calls the "classical" ("dramatic," "traditional") theory of the Atonement, as opposed to the "Latin" ("objective," "Anselmian") and "subjective" ("Abelardian") theories; he claims that it was the accepted teaching of the Church for the first thousand years of her existence, and was later revived by Luther.[87] Yet, in spite of the elaborate way in which the theory is developed, we cannot but agree with W. R. Maltby when he says it is but a "rhetorical explanation" of Christ's work.[88] Very little indication is given as to just how victory is achieved, or how salvation is linked up with it, or what exactly are the evil powers that are vanquished. There can be no question of any "God-ward" sacrifice on the part of Christ (this the author energetically rejects in connection with the "Latin" theory), in fact the whole Atonement is explained as a continuous divine movement towards man, a kind of triumphant revelation of Divine love, in Christ's overcoming evil.[89] "Victory," in fine, is but an idea, a theme—Aulén admits this, yet seems to belie the admission by instituting a full-scale comparison between his theory and the "Anselmian" and "Abelardian;"[90] as an idea, descriptive of an effect of Christ's atoning work simply, it has a certain role to fulfil. In actual fact, as the Gospels suggest, it was precisely because of the sacrifice offered by Christ to the Father "unto the remission of sins" that victory was achieved over the powers of evil (sin, death and Satan) and man was liberated, "ransomed" from their bondage.[91]

The "victory" theme has a part to play in several other modern theories. For instance, the Congregationalist, S. Cave, combining the theories of Aulén and of Dr. Franks,[92] and A. C. Headlam, former Anglican Bishop of Gloucester,[93] have both utilized this idea to portray the Death of Jesus as God's triumph over the forces of evil—the power of sin, to be precise—by the method of love, that is, of *non-resistance*. Calvary was "love in decisive and

victorious conflict," writes Dr. Cave;[94] it was "the decisive battle in
God's age-long conflict with human sin," declares W. E. Wilson,
the Quaker scholar, another keen protagonist of "non-resistance."[95] It was a grand assurance to man that Christ had, once and
for all, overcome the power of sin and evil; having persevered unto
death in exemplifying and embodying God's love for man in the
face of all that sin could do against him, He ultimately succeeded
in overcoming the sinner's obstinacy and winning him by love.
"Christ was victorious over evil on the Cross, because the only
power that can triumph over evil is love";[96] "love can overcome
only by non-resistance."[97] The victory-theme appears sometimes in
the "Eternal Cross" theories, in the shape of God's triumph over
evil through His suffering and transforming love—"a victorious
vitality transforming the evil thing into its own purposes," as E.
S. James puts it.[98] All these ideas, it is clear, add little fresh to what
has gone before.

However, there is one last development of the victory-theme
that calls for attention—the idea that Christ "broke the power of
evil and sin" by the *personal example* He has left us of how to
triumph in our own lives over the forces of evil by the power of
love.[99] This idea is sometimes expressed as follows. By His personal *resistance to temptation,* during His whole life, even to His
last breath, Jesus victoriously showed forth the love of God,
triumphing over a hitherto-undefeated sin, and thus bequeathing us
an inspiring example. This "victory over temptation," considered
as the greatest ordeal of Christ, more than the sufferings of His
Passion, is made central in the theories of the Presbyterian, A. B.
Macaulay,[100] and of many others.[101] It is the theory of a *Christus
salvus factus* becoming a *Christus salvum faciens,* as Dr. Bandas
put it.[102] Its basis is the very widespread rejection of the teaching on
the impeccability of Christ, and the representation of His whole
life as a real struggle against temptations "from the devil, the world
and the flesh,"[103] which He overcame "by faith and prayer,"[104]
just as you or I must do. For all this there is, I believe, no proof in
the Gospels. To take simply the two cases generally instanced, the
first, the initial "Temptation in the Wilderness"[105] certainly does not
read like an inward conflict between opposing ideals and attrac-
tions in the soul of Jesus; it seems to me to consist in a firm,
decisive and unhesitating rejection on three occasions of sugges-

tions of the Tempter coming from outside, the outcome being a resounding victory over the same diabolical Tempter. The other text sometimes adduced is to be found in St. Luke's narrative of the Last Supper: "You are they who have continued with me in my temptations."[106] Surely, the "temptations" (πειρασμοί) referred to here are the external persecutions, hardships and trials of the public ministry, for the disciples could scarcely be said to "abide with Him" (διαμεμενηκότες) in His inward conflicts of soul.

CONCLUSION: GENERAL RETROSPECT OF THE "MAN-WARD" THEORIES

Such are, within recent years, the main trends of interpretation of the Atonement within the general framework of what, for want of a better title, I have called the "man-ward" system. As I remarked at the start, there is no strict succession, no necessary cohesion or water-tight exclusiveness about these various "trends," though it is often possible to associate a particular author more immediately with one or other of them; e.g., we have the "experiential" theory of Dr. Franks, the so-called "clothes and peg" theory of A. T. Cadoux and others, the "non-resistance" theory of W. E. Wilson, the "divine redemption" theory of H. Wheeler Robinson, the "dynamic" theory of H. W. Clark, the "pledge" theory of W. R. Maltby, the "psychological" theories of C. Ryder Smith and F. H. Stead, the "victory" theory of G. Aulén, and so on. However, it is apparent that, to a certain extent, additions and modifications have been "forced on" the theory in its primitive form—and this has been largely due, as some of its exponents admit,[107] to the inadequacy and ineffectiveness of the system in practice, i.e., in actually leading souls to repentance and conversion of life. At the beginning, the Cross was simply a revelation of Divine love; at the end, it is a powerful demonstration and embodiment of holy, suffering, sin-bearing, sin-destroying, forgiving, compassionate, re-assuring and victorious love!

To examine the principles, religious and philosophical, upon which the "man-ward" system ultimately reposes, e.g., rejection of Original Sin, denial of the Divinity and Incarnation of Christ in the traditional sense, with all that this involves, erroneous concepts of sin, personality and even of the whole moral order, would carry us far beyond the scope of this essay. However, many of the more immediate arguments advanced in favor of "man-ward" Atonement have already been briefly examined in the course of the foregoing survey. One further argument of a more general character deserves mention here. It is that, during the whole of his public teaching (more especially during the "Galilean Ministry") Jesus preached a salvation from sin which required no other condition save true repentance on the part of the sinner. This teaching of "unconditional salvation" for the repentant sinner—intimately linked with the beautiful doctrine of the Fatherhood of God—was enshrined once and for all, they tell us, in the parable of the Prodigal Son. "Every separate point of doctrine," declares Dr. Franks, "even that of Our Lord's Passion and Death, must be developed in agreement with this fundamental truth."[108] In other words, the only possible atoning efficacy that can be attached to the Death of Christ is the power of an inspiring example, moving and encouraging the sinner to repent truly. Yet, is the question as simple as all that? Does emphasis on the necessity of repentance as a subjective condition of forgiveness and salvation exclude the existence and necessity of some divinely-ordained work of the objective order, that is (to avoid a debatable term), some "Godward" atoning act on the part of Christ, whereby that forgiveness and salvation is adequately merited? Certainly, the fact remains that not only does Jesus from the first imply that salvation is bound up with belief in His Person, but, during the last months of His life and chiefly to His faithful disciples, He declares roundly that "The Son of Man has come . . . to give His life a ransom for many" and, "This is my Blood of the Covenant, which shall be shed for many unto the remission of sins." When we interpret these texts in their true background—the times in which Jesus lived, the sacrificial system of the Old Law, and the great prophecies (especially that of Isaias 53)—and not in the light of certain modern psychological and religious ideas, it becomes clear that Jesus regarded His death as a God-ward sacrifice of atonement for the sins of men. "Let theologians make what they can of the death of Jesus," writes T. H. Robinson, the veteran Old Testament scholar, "the fact remains beyond dispute or doubt that Jesus died for many . . . to win the remission of their sins."[109] Another scholar, in the course of a doctorate dissertation on the Early Eucharist, declares: "The evidence that Jesus attached a sacrificial, redeeming, sin-remitting significance to His Death, and so expressed Himself at the Last Supper, seems beyond any reasonable doubt."[110] Moreover, the absence of clear reference to the sacrificial value of His Death in the public preaching of Jesus admits of a perfectly reasonable explanation, viz., that the minds of His Jewish audience were not prepared to receive such a doctrine. The idea of a "Suffering Messiah," one who would expiate sin (even the sins of the Gentiles!) by enduring an ignominious death, was abhorrent to the average Jewish mind;[111] so, like the wise Teacher He was, Jesus strove to prepare the minds of His hearers first, leading them gently and by degrees to higher things. He began by emphasizing the true spiritual nature of the Messianic Kingdom (about which, also, most of them had false notions), entrance to which required true repentance for the remission of sins; subsequently He meant to lead them on to faith in His Person. In actual fact, few, save Christ's immediate disciples, attained to that faith in Him which was needful for the hearing of the "mysteries of the Kingdom of God,"[112] among which the mystery of His redemptive Death occupied a prominent position. We must also remember the actual concrete circumstances of history under which Jesus met His Death—it would have been peculiarly difficult, if not impossible, to preach to the people of the atoning value of His Death to come, when, historically speaking, that Death would be the direct fruit of their unbelief and rejection of Him.

Let us turn now to some positive objections to the theory as a whole. In the first place, it is not really a theory of the Atonement at all—the Death of Jesus has no redemptive value in itself, as He said it had, it is simply an inspiring subject for meditation. Fundamentally, the Death of Jesus is simply a martyr's death, its religious value is essentially the same as that of the Christian martyrs of the early centuries[113]—an inspiring example of courage, love and virtue, when we reflect on it. Should it happen that no one ever reflected on it, the Death of Jesus would have no salutary value at all. The saving virtue attributed to it in the theories sketched above is, so to speak, projected back upon it by subsequent reflection and theorizing, with the aid of religious "experience" and a number of twentieth-century ideas and analogies. Perhaps the force of these objections will be recognized if the reader examines the Gospel narrative of the Passion, and tries to discover

for himself just what was the "moral influence" exercised by the
Death of Jesus on those who actually witnessed it, or who heard or
knew of it at the time. For the Ancients and the Scribes and
Pharisees, it was the occasion of revengeful gloating and of obstinate unbelief and hardening of heart—Jesus did not break the
social habits of his day, as the "psychologists" might lead us to
think. There were many more whom the spectacle left quite indifferent. Even the Centurion, and those who went away beating
their breasts, seem to have been influenced more by the miraculous
signs which followed the Death of Jesus, than by the Passion
itself.[114] The Good Thief stands out as the solitary exception. Yet
what of those who loved Jesus, those who must have known that
He was being put to death on account of fidelity to His God-given
mission, because of His putting into practice of that love and
meekness, that "non-resistance" in the face of evil which He had
preached to the people. The women of Jerusalem who wept over
Our Lord as He carried His Cross were inspired, not with repentance, but with sorrow, pity and regret on his account; He Himself
had to tell them, "weep for yourselves and for your children."[115]
The apostles and disciples were filled with sadness, disappointment,
despondency, the holy women with deepest sorrow on Jesus' account. How, then, can we maintain that Jesus hoped or expected,
purely by means of the spectacle of His sufferings, to move to
repentance and belief in Him those whom His life and preaching
had failed to conquer? Had He not, moreover, foretold the reprobation and chastisement of those who thus rejected Him and put
Him to death? Besides, as we suggested above, it was not Our
Lord's way to rely, with the buoyant optimism of certain modern
theorists, purely and simply on "holy love" to break down opposition to His teaching and lead men to repentance and faith. More
than once He had recourse to sterner measures—warnings of various kinds, threats of judgment and punishment, prophecies of
chastisement. Can it be, as some contemporary scholars prefer to
believe, that Jesus was not fully cognizant of the real redemptive
value of His sufferings? Could it be that it was God Himself who
afterwards "made use" of Christ's sufferings to stir men to repentance, in a way He (i.e., Jesus) did not foresee, at least in its
entirety.[116] May we not, then, distinguish the "will of Jesus" and the
"will of God" regarding the Crucifixion?[117] Surely, this is to escape

from the issue by abandoning the Gospels altogether, and journeying into the regions of pure hypothesis and unlimited speculation. Need we repeat that the Synoptic writers inform us that Jesus had most definite convictions regarding His Death, and leave never a suggestion that His mind on this subject was not completely one with that of His Father? Those oft-repeated and authoritative words, "I am come," spoken in connection with His mission,[118] imply full consciousness of what that mission involved; His many references to His sufferings and Death—the "things of God"—are couched in tones of complete assurance and absolute certainty.

My second general objection to the "man-ward" theories is that the Atonement they envisage cannot be said, by any manner or means, to be universal in scope and application, as the Synoptic evidence demands. Jesus' Death, in fine, was to be a ransom "for many," His Blood was to be shed "for many"—or better, for "the *multitude*" of sinners as contrasted with the individual innocent sufferer; such interpretation is borne out by the Hebrew background of the expression, and by its usage in the Servant prophecy of Isaias 53, which forms the true background for the interpreting of the thought of Our Lord.[119] Universality of Redemption is confirmed by the many earlier references to universality of salvation—universality of the Kingdom of God in the parables, world-wide preaching of the Gospel, the mission of the Apostles to teach all nations.[120] In the modern theories we have been considering, redemption is only for those who have heard the word of the Gospel; nay more, even then, it is principally, and in varying measure, for the benefit of the fortunate few who, besides the necessary leisure time, have minds sufficiently trained to follow the successive ramifications of the theory, and feelings and emotions sufficiently responsive to be suitably affected by the resultant "moral influence." As one Anglican missionary put it: "The Gospel as preached in the New Testament is simple and goes straight to the heart of the poor—modern re-interpretations of it are for the educated and the thinker only."[121] It is strange that a system which emphasizes to excess the love of God as Father should tolerate such manifest unfairness.

Thirdly, the man-ward system is seriously wanting in the provision of that assistance and strength, which, according to the mind of Jesus, the sinner requires in order to repent and lead a new life.[122] For, when there is no immediate and real connection between the Death of Jesus and the individual soul, where there is no belief in His Divinity in the full sense,[123] that much-vaunted mighty revelatory power, that "dynamic" and those spiritual forces which the Death of Jesus is supposed to generate, all become merely so many intellectual notions. If these notions demand no little "mental gymnastic," if I may say so, to decipher and understand, how can they supply the virtue and power necessary to bring about Christian repentance in the ordinary man?

The Passion and Death of Our Saviour, as the history of the Church shows, has always exercised a most powerful moral influence, and has had an unparalleled exemplary value in the lives of men—yet how illogical it is for those who profess a purely "manward" theory of the Atonement, and consequently deny that there was any real, independent virtue in that Passion and Death, to appeal to this historical fact in support of their contentions! The reason why men of good will have ever been deeply moved by the Passion of Christ is that they knew that—before ever they thought about it—the blood of Christ had there been shed as a real redemptive sacrifice to win the remission of their sins, and that He who suffered was the Son of God. Each faithful soul could exclaim, "He died for me—He died to expiate my sins!" "Walk in love," wrote St. Paul in the first century, "as Christ also hath loved us and hath delivered Himself for us, an oblation and a sacrifice to God for an odour of sweetness."[124] "In this have we known the charity of God," said the beloved disciple, "because He hath laid down His life for us."[125]

NOTES

1. *The Master Idea of St. Paul's Epistles, The Redemption* (Bruges, 1925), pp. 237–285.
2. *Modern Views on the Atonement*, no. VIII, pp. 237–285, in *The Atonement* (Cambridge Summer School, 1926), edited by C. Lattey, Cambridge, 1928.
3. See especially *Le Dogme de la Rédemption: étude théologique* (Paris, 1914), and Art. "Rédemption" in *Dict. Théol. Cath.*, XIII, col. 1912–2004, (Paris 1937). More recently, Fr. David O.F.M. Cap., "Vicarious Satisfaction and Reason," in *Irish Eccl. Rec.*, LXXIII (1950), pp. 116–128, 243–256, 331–343.
4. On the Atonement in the Synoptic Gospels, besides the works of Rivière,

see C. van Crombrugghe, *De Soteriologiae Christianae Primis Fontibus* (Louvain, 1905), and more recently, J. M. Vosté, *De Passione et Morte Christi* (Rome, 1937), pp. 331–368. Christ's allusions to the redemptive character of His Death—principally Mark 10:45 and 14:22–24—are brief, but will be found to be pregnant with meaning when considered in the light of the Old Testament prophecies and in the full context of His public ministry.

5. *The Historic Mission of Jesus* (London, 1943), p. 264.

6. *The Atonement* (Oxford, 1934—the Dale Lectures), p. 4.

7. This term is used in quite a different sense by the Anglican P. L. Snowden to denote Christ's enduring of the consequences of man's sin as an "experience" to qualify Him for his work as Saviour: *The Atonement and Ourselves* (London, 1919), p. 149.

8. These terms were suggested to me in part by the statement of the Quaker scholar W. E. Wilson, who wrote, "His death had a man-ward and sin-ward reference, but no God-ward reference." in *The Problem of the Cross* (London, 1929), p. 296.

9. "In Jesus the divine love takes concrete form for us" (R. S. Franks, op. cit., p. 164). It should be noted that, in these theories, the term *revelation* is not restricted to the manifestation of truth to the intellect, but applies also, and often principally, to the inspiring influence of example, which is frequently of an emotional character. In this sense, then, God is "fully revealed" only in personality, and "supremely revealed" in the personality of Jesus; it is in the latter sense, according to many, that Jesus is "divine."

10. Op. cit., p. 167.

11. *The Problem of the Cross* (2nd ed., London 1924), p. 103.

12. More noteworthy exponents during the period under review have been Dean Hastings Rashdall and Canon V. F. Storr, among the Anglicans; the Methodist, Principal H. Maldwyn Hughes; the Quaker scholars, Dr. E. Grubb and Dr. W. E. Wilson; the late Professor H. Wheeler Robinson, the noted Baptist scholar; and a large number of Congregationalists, e.g., Dr. R. S. Franks, and the brothers A. T. and C. J. Cadoux.

13. By this is meant, either that Christ offered Himself to the Father to be the means of revealing His love to men (cp. R. S. Franks, op. cit., pp. 172, 189), or that His death was a "piece of self-sacrifice" for others (cf. H. Rashdall: *The Idea of Atonement*, London 1919, pp. 37, 45), or that He offered His Father a "spiritual sacrifice" of perfect obedience or full dedication of will, with no value for man's salvation other than revelatory (cf. V. F. Storr, op. cit., p. 127).

14. *The Meaning of the Cross* (London, 1922), p. 154.

15. *Op. cit.*, p. 166.

16. *The Idea of Atonement in Christian Theology* (London, 1919—The Bampton Lectures for 1915), pp. 435–464.

17. E.g., R. Mackintosh, *Historic Theories of Atonement* (London, 1920), p. vi: ". . . very learned and very unsatisfactory." Cf. also W. E. Wilson, *op. cit.*, p. 27.

18. On pages 441 and 442, Rashdall does attempt to make out some case for what might be called the "historical necessity" for the Death of Jesus—it was "the direct and necessary consequence of faithfulness to His Messianic calling" (p. 441). At the most, this would argue some slight relation to the salvation of His fellow-countrymen, but not to that of men in general.

19. The expression derives from R. Mackintosh, op. cit., pp. 17–18.

20. W. E. Wilson, op. cit., p. 309.

21. E.g., those of W. F. Halliday, *Reconciliation and Reality* (London 1919), pp. 189–191, and A. T. Cadoux, *Essays in Christian Thinking* (London 1922), pp. 153–156.

22. Matt. 16:21; Mark 8:31; 9:12; Luke 17:25.

23. Cf. Luke 12:50; 13:32; 9:31 and 51; 22:37.

24. Luke 12:50.

25. Luke 18:31; 22:22 and 37; Mark 14:27–28.

26. Mark 8:33 (Matt. 16:23).

27. Mark 10:45 (Matt. 20:28).

28. W. F. Halliday, op. cit., pp. 185, 189–191; W. E. Wilson, op. cit., p. 296.

29. "Major trends which were not treated as sins, till Jesus showed into what they issued"—C. S. Herbert (Congregationalist), *The Drama of the Cross* (London, 1944), p. 20.

30. Cf. Matt. 15:14 and 16:24, and especially 23 (Denunciation of the Scribes and Pharisees) and 21:33–46 (Parable of the Wicked Husbandmen).

31. Matt. 25:25.

32. *Jesus and His Passion* (London, 1941), p. 108.

33. *The Good News* (Oxford 1945), p. 76: "Whether it be desirable to penetrate any further in to the designs of God," he adds, "must be a matter for the individual Christian."

34. *What is the Atonement?* (London, 1924), pp. 86–105. Principal Hughes also stresses the idea of God's "resisting sin" by His suffering love (pp. 93, 141, 147, 152).

35. *Op. cit.*, pp. 133–156.

36. *Op. cit.*, pp. 157–160; also *The Theology of Jesus* (London, 1940), pp. 294–298. Cadoux's favorite theme is that of the "frustration and defeat" of Divine love—it was only by enduring temporary "defeat" that Divine love could prove its sterling qualities to man: historically, this was realized through the Death of Jesus, which was an "unrepeatable experience . . . a unique opportunity for God to manifest His love for men." (*Essays*, p. 159).

37. Most fully developed in *Redemption and Revelation in the Actuality of History* (London, 1943), pp. 262–280.

38. Apart from the writers already quoted, I have found the belief accepted (to name but the more important) by the Anglicans Dr. Temple, Dean Rashdall and Dean Inge, Canon H. Maynard Smith and Canon B. H. Streeter; the Methodists, Professors A. McCrea and V. Taylor; the Presbyterians, G. H. Morrison and D. C. Mitchell; the Congregationalists, C. J. Cadoux and Dr. S. Cave; and the Quaker, E. Grubb.

39. W. H. Horton, *Contemporary English Theology: An American Interpretation* (London, 1940), p. 55.

40. "We recognize that this (i.e., belief in a Suffering God) carries with it a loftier conception of the Divine Majesty than that which would deny that suffering can enter at all into the experience of God . . . if He suffers, it is because He wills to suffer." *Doctrine in the Church of England* (London, 1938), p. 56.

41. E.g., Canon O. C. Quick, *The Gospel of the New World* (London, 1944), pp. 26–32; L. Hodgson: "The Incarnation," Essay VII in *Essays on the Trinity and Incarnation*, edited by A. E. J. Rawlinson, (London, 1928), pp. 377–8, 395–6.

42. "The Christian Gospel of Redemption," Essay VIII in *The Christian Faith*, inter-denominational essays, edited by Dean W. R. Matthews, (2nd ed., London, 1944), p. 136.

43. *Redemption and Revelation.* p. 276.

44. *Op. cit.*, 138.

45. According to Professor J. M. Shaw (Presbyterian), the one "absolute" attribute in God is "Holy Father-love"; all the rest—infinity, eternity, wisdom, justice, truth etc.—are "relative." See *The Fatherhood of God* (London, 1924), pp. 9–11.

46. V. F. Storr, *op. cit.*, p. 146.

47. "It is a Christ-like God, or nothing . . . In a world like this, God cannot refuse the cross and remain a God of love." See E. S. James, *Christ and Human Suffering* (London, 1933), pp. 188, 170.

48. "Why . . . rob God of the highest form of attainment which human life displays?" (H. Wheeler Robinson: *Redemption and Revelation*, p. 266).

49. "Self-limitation": writes Professor Wheeler Robinson, "is indeed the single and adequate answer to every form of objection to the passibility of God. . . . Sin is a partial or temporary defeat of the divine purpose." (*Redemption and Revelation*, pp. 265, 267).

50. *Op. cit.*, pp. 23–24; a statement repeated by many other writers.

51. E. S. James, op. cit., p. 183.

52. Professor H. H. Rowley, *The Relevance of the Bible* (London, 1941), p. 188.

53. Matt. 5:22, 25, 26, 29; 6:13–14, 19, 21–22, 27; 8:38; 10:15; 11:20–24; 12:36; 13:42; 23:13 ff.

54. Luke 14:15–24; 16:1–12 and 19–31; Matt. 13:24–30 and 36–43.

55. Matt. 21:28–46; 22:1–14; 23:29–39 and especially 24 (with parallels in Mark and Luke); Luke 12:6–9 (Parable of the Barren Fig-Tree).

56. Matt. 11:20–24.

57. Matt. 23.

58. Matt. 8:38; 16:4; 17:6; 23:33–36.

59. Mark 11:15–17 and parallels; cp. also Mark 3:5.

60. Op. cit., p. 168.

61. Cf. H. M. Hughes, op. cit., pp. 148, 152; H. Wheeler Robinson: *Redemption and Revelation*, p. 278.

62. H. W. Clark (Congregationalist), *The Cross and the Eternal Order* (London, 1943), *passim*.

63. *Op. cit.*, pp. 137, 168–9.

64. *The Cross and the Crisis* (London, 1940), p. 83.

65. "God wins our wills . . . by the love that bears and forgives." (E. Grubb: *op. cit.*, p. 154.)

66. Cf. J. M. Shaw, *op cit.*, pp. 110–111; W. E. Wilson: *op. cit.*, p. 37.

67. *The Death of Jesus in Three Aspects* (London, 1938), p. 146.

68. *Christ and His Cross* (London, 1936), pp. 96–97.

69. *Op. cit.*, pp. 80–90; 164–5. L. D. Weatherhead follows Maltby, while borrowing certain elements from the theory of V. Taylor, to be dealt with later: *A Plain Man Looks at the Cross* (London, 1945), pp. 116–7, 138–140.

70. Op. cit., p. 98.

71. *Suffering, Punishment and Atonement* (London, 1919), pp. 160–163. Jesus, standing for the "Law of the Ideal," saves man from the "Law of Sin, Suffering and Death."

72. *Reconciliation and Reality* (London, 1919), pp. 202–204.

73. E. Grubb, op. cit., p. 148. Many others uphold this "natural conse-quences" theory of moral retribution, even to the extent of stating that Christ's words on Eternal Retribution are but a figurative description of the "natural consequences" of men's actions.

74. *The Bible Doctrine of Salvation* (London, 1941), especially pp. 13–25

and 307–310. Man, C. Ryder Smith says, was made to live in "society" with God (hence the name *societary* theory of Atonement), but sin has marred this fellowship; God craves for its restoration, but the only way it may be restored is for the sinless Christ to enter into fellowship with sinful man, tasting his bitter experience to the full by self-identifying sympathy, and thus winning his heart and reconciling him with God.

75. Op. cit., p. 160.
76. *The Deed and Doom of Jesus* (Edinburgh, 1927).
77. Op. cit., pp. 9–33, 47–59.
78. Op. cit., pp. 61–66.
79. Matt. 6:26–30; 10:30.
80. Matt. 16:21; Mark 9:12; Luke 17:25 and 18:31; Matt. 16:23; Luke 12:50; Matt. 20:28 and 26:28.
81. Appeal is sometimes made to the experiences of Our Lord in the Garden and on the Cross as "sin-bearing" experiences; however, there is no suggestion of this in the Gospel narratives.
82. "He was wounded for our rebellions, he was bruised for our sins, upon him was the chastisement which made us whole, and by his stripes we were healed . . . though his own life be made a sin-offering, he shall see a seed that shall have length of days . . ." Is. 53:5, 10 (Mgr. Kissane's translation).
83. He explicitly alludes to Is. 53:12 as fulfilled in his Passion (Luke 22:37), and implicitly refers to the same prophecy in His predictions of his Death and Resurrection, e.g., Luke 18:31; Mark 14:21, and in the post-Resurrection sayings, Luke 24:24–27 and 44–47. The resemblances in character, life, word and deed between Jesus and the Servant are also very striking.
84. Matt. 20:28 and 26:28.
85. S. Cave, *The Doctrine of the Work of Christ* (London, 1937), p. 257.
86. *Christus Victor* (English trans., London, 1931), p. 20.
87. Op. cit., pp. 22–23, 118.
88. Op. cit., p. 147.
89. "The divine love prevails over the wrath, the blessing overcomes the curse by the way of divine self-oblation and sacrifice. The redemptive work of Christ shows how much the Atonement 'costs' God." (op. cit., p. 171).
90. Op. cit., pp. 160–176.
91. Victory over sin was realized by Christ's sacrifice "unto the remission of sins" (Matt. 26:28); His whole public ministry was a warfare against Satan, with His Death as the culminating-point, whereby man was ransomed from his bondage (cf. Matt. 20:28); death was conquered by His own Resurrection, which He had repeatedly foretold.
92. Op. cit., p. 267.
93. *The Atonement* (London, 1935), pp. 11–12, 185–186, 190. Like many others, Bishop Headlam looks upon the Death of Jesus as simply a *part* of his atoning work: "The Atonement, then, which reconciled men to God, was the whole life and work of Christ: His teaching, His revelation of the Kingdom, His founding of the Church." (p. 75).
94. Loc. cit.,
95. Op. cit., p. 313.
96. A. C. Headlam, op. cit., p. 190.
97. W. E. Wilson, op. cit., pp. 40, 309.
98. Op. cit., p. 82.

99. R. S. B. Sinclair (Anglican), *Victim Victorious* (London, 1940), p. 105.

100. Op. cit., pp. 136, 153, 157, 170, 177 ff. Dr. Macaulay's work also shows traces of the "vicarious confession" theory of J. McLeod Campbell, which will be dealt with later.

101. E.g., D. C. Mitchell (Presbyterian), *The Gospel of the Cross* (London, 1940), pp. 11–21; O. E. Burton, *The Conflict of the Cross* (London, 1939), pp. 110–113.

102. Op. cit., p. 146 (referring to the older theories of Holtzmann, J. Weiss, Du Bose and Morgan).

103. H. Maynard Smith, *The Atonement* (London, 1925), p. 81.

104. E. J. Bicknell (Anglican), *A Theological Introduction to the Thirty-Nine Articles* (new ed., revised by H. J. Carpenter, London, 1942), pp. 93–5.

105. Matt. 4:1–11; Luke 4:1–13.

106. Luke 22:28.

107. E.g., E. W. Johnson, op. cit., pp. 205–7.

108. "The Atonement" (Essay X in *Essays Congregational and Critical*, edited by A. Peel, London, 1931), p. 211.

109. *The Gospel of Matthew* (The Moffatt Commentaries, London, 1928), p. 217.

110. F. Cirlot, *The Early Eucharist* (London, 1939), pp. 154–5.

111. This fact, generally admitted by present-day scholars, may be proved by examination of the Jewish apocrypha and early rabbinical writings, and confirmed by the New Testament and the early Christian apologists.

112. Mark 4:11.

113. This is admitted by many of the exponents of the "man-ward" system; they are content to emphasize that there was a difference in *degree* between the value of Jesus' death and that of the martyrs—because of the Person of the Sufferer and of His life of love, or of the more universal appeal of His death, or because His sufferings revealed the Passion of God Himself.

114. Luke 23:47–48.

115. Luke 23:28.

116. Cf. C. J. Cadoux. op. cit., p. 264.

117. Thus A. B. Macaulay, in the fourth and fifth chapters of his work, treats of the "Will of Jesus concerning His Death" (pp. 89–148), and, in the sixth, of the "Will of God" (pp. 149–178).

118. E.g., Luke 5:32; Mark 1:38; Luke 12:49 and 19:10; Matt. 20:28.

119. In this prophecy the "many" represents the whole body of sinful men, in contrast with the individual innocent Servant, who expiates their sins; cf. v. 6, "We all like sheep had gone astray . . . and Yahweh made to light upon him the iniquities of us all."

120. The question of the universality of the "Kingdom of God" is dealt with in the doctorate dissertation of W. R. Galus: *The Universality of the Kingdom of God in the Gospels and the Acts of the Apostles* (Washington, 1945). The rejection of the Jews and the preaching of the gospel to the Gentiles is made explicit in Matt. 8:11; 10:18; 21:43 and 24:14; the command to "preach to all nations" is found in Matt. 28: 18–20; cp. Mark 16:15–18 and Luke 24:46–49.

121. H. E. Guillebaud, *Why the Cross* p. 180, (London, 1937).

122. The sinner is the "sick man," and Jesus the Physician who has come to heal him (Matt. 9:12); he is the lost "sheep," whom the Son of Man has come to "seek and save" (Matt. 18:12 ff. 10:6 and 15:24; Luke 19:10).

123. For the most part, the authors so far considered believe that Jesus was "divine" in a *revelatory* sense, i.e., that in His (human) Person, God was fully revealed, embodied and expressed, so that "in Him we meet God," and He has for us the "value of God." The remark of the Congregationalist, Dr. Nathaniel Micklem, is very apposite: "According to our conception or experience of Redemption, then, must be our doctrine of the divinity of Christ."—"A Modern Approach to Christology," p. 153 (Essay VII, in *Mysterium Christi*, Christological Essays by British and German theologians, edited by G. K. A. Bell and A. Deissmann, London, 1930).

124. Eph. 5:2.

125. 1 John 3:16.

14 *The Theology of Mysteries* *

CLEMENT TIERNEY

In his outline of the theology of Dom Odo Casel, Father Tierney states that Casel's contribution lies in having stimulated a train of thought and inquiry which bears promise of deepening and enriching both sacramental theology and the Christian life.

THE COMPARATIVE STUDY of religion has brought to light a common basic pattern among the pagan mystery cults. Each of them is a ritual presentation of the death and resurrection of a god. The followers of the god take part in a religious rite which associates them with the saving act of the deity. This is the process by which they themselves are saved. They are now considered as born again to a new divine life, the life of the god who triumphed over death.

According to Casel the pagan mystery religions cannot explain the origins of the Christian mystery or liturgical cult. But they were a providential preparation of humanity for the divine work of salvation. They show how the Christian mystery corresponds to the desires and needs of the human heart.

THE CHRISTIAN MYSTERY

The Christian life is not simply a matter of believing in Christ and receiving His grace into our souls. To be a Christian in the fullest sense demands a real participation in the saving acts of Christ. The Christian must come into contact with them and live by them. He must associate himself with Christ's mysteries.

We can distinguish three phases of the Christian mystery. In the first place is God Himself. He is infinite, inaccessible, all holy. But the word "mystery" implies equally a second notion, that of a

* *The Australasian Catholic Record,* 35 (1958) 15–22, 118–25, 276–86.

revelation. This mystery—the second phase—is realized in history by Christ, God Incarnate. The entire life of Christ is a progressive revelation of the mystery of God. Because of sin, however, the mystery of Christ is a mystery of redemption, a revelation of the saving act of God. The third phase is the cult mystery, or the liturgical mystery, which is an extension and application of the mystery of Christ.

The Son of God became man and savior for the sake of sinners. That is why He did not appear in a glorious body but in the flesh of sin, so that the sins of men might die in His own flesh. After the Resurrection His body is no longer the flesh of sin, but His entire humanity is transfigured by the divine glory. In the language of St. Paul, the Son of Man has become the *Kyrios Pneumatikos,* transfigured and exalted in glory.

Now this itinerary of salvation we too must follow. Since it is by His passion that Christ has entered into His glory, we in turn must live that passion mystically with Christ. We must pass through His passion to enter into His Resurrection. This is accomplished in baptism. The baptized Christian is no longer simply a man, but a man transformed and divinized. Thus salvation is attained by a real but mystical sharing in Christ's death and Resurrection.

The essential point is that we cannot really share in the saving acts of Christ's life unless these acts are objectively present and accessible to us here and now. Hence the theology of mysteries professes that the saving acts of Christ are present in the sacraments of the Church. The acts of salvation, which took place in Palestine under the veil of historical accidents, are made present in the sacraments under the veil of signs. As Leo the Great declared: "What was visible in our Redeemer has now passed into the sacraments." And St. Ambrose addresses these words to Christ: "It is in Your mysteries that I find You." The liturgical mysteries are simply the sacramental mode of Christ and His work of redemption. The difference between the mystery of Christ and the cult-mystery lies in their mode of existence, not in their essence.

THE SACRAMENTS IN GENERAL

God, Christ, the Church—the three phases of the Christian mystery—are intimately related. God, invisible by His nature, acts visibly in Christ for the salvation of men. He makes this activity present in the Church by means of the sacraments. The members of the Church are thus brought into contact with the saving actions of Christ so that they might draw life from them.

The sacramental sign is an efficacious sign, always involving the real presence of the reality which it reveals. This is the original sense of the axiom that the sacraments effect what they signify. Since the external rite of the sacrament manifests the work of our redemption, it must contain the work of redemption. To consider that the sacrament contains nothing more than the ultimate effect of sanctification, i.e., grace, is to limit both the significance and content of the sacraments. It is a concept introduced into theology by the late scholastics and at variance with the patristic notion.

Casel reproaches modern theology for limiting the real presence of Christ to the one sacrament of the Eucharist. The glorified Christ is really present in all the sacraments because Christ is acting in them. Moreover, the sacraments never confer grace independently of the presence of Christ.

The central element of Casel's theology, then, insists on the objective and real presence of Christ's saving acts in the liturgical mysteries. For other theologians the sacraments are *commemorative* signs of Christ's passion but not efficacious signs. With the exception of the Eucharist, the sacraments contain the power of Christ's passion; but the passion itself is not objectively present. For Casel the Eucharist is the key to the entire sacramental system. The real presence of Christ's body and blood demands the real and objective presence of Christ's passion. But what is true of the Eucharist must be verified, in an analogous manner, in all the sacraments. Otherwise the Eucharist is removed from the sacramental system and becomes an isolated reality.

This does not mean that there is no difference between one sacrament and the other. The death of Christ is present in baptism not as an objective sacrificial act, accomplished for and by the Christian community through the medium of her priests, but as a saving act, no less objective, but applied to the individual. Thus the passion of Christ is objectively present in every sacrament; but the formal aspect under which it is present, and even the degree of objectivity itself, may differ from sacrament to sacrament.

The saving acts of Christ are present in the sacraments for the sanctification of men. Grace is certainly communicated by the sacraments but only as the fruit of the saving act which is present. The sacrament does not contain grace abstracted and isolated from the redemption which is its source. It contains the very saving acts from which the grace emanates.

THE EUCHARISTIC MYSTERY

The Eucharistic mystery implies far more than the real presence. The body of Christ is present, but it is the body given and immolated in sacrifice. In the Eucharist the saving act of Christ's passion is both signified and made present, for the sacraments effect what they signify. The Mass, then, is a sacrifice because it signifies and makes present the sacrificial act of Christ on the cross. The Eucharist is the sacrifice of the cross made present in a sacrament, in a mystery. This is the thought of St. Cyprian and St. Gregory.

This re-presentation of Calvary which takes place in the Mass is understood by Odo Casel as a making present of the redemptive sacrifice in all its fullness as a saving act. Not only is the passion of Christ really present but also the love, the obedience, the devotion which animated and informed the sufferings of our Savior. According to Casel the exact statement of his own thought is best expressed in the words of the encyclical *Mediator Dei,* which states that the Mass is an act of sacrifice in which Christ does what He did on the Cross.

The Eucharist viewed as a mystery could never enter into conflict with the Cross as a second sacrifice of redemption. The redemptive sacrifice which took place on Calvary under the veil of historical accidents is made present in the Eucharist under the veil of signs. There is a perfect numerical identity between the two. The Eucharist is a real sacrifice; but the Cross retains its place as the unique sacrifice. The Mass is essentially a relative sacrifice. It is the real, objective commemoration of the sacrifice of the Cross. It is essentially a sacrifice insofar as it is a memorial.

All Catholic theologians admit that the Mass and the Cross have the same priest and the same victim, that the Mass represents and applies the sacrifice of the Cross. Very many theologians would maintain that the Mass is a sacrifice insofar as it is a sacramental representation of the sacrifice of the Cross. But Casel's doctrine is quite distinctive. In the Mass the saving *event* itself of Christ's passion is made present. The historical act of Calvary is realized in a mystery.

Casel believes that this is the traditional doctrine found in the primitive liturgical texts and in the patristic writings. The fathers of the Church consider the Eucharist as the *image* of the sacrifice of the Cross. For them the image is not a pure symbol. Rather it is the sensible appearance of a hidden reality. Hence, when the Fathers designate the Eucharist as the *image* of Christ's passion, they profess that the passion of Christ is objectively and really present under the sacred species. This idea prevailed till the ninth century. From then on it became more and more obscured owing to the Eucharistic heresies concerning the real presence.

THE MASS AND REDEMPTION

So far, the Mass has been considered as a re-presentation of the sacrifice of the Cross. But for Dom Casel the Mass involves a real objective presence of the entire work of redemption. This means that the Incarnation, the passion and death, the Resurrection and Ascension, all the saving acts performed by Christ, are really present again in the Eucharistic celebration. The Mass is necessarily a universal re-presentation of the entire work of redemption since the mystery of salvation is one indivisible whole. Each one of the individual mysteries of Christ is, in its own way, the cause of our salvation. In the Eucharist the Incarnation is present as the first condition of sacrifice; the passion of Christ as the central act; the Resurrection and Ascension as the acts by which the Father accepts the sacrifice; the parousia, the second glorious coming of the Son of God, as the final term of redemption. This view according to Casel is demanded by the prayer *Unde et memores* in the Mass.

Thus the life of Christ is conceived as a gigantic itinerary of salvation which goes from the womb of the Virgin to the throne of the divine Majesty, from the first coming to the second coming. While the Church lives in the joyful expectancy of the parousia, she celebrates the Christian mysteries through her liturgical cult. The Eucharist is, then, the sacred action which commemorates the great economy of salvation and makes it present for all generations until the end of the world.

PHILOSOPHICAL DIFFICULTIES

The theologian is faced with the task of illustrating the mystery-presence, essentially a mystery of faith, and demonstrating its nonrepugnance. This is all the more necessary because the metaphysics of time and place would seem to exclude all possibility of the past event of Christ's passion being really present in the Eucharist. However, many of these difficulties are stillborn if we remember that the mystery-presence is a sacramental presence.

The sacramental order is a supernatural order which lies midway between the symbolic representation of an event and its historical enactment. The mystery of Christ in its historical and physical reality is realized among us in the symbol. However, these symbols are not mere exterior and empty signs. Rather they contain and communicate to us the full reality of the new life which Christ our Mediator offers us. This special kind of participation in the life of Christ was called "mystical" participation by the early Christians. The very existence of such an order and the laws which govern it cannot be deduced from human reason. Although we can hardly find words to express such a mode of existence, our reason, guided by faith, can know that it is possible to God.

Sacramental presence means real presence, but reality of an altogether special kind, demanded by the very purpose of the sacrament which permits the faithful to participate in the life of Christ as Redeemer of their souls. For this purpose the historical accidents which accompanied the redemptive work have no importance. The only thing which counts is the act of Christ, the very quintessence of redemption. The passion of Christ is present in the Mass after the manner of a substance without temporal succession. The general tendency of this explanation is to illustrate the real presence of Christ's redemptive work in the Eucharist by analogy with the real presence of Christ's body and blood. Just as the body of Christ is sacramentally present beneath the sacred species, so the passion of Christ is sacramentally present beneath the same species.

FOUR BASIC PRINCIPLES

On the basis of this analogy some principles can be formulated to illustrate and clarify the presence of Christ's passion in the Eucharistic mystery:

1. The sacramental presence of Christ's passion in the Eucharist excludes a repetition or a renewal of the passion of Christ. The fact that Christ is now glorified and cannot die again does not constitute a difficulty if we keep in mind the sacramental perspective.

By transubstantiation the sacred species contain the body and blood of Christ. Yet the body itself of Christ is never multiplied or reduplicated. The body of Christ present in the Eucharist is the body of Christ present in heaven. Similarly, the consecrated species contain the passion of Christ. But the passion of Christ is never multiplied or repeated. Consequently it is not true to say that Christ suffers or dies again. The Eucharistic celebration is not to be envisioned in terms of a passion play.

BEYOND SPACE AND TIME

2. The sacramental presence of Christ's passion is a super-spatial mode of presence. One of the fundamental difficulties against the presence of Christ's passion in the Eucharist is founded on the limitation of place. Historical events are enacted in a particular place and cannot be transferred from one locale to another. However, the sacramental existence completely transcends the category of place. The body of Christ is locally present in heaven. The same identical body is present in the Eucharist, but it does not acquire any local presence. This is due to the fact that the body of Christ is not related to the sacred species by reason of its own quantity. Similarly, the identical saving act which took place on Calvary is contained beneath the sacred species. But it does not acquire a new localization, nor is it subject to the law of space. Hence the problem of multilocation does not exist.

3. The sacramental presence of Christ's passion is a supra-temporal mode of presence. An historical event, however, is enclosed within the barriers of time. The passion of Christ took place at a definite hour of a given month in a particular year. How can

the same historical event be made present at every hour of the day by the Eucharistic sacrifice? Moreover, if the entire redemptive work of Christ is really present, how can the thirty-three years of Christ's life be compressed into the short interval of the Mass?

Casel gives to the problem of time the same answer he gives to the problem of place. The sacramental presence transcends the order of time. Just as the sacred species alone are present in a place, so the *sacred rite alone* is enacted in the order of time. The *contents* of that sacred rite, the saving act of Christ's passion, completely exceeds the order of place and time.

The historical saving act of Christ's life is endowed with an eternal permanence by which it transcends the limits of time. Christ's redemptive work performed within the geographic confines of Palestine and within the time limit of thirty-three years is a mystery. It is the first mystery, the saving act of God manifested in history and time. Nevertheless the mystery is above history and time. The mystery shows us the great redemptive plan which is hidden in God from all eternity, which is revealed in time, and which finally returns to God. As man Christ is the way; as God He is the term. Thus the historical event reveals itself as the execution of the divine thought. Once it is realized in time, it becomes again *eternity*. When the liturgical year celebrates the succession of historical actions, it does not attach itself to them as such but to the eternal content which they express and conceal.

SACRAMENTAL MODE

4. The sacramental presence of Christ's passion is a substantial mode of presence. In the Mass the passion of Christ is present after the manner of a substance. The accompanying historical circumstances are not made present in the sacrament. These do not contribute to the salvation of mankind. For the purpose of the sacrament one act alone is important, the saving act of Christ. In the Eucharist, therefore, the passion of Christ is made present according to the manner of a substance without the historical accidents.

Casel believes that the conceptual difficulties which are brought against the theology of the Christian mystery are no greater than those brought against the real presence. The theological principles which illustrate the real presence can be extended to the presence of Christ's passion in the Eucharist. Every objection stems from a failure to distinguish between the natural mode of existence and the sacramental mode. The metaphysics of time and place have nothing to do with the sacrament.

15 *Ritual and Grace in the Sacraments** *

PIETER SMULDERS

Catholic theology is forever trying to explain how pouring water and saying a few words or anointing with oil is a certain sign that God is pouring grace into a human soul. To this age-old problem, Father Smulders proposes an answer inspired by the Church fathers. He suggests that the rite and the grace of a sacrament are linked together by the sacrifice of Christ, celebrated in the Church.

T HERE IS NO contradition in saying that the Church is both a juridical society and a Mystical Body. But few have attempted to explain just what the relationship is between these two aspects of the Church. When a Christian enters marriage, for instance, he becomes subject to the numerous laws that regulate it; yet essentially marriage is the receiving of a special grace, and getting married is a special way of worshiping God. Just how are these legal, spiritual, and liturgical aspects interwoven in the one act?

Before we can understand the Church, we have to understand how the sacraments operate. Since the sacraments are easier to understand, let us start with them and come to a knowledge of what the Church is.

The sacraments are first of all instrumental efficient causes of grace. This means that the principal cause, God, unites his action to that of these instruments to cause grace. But the action of the two causes is really but one action, and so only one effect results. Each cause produces the entire effect, and the influence of both causes is seen in the effect. Secondly, the sacraments are signs, and they cause what they signify.

In the Church, there are three levels of being and action, but they have an internal unity. The Church is a juridical society, a worshiping society, a society of grace. At the lowest (juridical)

* "Sacramenten en Kerk," *Bijdragen*, 17 (1956), 391–418.

level, the activity of man seems paramount; at the next level, it is the activity of Christ the High Priest; and at the highest level, the activity of the Holy Spirit. The same three levels of action can be seen in a sacrament. The lowest level is that of the rite performed by men; the next (intermediate) level is that of the sacramental character; the highest level is that of the sacramental grace. Perhaps an outline will make the pattern clearer:

Activity of	In sacraments	In the Church
Holy Spirit	Grace	Grace
Christ	Character	Liturgical
Men	Rite	Juridical

The relationship among these different levels is always that of instrumental efficient causes to principal cause and of signs to the signified. That which is juridical (the rite) is the sign and the instrument of what is liturgical (the sacerdotal action of Christ). That which is liturgical is the sign and the instrument of what is spiritual (the sanctifying action of the Holy Spirit). In other words, the action of the Spirit externalizes itself in the sacerdotal action of Christ, and the action of Christ externalizes itself in the juridical action of the Church. We shall now analyze these three elements of a sacrament, remembering, however, that they form a unified whole.

We begin with the juridical level, the level of canon law. This is the lowest, the human level, in which the sacraments have far-reaching social effects. Their general effect is to bind the community together, even outwardly, so as to make it an organized society with members of different degrees performing different tasks.

On this juridical level, the sacraments have many specific effects, as is clear from canon law. "Baptism makes a man a member of the Church with all the rights and duties of a Christian" (canon 87). The juridical effects of the other sacraments have lost much of their importance, but some effects do remain. Confirmation is a prerequisite for matrimony and holy orders. After extreme unction, a sick person is no longer bound by the Eucharistic fast, which indicates that he has acquired a new relationship to the juridical Church. The Eucharist, a sign of visible union with the Church, is denied to anyone in heresy or under censure. The sacraments, in fact, affect the public order of this visible society to such an extent that it is correct to say that all ecclesiastical law is based ultimately on the sacraments.

TO WORSHIP GOD

But the visible juridical effects of a sacrament are but one element in a more sublime structure. The real purpose of the Church as a visible society is to worship God, to give glory to God on earth. This was also the purpose of Christ, who said, "I have exalted thy glory on earth, by achieving the task which thou gavest me to do" (John 17:4).

We glorify God by recognizing him as the goal of our whole existence and by expressing this interior devotion by visible, social acts. Christ did this by his continuous obedience to the Father, especially by his death. The entire human family must do this in order to fulfill its destiny, and it is the Church's task to make this ideal a reality.

Law is concerned with men's relations to one another; worship concerns their relation to God. But this relation to God is necessarily social; it permeates the relations between men. In other words, we cannot separate the liturgical activity of worship from juridical activities. The sacraments are juridical acts; but they are at the same time acts of worship because they are a public profession of faith, hope, and love. More concretely, they are acts of worship because they are an application to us of the sacrifice of Christ, the most perfect act of worship. In receiving the sacraments, we are united to Christ in his death and resurrection and this is the essence of worship.

ALL PARTICIPATE IN SACRIFICE

Each of the sacraments is a unique way of participating in the sacrifice of Christ. Penance and the Eucharist are *acts of worship,* while the other five sacraments are a *consecration of worship.* The Eucharist is Christ's sacrifice become the sacrifice of the Church; in communion, we receive the lamb that has been sacrificed. Penance is also an act of worship because it is an application to the penitent of Christ's sacrifice. Jesus carried the sins of the world before the tribunal of the Father, who condemned sin itself and forgave sin in us. In confession, we carry our own sins to the same tribunal where the condemnation of sin is its extinction. The action of the Church makes the Cross present again.

The other five sacraments are con-secratory; they "set something aside for a holy purpose." Consecration, in this sense, really means nearly the same thing as sacrifice, for to sacrifice is also "to make holy." Sacrifice externalizes our whole relation to God, for a victim is separated from the world and passes to God. Similarly, to consecrate something is to detach it from the profane world and set it aside for God. The difference between the two is that a sacrifice externalizes the totality of our belonging to God, while a consecration merely expresses our belonging.

The five sacraments we are now discussing consecrate us because they mark us off for the worship of God. They enable us to participate in Christ's sacrifice by conferring a sacerdotal power on us. Baptism enables us to take part in this sacrifice because only the baptized can offer the Victim and receive the Victim in Communion. The other four—holy orders, confirmation, matrimony, and the last anointing—also consecrate us because they enable us to take part in Christ's sacrifice in some particular way.

Holy orders enable the priest to participate in the sacrifice as actual minister with power to consecrate and to offer the sacrifice on behalf of the people. Confirmation enables us to take part in the sacrifice as public witnesses of the faith. These two sacraments, like baptism, bestow a permanent character. This character is the stamp of Christ. In this way he designates different men for different roles in offering his sacrifice.

Matrimony and the last anointing do not give a character, but they do impose a relatively permanent state of life. The sick man, once anointed, is in a consecrated state. He submissively endures his illness and death together with Christ, having been publicly consecrated to this by the Church. The anointing prepares him to enter the kingdom of heaven, to attain by death his final union with Christ, to achieve the final and complete victory over sin.

Matrimony is also a consecration. It puts man and wife in a new state of life in the visible Church, for it gives them the privilege of bringing new life into the Church and of forming their children in Christian perfection. When they give themselves to each other in perpetual fidelity and with complete devotion, they thereby express their faith and devotion to God, as is done by sacrifice. Hence they take part in Christ's sacrifice in their own unique way; their faithfulness to each other is a sign of their faithfulness to God.

All the sacraments, therefore, are linked with worship. The Eucharist is Christ's sacrifice become our own. Penance brings the fruits of Christ's sacrifice to us. The other five consecrate us to divine worship and so accomplish in us Christ's sacrifice in some particular way.

The juridical acts, therefore, by which the Church confers the sacraments are the external signs of her public worship. When she worships through the sacraments, she acts as the instrument of Christ, because she cannot worship except in union with Christ, the eternal High Priest. Men cannot return to the Father except through Christ the mediator. The power to offer the sacrifice that we receive in the sacraments is therefore a participation in Christ's priesthood.

FROM GOD TO MAN

In showing that we are worshiping God when we receive a sacrament, we run into some danger of confusion. We have to insist that a sacrament is primarily an efficacious sign of grace, that its movement proceeds from God to man, not from man to God. The act of worship is not primarily an act of the recipient, but of Christ and the Church *in the recipient*. We may say, however, that we receive actively; what we receive is actually a motion toward God. The Church in the sacraments signifies to us her faith, hope, and love; and we participate by professing these virtues in the very act of receiving. The sacrament as an act of worship is actually a sign and instrument of the grace we receive.

When God re-creates us by communicating Himself to us, we call this gift grace. We know the sacraments confer the grace which they signify. But as acts of worship, the sacraments are acts of Christ and of the Church directed toward God. How, then, can they simultaneously be acts of God giving grace to men? St. Thomas asserts: "The sacraments of the Church are ordered to two things: to perfecting man in what pertains to divine worship according to the Christian religion and as a remedy against sin" (*Sum. Theol.*, III, q. 65, a. 1). Hence a sacrament achieves two purposes: God is worshiped and men are sanctified. We now must discover the intrinsic unity of these two purposes, worship and grace.

The sacraments are constituted as acts of worship by the sacramental character. Our problem is, therefore, to see how the character is related to the grace. Some theologians have said that the character causes the grace or is a condition of its being granted. But such solutions are unsatisfactory because they create a false cleavage between the character and grace. The solution must show the character as an instrumental sign by which the Holy Trinity gives grace to men. We can state our position briefly in a syllogism:

When we receive a sacrament, God gives us the power to perform Christian worship. *But* this power to perform Christian worship is of itself a sign of the life of grace. *Therefore* a sacrament, being a sign by which we are united to Christ in his priesthood, is an instrument by which God communicates grace to us, and therefore a sign that we are receiving grace.

Just as the rite is a sign of our incorporation into the sacrifice, so our incorporation into the sacrifice is a sign of our receiving grace. Conversely, God uses Christ's sacrifice as an instrumental cause of grace, and Christ uses the rite as an instrumental cause to unite all of us to his sacrifice.

SIGN OF SALVIFIC WILL

Man is unable to offer an acceptable worship to God until God enables him to do so. When the Word became incarnate and, as a man, offered sacrifice, he enabled other men to offer sacrifice by uniting themselves to him. The existence of the High Priest is an externalization or revelation of grace being given by the Father. The Father wanted to be served and worshiped; and to make this possible he created the High Priest, the man Jesus. The worship thus made possible is, therefore, a profession of devotion on the part of men and of Christ; but it is also a sign of the salvific will of the Father.

The fact that our worship is in itself a sign of God's grace can also be seen from the fact that we are the new Chosen People. "You are a chosen race, a royal priesthood, a consecrated nation, a people God means to have for himself" (1 Pet. 2:9). God himself separated from the rest of men the society of his Church, this visible society of public worship. To be a member of it is, therefore, a sign that one has been called by God to exercise the divine worship. The very existence of the Church as the society of divine worship is a visible revelation of God's plan to save men. Juridical reception into the Church, which is a sign and an instrument of reception into the priesthood of Christ, is an instrument by which God bestows grace on this individual and a sign that he is doing so.

The worship to which we are called is an external, social act of religion, an external sign of our internal devotion. And our internal devotion consists primarily in our faith, hope, and love, the virtues by which we live our relationship to God. These are the interior sources of our worship, and they are infused into us by God. Our worship, therefore, which is on the surface a sign of our devotion to God, is a sign that God's grace is given to us.

It may help to look at this worship from a different angle, as a manifestation of obedience. The human obedience of Jesus was the manifestation in human nature of the divine "obedience" of the Word to the Father. It was because Christ was both divine and human that he was the High Priest whose sacrificial offering was accepted. Our worship is a sign that we also are sons of the Father because we have put on Christ.

Hence, in order that we may worship properly, Christ made man must be formed in us—the Father must generate his Son in us out of the same love with which he caused his Son to be born of the Virgin Mary. This love is the trinitarian love of the Father and the Son; it is the Holy Spirit. The Spirit, as proceeding from the Father, forms the Son in us; and the same Spirit, as proceeding from the Son, is our love of the Father.

CHURCH, CHRIST, HOLY SPIRIT

This filial devotion Christ manifested in his sacrifice; we manifest it, with and in Christ, by our Christian worship. This worship is a gift from the Father. As such, it is a sign of grace, of the Holy Spirit, in us. By baptism, for instance, a person becomes: juridically, a member of the Church; liturgically, a participant in Christ's priesthood; spiritually, a temple of the Holy Spirit by grace. This analysis makes it easy to see that the sacrament is a consecration. When Christ and the Church bestow on us this sign of membership in the Church and of participation in the royal priesthood, the same sign is an instrument in God's hand by which he sanctifies us.

In our attempt to see how the character is related to the grace of the sacrament, we can be misled by the fact that the character is sometimes conferred when the grace is withheld (the case of valid but nonfruitful conferral of a sacrament). Likewise, the grace may be obtained without the character, as in baptism of desire. But what we have to remember is that both of these cases do violence to God's plan. The character is an external manifestation of the Holy Spirit possessed by us for purposes of worship. So, to have the character without the interior grace is something of a lie; and to have the Spirit without the character is like having a fire without flames.

CRIPPLED WITHOUT SPIRIT

The sacramental character makes it possible to take part in worship, and this worship is an expression of the Spirit within us. But if we do not have the Spirit, then the power to worship remains, but it is crippled. A priest bereft of grace can confer the sacraments validly; his unworthiness does not prevent the recipient from receiving the sacramental character and grace. But it distorts the true image of a sacrament, which requires that a priest, as minister of the worshiping Church, whose unfailing love, faith, and hope worship God in truth and in Spirit, should himself possess love, faith, and hope.

Since character and grace form a unity, it follows that the life of grace, without the character, is imperfect. What, then, should be said of those who have baptism of desire and are later baptized sacramentally? What does the sacrament add? It certainly adds the character and juridical membership in the Church. It also perfects the life of grace. More important, though, it gives more perfect graces, graces that unite one with Christ not only spiritually but also corporally. Such graces redeem the whole man, body and soul. They sanctify the person as an individual and as a member of the worshiping society.

Membership in the juridical, visible, social, human society of the Church is, therefore, one of the essential effects of sacramental baptism. Only with this visible membership can a man worship the Father in union with Christ and ascend to the Father joined to Christ. Only with it is he one of the "people of God." Only with it can he perfect his love of God and neighbor by manifesting it in the common sacrifice and at the Lord's table.

We may be able to tie together all we have said about grace, character, and rite by offering our own definition of the sacramental grace: The grace of each sacrament is sanctifying grace and the theological virtues, modified by the distinctive way in which one particpates in the priesthood of Christ owing to this individual sacrament. It is in this sense that each sacrament causes instrumentally the grace that it signifies.

The full causality of grace through the sacraments begins with God. He manifested his will to save men when the eternal High Priest became man and offered an acceptable sacrifice. The High Priest manifests his will to share his priesthood with you when you receive one of the sacraments at the hands of his Church. Conversely, the sacramental ritual is a sign that you are being united to Christ in his sacrifice, and this union is a sign that you are receiving grace.

Each sacrament is simultaneously a juridical act, an act of worship, and a gift of grace. Similarly, the Church is simultaneously a juridical society, a worshiping community, and a sanctified Mystical Body. Membership on the lowest (juridical) level is an efficacious sign of union by grace in this body. It is up to each individual to see to it that the external sign is not, in his case, a lie. He must be sure that the grace that is signified is really there, and he does this by being obedient to the teachings of the Church. Christian grace wears two garments—the sacrifice of Christ and, over that, canon law.

16 The Sacraments: An Encounter with God*

EDWARD H. SCHILLEBEECKX

The divine plan of the sacramental presence is not always appreciated even among Catholics. Its rich content is hardly even suggested by the classical definition of a sacrament: "an efficacious sign of grace." Father Schillebeeckx' exploration into that content should prove revealing to Catholic and Protestant alike.

CATHOLIC THEOLOGY HAS not always clearly distinguished between the mere presence of things in the world and the personal call to *human* existence that comes from the living God. Such lack of clarity has had its unhappy effects. Specifically, in the doctrine of the sacraments it has resulted in a one-sided view that tends to depersonalize the sacramental encounter between God and man, to regard it as nothing more than a cause-effect relationship. This view, in turn, could easily give rise to the attitude that mere passivity suffices for a sacrament's reception. Our object is to explore the sacraments as a living, personal encounter with God.

SACRAMENT AND WORD

In the order of grace established by God, it is in this personal encounter that man finds his salvation. From God's viewpoint, the encounter is revelation; from man's viewpoint, religion. Both revelation and religion then, as the mutual encounter of the created historical man with the uncreated God, are essentially historical

---

* The above chapter is a summary of a longer article by Father Schillebeeckx: *Fragen der Theologie Heute.* Edited by Johannes Feiner, Josef Trütsch, and Franz Böckle (Zurich: Benziger Verlag, 1957), 379–401. This abridgment was approved by him for publication although he himself did not prepare the summary.

and genuinely sacramental. By *sacramental* we mean every supernatural, salvific reality that takes place historically in our lives. For
it is only in some earthly form (sacrament) that we can grasp in
space and time the mysteries God has revealed to us (word).

The dialogue structure of revelation, viewed as word and sacrament, is already present in the Old Testament. In its history Israel
meets with the reality repeatedly expressed in the prophetic word:
"I will be your God, you will be my people." God extends a loving
invitation to his people, and it is for them to respond or refuse.
Clearly, then, the revelation that leads to Christ is an historical
salvific dialogue, an existential struggle between the ever-faithful
God and man who resists him.

In the man Jesus, God's fidelity finally finds the perfect human
response. In this single person both the invitation and the answer
become the constitutive content of the full revelation of God. As
the Second Person of the Holy Trinity, Jesus reveals to us the
divine proposal of love; as man, he accepts it in the name of all of
us. Thus his sacrifice on the cross is at the same time our redemption. Only in union with the man Jesus, who is the head of mankind, does our own fidelity become possible.

To be addressed personally by the man Jesus is for the believer
a personal contact with God, for Jesus is God himself. Consequently the inter-human exchange between Jesus and the men with
whom he comes in contact is the sacrament of their encounter with
God.

Interhuman relationships take place in and through corporal
signs. The encounter of the Son of God with his fellow men demanded a bodily expression. But the specifically human operations
of Christ remain the personal deeds of the Son of God, even
though expressed in human form. As an action of the Son of God,
the interhuman encounter of Christ possesses divine salvific power.
This is true especially of those operations of the God-man, which,
though realized in a human way, are nevertheless specifically operations of God—his miracles, for instance, and above all the redemption itself, completed in the sacrifice of the cross.

PRIMAL SACRAMENT

These operations of Jesus in their human form are "sign and
cause" of the divine grace in such wise that the externally palpable

is itself the inner power of salvation in visible form; it is the imparting of a corporal dimension to the event of grace. The encounter of the believer with Christ, the primal sacrament (*Ursakrament*), remains the fundamental act of the Christian religion as a personal communion with the three divine Persons.

The body is not only the manifestation of the human person who reveals himself; it is also the medium in which the soul externalizes its personality development. Thus corporeity becomes a sign of the innermost acts of the person. The mutual encounter of persons takes place in and through the body. Therefore, although spiritual interchange among men may in itself be quite independent of bodily encounter, nevertheless it reaches fulfillment precisely in such an encounter.

Now though Christ is true God, he is also true man. Hence in him, too, we find this anthropological dimension in his human interchange with men. For the apostles, the moments of body-soul engagement with Christ were decisive high points in their experience with him. The Last Supper is a vivid example of this. Such body-soul encounters meant for both Christ and the believer the vitalization and perfection of spiritual encounter. The man Jesus is the redeeming God. Therefore his spiritual human action is an action of grace, the sacramental realization of God's will concerning the salvation of mankind. The religious life consequently can best reach maturity in the human interchange which is the sacramental encounter with Christ Jesus. In the last analysis, Tertullian's aphorism is verified: "The flesh is the hinge of salvation."

It could be objected that, since we have not yet been glorified, our encounter with Christ should take place in a purely spiritual contact through faith. The objection is in one sense true, just as the salvific character of the Old Testament had to be attributed to Christ even though no corporal encounter with him was possible. In this analogy we discover the fundamentally advent character of Catholic life; the spirit of Christianity is the spirit of the *maranatha:* "Come, Lord Jesus" (Apoc.: 22–20). The encounter is not yet perfect.

PRELUDE TO THE PAROUSIA

But that is only one aspect. This active expectation of the perfect encounter, though inspired by faith, is nourished by corporal contact with the living Lord. Precisely in and through the sacraments we experience an earthly prelude to the perfect eschatological encounter. From the cloud of his glorification behind which he disappeared from our earthly eyes, our Lord in this visible Church reaches for elements that are earthly, unglorified—a little bread and wine, oil and water, a father's hand on the head—and in them he makes his heavenly act of salvation present and effective for us. The sacraments, therefore, are in fact corporal encounters with the glorified Jesus; and since he is himself the *Eschaton* (the Ultimate), they are a mysterious celebration of the parousia. Especially in the Eucharist do we possess the acme of this encounter.

So now we see the reason for the sacraments of the Church. Without them one of the unalterable human dimensions of the Incarnation would be lost to us. But God has remained faithful to his pedagogy of salvation. Out of consideration for the nature of man who must live and perfect himself in a world of men and things, God presents the kingdom of heaven to us in an earthly garment. Thus the divine institution of salvation is essentially a sacramental economy.

THE CHURCH AND THE SACRAMENTS

We have seen that the sacraments are not things, but rather personal living encounters with the glorified Jesus and, in him, with the living God. Now we shall investigate the objective structure of the sacraments and then explore them in their subjective religious element.

The Christological dimension of the sacraments can be better appreciated after we have explained their ecclesiastical dimension. When we spoke above of the sacraments as the earthly garments in which God clothes his revelation, we meant above all the Church herself. For the Church is the visible historical representation of the accomplished redemption. As the earthly channel of God's revelation, she is essentially both sacrament and word. Both of these are the specific operative sphere of the apostolic office as Christ has fashioned it through his Spirit.

Through the mediation of his Holy Spirit and of the apostolic office of his earthly Church, he builds up in this world a living temple, a people of God. Christ sends the Holy Spirit, but he also sends his apostles. Both missions are organically connected: Pentecost, the day on which the Church is fully revealed in her sacramental and kerygmatic action, is the mystical manifestation of both missions precisely in their cooperative union—a union whose vitality springs from the common source of the Christ-life. Whatever the visible Church performs in the historical order is performed interiorly in the superiors of the Church as well as in the souls of the faithful by the Spirit sent forth from Christ.

Therefore the Church may herself be called a primal sacrament, inasmuch as she is the "sacramental Christ" and the recipient of the seven sacraments.

This means that the seven sacraments, even before they are specified individually, are fundamentally an operation of the heavenly Christ that is sacramentalized in the visible, authorized operation of the Church. Hence in every sacrament the power of orders as well as that of jurisdiction are at work, and the validity of a specific sacrament will depend on whether or not it is administered as an operation of the Church. The minister must intend "to do what the Church does." Thus every sacramental contact with the visible Church is also an encounter with the living Christ.

This immediately involves the fact that the basic order of the seven sacraments was established by Christ in founding his Church. But the fundamental factor, which takes on a specific coloring in each of the seven sacraments, is the personal contact with the essential dynamism of the Church as the effective symbolic moment of our personal encounter with the glorified Jesus and, in him, with the living God.

The use of sacramental symbols, especially the symbols of the Eucharist, implies in some sense a "presence of mysteries." The Son of God became man at a definite point of time. Time, however, is irreversible and not even God can call back an historical event. Hence, since Christ was truly man, his sacrifice on the cross is, as an historical event, a past reality which cannot be made present again, not even "in mystery."

On the other hand, the historical-human deeds of Christ are the personal deeds of the Second Divine Person. Consequently, the sacrifice on the cross, as a personal action of God, is also an eternally existent and indestructible reality. Although it took place in time in the humanity of Jesus, the redemption is an act that is

God's, for only God can redeem us. Therefore, the death on the cross possesses a content of mystery that is elevated above time.

ETERNAL REDEMPTIVE POWER

But Jesus does not cease to be man after his resurrection: "Jesus Christ, the same yesterday, today and forever" (Heb: 13–8). The historical-human form of the interior act of Christ's sacrifice has passed away forever, but as an operation of God it remains in its content of mystery; it possesses an eternal actuality in the Christ who is now living. What was done for us in sacrifice is still intended for us now, and it is precisely in the seven sacraments that the entire redemptive mystery of Christ is made actively present to us. Plainly, then, the essence of the sacramental power is the eternally active redemptive act of the Son of God—an act that is identical with the salvific mystery of the historical sacrifice on the cross, of the Lord now living in glory, and of the sacramental Church.

Nevertheless, the sacraments are also a "celebration of mysteries," of the temporally past actions of Christ, especially his action on the cross. Hence, St. Thomas and tradition testify that the sacraments derive their salvific efficacy from the death of Christ; but in the same breath we must also say that it is the Christ now living in glory who gives them this efficacy. "It is Christ himself who baptizes, teaches, rules, absolves, and sacrifices through his Church" (Pius XII, *Mystici Corporis*, AAS 35 [1943], 218). Hence we should place sacramentalism not so much between the historical action of the cross and our world of the twentieth century as between the Lord now living in glory, the *Eschaton,* and a humanity not yet glorified but reaching out for the *Eschaton*. In other words, we must conceive of sacramentalism as a "mediation" in a real encounter between living persons, between Jesus and us, and therefore as a moment of this encounter itself.

Only thus can we explain the historical salvific perspective of the sacraments, inasmuch as they are:

(1) A celebration of the mystery of the cross (a commemorative sign), since the eternally existent redemptive deed of the Son of God became an historical, genuine sacrifice on the cross;

(2) Actual giving of grace (a demonstrative sign), since the

recipient of sacraments is actually included in the eternally abiding redemptive deed;

(3) A germinating anticipation of the parousia (a prognostic sign), since they cause the actual presence of the *Eschaton* himself (in the Eucharist) or at least (in the other six sacraments) his eternally existent redemptive action.

WORSHIP AND SANCTIFICATION

We have already seen that Jesus is the person who in his humanity not only offers us God's grace, but who also in our name accepts it in a loving spirit of religious obedience. In his salvific actions, therefore, we find a double aspect: cult or worship with reference to God and sanctification with reference to men.

Clearly, then, in this primal sacrament that is Christ, the redemptive deed is a liturgical cult-mystery because it is done in our name (*leiton* or *leiton ergon*: the work of the people); at the same time it is the redemptive gift of sanctification. Both are performed by God in a human nature.

These two aspects appear again in the sacraments of the Church as a mystery celebration of the redemption, in which Christ remains the actual high priest or liturgist. In and through the Church, which makes historically perceptible the redeeming grace of the cross, Christ sacramentalizes his heavenly "intercession for us." The grace which works in the sacraments is the fullness of the grace of Christ, shared by the living Church. Hence the sacraments are not only salvific signs of the sanctifying cult of Christ; they are also signs of the cult proper to the Church herself in union with Christ. They are the cultic expression of inner worship of God.

DISPOSITIONS OF RECIPIENT

All this belongs to the constitution of an ecclesiastically valid sacrament, which grants its grace effectively by its own operation (*ex opere operato*), unless the recipient places an impediment by failing to incorporate himself into the cultic prayer of the Church. But precisely because of this prayer value, a valid sacrament unfruitfully received can later "come to life." No single sacrament is ever completely unfruitful because it has worth as the sacramental prayer of Christ in and through his Church.

The meaning of the traditional formula—"The sacraments cause what they signify"—now becomes clear. In their visibility (sign), they are the redemptive will of Christ himself for the faithful who receive them.

The interior religious state of one who receives a sacrament is not merely a disposition that exists prior to or apart from the sacrament; it enters into the very nature of the fruitful sacrament. Although the religious experience contributes in no way to the sacrament's validity, nevertheless only by an authentic religious impulse does the recipient's participation in the Church's cult-mystery become a worthy sacramental expression of his longing for grace and his will for encounter with Christ. The personal religious dispositions (which vary in sacraments of the living and of the dead) are thus sacramentalized to effect a real, personal encounter with Christ.

Evidently, then, the sacraments are not automatons, dispensing us from the religious striving necessary to attain the grace of reconciliation and intimacy with God. In human life, besides ordinary acts, there are those decisive acts in which the person achieves a more intense expression of himself. Such are the sacramental acts intended to be in the Christian's life. They are intended to bring us into vital contact with God's own decisive act of salvation. Each of them is a concealed encounter on our Emmaus path to the *Eschaton,* where the believing heart will burst into flame. Each is an encounter that brings a comforting moral certitude (lacking in extrasacramental grace) of Christ's redemptive will for us. "It is you, O Christ, that I find in your sacraments" (St. Ambrose, ML 14, 875).

17 The Sacraments in the Early Christian Tradition

HERBERT MUSURILLO

Most recent research has reoriented sacramental theology to a fuller appreciation of the symbol and its role in theology.

THE PROBLEM OF the sacraments of the Church cannot be understood without reference to the historical evolution reflected in the writings of the primitive Church. The Latin word *sacramentum* early gained currency as the translation of the Greek μυστήριον in the African version of the Old Testament.[1] The meaning of the Greek word is clear:[2] in classical Greek it refers primarily to the "secret rites" of the mystery religions, and especially those of Eleusis; next it might apply to any religious or magical objects used during the rites; and, finally, in Roman times we find that it is the equivalent of the military oath or *sacramentum*. In the Old Testament book of Tobias 12:7 it refers to the "secret" of the king; whereas in the late Greek book of Wisdom (2:22, 6:22) the word is used of the "mysteries" of God and the universe. New Testament usage varies. In the Apocalypse (1:20, 17:7) it seems apparently to mean a secret riddle or sacred allegory—a usage which anticipates the manner of the Alexandrian school. In the Gospels the word is used in one context only, in reference to the "mystery of the kingdom of God" as revealed through the parables (Mark 4:11; Matt. 13:11; Luke 8:10). But we find it used twenty-one times in the Pauline epistles, usually in a sense which shows the derivation from Wisdom and other Jewish Hellenistic writings: here it means the secret dispensations of the Lord which are hidden from human reason and can be revealed to men only by a special act of God. In Colossians and Ephesians, the concept of mystery is of prime importance! In Col. 1:26, it is the entire plan of redemption culminating in the presence of Jesus among men; in Eph. 5:32 the marriage bond is the great symbolic mystery with reference to Christ and His Church.

Thus among the early Christian Greek writers that use *mystêrion* to refer to the sacrament of Baptism or the Eucharist, the word carries the extensive overtones of the entire cosmic mystery of God's operation within the Church: the divine transformation of the spatio-temporal into a revelation of His hidden designs for men. In this sense *mystêrion* is the ideal designation for the Christian symbol in which man and God can communicate and unite.

The history of the Latin *sacramentum,* however, is far more difficult and complex. In accordance with the general rule,[3] in the transition from Greek to Latin, especially in Africa of the middle second century, Greek abstract words were regularly translated into Latin, while concrete terms or objects (e.g., baptism, eucharist, deacon) were more regularly retained in their Greek form. From the Latin versions of the Old Testament and from the works of Tertullian it is clear that *mystêrion* was regularly translated as *sacramentum,* even though the Latin word had a context and history of its own. The meaning seems to have moved from "sacred obligation," to "oath of initiation," "sacred rite," or even "sacred union." And from the evidence available it would seem likely that it designated "oath" (especially the military oath of allegiance in the Roman legions) only in its secondary sense.[4] In any case it becomes clear that the connotations of the Greek *mystêrion* and the Latin *sacramentum* were quite divergent. In a sense the Latin word is perhaps the more precise as the designation of "sacrament," since by etymology it refers primarily to a sacred bond, often reinforced by an oath or other ritual of initiation. It is only later that the Latin words *mysterium* and *mysteria* find a place in the sacramental terminology of the West.

In a general sense sacraments are the liturgical or ritual signs by which the graces of the Atonement are channeled to men, and by their very nature they demand some authoritative designation by the founder of the Church, the author of our Redemption. It is in this sense that the sacramental sign is said to have been instituted by Christ; but how far Jesus in His earthly life actually determined the specific elements of each rite can emerge only from an historical study of the process of liturgical evolution. For the Church had inherited from her founder a vast undifferentiated complex of saving gestures, which were only in the course of time to be analyzed and understood.

In the profoundest sense it is the Church itself, the people of God, that constitute the primary *mystêrion,* the great sacrament between human and divine. It is through this Body that God becomes present to men, and men find the means by which they can have access to God. The Church is thus the great outward sign, the great vehicle of the graces of the Atonement to men. It is the continuation of the *anawîm* of the Old Law, the just who were especially blessed by Iahweh, and it has taken up the prerogatives once reserved to the seed of Abraham. Indeed, in the Church's sacramental system it has inherited so many of the liturgical gestures of the Old Law: the raising and imposition of hands, blessings, oil, bread, and water, washing, kisses, and greetings—all of these enrich the texture of the Christian's ceremonial life. From the Old Law, too, we derive the concept of the symbolic meal and the propitiation of God by means of sacrificial offering. The banquets and ritual washings of the Convenanters of the Dead Sea also serve to remind us that the early Christian Church drew its symbolic gestures from many different sources.[5] In fact, the communication by symbolic gesture is at the heart of all religions. Gesture is instinctive to man and most probably preceded actual speech as the intelligent binding force of primitive societies.[6] To attract the attention of the gods, to worship and to pray, to curse and to bless, gestures for all these come spontaneously and are deeper than speech. It is no wonder then that the social texture of the early Christian liturgy was formed of symbolic gestures, inaugurating, uniting, and blessing the people of God, as a way of making them share in the good things of Christ, washed as they were in the blood of the Lamb and coheirs of the kingdom.

In early Greek Fathers like Methodius of Olympus, the Church exercises her sacramental functions as a virgin mother, bringing her children to birth from the seed of the Word, nursing them on the milk of her doctrine and her grace, renewing with them the memorial of Christ's passion, and perfecting them for that final day when they will be reunited with Christ the Bridegroom in heaven.[7] All this, however, implies the ordered and hierarchic functioning of the various members of the body, cooperation and obedience, self-discipline and love. It was only the analytic mind of a later age that would dissect and isolate the different sacramental actions, define their precise natures and their effects. But in one sense the sacraments of the Church are not to be fragmented: they are all partial functions of a single principle and operation, and their effects cannot be understood except as the meager distribution of a vast and comprehensive system. But considering them in their totality we can understand how the sacraments channel the effects of the Atonement, and hence their causality is secondary and derivative. Christ's redemptive act, as obedient servant of God and symbolic paschal lamb, secured reconciliation and grace for all men; but His blood cannot become a laver of redemption for many until they are initiated in the name of the Trinity and participate in the memorial of His death. Thus the effects of the sacraments, though incomplete and partial, are physical and real: they look backward to Christ's achievement, and forward to the reality of ultimate union with God.

From the very beginnings of the Church, the inspiration of the first Christians was the catechesis and the liturgical communal acts which were the center of their existence. St. Luke gives us a highly idealized picture in the early chapters of Acts, but one that enshrines the early ecstasy and enthusiasm of the new religion. The announcement of the Good News would terminate in the charismatic descent of the Spirit, speaking in tongues,[8] and the symbolic washing of baptism. Those who had already been buried in the waters and had risen again would assemble in private houses in the evening, and preparatory prayers and readings from the Scriptures would culminate in the *agapê* or love-banquet, at the close of which the leader or "president" would celebrate the Eucharist. From our earliest anaphoras (in Justin, Ambrose, Serapion, and others) it is clear that this *eucharistia,* or prayer of thanksgiving, would be normally in narrative form, recounting the great acts of God's mercy toward His people, and this would culminate in the narrative of Jesus' last supper with His disciples, concluding with a reference to His death and resurrection. After an invocation of the Spirit to descend upon the gifts, the faithful would partake of the bread and wine and then depart. Thus the center of Christian life from the earliest days was the ritual commemoration of Christ's

Atonement with the subsequent effects for all mankind. In a community that lived so closely together, the sacramental signs constituted one vast symbolic gesture which the enlightened understood and participated in to varying degrees.

The *baptisma,* the symbolic immersion, was the entry-rite, the signal by which a man signified his acceptance of the Good News and by which the people of God acknowledged his new membership. Thus he expressed his death and resurrection with Jesus and obtained the right to participate in the mysteries of the community. The Mass or the Liturgy becomes thus the Chruch's archetypal sacrament: the central *mystêrion* in which the union between man and God is both symbolized and achieved in virtue of the redemptive act of Jesus. All the other sacramental acts cluster about this central mystery, as gestures which prepare for it, support and confirm it, or further channel the graces of the Atonement into all areas of Christian existence. The act of ritual anointing in Confirmation is supportive of Christian baptism; Orders must create new elders and priests to lead the sacrifice; Marriage, a symbol of God's union with man, strengthens the physical growth of the Church in the world; the sacrament of Reconciliation bridges the gap between the experience of baptism and the temptations of daily life; and, finally, the Last Anointing heartens the ailing Christian and girds him for the final battle with death.[9] There were innumerable other symbolic gestures which bound together the early Christians: blessings of bread and the fields, the hospitable kiss and the washing of feet, the anointing of rulers and the reception of monks and consecrated women. All of these formed a part of the primitive sacramental texture; though some were of but passing importance and fell into disuse. Only those great Seven were to survive into the early Middle Ages,[10] when sacramental theology was first discussed in the schools. The process of growth was a natural and unself-conscious one. And Luther and the Reformers, in their eagerness to give the lie to the Roman theologians, misrepresented the historical problem; yet their insistence upon the two "dominical sacraments," and their reaction against some of the exaggerated sacramental theology of their opponents, has proven salutary in the light of the past three centuries. The study of Scripture and the Fathers has more and more revealed the reality of the total sacramental complex, in which all the ritual signs form, as it were, a spiritual galaxy revolving about the two central mysteries, Baptism and the Eucharist.

In the light, therefore, of current knowledge, many of the ancient philosophical controversies on the manner of sacramental causality present a false problem. For the cluster of sacramental signs were accepted by the primitive Church in their totality, often without precise definition; and they were believed to bind, restore, and heal, and to communicate the effects of Jesus' atoning act. What further need was there to enter into the precise nature of the operation in terms of current philosophical controversies? Both the Greek doctor Galen and the pagan writer Celsus had accused the early Christians of being an uncritical race, and ignorant of philosophy, for their new life was a *philosophia* of its own, a love of wisdom in a larger, deeper sense. Theirs was a sharing in the mystery of God's dealing with men from all ages. And yet the aid of philosophy would be enlisted in the analysis and explanation of the meaning of the *kerygma*—and, if need be, to prove the truth of the Christian message by Aristotelian-Stoic logic, and to attack all oponents with the weapons of the pagan arsenal. This philosophical direction of early Christianity, if we may so term it, entered into the Christian stream with the early Greek apologists of the second and third centuries, and was developed by the Platonic leanings of the Alexandrian catechetical school. But after the close of the patristic period in the middle of the eighth century, its home was largely in the Latin West; here philosophy, as theology's *ancilla* or handmaid, grew stronger in her service to Christian doctrine, especially in the lecture halls of the medieval Schoolmen, and in the seminaries of the early monastic orders.

There is no real difficulty about the essential role of sacramental signs in the general scope of the Church as the vehicle of God's grace to men: this is clear from the Scriptures, and from the way in which the Fathers have spoken of these symbolic rites from the earliest days. But to set the sacramental system, this precious complex of hieratic signs, into a framework of a philosophical (and sometimes mechanical) causality can cause difficulty to some. Indeed, here was the chief stumbling block for the sixteenth-century Reformers: distracted by some of the exaggerations of Renaissance theologians, they failed to see the fundamental structure of the sacramental system as it had existed from the primitive

Church. It is only by a recall to a study of our Christian origins that there can be any hope of union within the modern Church. It is with this in mind that we must review the entire plan of the Atonement insofar as it can be understood in human terms. For the Church is nothing less than the living embodiment of the mystery of Christ's Atonement: it is her function to channel its effects, and to incorporate all men who have been redeemed by the blood of the Lamb.

Christ's historic act stood at the convergence of many lines of ancient thought. As St. Paul and the Fathers constantly emphasize, Jesus' gesture was the historic expression of man's reconciliation with God. In the person of Jesus, suffering becomes the means of man's redemption by His vicarious satisfaction and sacrifice in the spirit of the second servant song of Deutero-Isaiah (53):

> He has borne our griefs
> And carried our sorrows;
> Yet did we esteem him stricken,
> Smitten by God and afflicted.
> For our sins was he wounded,
> And bruised for our transgressions. . . .

Here we see the symbolism of the sacrificial victim and later of the lamb, applied to the messiah of Israel. It was the doctrine of Isaiah, together with the image of the paschal lamb, which Jesus made His own: *This is the body broken for you, the blood shed for man for the remission of sins.* Thus Jesus' innocent death at the hands of the Jews and the Romans becomes a vicarious sacrifice in the Jewish sense. And as a sacrifice its essence is both immolation (as lamb) and oblation (as servant of Iahweh). In the Cross, history and symbol become one. For Christ's historic gesture, from the Supper to Calvary, would not only symbolize the atonement by sacrifice foreshadowed in Isaiah; it would achieve it. Thus it follows that in the Christian economy the sacred Liturgy is the archetypal sacrament. For in the Last Supper, Jesus replaced the sacred Hebrew ritual by a new ritual which would be not only an eschatological banquet—a ritual perhaps dimly echoed in the Dead Sea Scrolls[11]—but would express both by word and gesture His own historic act of atonement. As the writings of the Fathers attest, in the bread and wine there is present both Lamb-Scapegoat and

Victim-Servant; and by this presence, held by faith, the meaning of the original bloody sacrifice is cherished and renewed.

But this messianic banquet, to celebrate the mysteries of the Lord until He come, is also the outward sign by which all the faithful could unite and participate in the effects of the atonement. Thus its causality (if this is the word we are looking for) must be analogous, as a ritual of commemoration, with the very act of atonement itself. And this causality is historico-symbolic, corporate, and transcendental. It is historico-symbolic insofar as an event in history was so designated by providence as to produce a transcendent, spiritual effect. So too the Liturgy of the Mass, as a memorial and commemoration of God's redeeming gesture, not only symbolizes, it also achieves. Hence the way in which it produces its effects upon the faithful must also be historico-symbolic, though of a secondary order. The action of the Church in the Liturgy is corporate and mystical, although mediate, dependent, and secondary. This causality is real and "physical"; it is also symbolic, insofar as the outward rites (not the effects) are sensuous vehicles of a deeper meaning.

And so it is with all the other sacraments that have, in the course of time, been accepted by the Church as fragmented planets revolving about a central star. They are all, in a sense, commemorative of the life and achievement of the Lord, and function as continuing His saving presence. As symbolic gestures that dispense the graces of the atonement, they have a threefold reference: historically to Christ, liturgically to the Church, and personally to the individual member of God's people. As corporate gestures shared in by the faithful they can be understood as symbols of initiation and decision, union and commitment. It was especially through the technique of allegorical exegesis that the patristic writers enlarged on the symbolic dimension of the sacramental signs by referring them backward to the salvific events of the Old Law, and forward to the messianic banquet of heaven. Especially important for such symbolism are the catechetical sermons of St. John Chrysostom, the catechetical lectures of St. Cyril of Jerusalem, the treatise of St. Ambrose *On the Mysteries,* and passages in the works of Gregory of Nyssa and St. Augustine. In the newly discovered *Baptismal Homilies* of Chrysostom, for example, the baptized, "the illumined," are as new stars in the firmament (*Instr.* 3:1–4), they are

Christ's newly recruited infantry (12:30–32), His picked athletes for the battle of the spiritual arena (2:23). The fresh baptismal tunics are the symbols of the new man, the new life they are to put on, the spiritual nuptials with Christ, the royal banquet of heaven (12:17–20); and by the sacrament they are transformed as tarnished metal in a furnace (9:22). The ceremonies of the liturgy are a representation of the events that took place in the days of Moses and God's chosen people (3:23–26). The list could be expanded indefinitely: for there is a wealth and richness in the symbolic dimension of the sacraments which the Fathers are at constant pains to exploit, especially for the instruction of the laity. The long list of symbolic comparisons are intended to demonstrate the effects of the sacramental rites in their channeling of the graces of Christ's Atonement to men.

But the symbolism also manifests the relationship of the Church, as Mother of men and virginal Bride of the Savior, to those who have been redeemed. If the sacraments designate a commitment on the part of Christ's soldiers, or athletes, they also point to an organic relationship with the total body, the Church, in which they take on their reality. From the viewpoint of the Church, the sacraments are tokens of the Church's willingness to incorporate, to seal and confirm, to reconcile and to appoint, to heal and to bless her children in the way specific to each rite. Here we can glimpse the true meaning of the term *opus operatum,* which began to be applied to the sacraments from the latter half of the twelfth century. For the sacramental rites are not merely arbitrary, casual prayers or petitions by the faithful for God's grace, but they are unambiguous signs whose meaning and effectiveness are guaranteed by the Church and, therefore, by God Himself. Here and now, by virtue of Christ's promise and the force of the new dispensation, grace is offered to the worthy recipients of the sacrament in a way that is public and open to all. The sacraments are truly the official, designated vehicles of God's people; that they operate apart from the subjective disposition of the minister and the recipient is merely a negative way of saying the same thing.[12]

And yet this is not to deny the contention of the Reformers, that these ancient rites and ceremonies are instructive as cues to prayer and to perfection, and express our historic link with the primitive liturgy and catechesis which was the final testament of the Lord.

Though the sacramental process and its effects may in some cases
have been distorted by medieval theologians, the study of the
Fathers demonstrates that the Church would not be as Christ
founded it if were deprived of this rich liturgical texture that
binds it infallibly to its bridegroom and Lord. These rites, which
time and growth have specified and modified, are an integral part
of the *mystêrion* as Christ formed it before His departure from this
earth. Indeed, it is like the green foliage of the great willow tree
described in the *Shepherd* of Hermas: it bears witness to the
healthy life-giving sap within, and cannot be cut away without
necessarily harming the entire living structure.

Although in many cases the precise ritual and proper scope of
the sacraments were not determined until patristic or even medieval times, it is interesting to note that Holy Scripture refers to
every one of the signs that were afterward to be called sacraments.
We have Baptism in John 3:5; Romans 6:3; Acts 2:41, and elsewhere; the forgiveness of sins in John 20:23; the reception of the
Spirit through the imposition of hands in Acts 8:14 ff.; final
anointing in James 5:14; Orders in 2 Tim. 1:6, and elsewhere;
marriage in the classic passage, Ephes. 5:31 ff. The Eucharist is
perhaps the clearest of all in Matt. 26:26, and the parallel synoptic
passages, and especially in 1 Cor. 11:23 ff. But it was not to be
expected that later historians should be able to reconstruct all the
stages in the evolution and growth of these rites: the Church was
the community of God's chosen people and not an academic body.
It would take centuries for the precise concept of the sacrament to
become clear. Even in the fourth century no less an authority than
St. Ambrose of Milan in his work *On the Mysteries* 6:32 (ed.
Srawley, p. 136) should believe that the washing of the feet was a
sacrament. But it seems clear from other patristic writers and especially from St. Augustine (*Ep:* 55:33; *P.L.* 33:220) that Ambrose's view was unique and perhaps restricted to local Milanese
practice.

The lack of patristic evidence for the actual practice of some of
the sacraments is embarrassing, but this again is consistent with
the silence we encounter on many other details of the life of the
primitive Church. Jesus Himself spoke explicitly of the Eucharist
and its effects, of Baptism, and of the reconciliation of sinners with
the Church.[13] These can, if one prefers, be called the dominical

sacraments *par excellence*. We are not so fortunate in the evidence for Confirmation, Orders, Marriage, and Extreme Unction. Similarly, in the early patristic period there is abundant testimony for the Eucharist and Baptism, and (at least public) Penance. Documents of the apostolic period, such as the *Didache* (ch. 7), the *Shepherd* of Hermas (931-4 = *Similitudes* 9:16), Justin's *Apologia* 1:61, and the so-called *Epistle of Barnabas* 11:11, offer abundant evidence for the sacrament of Baptism. Tertullian wrote an entire treatise on the sacrament; the controversies in Africa dealt with the rebaptism of heretics; and the catechetical sermons of Gregory of Nyssa, Cyril of Jerusalem, and John Chrysostom treat the ceremony and the effects of Baptism from many points of view. It is St. Augustine, however, who formalized much of the theology of Baptism, dealing with its effects (especially the sacramental character) and the relationship of the baptized to the Church, the requisite conditions in minister and recipient, and the theological symbolism. Though he drew widely from the tradition that had preceded him—from Tertullian and the Cappadocian Fathers—Augustine has rightly been called the founder of sacramental theology. Some of his more important works in this area were those composed against the Donatists, who held (among other things) that only their schismatic sect possessed true sacraments; among these were *On Baptism against the Donatists* (about A.D. 400), *Against Cresconius* (about 406), and *Against Gaudentius* (about 420). Especially valuable are his *Commentaries* on the Psalms and on the Gospel of St. John. Baptism is, in fact, the most documented sacrament during the patristic era.

Hippolytus of Rome, who died about 235, opposed Pope Callistus and reigned as antipope until his exile during the persecution of the emperor Maximinus Thrax; he was however reconciled to the Church before his death and is revered as a martyr. His exegetical work reflects the allegorical tendencies of Alexandria. But as a witness of primitive doctrine his most important work is the *Apostolic Tradition* (written about 215) largely or wholly preserved in the so-called *Egyptian Church Order,* as the work was formerly known in its Ethiopic and Coptic versions. It is the oldest ecclesiastical Ritual or Church Order after the *Didache* and has been the source of many of the later ones. The first part deals with the consecration of bishops, the sacred Liturgy, the ordination of priests and deacons, and many other blessings and consecrations. The second section treats the rules for the administration of Baptism, Confirmation, and the Eucharist. And the third part deals with miscellaneous other practices, e.g., fasting and the celebration of the *agapê* or banquet. The rite mentioned in the *Apostolic Tradition* involves the imposition of hands and the anointing with consecrated oil by the bishop seems clearly distinguished from the baptismal unction performed by the priest after Baptism, and hence the text remains an important witness for the rite in the third century of our era. Similarly Cyprian, the saintly bishop of Carthage, martyred in 258, discusses Acts 8:14 ff. in his *Epistles* 73:9 as a ceremony that is still alive in his community: "Those who have been baptized in the Church are presented to the elders of the Church and by our prayer and imposition of hands receive the Holy Spirit. . . ." St. Cyril of Jerusalem, who died in 386, is chiefly known for his twenty-four *Catecheses* or *Instructions* delivered for the most part in the great Church of the Holy Sepulchre in Jerusalem some time in the years 348–50. In addition to most important chapters devoted to the Liturgy and the Eucharist, his entire third *Catechesis* treats "Unction," that is, the sacrament of Confirmation. There is further abundant testimony from Ambrose, Augustine, Jerome, and many other ecclesiastical writers. Modern theologians dispute on the essential "matter"[14] of the sacrament of Confirmation, but most would hold that both the imposition of hands (which is the rite as we know it from apostolic times) and the anointing with chrism are essential for the sacrament, even if we are to assume that Chrismation was a later development in Church practice, no later, of course than the third century. In the Orthodox churches a child is confirmed immediately after baptism, and the anointing is performed by a priest with myrrh consecrated by a bishop. The priest anoints various parts of the child's body with the words: "[Behold] The seal of the Holy Spirit's gift!" In a certain sense, the sacrament of Confirmation may be thus considered as an integral part of the complete ceremony of Baptism, the special anointing being conferred as a special seal on those who have already been received into the Church.[15] But the question of terminology is here not an important one, and there has never been any essential dispute on the question between the East and the West.

It is interesting to note that Chrismation is also employed in the Eastern separated churches in the ceremony of reconciliation of the lapsed.[16] Apostates to Mohammedanism, Anglicans, Protestants, and (in the Greek church) even Roman Catholics are received after a profession of faith and a ceremony of anointing. Interestingly enough, there is evidence for a rite of Chrismation in the reconciliation of sinners in Origen (*In Lev. hom.* 2:4), Chrysostom (*On the Priesthood* 3:6), in the writings of the Syrian Father Aphraates, and in other sources, where the anointing of the penitents with oil can hardly be understood in anything but a literal sense.[17] The rite seems to be clearly distinguished from either Confirmation or final anointing; but in any case, it was soon to fall into desuetude, and survives solely in the rite of reconciliation in the Eastern churches.

The sacrament of the Eucharist or the Lord's Supper is perhaps the clearest inheritance from the early Church and most Christian churches have retained the Liturgy in one form or another. The words of institution have been so clearly preserved in St. Paul (I Cor. 11:23–5) and the Synoptics (Matt. 26:26–28, Mark 14:22–34, Luke 22:15–20) that the reality of the change was doubted by no one in the earliest days of the Church save the Docetes; and indeed they were committed to their position because they believed that the Lord in His earthly life possessed no true body. St. Ignatius of Antioch, St. Justin, Irenaeus, and Tertullian are all early and clear witnesses to the belief in what is today known as the Real Presence. Of the Docetes, Ignatius says, "They avoid the Eucharist and the Prayer, for they do not believe that the Eucharist is the flesh of our Savior Jesus Christ, who suffered for our sins and who was raised from the dead by the Father in His goodness" (*Smyrn.* 7:1). The texts of Justin and Irenaeus are equally clear. Of the Gnostic heretics Irenaeus says: "How can they be convinced that the bread over which the eucharistic prayer has been said is the body of their Lord, and the chalice is His blood, if they do not confess that He is the Son of the creator of the world?" (*Against Heresies* IV:18:5). The doctrine of the Eucharist as a sacrament is one of the best attested in the history of the Church. The actual explanation of the sacramental change of bread and wine into the Body and Blood of Christ is discussed by the Fathers of the Golden Age, especially St. Cyril of Jerusalem, St. Gregory of Nyssa, and St. Cyril of Alexandria in the East and Ambrose, Augustine, and pseudo-Eusebius of Emesa in the West. They speak of a change of the bread and wine into the body and blood of the Lord: a conversion, a transformation, an elemental mutation. Cyril of Jerusalem, for example, in his *Catecheses* (4:2) was the first to compare the process to the miracle at Cana in the gospel of St. John: "He once changed water into wine at Cana in Galilee by a mere nod of His head. Is it then incredible that He now changes wine into His blood?"[18]

It was ultimately this concept, of the miraculous conversion of one object into another, which was to be normative in Eucharistic theology. St. Ambrose compared the change to the transformation of Moses' staff into a serpent in the book of Exodus (7:10) or the changing of the waters of Egypt into blood (Exodus 7:20). It is easy to see how the twelfth-century theologians, as, for example, Rolando Bandinelli (later Pope Alexander III), Stephen of Tournai, and Peter Comestor should have hit upon the term "transsubstantiation," which was then taken up in the Decretals of Innocent III and the decrees of the Fourth Lateran Council in 1215. This explanation of the sacramental change was taken over by Greek orthodox theologians after the Second Council of Lyons, and became more and more widespread after the synod of Jerusalem in 1672, although the churches are at pains to emphasize that such a doctrine does not commit the faithful to the philosophy of western Scholasticism. Further, some Orthodox catechisms stress the incomprehensibility of the mystery, citing the words of John of Damascus (*On the Orthodox Faith* 4.13): "Suffice it to know that this is done through the Holy Spirit. . . . The word of God is operative, omnipotent, and true: but the mode of its operation is inscrutable."[19]

The literal acceptance of Christ's words at the Last Supper did not prevent some of the Fathers, especially those of the Alexandrian school, from taking the words of the Gospel as referring to a spiritual nourishing with the doctrine of the Lord: thus the body and blood of Jesus possibly signify His sacred teaching in Origen's *Against Celsus* 8:33, and elsewhere. At the same time Origen and Clement testify to the general belief of the Church that the bread and wine are truly the body and blood of the Savior. In fact, the doctrine of the Eucharistic presence continued all but unchallenged until the famous heresy of Berengarius of Tours in the eleventh century. A student of Fulbert of Chartres, Berengarius became archdeacon of Angers about 1040; his novel doctrines were condemned frequently at local synods, and he finally recanted before his death about 1088. In his major work, *On the Sacred Banquet against Lanfranc,* he insists that the sign and the thing signified cannot be identical; hence the bread and wine, which *signify* or symbolize Christ, cannot be the body and blood of the Savior. Just as the washing with the waters of baptism signifies (and effects) the regeneration of the soul in Christ, so too the bread and wine symbolize and effect the union of the faithful soul with Jesus; but the *sign* of the body and blood cannot *be* the body and blood.[20] But the majority of medieval theologians replied with the famous distinction that though the appearances of the bread and wine (after consecration) are the "sacrament merely" (*sacramentum tantum*), the body of Christ present under the appearances is both sacrament (sign) and reality, *res et sacramentum*; though truly present, the body of Christ points to and achieves in the soul the spiritual nourishment of the faithful by the reception of the sacrament. This solution was finally adopted by Innocent III in a doctrinal letter of A.D. 1202 (Denzinger 415), and was widely accepted as the best presentation of the traditional doctrine. In any case it would seem clear that the famous Lutheran theory of "consubstantiation," according to which there is no conversion but rather the simultaneous coexistence of the bread with the body of the Lord, however defensible on other grounds, finds little or no support in the writings of the early Fathers and theologians.

Similarly, the belief that the sacramental presence abides even after the termination of the Liturgy is supported by the practice of carrying the Eucharist to the sick and to those in prison (Justin, *Apol.* 1:65), and of keeping some of the elements left over until the following day (Cyril of Alexandria, in his *Letter to Calosyrius,* and elsewhere). Though it is true that the external veneration of the Eucharistic species developed largely in the West from the eleventh and twelfth centuries, and especially with the establishment of the Feast of Corpus Christi in the year 1264, the practice of reservation in the eastern churches is very ancient and there is no theological reason against public worship from the Orthodox point of view.

It was Adolf Harnack who held the position that the Church of the first two centuries held the eucharistic liturgy to be merely a spiritual sacrifice of praise and adoration. But he is contradicted by the clear and constant testimony of the documents, beginning with the *Didache* or *Teaching of the Twelve Apostles* (14:1–3), which speaks of the liturgy as fulfilling the prophecy of Malachi, and by St. Ignatius of Antioch, Justin Martyr, Irenaeus, Tertullian, Cyprian, and many more. St. John Chrysostom is especially emphatic in teaching that the sacrifice offered in the Christian Churches is identical with the one offered at the Last Supper (*In 2 Tim. hom.* 2:4). The victim, he teaches, is always the same; and hence the sacrifice is one, even though now we accomplish a memorial of what was done then (*In Hebr. hom.* 17:3). Augustine is particularly clear in teaching the unity of the sacrifice, even though it was offered historically in a bloody manner (*City of God* 17:20:2) and now in a bloodless fashion, incorporating the oblation of all the faithful in union with His mystical body. The doctrine is reflected in all the early anaphoras, especially those in Hippolytus, Ambrose, and Serapion of Thmuis. The medieval theologians merely reiterated the general doctrine on the sacrifice of the Mass as found in the early patristic writers. Further discussion of the precise nature of the sacrifice was to be reserved for the theologians of later centuries.[21]

According to the sixteenth-century Reformers, Penance was not a sacrament really distinct from Baptism, nor was there any special mode of reconciliation of the sinner after baptism apart from personal contrition and faith. The sacrament of Reconciliation indeed poses a problem; but such a position would be in danger of grossly oversimplifying the evidence. Among the apostolic Fathers, for example, it is clear that all of them envisage some possibility of serious sin after baptism with the opportunity of penance and salvation for those Christians who would appease God and perform certain penitential exercises: so the *Didache,* the first epistle of Clement of Rome, the so-called second epistle of Clement to the Corinthians, Justin, and Hermas.[22] The entire burden of the *Shepherd* of Hermas is to arouse the lukewarm Christians into realizing the necessity of penitence—not only for the great sins (apostasy, murder, and adultery), but also for lesser and interior ones. Throughout, of course, it is always God who forgives; and yet it is the Church, in the person of the elderly woman (who remains forever young), that is most concerned that the penitence should be practiced. Ultimately penance achieves reconciliation with the Church and the restoration of full Christian life and membership as Christ had envisaged it. But this great act of repentance is allowed but once after baptism: only the forgiven can re-enter the great Tower of the Church, and all outside it will be lost.

Tertullian (who supported Hermas' doctrine of a single penitence) is one of the clearest testimonies to the practice of public reconciliation in the early Church, especially in a work written during his Catholic period, the treatise *On Penitence*. The guilty Christians must confess their sins publicly, and after the performance of certain works they would be openly absolved and restored to the Christian community. In his book *On Chastity*, written during his Montanist period, there is further evidence of the penitential practices of the Church inasmuch as it attacks what Tertullian feels is laxity, in allowing adulterers to be reconciled to the Church, and lays down three sins that may not be forgiven after baptism: idolatry, adultery, and murder. But common practice was against this rigorist trend, and Tertullian's plea bore no fruit. In this and the controversies which followed over those who had lapsed during the persecutions, Rome was more lenient than the African churches. The procedure for public penance during this early period was quite complex and differed from region to region. The bishops usually regulated the amount of penance and the establishment of the grades or divisions of the penitents: at least for Asia Minor we have evidence of four grades or stations, the bystanders, the kneelers, the hearers, and the mourners, although the importance of these has perhaps been exaggerated in the past.[23] We have good evidence that the ordinary priests, at least by the third or fourth century, cooperated with the bishop in imposing satisfaction on sinners and even absolving them in his name.[24] But the practice of public penance began to decline by the fifth and sixth centuries, and all but disappeared about the year A.D. 800. Already in the eighth century we have evidence that persons of high rank enjoyed the privilege of having their own confessors; other authors comment on the obligation of confessing at stated intervals. It seems almost certain that the practice of the Celtic church and the Anglo-Saxon penitential books which date from the sixth century had an enormous influence on the growth of private confession and penance throughout the Church at large, both in the East and the West.

We learn of another custom from Tertullian in connection with the sacrament, and that is the reconciliation a penitent could obtain during the persecutions through the intercession of the martyrs, even by obtaining from them a *libellus pacis*, "a certificate of peace." This was, however, only an interlude in the growth of a practice later called an "absolution," by which popes or bishops signified an intercessory prayer for the remission of sins on the part of those who were ill, special benefactors, or those who fought in holy wars.[25] It is only from the eleventh century, however, that we have a record of bishops in the south of France and northern Spain issuing real *indulgentiae*: these were remissions of specific amounts of penance to be performed for sins confessed, or the reduction of the length of time involved. These "indulgences," which were granted for visits to churches, for almsgiving, and for other good works, were only later measured simply by the number of days or years. It was, however, the Schoolmen of the thirteenth century who developed the concept of indulgence in its theological dimensions: it was interpreted as effecting a direct remission of the pains of purgatory, deriving its efficacy from spiritual treasury of merit entrusted to the Church by the Savior and the martyrs of Christendom. Of the later, fifteenth-century exaggerations, especially those connected with the name of Raymond Perraudi, dean of the cathedral church at Saintes, it is not our purpose to speak.

There can be no doubt that reconciliation was always an integral part of the Church's sacramental system, justified by a continual appeal to the power of the keys, and to the power of binding and loosing entrusted by the Savior before His death. And yet Penance was always different from the other rites insofar as reconciliation with the Church, as the effect of the sacrament, was a judicial process, which left the subjective attitude of the penitent somewhat undefined and therefore the object of controversy. This conflict between the juridical and the penitential factors of the sacramental rite has continued within the theological schools to the present day in the discussion of the "matter" of sacrament, the requisite nature of the penitent's sorrow, and the nature of extra-sacramental contrition. That perfect contrition is possible for men and is sufficient for justification outside of the sacrament has been the general teaching of theologians. But, within the sacrament, it is the agreement of perhaps a majority that the penitent's interior sorrow (at least imperfect contrition) is of the essence of the sacramental sign, together with the priestly absolution. This solution, which has come down from St. Thomas and the scholastics, has been the dominant one, even though in view of the history of the sacrament it seems more likely that the immediate end of the rite, the so-called *res et sacramentum* (both signified and signifying), should be the reconciliation with the Church, the *pax ecclesiae* of which the early documents so often speak.[26] For it is clear that reconciliation of sinners after baptism was always associated with the public weal of God's people, and the power and responsibility for this was always assumed by the episcopate as touching the holy character of the Church. Thus the judicial act of the priest is the logical continuation of the healing and forgiving gestures of Jesus, but not now for the good of the person alone but also for the integrity of God's people.

The earliest evidence for the sacrament of Final Anointing on the Anointing of the Sick can be found in the references to the blessing of oil for the sick and for other purposes (the *Apostolic Constitutions* 8:29; Hippolytus, *Apostolic Tradition*; the *Euchologion* of Serapion of Thmuis nn. 5 and 17). The references are, of course, not unambiguous; although the *Euchologion* speaks of the effects of the oil as "health of soul and body," as well as the "remission of sins." It is strange that both Origen (*In Lev. hom.* 2:4) and John Chrysostom (*On the Priesthood* 3:6) seem to understand the famous passage in the epistle of James (5:14 f.) as referring to an anointing in connection with the reconciliation of penitents—a ritual to which we have alluded earlier.[27] It is only when we come to an epistle of Pope Innocent I (d. 417) to Bishop Decentius that we have clear evidence of a ritual anointing of the sick. In commenting on the meaning of James 5:14, Innocent speaks of the oil blessed by the bishop as a *genus sacramenti* ("a kind of sacrament") which may be applied to the sick by priests, bishops, and also by the infirm themselves. There is further evidence in the *Life of St. Augustine* by Possidius (§ 27, and in the sermons of St. Caesarius of Arles (d. 542). But in Caesarius, as in many of the other early witnesses, it would appear that the effect of the oil could be obtained even by private anointing by the sick person himself or by a member of his family. It was not until the Carolingian reform of the eighth century that the rite of anointing by priests becomes clear with clear regulations set down for administration.

The purpose and the effects of the sacrament, however, continued to be discussed down through the medieval period. The spiritual healing, which most agreed was its primary effect, was interpreted by St. Thomas and the majority of theologians as implying the removal of all obstacles (including serious sins) to an immediate entrance into heaven. St. Bonaventure and the Franciscan school, however, insisted on the removal of the "infirmity of sin," that is, of the lesser faults and venial sins of the sick person; and for this reason tended to restrict the reception of the sacrament only to those who were in imminent danger of death. All Latin theologians agree that only those can receive the sacrament who are capable of sin and are somehow in danger of death from illness or age. The Orthodox churches represent the opposite pole to the earlier Scotist view in allowing anyone who is ill to receive the sacrament, on the grounds that bodily healing is the primary effect; indeed, it is sometimes administered to the healthy and occasionally serves as a preparation for the reception of the Eucharist. But apart from the minor dispute on the primary effect of Final Anointing, the Western theologians have been in substantial agreement, supported by the decrees of the Council of Trent.[28]

That presbyters and bishops were appointed by the imposition of hands is clear from the Acts of the Apostles (14:22; cf. 6:6) and from the Pauline epistles to Timothy (1 Tim. 4:14; 2 Tim. 1:6; cf. 1 Tim. 5:22). The use of the Greek word χάρισμα in the first two of these passages to designate the "grace" that is in the minister through the imposition of hands indicates the basis on which future theological speculation was to be founded. The various orders of bishops, presbyters, and deacons is recognized by St. Ignatius of Antioch in various letters: indeed, his doctrine of ecclesiastical harmony and love is based upon obedience to legitimate superiors (*Ephes.* 3, *Trall.* 3, *Smyrn.* 8). The importance of obedience to bishops and presbyters is stressed by Clement of Rome in his epistle to the Corinthians about the year A.D. 90 (21:6), for these orders come ultimately from the Apostles, who were appointed by Christ Himself. Tertullian's Montanist view (*On Monogamy* 12) that all Christians were priests was never accepted in the early Church, and even Jerome's view that bishops were superior to priests "by custom rather than the truth of the Lord's dispensation" (*Epist.* 146 on Titus 1:5) was not considered the normal doctrine. St. Augustine compares Orders with Baptism: "Both are sacraments that are conferred on a man with a kind of consecration. . . . Thus in the Catholic Church they cannot be repeated" (*Contra ep. Parmeniani* 2.13.28). Perhaps clearest of all on the sacramental nature of Orders is Gregory of Nyssa in his *Sermon on the Baptism of Christ* (PG 46.581 ff.). He compares the ordination of the priest to the consecration of the bread and wine in the sacrament of the Eucharist. The comparison is apt in many ways: for just as the wine and the bread remain externally the same, so too the consecrated priest. But he is internally changed, marked off from the rest of men; and by his consecration he becomes a teacher of men, an overseer, and the minister of the mysteries. Surely there is no greater reason than this that Orders should be a sacrament, conferring the same sort of "character," or designation, as Baptism and Confirmation. Unlike Penance, Final Anointing, and Marriage, Orders is conferred for the good of God's people for the propagation of the sublime *mystérion,* the Church, and the administration of the focal sacrifice from which all sacramental graces, in a sense, derive.[29]

The four minor orders (porter, lector, exorcist, acolyte) and the subdiaconate are, of course, of later institution. Tertullian mentions the lector (*On the Prescription of Heretics* 41), Hippolytus of Rome the subdiaconate, and Pope St. Cornelius in a letter to Bishop Fabius of Antioch mentions the seven "grades" (in Eusebius, *Eccles. Hist.* 6.43.11). In the Orthodox Church there are in modern days five orders: reader, subdeacon, deacon, priest, and bishop. In cases of necessity certain priests with the honorific title of archimandrite or archpriest may ordain a reader. Bishops, at least from the sixth century, have been chosen from the unmarried or the monastic clergy; outside of the monastic clergy, priests may get married (provided normally that they signify their intention before ordination). In the West the ancient custom of an unmarried clergy has prevailed universally from the days of Ambrose, Augustine, and Jerome. At least by the fourth century the impact of these three great Fathers of the Church, with their extensive interest in the guidance both of clergy and of the monks—Augustine in northern Africa, Ambrose in the area of Milan, and Jerome both at Rome and in Bethlehem—effectively formed the ideal of the celibate priest in the West at a time when this was uncommon in the Greek-speaking Church outside of the monastic settlements. This early ideal soon became customed-hardened into law, and through the vigorous efforts of Roman Pontiffs, as for example Pope Gregory VII (Hildebrand) and the wide missionary activities of the Gallic and Celtic monks in the West, the modern legislation gradually came into being.[30] The Council of Trent (especially in *Sessions* xxi, xxiii, and xxiv) dispelled the final lingering doubts, thus paving the way for current Western Canon Law. Clerics in major Orders are obliged to take a vow (or solemn promise) to observe chastity (*Code of Canon Law* 132) and remain unmarried, and this status constitutes a diriment impediment to any subsequent marriage (*Code* 1072), subject, of course, to special provisions granted by the Holy See in extraordinary cases. The Eastern Churches, however, both those in union with Rome and those that have been separated, have retained their ancient custom of a married diocesan clergy.

So far as the nature of the Orders themselves is concerned, the opinion of all theologians that all three of the major Orders constitute the sacrament has been supported by papal and conciliar decrees: but whether deaconate, priesthood, and episcopate each constitute a separate sacrament or, as seems the more plausible, each is a grade or degree in the perfection of a single sacrament, has been left undecided. The grade of deaconesses was current in the Eastern church from about the third to the sixth centuries: designated women were consecrated by a special rite with the imposition of hands and prayer (*Apostolic Constitutions* 8.19 f.); but the order soon fell into desuetude, for most of their duties (as the care of the infirm, the poor, and children) were assumed by the increasing communities of consecrated women or nuns. In recent times the question has arisen of restoring the custom of an active, married deaconate both for men and for women, for the purpose of assuming duties in missionary countries. Provided the practical details can be worked out, the revival of this ancient custom would seem advantageous to the growth of the Church at large.

The sanctity of the marriage bond was attacked by the early

Gnostics, Montanists, Manichaeans, and again in the Middle Ages by the Albigensians.[31] These heretical opinions should, of course, be distinguished from the view of patristic writers like Origen, Gregory of Nyssa, Chrysostom, Jerome, and others who, though they defended the sanctity of Christian marriage, firmly believed that sexual union was the result of Adam's sin, and that in the state of pure nature God had intended men to procreate their species in an angelic manner. Of the earlier Fathers, St. Ignatius of Antioch and Tertullian speak of the necessity of contracting marriage before the Church. St. Leo, in a letter to Rusticus of Narbonne, uses the word *sacramentum* of the unity of man and woman following the epistle to the Ephesians 5:22. And even St. Augustine, despite his severity with regard to the enjoyment of sexual pleasure within marriage, staunchly defends the sanctity of the sacrament as a source of holiness and as a symbol of Christ and the Church.[32] There is a general agreement on the monogamous character of Christian marriage. The early councils (for example, the synod of Carthage in 407) vigorously condemn divorce, and the general doctrine of the western Church stresses the indissolubility of the bond.[33] The analogy (following Hinemar of Rheims who died in 882) was always the indissolubility of the union between Christ and the Church.

It is true, however, that some of the early synods (for example, the synod of Arles in the year 324, and Rome in 826), and some of the Greek Fathers seem to permit divorce and remarriage in the case of adultery; at the very least, they appear to condone what was the practice in some localities: so, apparently, St. Gregory of Nazianzus (*Sermons* 37.8), St. Basil (Epistles 188.9, 199.21 ed. Deferrari), and St. John Chrysostom (*In epist. 1 ad Cor.,* hom. 19.3).[34] Though the Latin Church will allow the dissolution of the bond only in quite exceptional cases (e.g., *ratum et consummatum* only for entrance into clerical or religious life, without the permission to remarry; *ratum non consummatum* for grave reasons if nonconsummation can be proven), the ecclesiastical law of the Orthodox churches has developed in quite a different way. Here divorce is allowed in the case of adultery—and even, exceptionally, for other grave reasons—with the possibility of remarriage *coram ecclesia* three times. This custom in the East would appear to go back to the period before the separation from Rome.[35]

But the sacramentality of marriage in the strict sense was not formally recognized until the twelfth century with the theological speculation of the school of Peter Abelard, Rolando Bandinelli, and Peter the Lombard. But their reasons for so doing were clear. Beginning with the Pauline symbolism of the marriage bond, they pointed out the sanctity in which matrimony was held throughout the patristic period; the Church had always exercised a close watch over the formalities, the impediments, and the rite of marriage, and carefully protected the indissolubility of the bond. Finally, there was the essential role which Christian marriage plays in the Church as the physical and spiritual source of her increasing membership, both clerical and lay, throughout the course of time until the final coming of Christ the Bridegroom. Thus the Christian family is, in a sense, the Church in microcosm; and it was eminently fitting that the natural contract should have been elevated to the dignity of a sacramental sign.[36]

Sacramental theology was largely a development of the post-patristic period. Indeed, many of the relevant problems were to be solved only in recent times. Others, like the nature of the Eucharistic sacrifice, the primary effect of Extreme Unction, the problem of penitential sorrow, the relationship of the Orders, still remain controverted. But it was the merit of the theological schools of the twelfth century to have made the distinction between the great seven *sacramenta maiora*, or "major rites," and those of lesser importance, which we call sacramentals. The major rites were correctly defined as those which were instituted by the founder of Christianity—at least in a substantive, generic sense—and were intended to remain with the Church in some permanent, unchanging mode as an efficacious sign of the graces of the Redemption. But as most modern theologians hold, the fact that Christ instituted the sacramental system does not necessarily mean that He specifically and immutably determined the matter and form of the rite of each sacrament.[37] What is agreed, however, is that whatever Christ Himself determined—the substance of the sacrament and its purpose or effect—may not be changed by the Church; but it seems reasonable to hold that the Church in the course of time did make more specific and definite the significance, ritual, and scope of some of the sacraments where Christ's determination was less precise, and will perhaps continue to do so. For as the authoritative voice of Jesus throughout time, the Church must surely be allowed to declare when and in what circumstances the expression or the ritual of a sacrament will or will not be in accordance with Christ's original institution.

It was then the school of Peter Abelard and, following him, Peter the Lombard in his *Sentences* about the year 1148, who first clearly set forth the list of the great seven sacraments. As he wrote (*Sent.* IV, Dist. 2, 1):

> Now let us proceed to the sacraments of the
> New Law, Baptism, Confirmation, the blessing
> of the bread or the Eucharist, Penance,
> Final Anointing, Orders, and Matrimony.
> Of these some offer a remedy against sin
> and confer auxiliary grace; some, like
> Marriage, are merely for a remedy; others,
> like Orders and the Eucharist, strengthen
> us with grace and virtue.

Peter gave a new formality to a doctrine that had long been held, and indeed had been accurately set forth in the anonymous *Summa Sententiarum* of the first half of the twelfth century; hence it is wrong to speak of him as the creator of a new dogma, as A. Harnack and others do.[88] The list of the major sacraments made clear, once and for all, the role of the lesser sacraments or "sacramentals," which had long been held in honor in the Church. These were, to name but a few, the minor orders (differently understood, however, in East and West), the washing of feet, the blessing of fields and other objects, the extermination of vermin, and various acts of prayer, penance, and pilgrimage performed under the guidance of the Church. The effectiveness of these signs was more intercessory in nature; they implored God's grace for the individual and, like indulgences, tended to remit the earthly and temporal punishment due to sin. But their efficacy was defined as *ex opere operantis,* that is, it was not guaranteed by the Church but depended upon the fervor and intention of the faithful.

The doctrine and practice of the separated churches have remained very close to the Roman Catholic Church in the matter of the sacraments and the sacramentals, and, indeed, this is a further confirmation of their primitive authenticity. In particular, the adherence to seven sacraments was explicitly affirmed at the Or-

thodox synods held at Istanbul in the years 1638 and 1642, and
again at Jerusalem in 1672, at which time the heretical teaching of
the patriarch Cyril Lukaris was condemned. Substantially the same
doctrine has been reiterated in the famous *Catechism* of Peter
Mogila and the *Confession* of Dositheus in the seventeenth century, and in other noted documents of the Orthodox Church of the
nineteenth and twentieth centuries.[39] The witness of the Eastern
churches is especially precious in this highly controversial area,
and offers firm ground for that eventual union which was so
earnestly desired by Pope John XXIII of happy memory.

In summary, the patristic doctrine on sacramental symbolism is
found in its richest form in the Greek Fathers, and especially in
those like Gregory of Nyssa under the allegorical influence of the
Alexandrian school. The entire Church in its union with the Savior
is the great *mystêrion* or sacramentum, born from the side of
Christ on Calvary. More specifically, the entire supernatural life of
God's people consists of a complex texture of symbolic acts and
gestures, involving the use of sacred and symbolic objects as water,
oil, bread, and wine. Both the actions and the objects derive their
power or effectiveness from the mystical words handed down by
the apostolic tradition. It is the intention of Christ that by their
gestures the faithful imitate and participate in His life; by their
actions and prayers they fulfill the mystical types of the Old Law;
and by the special consecration of the hierarchy the water, oil,
wine, and so on become possessed of special "vivifying grace" to
transform the faithful into a member of Christ, into a militant
Christian, into a high priest of sacrifice. Certain of these ancient
rites, as that of Baptism, Chrismation, and Ordination bestow
upon the participant a special, invisible mark, a "seal" of the
spirit, a "spiritual anointing," such that even should he fall from
grace they may not be again repeated. Finally, Augustine's doctrine of symbols (*signa*) in his treatise *On Christian Doctrine* sets
the sacramental system within the entire context of man's coming
to a knowledge of God both within the world and within the special context of the Church. For Augustine the divine signs are given
to men in order to know, and it is by their operative grace that
men are enabled to live in a new dimension—a supernatural dimension whose terminus is the possession of God.

NOTES

1. For the literature, see especially Christine Mohrmann, *Études sur le latin des chrétiens*, 2 vols. (Rome, 1961); on the evolution of *sacramentum*, see "Sacramentum dans les plus anciens textes chrétiens," I, 233–44, with the bibliography cited.

2. See W. F. Arndt, and F. Wilbur Gingrich, *A Greek-English Lexicon of the New Testament and Other Early Christian Literature* (Chicago, 1957), *s. v.* See also P. Pourrat, *The Theology of the Sacraments: A Study in Positive Theology* (London, 1924), pp. 2–21.

3. C. Mohrmann, *loc. cit.* 235–36.

4. See Livy 10.38.2; Tertullian, *Apology* 7.1; and cf. Mohrmann, *loc. cit.* 237–39.

5. See now William H. Brownlee, *The Meaning of the Qumrân Scrolls for the Bible* (New York, 1964), especially, pp. 110 ff., with the literature cited. The views of A. Dupont-Sommer, *The Essene Writings from Qumran* (trans. G. Vermes, Oxford, 1961), pp. 368–78, are perhaps too extreme on the debt of Christianity to the Essenes.

6. See H. Musurillo, *Symbolism and the Christian Imagination* (Baltimore, 1962), pp. 5 ff., with the literature there cited.

7. See H. Musurillo, *St. Methodius: The Symposium: A Treatise on Chastity* (Ancient Christian Writers 27, Westminster, 1958), pp. 16 ff.

8. This gift (*glossolalia*), whose manifestation at Corinth at times tried Paul's patience, has been interpreted in various ways. The older view, that the inspired actually spoke new languages (or were miraculously understood by speakers of different languages) has now yielded to the theory of ecstatic speech of the sort manifested in persons subject to trance or ecstasy.

9. See H. Musurillo, *op. cit.*, pp. 9 ff.

10. See Bernard Leeming, *Principles of Sacramental Theology* (London, 1956), pp. xxxviii ff., and cf. Pourrat, *op. cit.*, pp. 256 ff.

11. See, for example, Brownlee, *op cit.*, pp. 114 ff., with the sources quoted.

12. See Karl Rahner, *The Church and the Sacraments* (Quaestiones Disputatae 9, New York, 1963), pp. 24 ff.

13. On the patristic evidence, see M. Schmaus, J. Geiselmann, and P. A. Grillmeier, *Handbuch der Dogmengeschichte: Band IV (Sakramente*, Freiburg, 1951 ff. in fascicules). Cf. also J. N. D. Kelly, *Early Christian Doctrines* (New York, 1958), pp. 422–55, with the sources cited. There is an excellent selection of texts in Paul F. Palmer, *Sources of Christian Theology* (2 vols., Westminster, 1959, 1963), covering Baptism, Confirmation, and the Eucharist, and (in vol. II) Penance, Unction, and Indulgences.

14. See B. Neunheuser, in M. Schmaus and others, *Handbuch der Dogmengeschichte* Band IV, Faszikel 2 *Taufe und Firmung*, (Freiburg, 1956); cf. Leeming, *op. cit.*, p. 426. See also Ludwig Ott, *Fundamentals of Catholic Dogma* (ed. by James Canon Bastible and trans. P. Lynch, St. Louis, 1955), pp. 361 ff.

15. See the discussion of Rahner, *op. cit.*, pp. 51 f.

16. See Timothy Ware, *The Orthodox Church* (Penguin Books: Baltimore, Md., 1963), pp. 285–86.

17. For a discussion, see Bernhard Poschmann, *Penance and the Anointing of the Sick* (trans. Francis Courtney, New York 1963), pp. 238–39.

18. There is a good collection of texts which deal with the "conversion" of the elements in G. W. H. Lampe, *A Patristic Greek Lexicon* (Oxford, 1961 ff.), fasc. 3, *s. vv.* See also Kelly, *op. cit.,* pp. 440–49.

19. See Timothy Ware, *The Orthodox Church,* pp. 290–92; see also Ernst Benz, *The Eastern Orthodox Church: Its Thought and Life* (trans. R. and C. Winston, Anchor Books: New York, 1963), pp. 36–39. For an historical survey of the doctrine in the Eastern churches, see B. Neunheuser, in M. Schmaus and others, *Handbuch der Dogmengeschichte:* Band IV, fasc. 4b, *Eucharistie in Mittelalter und Neuzeit,* pp. 1–11.

20. On Berengarius, see the bibliography in Ulysse Chevalier, *Répertoire des sources historiques du Moyen Age: Bio-bibliographie* (Paris, 1903; reprint New York, 1960), I, 537–38. For a discussion of his work, see Leeming, *Principles of Sacramental Theology,* pp. 252 ff., and B. Neunheuser, *Eucharistie in Mittelalter und Neuzeit,* pp. 19–22.

21. See Neunheuser, *Eucharistie in Mittelalter und Neuzeit,* pp. 51 ff., for a summary of the controversies.

22. For a discussion of the sources, see Bernhard Poschmann, *Busse und Letzte Ölung,* in M. Schmaus and others, *Handbuch der Dogmengeschichte:* Band IV, Faszikel 3 (Freiburg, 1951), pp. 10 ff. (*Penance and the Anointing of the Sick,* pp. 19 ff.), with the literature. Cf. also Paul F. Palmer, *Sources of Christian Theology,* II, 9 ff.

23. See Poschmann, *Penance and the Anointing of the Sick,* pp. 89–91.

24. *Ibid.,* pp. 97–99.

25. *Ibid.,* pp. 212–215.

26. See Leeming, *op. cit.,* pp. 361–66; Rahner, *The Church and the Sacraments,* pp. 93–95; Poschmann, *Penance and the Anointing of the Sick,* pp. 202–9.

27. Poschmann, pp. 208–9.

28. See Paul F. Palmer, *Sources of Christian Theology,* II, 394–98.

29. See also Rahner, *The Church and the Sacraments,* pp. 95–106.

30. For a summary of the historical problem, see Egidio Caspani, "Celibato," *Enciclopedia italiana* 9 (1951), 659–60, with the bibliography, and the addendum on the Orthodox churches by Cyril Korolevsky (660).

31. See Pierre Adnès, *Le mariage* (Tournai, 1963), especially pp. 43–58 for the evidence of the patristic period. See also Arturo C. Jemolo, "Matrimonio," *Enciclopedia italiana* 22 (1951), 582–85.

32. For the textes, see P. Adnès, *Le mariage,* p. 75.

33. *Ibid.,* pp. 59 ff.

34. For a more favorable interpretation of these texts, see P. Adnès, pp. 59 ff., with the bibliography.

35. See Ware, *The Orthodox Church,* pp. 300–302.

36. See also Rahner, pp. 107–12.

37. For this section I am indebted to the very lucid discussion of B. Leeming, pp. 385–431, especially the conclusions on pp. 424 ff.

38. Cf. the historical survey in P. Pourrat, *Theology of the Sacraments,* pp. 272 ff.

39. See the sources as quoted and discussed in Leeming, pp. 578–81; And cf. Ware, pp. 281 ff.

18 *Focus for Contemporary Ethics*

JULES TONER

The basic need for the Christian philosopher in the study of ethics is a new focus more in accord with our times—a focus on love.

In THEORY IF not in practice all would agree that it is unreasonable to affirm or deny the validity of a philosophy because the philosopher happens to be of a certain temperament, comes from a certain social, or religious, or cultural background, has certain peculiarities of style. The only valid reasons for affirming or denying a philosophy are objective reasons. One may reasonably, however, for nonphilosophical, even for subjective reasons be more interested in one philosopher than another, emphasize one part of philosophy more than another, or look at reality under one aspect rather than another. It is, perhaps, necessary to go further and say that it is not possible, and even if it were possible, would not be desirable, that a man should philosophize as if in a vacuum, uninfluenced by his own personal inclinations, problems and commitments, or by the needs, problems, and intellectual currents of his historical setting. Surely his thinking ought not to be fully determined by these factors, but it inevitably is influenced by them; and this influence ought to be consciously felt and reasonably responded to. Plato could not escape being a fifth-century Athenian, the heir of Socrates and the pre-Socratics, a member of the ruling class in a state that was showing signs of need for moral reform. Immanuel Kant could not escape being a German Protestant, of pietistic background, living in an age that was awed by Newtonian physics and troubled by the skeptical conclusions of Empiricist philosophy. I do not imply that either of them was fully justified in their manner of reacting to the influences of their worlds, but I do say that if either of them had tried to philosophize as if these influences did not exist, they would very likely have said nothing of value and certainly would have had no influence on their contemporaries.

THE CURRENT SITUATION

Now it seems to be a notable fact that moral philosophy in general has a very slight impact on the lives or even the thinking of educated persons in our time, and that philosophers of the Christian tradition have done little to change the situation. This is not to say that our times are more wicked or less interested in moral life than earlier ages. There is considerable evidence available for one who wishes to argue the contrary thesis. However that may be, all I am maintaining is that the world is not much influenced by what the contemporary moral philosophers are saying, neither in its thinking nor in its acting. And the reason seems to be plain enough. Moral philosophy as it is practiced in our times has very little to say that answers the deep problems, needs, and desires of our world. The analytical philosophers go on playing their very intellectual word game, and those who do not play the game have slight interest in what they are doing, because, while analysis has a limited value for making discussion precise, it gives no real direction or inspiration for living to a world hungering for a meaning to life. Existentialists have some impact, because they are passionately concerned about existence as we experience it, because they express dramatically our loneliness, our confusion, our despair and our hope. But the most prominent of them fail to find any genuine meaning to life.

The one group of philosophers which might be expected to be influential at such a time of crisis is the one composed of those who philosophize under the influence of Christian faith and a tradition of great thinkers stretching back for 2,500 years, and who have the amazing opportunity of teaching their moral philosophy to many thousands of students every year. To say that we are totally ineffective would be an unfair exaggeration. But that the effect on the lives of our own students or even on their thinking is very disappointing must be admitted, and much more so, the influence on the intellectual milieu of our time.[1]

I would like to suggest a reason for this situation and, in doing so, to suggest a remedy. To me, the basic need in our teaching and writing on ethics is a new focus more in accord with the need of our time—and, I am convinced, of all times, because it gives the fullest insight into moral reality.

What, then, is the present focus in Scholastic ethics? If I am not mistaken, the general focus can be expressed by the following questions. In what does my end consist? That is, what will fulfill me? What is the most I can demand as a right from others? And what is the least I am required to render to others, whether it be owed to the individual or to the common good? Put in a universal manner, in what does man's fulfillment as a being capable of thought consist? What is the minimum of obligation which each has to the others and they to him, so that each may be enabled to seek his own fulfillment? This approach is referred to as the "rights-and-duties" approach. And it is, of course, valid and useful as far as it goes. We cannot do without these considerations in ethical theory.

Some make what is an important advance over this approach. Without eliminating what is valid in this latter, they focus more on the ideal of moral development, on virtue, on the heights of moral achievement, rather than on minimal obligation. However, while allowing for a more complete and more effective ethics than the former, even this focus, in practice if not in theory, fails to make clear what, as Christian philosophers,[2] we ought to see is obviously the heart and soul of moral greatness, and as men sensitive to our times, we ought to see is a conscious and intense need of our world, a need which is also a call.

There are, then, several questions which arise and to which I will attempt to offer answers in this article. (1) What is the focal point of ethics which the Christian philosopher should see in the light of, but without proving it by, Christian faith? (2) How did Christian philosophers lose this focal point? (3) What are some of the currents of thought in our time which call for a return to this focal point, currents which could flow together with an ethics so focused as to strengthen it and, in turn, to be guided by it?

The Christian Focus

First, what should be the focus of a moral philosophy which arises under the influence of Christian faith, its power to heal fallen nature, consciously and confidently submitted to, but without using that faith as a premise? Should it not, without any doubt, be a focus on love? If, after reading what Christ and St. Paul and St. John have to say about charity, should we not think that anything other than a love-centered ethics at the natural level should bear the burden of proving itself against the latter?[3] I, for my part, have not found any convincing or even persuasive argument to sustain that burden of proof. On the contrary, I find more and more philosophical reasons to confirm and fill out the lines of ethical thought toward which the Christian faith points.

As was mentioned previously, the rights-and-duties orientation in moral philosophy is valid and necessary but inadequate. The virtue orientation includes and surpasses the former. But both lack depth and force unless they are vitalized by love at their center—and not only at their center, but working out from the center, through all their parts. A morality of rights and duties, once it loses the focus on love, readily becomes a sterile legalism in which a man readily forgets that others—strange as it may sound to those who identify love wholly with spontaneous feeling—have a right to be loved and he has a duty to love and vice versa. A morality of virtue which allows the focus on love to be lost or even to become vague tends to turn the ideal image of moral man into that of a self-seeking perfectionist at best and at worst that of an arrogant, egotistical snob—as some see Aristotle's magnanimous man of virtue[4]—or a self-righteous, puritanical prig—as Toby Belch saw Malvolio.

Nor is it enough to assert in the proper place that love is the most important moral act of man or that love must inform every virtue—and then let all proceed just as it would have without such an assertion. The focus on love must be constant. Every part of moral philosophy must be understood in relation to love and every moral problem solved in the light of love.

It is not my purpose in this article to elaborate a positive theoretical justification for a love-centered ethics or to draw up an outline of such an ethics. No doubt both of these tasks must be done, and I hope to present something on them hereafter. The present discussion may help to prepare the way by offering some explanation for the present lack of focus on love and by calling attention to some developments in our time which point us back to the focus on love in moral thought.

Some Reasons for Loss of Right Focus

It could be that we are afflicted by the same difficulties which afflict most of our contemporaries when the subject of love is discussed. One reason for avoiding discussion of love is that which has plagued everyone from the Greeks to the present, the difficulty of grasping the experience clearly. Ortega y Gasset suggests a reason for this.

A store of crude ideas fixed in peoples' heads prevents them from seeing the facts with normal clarity. Everything is confused and distorted. There are many reasons for this. In the first place, love, by nature, is part of one's secret life. One cannot tell about one's love; in the telling it vanishes or vaporizes. Everyone has to rely upon his personal experiences, almost always meagre, for it is not easy to profit from that of one's neighbor. What would have happened, however, to physics if each physicist possessed only his personal observations? In the second place, what happens is that the men who are most capable of thinking about love, are the ones who have experienced it the least; whereas those who have experienced it are usually incapable of thinking about it, of subtly analyzing its iridescent and ever vague plumage.[5]

Gordon Allport expresses this difficulty by saying that love is the very groundwork of all psychological activity and that we do not ordinarily perceive the groundwork of our activity.[6] It is this difficulty of studying and understanding love, according to A. H. Maslow, which accounts for the sometimes "sad and irritating," and more often "completely ludicrous," silence of the empirical sciences on the subject of love. Especially strange, he thinks, is the silence of the psychologist who might be thought to have a special obligation to study love. "Probably this is just another example of the besetting sin of academicians, who prefer to do what they are easily able rather than what they ought . . ." but what is exceedingly difficult.[7]

Not only is it difficult to understand love, it is difficult to express one's understanding without being misunderstood by others. The word "love" has such a variety of related meanings and is used in so many diverse senses that confusion abounds.[8]

The difficulty of the subject, however, can hardly be an adequate justification for the fact that the empirical scientists, philosophers, and even the Christian theologians, have let love slip out of its central position which it formerly held in Western thought. The difficulties have been there in every age, and yet every age save our own has had its great philosophy of love and of the affections in general.[9]

What the reason is might take some social psychoanalysis as well as history to unravel. For it would have to take account of the strange embarrassment of our contemporaries when love is discussed seriously, an embarrassment which tends to turn the discussion into a joke, as though love were something a bit indecent to bring up and had to be passed off with a witticism. All the brave Freudian disclaimers of reticence about sex sound very hollow in our time. But how explain our reticence about love? How explain why serious scholars and scientific men who dare to discuss the subject feel that it takes great courage to do so in the face of the inevitable reaction of their colleagues? The members of the Research Society for Creative Altruism[10] have remarked this. Ian Suttie characterizes the attitude as science's "flight from tenderness," and ascribes it to a reaction against theology.[11] I might add my own experience when I began to give a course on the philosophy of love. On all sides, there were lifted eyebrows, sly smiles, and many witty remarks at my expense. And all this, not from adolescents, nor from light-minded persons, but from quite mature and good persons, both faculty and students.

Over and above the general attitudes toward love characteristic of our times, though closely bound up with these, there are two other reasons for the strange reticence about love found even in Christian moral philosophy. Both arise from historical accidents. The first arises from the development of theology in modern times. The teachers and writers of scholastic ethical treatises were until relatively recent times principally if not almost exclusively clerics trained in moral theology, who transposed that moral theology into philosophy. When theology lost its focus on charity as its center and vitalizing principle,[12] moral philosophy suffered a similar loss. A second historical accident which is at least a likely reason, if not for love losing its primacy in ethics—that was already lost— at least for stabilizing the bad situation, is the uneasiness of the Christian philosopher in a secular culture. Have we, perhaps, in order to allay suspicion of our ethics as not being purely philo- sophical—which of course it ought to be—tried to philosophize as if we were not Christians philosophizing, as if we were just a bit embarrassed for fear our unbelieving colleagues would accuse us of theologism should we say anything which too much resembled revealed truth? Are we so accustomed by now to the bent-over- backwards posture that we feel uneasy when we abandon it—even when we find unbelievers saying what we should have been saying all along, and, ironically, speaking of our ethics as legalistic and utterly ineffective for helping men to live humanly and strive productively for a human world in which men truly love one an- other and live in peace?

In reality we are Christians, who have from our supernatural faith insights into the nature of man and human life at the natural level; to be guided by these insights without employing faith as a premise is no more illicit philosophically than for Socrates to be guided by his demon or any philosophical or scientific genius to be guided by some brilliant insight that he cannot yet establish. When the philosophical grounds for a guiding insight are found and shown then it should be judged philosophically on those grounds alone. Until then it is not philosophically grounded; after that it is stupid to argue that it is not philosophical because inspired by faith or by a brilliant guess.

I am well aware that you might find particular illustrations of the opposite mistake in some Scholastic books where positions which are really held by the author only because he is a Christian are presented as if philosophical arguments justify the firmness with which he asserts the conclusions. The confusion of faith and reason does no real service to either. Nevertheless, I think you will ordinarily find even such writing embedded in an overall frame- work which would do considerable credit to a pre-Christian pagan but not to a twentieth-century Christian.

Let me make my point by referring to a remark in a text widely used in Catholic schools, one which is, in many ways, an excellent piece of work, by a man who is an excellent scholar, philosopher, and Christian. In his Preface, the author acknowledges Aristotle's *Nicomachean Ethics* to be still the best formulation of the practical science of ethics. He seems to see nothing strange about such a remark. Certainly it was not the author's intention, but I could hardly think of a more devastating comment on the failure of Christian philosophers in the field of ethics. Think what it would mean if we had to say that Aristotle's metaphysics was the greatest formulation of the science of metaphysics. Whether or not this author's remark about the *Ethics* is true, it could pass with no one, to my knowledge, taking violent objection to it. So here we are even now able to say, at least without sounding absurd, that perhaps the best formulation of ethics yet achieved is one in which God plays no part, in which unselfish love for persons just as persons is undreamed of—as if we had not learned anything of God, of love, of personality, and the meaning of life since Aristotle.

As a matter of fact, there is sound reason for thinking that the overwhelming influence of Aristotle on Christian thinkers is to some extent responsible for our confusion. Even a deeply Christian man, once he has submitted his mind to the framework of thought in Aristotle's *Ethics,* will have a hard time keeping anything like a natural charity central to his thought or even making the *Ethics* fit in coherently. The more general opinion is that St. Thomas succeeded in transforming Aristotle for Christian use. Some think he did not altogether succeed. However that may be, it seems certain that the Scholastic ethics as developed in more recent centuries has not succeeded. In fact, some are of the opinion that it has retrogressed in a certain respect by losing the Aristoltelian emphasis on virtue.

Converging Currents

There is reason to hope that the regrettable situation about which we have been speaking is on the way to becoming obsolete. There are signs on all sides of an awakening interest in the study of love: in theology, philosophy, psychology, and sociology. Books and articles have begun to multiply, and the quality of the work is very good.

This brings us to our last question, a question about the need and the opportunity of our time for an ethics with love as its focal point. I shall try to answer this question by calling attention to some developments in the fields of psychology, sociology, and philosophy. I shall try to show how certain movements in these fields underline the central importance of love in human life; how they tend toward a normative as well as a descriptive treatment of love; how, as a consequence, their conclusions converge with or show the need for a love-centered ethics. No doubt there are ideas, even basic ones, in the thought of those men whom we will be discussing at which a philosopher in the Scholastic tradition, and certainly a Christian, might demur, some to which he would object strongly. But he will find much also which can strengthen and enrich his philosophy and help him to bring it to bear on contemporary life with an emphasis and focus which is appropriate to our contemporaries.

The principle figure among those concerned with love as a social force and an object of sociological study is Pitirim Sorokin. He himself relates how he was led to his sociological concern about love.

The loss, exterminations and the horrors of the First World War, and especially of the Russian revolution—in both of which I participated as an observer and actor—had led me to the conclusion summed up in my *Leaves From a Russian Diary* (1924) that cruelty, hatred and injustice never can and never will be able to create a mental, moral, or material millennium, and that the creative, unselfish work of love for humanity at large is the key to the reconstruction of the world.

Subsequently, my studies of social and cultural dynamics and the nature of the epochal crises of our age . . . reinforced the conclusion that, without a transformation of modern sensate man and of the dominant sensate culture, this crisis could develop into an apocalyptic war capable of terminating mankind's creative history. A few years later, these conclusions were to be tragically confirmed by the Second World War, by a multitude of hot and cold wars, and by a legion of bloody revolutions and disorders. The unprecedented destructiveness, bestiality, and moral insanity of these convulsions—and the millions victimized by them—led me, in February, 1946, to the decision to devote my free time from then on to the study of unselfish, creative love, and of effective techniques for transforming the motivational systems of man—and thus transforming his sociocultural universe.[13]

In his book published in 1948, *Reconstruction of Humanity,*[14] Sorokin described the crisis which society faces, indicated what he considers false lines of meeting it, what the true solution is, and finally laid out the general lines of a program for effecting this solution. The solution is altruistic love, and the program consists of methods for studying this love and bringing about such love in society.

To carry out this plan he founded in 1949 the Harvard Research Center in Creative Altruism. From this center has come a series of books by Sorokin on altruistic love, and of symposia on the same subject by scholars in a variety of fields, such as philosophy, theology, social studies, and the natural sciences.[15] All of these books discuss, and develop in detail, the ideas set out in the *Reconstruction of Humanity.* The main book for Sorokin's own views on altruistic love and the methods for developing it is entitled *The Ways and Power of Love.*[16] In this work he presents a sociological study of love itself and of the methods for generating, preserving, and releasing the power of altruistic love—or, to use his sociological terms, of producing, accumulating, and distributing altruistic love. What Sorokin seems to be aiming at in these writings is a normative, love-centered sociology, which tends to become a sort of social ethics.

In 1955, with the help of a group of other distinguished men, Sorokin founded the Research Society for Creative Altruism, which he calls "the cultural child and a successor of the Harvard Research Center in Creative Altruism." Sorokin gives his reasons for this move:

With the development of this research, my conviction that its goal—fostering the spirit of altruism in man—is indeed the paramount business on today's agenda of history, has been increasingly reinforced and confirmed. This logically suggested the next step in the development of scientific study of this "mysterious, powerful grace," namely, the establishment of a national, even international, research society in this field, which could be an independent institution and could do the research and educational work of the Center on a larger and deeper scale.[17]

The first Scientific Conference on New Knowledge in Human Values was held by this research society in October, 1957, and the results published in 1959 under the title *New Knowledge in Human Values*. The contributors are an impressive cross-section of scholars in this country.[18] Walter Weisskopf, one of the contributors, in his "Summary and Comment," says: "From the deliberations of this symposium emerges union through love as the ultimate value."[19]

Among the contributors to *New Knowledge in Human Values*, as also in the symposia published from the Harvard Research Center in Creative Altruism, there are a notable number of well-known psychologists. And in recent psychotherapeutic literature we find great emphasis put upon love in studying the symptoms, the causes, and the cure of neurosis. All this is both a development from, and a correction of, the original insights of Sigmund Freud, who did much both to promote and to hinder focusing of attention on love in psychological study. He promoted it by presenting love as the basic, or even the sole positive driving force in man; hindered it by a stunted, and to some neo-Freudians an absurd, notion of love, reducing it, as he did, to *libido,* the energy springing from sexual instinct.[20] In the long run, however, his influence may have been more a help than a hindrance; for those of his followers who have not settled into static orthodoxy have held on to the basic importance of love and brought their notion of love more into conformity with the facts which Freud's dogmatic materialism forced him to ignore, or to interpret in accord with the dogma. This development has taken place in conjunction with a new orientation in psychology, an orientation which in spirit parallels what Sorokin has been urging in sociology. I refer to the shift from the concentration on pathology and what Ira Progroff speaks of as a "diagnostic attitude cast . . . in terms of medical materialism" to a concentration on the positive unfolding of the human personality in its spiritual dimensions. In this new view, the unconscious is seen as a seat of "hidden propensities to growth which set the direction and possibilities of human development." This orientation demands what Smutz spoke of as a "science of personology," a study of persons who have achieved spiritual, personal, greatness.[21]

An example of this new orientation is A. H. Maslow's study

reported in his book *Motivation and Personality*.[22] The data
which he gathered led him to agree firmly with those who clearly
distinguish love from sex as against the Freudian tradition. It also
made evident to him that human beings have a psychic need for
being loved comparable, for instance, to the bodily need for salt;
and a fulfillment of this need is a condition for healthy psychological growth. And what is most significant for our topic, it led him to
see that those who have grown to psychological health exhibit
notably a "power to love and the ability to be loved."[23]

Insistence on the inability of the neurotic to love, the source of
neurosis in not being loved, the therapeutic power of love, the
ability to love altruistically as a mark of psychological maturity
and health—all this has become so commonplace as to make doc-
umentation superfluous.[24] Several remarks, however, about this
development will be relevant here. First of all, the interest of clinical and social psychology in love had developed with a normative
orientation—so much so that psychologists begin speaking like
ethicians. In Erich Fromm we even find a psychologist who conceives of ethics as applied psychology and presents what he calls a
"humanistic ethic" in his widely influential book, *Man for Himself*.[25] It is obvious, then, how these psychological currents, especially of the love-centered clinical sort, tend to merge with ethics—
even, in the extreme case, to identify with it.[26]

Certainly, then, there is a mutual benefit to be sought in this
situation. On the one hand, psychology needs philosophy, a philosophy with a genuine metaphysics, to keep clear the distinction
of the two fields; to indicate the areas of cooperation; to provide a
larger, metaphysically founded framework within which the moral
norms for man's activity can be developed more adequately than
psychology by itself is capable of doing; to give a deeper and
clearer understanding of love and its meaning in personal life; to
correct any invalid conclusions resulting from a lack of metaphysical perspective. On the other hand, the philosopher can benefit
from the data and insights of the psychologist, whether as confirming his own philosophical positions, or suggesting corrections, or
as opening up new paths of speculation on the nature of love, on
love as a value—its importance in the ideal person and as the
ultimate fulfillment of man—on love as the core of character, and
so on.

Evidence of possible fruitful cooperation between philosophy and psychology in this way can be glimpsed in the current interest which some psychologists are showing in the philosophy of encounter, of intersubjectivity, of the "I-Thou" relation, as it is variously called.[27] The effort to understand this experience with all its implications about the person as person and personal life as constituted by relation with other persons has become a major interest for a number of the most sensitive thinkers of our time.[28] John Macmurray speaks of the "form of the personal" as the emerging problem of philosophy in the new age which is evolving out of our present crisis[29]—and in his thought personal existence is constituted by relation with other persons. It is true that this contemporary study of the experience of interpersonal knowledge and love is not strictly an ethical study, but it is true that the full meaning of this experience is not grasped without an ethical understanding of it, and that it, in turn, has many profound implications in ethics, as well as in philosophical or clinical psychology. Inevitably those who are concerned with the study of interpersonal communion are led to ethical considerations. It is time, perhaps, that all those seriously interested in ethics should be led to a study of the interpersonal communion as it is found in the "I-Thou" relationship. This contemporary concern for understanding and promoting genuine interpersonal experience is another sign of the times, another expression of the intense and conscious—even when not understood —need of our contemporary world. It is another call to the Christian moral philosopher to respond to this need and opportunity of our time.

Summary

One might summarize the main point of this article as follows: we cannot and should not try to philosophize independently of our actual situation in reality. In reality we are Christians and as such know the primacy of charity, whether supernatural charity in Christian life or natural charity in the natural ethical life of man. In reality the conscious need of men in our times and the currents of intellectual life as exemplified in psychology and the social sciences and philosophy of intersubjectivity point toward the same kind of ethics as does the Christian faith.[30]

NOTES

1. These remarks are not made with the intention of adding another voice to that chorus of those who criticize Catholic universities for their lack of scholarship. In the matter under discussion our failure is certainly less than that of the secular schools. And this is one deficiency that can be remedied without a great addition to present financial resources—which cannot be said of scholarly production on any notable scale.

2. This term, "Christian philosopher," because of its close relationship with the term, "Christian philosophy," could be a cause of misunderstanding and debate and might better be avoided if there were a convenient substitute. I do not wish to take any position here on the legitimacy of the term "Christian philosophy." But certainly there can be no question about whether or not there are Christians who philosophize, and I see no reason for avoiding the term "Christian philosopher" any more than for avoiding the term "Christian lawyer," "doctor," "bricklayer" or "carpenter."

3. The love of which Holy Scripture is speaking is, no doubt, a supernatural love; but if the supernatural presupposes and builds upon and fulfills the natural, then it cannot contradict nature. And if supernatural charity is the fulfillment of all the law and the prophets, the summation of Christian perfection, then it would be surprising indeed to find natural charity playing a subordinate role in the natural moral life of man.

4. Cf., e.g., Maurice B. McNamee, *Honor and the Epic Hero* (New York: Holt, Rinehart & Winston, 1960), Chapter I.

5. Ortega y Gasset, *On Love* (New York: Meridian Books, 1957), p. 183.

6. Gordon Allport, "A Psychological Approach to the Study of Love and Hate" in *Explorations in Altruistic Love and Behavior,* ed. Pitirim Sorokin (Boston: Beacon Press, 1950), pp. 145–146.

7. Abraham H. Maslow, *Motivation and Personality* (New York: Harper, 1954), p. 235.

8. Most writers on the subject of love will mention this difficulty. Cf., for instance, the remarks in Paul Tillich, *Love, Power and Justice* (New York: Oxford University Press, Galaxy Books, 1960), pp. 1–6; Rollo May, *Man's Search for Himself* (New York: W. W. Norton, 1953) pp. 239–246.

9. There are those who would count the Freudian theory as our great theory. If by great one means influential, then there is no argument. But, for all Freud's genius as a pioneer psychologist, the fact that his notion of love could be taken seriously as anything like an adequate one is one of the worst comments possible on the culture in which his thought has flourished. There is reason for the opinion that contemporary interest in the "I-Thou" experience may be the beginnings of the great theory we have so long been waiting for.

10. Concerning this Society, cf. below, the section on "Converging Currents."

11. Ian Suttie, *Origins of Love and Hate* (London: Kegan Paul, 1933), pp. 1–2.

12. For an account of how this took place, cf. Gerard Gilleman, *The Primacy of Charity in Moral Theology* (Westminster, Md.: Newman Press, 1959), pp. xxviii-xxxii; John C. Ford and Gerald Kelly, *Contemporary Moral Theology* (Westminster, Md.: Newman Press, 1958), pp. 44–46. For an

account of some criticisms of the modern development in moral theology, cf. Ford and Kelly, *op. cit.*, pp. 42–59; and for some new approaches, with reflections on these, cf. *ibid.*, pp. 60–103. For a developed attempt at working out the lines of a moral theology which gives full primacy to charity, cf. Gilleman's book. Further bibliographical direction can be found in these two books.

13. *New Knowledge in Human Values*, A. H. Maslow, Ed. (New York: Harper, 1959), pp. xi-xii.

14. Pitirim A. Sorokin, *Reconstruction of Humanity* (Boston: Beacon Press, 1948).

15. The principal publications of the research center following upon the *Reconstruction of Humanity* which are directly concerned with the study of love are the following: P. A. Sorokin, *Altruistic Love: A Study of American Good Neighbors and Christian Saints* (1950); P. A. Sorokin, (editor), *Forms and Techniques of Altruistic and Spiritual Growth: A Symposium* (1954); P. A. Sorokin, *The Ways and Power of Love: Types, Factors, and Techniques of Moral Transformation* (1954). All volumes are published by the Beacon Press, Boston.

16. Cf. Note 15 above.

17. *New Knowledge in Human Values*, p. xiii.

18. Henry Margenau, Jacob Bronowski, Robert S. Hartman, Pitirim A. Sorokin, Ludwig Von Bertalanffy, Theodosius Dobzhansky, Gyorgy Kepes, Suzuki, Walter A. Weisskopf, Abraham Maslow, Gordon W. Allport, Erich Fromm, Dorothy Lee, Kurt Goldstein, Paul Tillich.

19. *Ibid.*, p. 223.

20. The theory of instinct went through several changes in Freud's writing. What is said here holds true at least of the later form which the theory took. For a brief statement of the meaning of love for Freud as seen from an ethical point of view, cf. James V. McGlynn and Jules J. Toner, *Modern Ethical Theories* (Milwaukee: Bruce, 1961), pp. 118–124.

21. Cf. Ira Progroff, "An Evolutionary Psychology of Wholeness," *Main Currents*, XV, No. 2 (November, 1958), 29–30.

22. Abraham H. Maslow, *Motivation and Personality* (New York: Harper, 1954). Cf. also his continuation of this study in *Toward a Psychology of Being* (Princeton, N. J.: D. Van Nostrand, 1962).

23. *Ibid.*, p. 241.

24. Besides Maslow, cf. the writings of Rollo May, Karen Horney, Carl Rogers, Clemens Benda, Erich Fromm, Gordon Allport, Percival Symonds, Viktor Frankl, etc.

25. Erich Fromm, *Man for Himself* (New York: Rinehart & Co., 1947).

26. For an account of Erich Fromm's ethics, cf. McGlynn and Toner, *op cit.*, pp. 126–138.

27. Cf. e.g., Michael A. Machado, "Existential Encounter in Gabriel Marcel: Its Value in Psychotherapy," *Review of Existential Psychology and Psychiatry*, I, No. 1 (Winter, 1961), 53–62.

28. Cf. the writings of Gabriel Marcel, Martin Buber, John Macmurray, Maurice Nédoncelle, Gabriel Madinier. A book to which attention should be drawn, because it is not as widely known and appreciated as it deserves to be, is Robert Johann's *The Meaning of Love*, an essay at providing a metaphysical basis for the phenomenological treatment of the "I-Thou" relation. Even when one disagrees, the book is enlightening and moving; and it is an excellent model of Thomism which is both aware of the limitations of

Thomas and yet draws upon his riches to form a creative synthesis with contemporary thought.

29. John Macmurray, *The Self As Agent* (New York: Harper, 1957), pp. 17–38. One can accept this historical judgment even if not ready to accept Macmurray's "preliminary and tentative reconnaissance" which is his contribution toward "the task set for philosophy in our time." See *Persons in Relation* (New York: Harper, 1961) pp. 12–13.

30. Distinct from and perhaps even more significant than the signs we have considered in the intellectual world are the startling signs in the religious and social events of our time, both in the world and in our own country. We see the breaking down of centuries-old barriers between men of different creeds and races. We note the collective sense of guilt for allowing these defects of pride and selfishness and hatred to exist, these obstacles to a union of all men.

19 *Authority and Power in the New Testament**

JOHN L. McKENZIE

The most controverted topic in Christianity today is presented in the framework of the New Testament concepts of power and authority.

B IBLICAL SCHOLARSHIP LIES very near the center of the campaign for the *aggiornamento* of the Church and the ecumenical movement. Depending on the point of view of the observer, biblical scholarship is thought to be either the Moses of a new exodus or the Pied Piper of a new Hamelin. We really do not deserve either the credit or the blame which we have received; but we have a modest role in contemporary theological events, and we ought to be aware of our responsibility. Our role is, I think, less modest than one would judge by the number of biblical scholars included among the *periti* of the Second Vatican Council. This illustrates rather well a common conviction that biblical scholarship is a fringe activity tolerated to prevent a greater evil. Biblical scholars are not thought to speak for the Church, nor even in the Church. Most of us, I am sure, can accept our uncertain status graciously and continue to do what we can. And what we can achieve is considerable. The absence of biblical scholars in numbers among the advisers of the Council does not represent the influence of biblical scholarship in the Church; and those who think that biblical scholars do not belong with the *periti* know this.

Our place in the ecumenical movement is large and evident. Most of us have found ourselves more and more frequently engaged in panels and discussion groups with Protestant clergymen and

* Presidential Address, given at the twenty-seventh general meeting of The Catholic Biblical Association of America, at the Vatican Pavilion, New York's World Fair, on September 1, 1964.

scholars. The reasons for this deserve to be recalled. We deal professionally with that theological source which Protestants accept as primary. They believe they can talk with us; they have or think they have a genuine problem of communication with our colleagues in dogmatic theology. More important is the widespread impression that biblical scholarship has become the very model of ecumenical discussion. The consensus of principles and methods of interpretation which exists and the exchange of opinion which flourishes, the free use of literature written by members of different confessions—these have no parallel in other areas of study. Theological ecumenism, if it is to advance at all, must follow the lines laid down by biblical scholarship; so at least many theologians, both Catholic and Protestant, are convinced. In biblical studies we have reached a degree of mutual respect based on candor and communication in a common body of learning which is not yet found elsewhere.

Just as most of us have engaged in ecumenical discussion, so I am sure many of us have found that it is at times embarrassing to have the respect and friendship of Protestants. A witty colleague of St. Vladimir's was kind enough to say in an article published two years ago that he hoped his approval of the theories of some Catholic scholars would not get them in trouble with their own superiors. The remark is partly serious; and I am sure that some of us continue to circulate freely only because Protestant exegetical journals are not widely read in certain ecclesiastical offices. Where ecumenism is thought of as capitulation rather than discussion, it is often believed that a Catholic scholar can win the approval of his Protestant colleagues only by compromising the faith, or at least by compromising *doctrina certa et communis;* and the line between these two doctrinal areas has grown incredibly thin here and there.

As a consequence of exegetical collaboration we are faced with a paradoxical situation; I do not wish to exaggerate its import, but I do not think that it should be entirely ignored. Catholic exegetes, while they move toward a greater consensus with Protestant exegetes, are drifting away from the theological positions held in some Catholic circles. Perhaps the word "position" is too flattering here; we are often puzzled by the problem of how to deal with irrational prejudice and tribal attitudes. I observe that we have had more

genuine theological dialogue with Protestants than we have with
some segments of Catholic theological opinion. The phenomenon
will probably become more disturbing before it ceases to attract
attention. The rift does not seem to be growing—if anything, it is
narrowing; but it is still there, and every now and then one is
astonished to notice how wide and deep it is.

A number of theologians and exegetes have voiced their concern
over the relations between theology and exegesis and their desire
for a closer integration of the two disciplines, or at least for
friendly relations. The existence of this division could easily create
a false impression; and this impression, in turn, could hamper
exegesis in its work. It is no secret, although no one to my knowledge has published it, that the encyclical *Divino afflante Spiritu*
has never been entirely received within the Church. This phenomenon ought to be considered whenever such topics as obedience
and devotion to the Holy See are discussed. We know that we
cannot afford to dismiss the problems of the relations between
theology and exegesis; and I trust we know also that the problems
will not be solved by granting control to one theological method.

The Bible, which was once a point of division between Catholics
and Protestants, is now becoming a point of union. But the same
Bible is still a point of division between Catholic theologians and
Catholic exegetes. This is the paradox of the present situation; and
we exegetes cannot expect others to resolve the situation for us.
The resolution could take the form of a power play which will
interdict the most important factor in contemporary biblical interpretation, the free study of biblical questions and the unimpeded
discussion of the problems of learning by scholars. Should such
an unfortunate development occur, we shall see no more either of
the ecumenical movement or of the biblical movement in our generation.

The relations of Catholic exegesis with Protestant exegesis on
the one hand and with Catholic theology on the other seem to
come to a focus at a single point; and it is to this point that I direct
your attention, because it is a point which exegesis has not yet
explored. Ecumenical discussions rarely fail to uncover the vital
point of division between Catholics and Protestants; it is the problem of authority in the Church. Similarly, the position of Catholic
exegesis in the Church is obscure not so much because of anything

in exegesis itself or in theology itself as because of some very common and some extremely distorted conceptions of authority in the Church, the same misconceptions which make Protestants hesitate. The discussion may take the form of a study of the structure of the Church, and even of the nature of the Church; or it may deal with the idea of power, or with the relations of obedience and freedom. But in the last analysis it is a single problem with numerous aspects; and this problem deserves the attention of exegetes as much as it deserves the attention of anyone else—assuming, of course, that the nature of power and authority can be legitimately discussed by others than the bearers of authority.

That this problem lies within the area of exegesis should need no explanation; but the number of studies carried on by Catholic exegetes is small enough to permit one to mention the reasons why exegesis should be concerned. The original grant of power and authority to the Church is conferred in the New Testament, and the books of the New Testament show the exercise of power in the apostolic Church. We cannot deny the evolution of power and authority in the Church; this belongs to legitimate doctrinal development as do other theological ideas, and no biblical study of any theological problem can be conducted with the presupposition that legitimate development ends with the apostolic age. But the genuine nature of the power of the Church cannot be seen unless the original state of that power is examined; and the legitimacy of the evolution of power is most clearly perceived in the unity and continuity of power throughout the history of the Church.

It is necessary to insist firmly on the distinction between the nature of authority and the exercise of authority. The nature of authority in any human society is more or less obscured by the practical use of authority; purely theoretical discussions become unreal, and the question of what authority can do is usually and quickly answered by seeing what authority has done. Sacral authority is more liable to be obscured by practice than secular authority because of the sacred character of its personnel. The theoretical implications of the use of sacral authority are closely scrutinized by theologians, who then make these implications a part of the teaching of the Church. They are, of course, no such thing. To base theory upon the actions of men who in their actions are subject to error and to malice is to make it impossible to distinguish between the nature of power and the abuse of power. Power which justifies itself by what it does is absolute and unrestrained. Unless one admits that power can be and has been abused in the Church, no reasonable discussion of the nature of authority is possible. Without this admission, whatever is done is then right because it is done; the agents are by hypothesis incapable of doing anything which is not right.

I spoke of misconceptions of power and of the theological development of the idea of power. Surely one basic misconception touches the development of the idea. For there has really been very little development of the idea of ecclesiastical power for several hundred years. I see no theological development corresponding to the evolution of man in civil society. And I trust no one will say that theological development has never been affected by the evolution of civil society. At the height of the Renaissance, at the moment when the power of the Church was challenged by the Reformers, ecclesiastical power had become a counterpart to secular power and had followed rather than led in the evolution of the idea of power. Both temporal and spiritual power stood as absolutes in their own realms. The subject of a Renaissance prince saw no difference between the power of his prince and the power of his bishop. Both powers were from God, and the subject owed absolute obedience to both. There was no appeal from either absolute except to the other. The theory of civil power was evolved later, principally by revolution; the theory of ecclesiastical power has more or less adhered to the medieval and Renaissance idea of absolute power. It is somewhat strange that only in this area of theology is theoretical evolution inhibited.

But man in civil society is no longer the subject of an absolute Renaissance prince. It would be foolish to suggest that most men in the modern world have achieved stable democratic institutions; it would be historically unsound to assume that democracy itself is a terminal political state. But modern man is wedded to democratic processes for better or for worse, and he has learned to think of himself as a citizen and not as a subject. The members of the Church also have evolved, and this itself is enough to suggest that they may have difficulty in understanding how they are to act when they are confronted with a society which they think is absolute.

In touching upon the abortion of development in the idea of

ecclesiastical authority, I risk committing that fault for which we exegetes will surely be rebuked: the fault of talking about things outside the field of interpretation. We have enough trouble vindicating our office of talking about biblical interpretation. Therefore I do no more than suggest this as an interesting area for our colleagues in theology and ecclesiastical history to explore. We exegetes can examine the idea of power and authority in the Bible. A full-scale exploration of this idea would be a book-size job. All that can be done here is to point out a few leads for such a study; this address, if it succeeds, will be the type which is dignified by the term programmatic. A study of authority in the Bible need not be and should not be militantly critical of existing institutions and practices. I observed that we must explore the idea, not the practice; and we are in danger, if we discuss the practice, of speaking about something which we do not know. If what we find is relevant to existing practice, it will be recognized as relevant.

I suggest first that we locate authority and power in the Church within the controlling theme of the New Testament idea of community. It should not be necessary in an assembly of biblical scholars to prove that this controlling theme is love, and that the Church in the New Testament is a community of love before it is anything else. If the Church should arrive at a point where its nature as a community of love is no longer perceptible, then it would lose continuity with the Church of the New Testament. The continuity of the Church need not be more perfect than we can expect in a society of men; the notion has to be flexible. Continuity can be obscured in various periods and in various areas of the Church. Quite clearly the Church has had members and does have members, some of them in official positions, to whom the idea of a community of love comes as a surprise, and perhaps an unpleasant surprise; the existence of such members does not destroy continuity. The Church maintains her identity in spite of her failures to achieve the perfection of love; but we must be concerned with maintaining the primacy of love.

Love is the quality by which the genuine Christian is tested and judged, and no other quality is relevant unless it is a function of love. When I read a letter in a clerical journal in which the writer reaffirms as traditional his conviction that obedience is THE WAY (*sic*), I can only reflect that Father has not been reading the New

Testament lately. I know the sources of his conviction, I think, and I know that he, like many others, has mistaken the part for the whole. Unless authority commands in love and the subject obeys in love, we are not dealing with a Christian obedience. And at this point one must risk being banal by recalling that love is directed toward persons, not ideas or objects. Christian obedience is intelligible only as a work of love, not as a substitute for love.

Authority reposes on power; and the power base of authority in the New Testament must be clearly recognized. The number of texts which deal with authority and power is not great, and I think I may be dispensed from treating them here; if any texts have received their due attention in theology, they are the texts on which authority is based. I would like to see the treatment expanded by some other texts not usually found in theses which deal with *potestas ecclesiastica*. These would include the lines which say that the greatest among the disciples should be a child (Mark 9:33-37; Matt. 18:1-5; Luke 9:46-48) and that the disciples should not lord it over one another like the great men and kings of the nations, but that the first among them should be the lackey and the slave of others (Mark 10:42-45; Matt. 20:25-28; Luke 22:24-30). Children and lackeys are not the bearers of power in secular society. What Jesus meant was at least that power and authority in the Church should have no resemblance to secular power and authority. Ecclesiastical power has a different end, and it disposes of different means.

The power base of authority in the New Testament is love, not the power to command or the power to coerce. Had Jesus wished to express dominative and coercive power, the words child and lackey are singularly inept for the purpose. For a practical demonstration of the power of love in action one can usefully study the letters of Paul. The efforts he makes to explain his position to his churches offer an interesting contrast to many communications from modern church offices. He meets the members of his churches person to person, and not through official channels. That they criticized him is evident, and that he took fire at the criticisms is also evident. But he responded to the criticisms; it did not occur to him to deny that the members of his churches had a right to criticize. He was much more sensible of his responsibility than he was of his dignity. The only power which he saw in himself was the power which entered the world in Jesus and endures in the Church; it is the power of love which saves. The apostle is expendable; he exists not to be served but to serve, and to give his life as a ransom for the many.

Love has its own way of commanding and its own way of coercing. And it is sadly true that those who do not know it cannot be taught it. The weight of love is far greater than the weight of mere authority, and the response of love is far in excess of the response of obedience. These things seem so obvious that I am almost ashamed to utter them; but why are we so often reminded of our duty of obedience, submission and respect, and so rarely challenged by love? Do we fear the reality of Christian love, or are we deeply aware that we lack it, or are we too self-conscious to admit that it is meaningful to us? And when I speak of the challenge of love, I do not mean exhortations to our duty to love—as if love could be conceived as duty; I mean active love which overpowers the reluctant by the depth of its devotion. The New Testament shows us leadership in love, and it shows us no other type of leadership. Love empowers some members of the Church to occupy hierarchical positions, and it vindicates their management of their office.

A second aspect of power which deserves study is power as the operation of the Spirit. In the New Testament the Spirit by its coming evokes the Church into existence. Every work of the Church is a work of the Spirit, just as every Christian work of the individual members of the Church flows from the dynamism of the Spirit. If authority in the Church is not an operation of the spirit, then it ceases to be authority in the Church; it would no longer be truly Christian leadership. Authority in the Church must be charismatic; its power is not from any human factors of intelligence, experience, or organization, but from the indwelling Spirit which enables the bearers of authority to achieve that which is impossible by merely human means. Charismatic leadership does not make these human qualities unnecessary; but it means that the leaders and the other members of the Church should not depend on the Spirit for that which human qualities can achieve, nor should they depend on human qualities for what is achieved by the Spirit.

St. Paul presents the charismatic Spirit as a unifying principle. There are different gifts, but the same Spirit; and the one Spirit is the one life of the body, whose members fulfill diverse functions in harmony. No member can say of the other members that it does not need them (I Cor. 12:4-31). Not all receive the same gifts, nor should one envy the gifts of another; the gift which all share is the highest of gifts, the gift of love. The gift of authority is completely safeguarded in the Pauline conception; but other gifts are just as carefully safeguarded. Authority has its proper position as one of the charismatic offices which the Church needs; and without other charismatic offices in the Church authority cannot fulfill its task. The principle of unity is the principle of the Spirit of love, not authority itself. The Spirit belongs to the whole Church and is possessed by each of its members; it is not the privilege of authority alone. Nor is the Spirit, the dynamic principle of life and action in the Church, subject to the authority of the Church. The Spirit can and does act outside the channels of authority.

This introduces us to the relation of authority to the prophetic office in the Church. It is an easy assumption that prophecy as a distinct function has ceased in the Church, or that the prophetic function has been subsumed into the official teaching office. The gift of prophecy is not as clearly described in the New Testament as some other charismata. But it is obvious that the Church needs prophets and has had prophets. It is clear also that the relations of prophets and official leaders have been hostile more frequently than they have been anything else. If there is no prophecy in the Church, then the indwelling Spirit dwells only in the officers of the Church, and the Spirit is under the control of the officers of the Church. Prophecy is the voice of the Spirit which speaks to the officers and to the members of the Church when either officers or other members are unfaithful to their own charisma. No conception of ecclesiastical authority is complete unless it leaves room for the prophetic utterance. Surely the prophetic office deserves serious study; and biblical scholars are better equipped than others to state clearly the place of the prophet in the Church. Perhaps we shall never accept the function of the prophet any more gracefully than it was accepted by the kings and priests of Israel and Judah; but even if the prophet must always be an outsider, the legitimacy of his role in the Church must be affirmed.

For the prophet is the means by which the Spirit protects the Church against corruption; and it takes a prophet to point out that there are other forms of corruption besides concubinage, nepotism and simony. The Church possesses within herself the principle of regeneration; but the authority in the Church does not possess this principle detached from the whole Church. Life is renewed by an exchange between the members. The officer of the Church can indeed receive the prophetic charisma, but he does not receive it in virtue of his office. It must be understood that prophecy is not normal and regular, like other offices in the Church; it is rare and exceptional, and belongs to times of crisis. But prophecy has its place, and it must be recognized as such when it appears. That there are false prophets does not take away the office; popes, bishops and priests have been false to their trust, but this does not take away the clerical offices. The Spirit often speaks to the officers of the Church through those whom the officers govern; if the officers do not hear the voice of the Spirit from this source, they will not hear it at all.

Our study of the authority of the Church in the New Testament ought to make it clear beyond dispute that Jesus established something entirely new in the authority which he conferred upon the Church. Authority as a function of love and as an operation of the Spirit has no precedent in societies which existed in Old Testament times or in the Hellenistic world, nor does it appear in social ethics of ancient or modern times. The relations of the officers and of the governed are totally dissimilar to the relations of officers and governed elsewhere. The Church has its own unique end and it has its own unique means of achieving that end. The use of means other than those with which Jesus endowed the Church not only do not advance its end, they may positively retard it. This danger, present in all the activities of the Church, may be peculiarly acute in the area of ecclesiastical authority.

Jesus commissioned his Church to create an entirely new social structure; and this means an entirely new conception of authority and leadership. The Church has indeed created such a structure; and it exists, even if not all the members of the Church nor all her officers are aware of it. The Church is a community of love in which the Spirit dwells. But our realization of the Church is still imperfect. We face the danger that the structure of the Church will take on the forms of secular society and that the Church will employ means proper to secular society. When the Church becomes a power structure, unless that power be the power of love, it takes on a secular character. When coercion replaces inspiration and love, the Church takes on a secular character; it can even take on the unpleasant aspects of the police state. When the officers of the Church dominate the faithful rather than become examples for the flock (I Pet. 5:3), the Church takes on a secular character. I suppose the one thing that is clear from the New Testament description of ecclesiastical leadership is that one person does not impose his will on another. If the members of the Church are not united in that love which makes all seek to serve each other, then coercion and control are no substitute for what is missing.

I said that we must distinguish between the idea of authority and the practice of authority, and I mean to maintain this distinction with no reference to any concrete situation. But one must point out that the new and revolutionary idea of authority which the New Testament discloses is constantly threatened by assimilation to that society which most resembles the Church externally, the political society. I have already alluded to certain assimilations which have occurred and which can scarcely be denied. The political society is an existing structure for the management of large numbers of people which appears, with certain adaptations, to be well suited to the management of the Church.

In modern times we have in addition the theories of corporation management; and I wonder if it is a tribute to the Church when it is said to meet the standards of good management practice. No doubt the Church must grow with history and live in it; but to yield to creeping secularism in its authority is not to grow with history. To adopt the workings of the political society converts the Church into a power structure. It introduces politics in the vulgar sense of the term, by which I mean the manipulation of people and things in such a way that one gains and keeps office. It means that office is conceived primarily as power over others and as control, not as service, and certainly not as a function of love. The enumeration of the effects of the introduction of political structure could go on and on and could become much more concrete and particular, but this I wish to avoid. All of us are aware of certain realities, unless we have deliberately refused to recognize them. We may not be as well aware of our duty in these realities, and of our resources. Exegetes have little to say; but they can study the power and

authority of the Church in the New Testament, and they can
present their conclusions as studies of theological sources which
never lose their value. They are as relevant now as at any time in
the life of the Church.

20 The Apostolate of Laymen*

KARL RAHNER

*In this article—which has been the occasion of much interest
and some controversy in Europe—Father Rahner gives a new
insight into the layman's vocation in the Church.*

I F W E W I S H to study the apostolate of laymen from a
strictly theological viewpoint, we must examine: (1) the
notion of the layman, (2) the notion of the apostolate in general,
(3) the nature of the apostolate of the layman, and (4) the importance of the lay apostolate today.

THE LAYMAN

The layman is a member of the Church. The theological concept
"lay" has nothing in common with that of "profane." Nor is the
layman a man devoid of knowledge and experience. He is not one
who has no interest in the Church or in religious questions. He is
not simply a tool in the hands of a powerful hierarchy. If this were
the case, there would be no place for the layman in the Church.

The layman, in a theological sense, is a member of the holy
people (.) of God. He is, in an eminent sense, consecrated,λαός
sanctified. His vocation to Christ's Church has snatched him up
from a sinful world given over to death. Baptism has called him to
salvation in a visible and tangible way. To speak of the laity does
not imply opposition between the profane and the holy. Rather it
indicates a man who occupies a determined and consecrated place
in the Church.

* "L'apostolat des laics," *Nouvelle Revue Théologique,* 78 (1956), 3–32.
This article appears also in the second volume of Father Rahner's *Schriften
zur Theologie* (Einsiedeln: Benziger, 1955), 339–73 and was previously published in three parts in the Austrian review, *Der grosse Entschluss.*

We must distinguish the laity from those who hold strictly hierarchical powers. These powers include those of orders and jurisdiction. Orders are primarily sacramental; jurisdiction pertains to
sovereignty in teaching and authoritative direction of the other
members of the Church. To be a layman in the strict sense one
ought not possess these powers.

But one can belong to the hierarchy without being ordained. For
certain powers in the Church need not be transmitted by the sacrament of orders, e.g., the powers of acolyte and sacristan. Other
powers cannot be transmitted by the sacrament, e.g., powers of
jurisdiction. Thus the laity and non-laity are distinguished with
respect to these powers not by the *manner* of acquiring them but
by their *content*.

In exact theological language we must say: Each time a person
is in legitimate, *habitual* possession of any part of liturgical or
juridical power which exceeds the fundamental rights arising from
baptism, that person ceases to be a layman in the proper sense of
the term. A cathechist or sacristan, for example, is not ordained;
nonetheless, if the duties of catechist or sacristan constitute their
principal function in life, they are no longer, strictly speaking,
laymen. This is apparent in the early Church where the ancient
minor orders were not temporary degrees leading to the priesthood, but permanent, though inferior, offices.

In the second place, we must distinguish the layman from the religious (and members of secular institutes who vow observance of
the evangelical counsels). The vows to observe the evangelical
counsels have essentially a "church" aspect. Not that this state of
life is founded upon hierarchical power; but the evangelical counsels express a very precise essential property of the Church: the
transcendence of its origin and destiny. These counsels are necessary in the Church in so far as the Church is the historical manifestation of the transcendent and eschatological grace of Christ. And
in this way they establish *in the Church as such* a state of life
distinct from that of the faithful in general.

ROOTED IN THE WORLD

Thus, negatively, the laity is distinguished from two "states,"
two stable and permanent forms of life. Both of these states re-

quire their subjects to leave the "world." Likewise, by positive concept, the layman will be that Christian who remains in the world.

To be a layman from this point of view does not mean to be a passive Christian, occupied with worldly and profane affairs devoid of religious significance. A layman is a member of the Mystical Body who exercises his ecclesiastical function on the spot where he lives in the world.

This world is not just a sinful thing; it is primarily a creation of God. In this world the layman has a determined place corresponding to his historical relation to family, profession or occupation, and so forth. He was born into this world independently of his Christianity. For him to be a Christian consists in christianizing this original, pre-Chrisitan environment, the very source of his being a layman.

The layman is distinguished by retaining his original position in the world and not abandoning it for a kind of life whose permanence would create a new state. If we say "the lay Christian remains in the world" we do not mean that he is a Christian, and then a man, a father, a politician, and so forth. Rather we mean that his situation in the world, given prior to his Christianity, is not changed by the fact that he is a Christian. His engagement *in the world* is what determines his being a layman. It marks the limits of his exterior life. If he passes these limits fixed by his original situation in the world, he ceases to be a layman.

POSITION IN THE CHURCH

A definition of the layman must not stop at showing how his situation in the world conditions his Christian existence. It must show also his position and contribution in the Church.

(1) A layman is a son of God, gratuitously called by God in Jesus Christ to eternal life.

(2) The layman contributes to the "Epiphany" of the Church. He participates in her life. He is commissioned by sacramental mandate in confirmation to the Christian mission. He contributes to the manifestation of the Church by sanctity in and with her, by interest in her activity, by his very existence.

(3) The layman can be a bearer of charisms. Granted that the

Church has received its proper structure from Christ for all times, she must remain ever open to the initiative of the Lord. Besides the stable element of the ministry there must be the mobile element of charisms.

Doubtless, ecclesiastical authority has the duty, right, and ability to discern spirits. But this authority is not the original, nor the unique bearer of the Spirit. Laymen also can receive charisms, the functions of which are as irreplaceable in the Church as her ministry, her law, her government. These charisms are free gifts of God. They cannot be foreseen. If they are given to the layman, they do not change his original situation in the world. He does not cease to be a layman.

(4) The layman is necessarily a part of the mission and responsibility of the Church. He must play an active part in it. But this does not mean that as a layman he participates in the mission of the hierarchy and clergy.

(5) The positive human law of the Church determines certain rights for the layman in the Church. He can be a godparent. He can perform functions in ecclesiastical organizations. He can collaborate legitimately in the administration of ecclesiastical goods and perform other functions which may devolve upon him by reason of positive law. These functions of themselves do not surpass the limits of the lay state. On occasion he can also undertake responsibilities that surpass those of the lay state.

RESTRICTIONS ON AUTHORITY

But if the Church wishes to impose on the layman any charge which would involve a change from his specific status as a layman, she must have his *free* consent. Doubtless the Church can impose certain responsibilities on a layman unilaterally. But this power is not unlimited. It has an intrinsic limit beyond which ecclesiastical power cannot go. If the Church, for example, would impose ordination to the priesthood on a layman without his free consent, such use of authority would be immoral.

CODE FOR THE LAYMAN

In this connection another observation suggests itself. The code of the Church now in force determines but to a slight extent the responsibilities, rights, and duties that otherwise could be given the layman without violence to divine law. I humbly suggest that as long as this situation continues we will never have the kind of Catholic Action we so much desire. To accept a responsibility presupposes the right to a certain amount of freedom in the accomplishment of the obligations and tasks involved. Catholic Action should not make the layman merely the executor of another's will, be it priestly or episcopal. Catholic Action cannot be deprived of all autonomy. Obviously the hierarchy alone can fix the limits of this independence. But once limited, it should be respected. In other words, it is of prime importance to establish in Catholic Action exact norms regarding the rights of laymen, a code which will protect these laymen in the face of the hierarchy, if need should arise.

Nor should one expect Rome to promulgate immediately such a code for the whole world. Situations around the world are too diverse. Cannot we hope nonetheless that these rights be slowly, prudently, but resolutely determined in particular dioceses and countries? The day the layman realizes what concrete powers he has in the Church, he will seriously assume obligations in greater measure.

THE APOSTOLATE

There is an apostolate that must not be confused with that of the layman. For clarity, let us call it the "official apostolic mission." What is reserved to this apostolate? How is it related to the apostolate of the laity?

To characterize the official apostolic mission we could simply list the actions and powers of non-laymen who possess some degree of hierarchical powers, e.g., sacramental absolution and transubstantiation. This method, however, does not suffice. It does not give the fundamental structure common to the diverse functions of the non-lay apostolate.

Christ himself marked these non-lay ministers with a double sign:

In their origin: It is of the nature of the ministry to absorb the whole life of the minister, to take him from the place he originally occupied in the world, and to identify the minister's life with his mission. The mission is realized not only *in* his life, but also *by* his life. The official apostolic mission lays claim to the entire existence of the man, and changes the place he originally occupied in the world.

In their consequent destination: The official apostolic mission sends its envoys afar. They depart for regions and areas of human experience with which, of themselves, they would otherwise have had nothing to do. Such an envoy testifies not to *his* religion, but to Christ alone—at all times and in all places. The minister must always be ready to pay the price of being taken for a fanatic, or for one who meddles in "private affairs" of others or excites anti-clerical sentiments. This new situation is justified only in view of the Faith.

COMPARISONS

We must exercise prudence in applying this definition of the hierarchical apostolate in practice. In comparing it with the negative notion of the lay apostolate it does not always give the clarity desirable. The Legion of Mary, for instance, is aggressive and praiseworthily so. Its apostolate has an intensity such as to make it a real "vocation." But does the obligation to engage in such a mission flow automatically from baptism and charity? Is such an apostolate strictly that of laymen, or is it on the frontier of the hierarchical apostolate?

Many forms of the apostolate which we are inclined to consider as lay are in reality, according to our principles, apostolates of the hierarchical mission. Ordination and celibacy are no help in making a distinction. As a matter of fact deplorable results often arise from the belief that unordained workers in ecclesiastical affairs cannot manage some aspect of the hierarchical apostolate within a zone clearly marked out by authority, with rights proportioned to responsibilities.

In practice, the line of demarcation between the two apostolates is not precise. In a given situation an apostolate of the laity might be more intense and more productive in its *final effect* than a hierarchical apostolate. This changes nothing essentially. The hierarchical apostolate is constituted by the mission that succeeds that of the apostles and sets up the ministry. The apostolate of the

layman is the apostolate of a man in the place that he has received
in the world.

THE APOSTOLATE OF LAYMEN

Strictly speaking, the apostolate of the layman does not consist
directly in recruiting, propagandizing, counseling, and so forth.
The layman realizes his proper apostolate when he leads an exemplary Christian life. This does not mean that the Christian cannot
speak of his Faith. Every man has occasion to make known the
intimate resources of his heart and of his life. But his duty as an
apostle does not extend beyond this.

The apostolate of the layman today is called the "action of
Catholics" in contradistinction to "Catholic Action." It involves
the obligation which baptized Christians have of caring for the
salvation of others. It is the apostolate of charity in the setting of
the world. Baptism and confirmation give to each Christian without further mandate the right and obligation to testify to the Faith
and to care for the salvation of the neighbor.

The layman must evidently present himself in all situations for
what he is—a Christian. He is a missionary in leading an exemplary Christian life. This apostolate is obligatory. It arises from
supernatural charity. It makes the layman an apostle in the concrete and familiar circumstances of everyday life, not in some
abstract theory.

AREAS OF ACTION

Science, art, medicine, politics, work, marriage present so many
open questions in the concrete order, questions of salvation or of
sin. Only the Christian can offer an answer to these questions in
terms of God's grace. If he responds by bringing patience, interior
freedom, and endurance to the accomplishments of his human
tasks, then he exercises his apostolate of the laity.

The field open to the layman is infinitely broad. His apostolate
embraces not only his private but also his public life. Whenever he
acts as a man, he acts as a Christian.

If these principles are grasped, we can see right away that education to a lay apostolate which is empty of education in an interior, saintly life is meaningless from the start. The education of the

lay apostle involves the formation of the full, authentic Christian, who is necessarily dynamic.

ORGANIZATIONS OF LAYMEN

We now come to a division of ecclesiastical organizations of laymen into two distinct groups:

(1) There are ecclesiastical organizations in the proper and strict sense. Created by the hierarchy, they aim at the realization of apostolic tasks proper to the hierarchy. Some laymen find their principal work here and thus cease to be laymen. Others consecrate only part of their time and energy, and hence remain laymen.

These organizations do what the hierarchy says to do. In return, what they do becomes a manifestation of the Church as such. These ecclesiastical organizations in the strict sense include, for example, third orders, sodalities, confraternities, associations for sustaining the missions. As much as they encourage their members to exercise the apostolate of laymen, they are rather organizations of the hierarchical apostolate than of the apostolate of the laity as such.

(2) There are organizations of laymen as such. They aim to promote the Christian life of laymen. We are thinking here of study groups, national federations for youth, university unions. There is a two-fold sign distinctive of such organizations: First, their primary end is not strictly religious, but rather profane, civil, cultural. Second, they see in this temporal affair a Christian work wherein ultimately salvation is involved. The concrete expression of such a mission cannot be determined by the hierarchy on the basis *only* of the general principles entrusted to their teaching and custody. For in the temporal realm the layman has a task to perform as a Christian and in performing it he should enjoy a real autonomy.

WHAT IS CATHOLIC ACTION?

Catholic Action is:

(1) an organization that proposes to form and instruct Christians in their apostolic duties in the world, marriage, professions, public life;

(2) an organization which sets about to safeguard the rights of the Church in public life;

(3) an organization of laymen who aim to help the clergy in their apostolic work without ceasing to be laymen.

The very nature of the first two aims demands that Catholic Action try to reach as many Catholics as possible. The third task mentioned is neither an obligation to be imposed on every Christian nor a service expected of each.

Clearly, Catholic Action points out some particular Christian organizations for the accomplishment of its first aim. In this respect it plays a double role. On the one hand it is subsidiary, trying to reach those in the world who, for one reason or another, do not belong to such particular organizations. On the other hand, it will be a superior organization coordinating these particular organizations that aim to form laymen for their mission in the world.

Catholic Action ought to be a superior organization coordinating and harmonizing a great number of other groups for the attainment of its second end, the protection of the Church's rights.

"A superior organism of coordination" means in this case that groups pertain to Catholic Action while still retaining their autonomy. They are not subordinate functions of an organization founded by ecclesiastical authority called "Catholic Action." Catholic Action cannot be an organization of the apostolate of the laymen as such. Catholic Action and action of Catholics do not coincide.

Catholic Action can educate towards a Christian life in a temporal situation. But it is incapable of taking charge of the life itself. In one sense the life of a layman cannot be organized, just as, for example, the role of a father in a family cannot be organized.

But in another sense, the life of a layman can be organized. For laymen can exchange views and aid themselves in coordinating their work. But the nature of such organizations should begin from below. They depend on the inalienable decision of laymen themselves. The Church cannot bear responsibility for them as she does for Catholic Action.

There is no need to develop at great length the importance of the apostolate of laymen. We will content ourselves with two remarks.

(1) Today for the first time a "world" exists which is historically brand-new. Men of former ages held one question to be vital: the religious question. Today there is a limitless number of interests that absorb men. These new realizations of human existence call for new attitudes. Man must invent new means for conquest.

The task of the priest is no less urgent in these changed circumstances, but because the life and duties of a priest do not bring him into such immediate contact with the problems of science, art, civil life, economics, etc., the layman has an indispensable role to play in Christianizing our age. He it is who has an entire, original relation to these new dimensions of human existence. And without the benefit of this new relation it will be impossible to control all the human possibilities of which there is now question.

(2) Catholic Action can have a great importance. But we must observe well that this importance arises from the service it renders to the action of lay Catholics. Catholic Action ought to enlighten, educate, coordinate. Every organization that is superfluous from this point of view is superfluous in reality and even harmful because it wastes the energy of both priests and laymen. In brief, Catholic Action will be important in exact proportion to its contribution to the action of Catholics.

FINAL REMARKS

In conclusion, let us return to two important points at the very heart of these reflexions.

(1) We must seriously consider the possibility and manner of establishing at least a definite diocesan code for laymen, especially for those laymen who find their principal function in directing Catholic Action. It seems to me that if we want to have directors of authentic personality, men of ideas and initiative, we must place a proper zone of activity under their responsibility with rights corresponding to those responsibilities. There they could enjoy the necessary autonomy. If a man is given a task he must have the power to perform it.

(2) We must not impose on the layman an apostolate that is not really made for him and to which he is not generally called. To assume such responsibilities can appear heroic and fruitful, but

this enterprise eventually disappears. Let us rather take the longer but more efficacious path. Let us teach the layman to be a Christian in the place that is or should be his: in the world. This is where he testifies to Christ by his life. If he so testifies, he is a lay apostle.

21 Death: A Test for Love, A Condition of Freedom

ROGER TROISFONTAINES

Eschatology is receiving an entire new dimension as a result of modern analysis of liberty and its culmination at death.

However different our human lives may be, they all, without exception, start with birth and end with death. But for my birth, I have no responsibility whatever, and I keep no remembrance of it. Its circumstances (time, place, race, family, etc.,) will influence—as we well know—the whole of my destiny; yet in no way does *it* depend on me. Blessed or cursed, it stands irreversible, unreformable. For ever, it is what it has been. It belongs to the past.

It is altogether different with my death. Certainly inevitable, my death however, *is* not yet. It will be: it is up to me to foresee it and to prepare for it. My freedom which had nothing to do with my birth, finds here a possible ground for action—at least, in that if I wanted to, I could, at this very moment, bring about my death. Suicide is a permanent possibility for man—and who has not thought of it at the time of his first deceptions or of his most bitter disappointments? Similarly, the conservation of life may be looked upon as the result of a progressive acceptance.

Actually though, rather than assenting to life or refusing it, many cling to it with a frenzy which is all anguish and voluntary blindness. We are afraid of death and we try all we can to forget it. "Sure, I will die, too"; however, there is no *divertissement,* be it noble or vulgar, that we have not dared to invent in order to cloud this too obvious necessity. Avoiding what reminds us of it, we always pretend that this possibility concerns others, only others, and we live on more or less duped by our insincerity. But in this matter as in all others, repression or insincerity profoundly disturbs conscience and life. For the onlookers, we behave as though we were in full possession of ourselves, but secretly we ceaselessly measure the proximity of the abyss and we apprehend—sometimes more, sometimes less—an insane vertigo. Rather than lying to oneself, rather than playing a comedy or a tragi-comedy, would it not be more simple, more courageous, more human to serenely meditate the mystery of death—of my death?

Very well, but how can I throw light on this subject? For, though my death is absolutely certain, its modalities remain covered with incertitudes and it possesses the unique character of being in its integrity "unexperimentable." Those who cross it do not come back to tell us how the affliction came about nor how they responded to it, nor how we should meet it when our turn comes. Strictly personal, death is an action where the experience of others is for us of very little help. Whoever, on the other hand, wants to "think" death, to discover its meaning, can do so only in relation to a metaphysical or religious world-view, in which death will be an inseparable part of the whole. Nonetheless, a concrete philosophy has to explore all the paths, to pick up all the indications which may bring us a little closer to the mystery. A few of these will be pointed out here.

I

The great suffering which is feared at the very thought of our death, the suffering we already feel when around us beloved friends or relatives pass away, is separation. A thorough investigation of all forms of pleasure, satisfaction, happiness and joy would show that, in spite of apparent and explainable contradictions, the element of bliss is always found in the birth or deepening of a union, whereas a separation on the contrary, is always marked with suffering, pain, unhappiness, sadness. However we explain it, death will remain the breaking of a modality of the union of man with the world, with his loved ones, with his own body. For this, death will always be distressing. Christ was not ashamed of crying before the tomb of Lazarus. But according as this mode of union broken by death will concretely be thought of as the only one possible to man, or as a particular mode subordinated to others, the suffering will be altogether different.

In the first case, death is the definitive misfortune, for which there is no way out, no remedy. It is annihilation. I identified myself with my wealth, with my belongings, with what I *had,* and I will *have* nothing any more (which within this hypothesis means: I will be nothing). I loved mainly his body, our love hardly went beyond the level of sexual relations and physical caresses, and this body lies there, inert, and soon will be placed in a coffin and buried underground: nothing of him will remain for me. This woman furiously throws herself on the corpse of her lover, clings to him, roars her animal despair. Indeed nothing will remain of the possessions and caresses, and for those who here on earth knew no other joys but these, death presents itself as the absolute end, *Evil* itself.

But if love has been spiritualized, if it rises to the level of friendship, if the objective fact of *being there* and of exteriorly manifesting one's presence—however precious this may be—is entirely or almost entirely subordinated to the fact of *being-with* (which cannot be objectified or described), of merging *our* existences into a common destiny, of being *we* rather than two juxtaposed I's, of being together opened to love rather than imprisoned into an egoism for two, then the tearing apart of death, however crushing and painful it remains, does not reach the very depth of this love, of this friendship. The experience—to which bear witness, among others, the *Lettres à l'absent* (*Letters to the Absent one*) of Mireille Duponey or *Liens immortels* (*Immortal Bonds*) of Alice Ollé-Laprune—of a communion which stays alive after the death of one of the espoused, is not so rare among the Christian communities. Death, this time, far from being felt as a definitive absence, rather makes manifest that I was reaching the beloved more intimately than I could be conscious of, and above all, could express. The disappearance of the apparent means of our love discloses to me (as was already indicated by the spotless fidelity that was ours at the occasion of temporary separations) that our reciprocal presence could do without the exterior signs without being really changed.

Once the first numbness of this sweeping distress which overtakes us at the death of a very dear husband, child, father or mother has passed, are they not many who have the experience, sometimes as soon as they collect themselves by his death bed, that the loved one is still very close to them, no more in this lying corpse, but *with* them in the interior dialogue? The preservation of communion with this missing one now depends on the survivor, on his faithfulness. If I declare him to be nothing any more, or that at least no intimacy with him is still accessible to me, he will not be anything for me any more, in fact, and I will have freely accomplished his death, his annihilation for me. But if far from considering his memory as an inert and silent relic, I inspire myself with his spirit, I keep myself within his radiance, I consult him in the depth of my heart, he does not die for me. "Illusion," will say all those whose mind has been shaped by positivism. Experience would have something to say, but it is clear that the very postulate of rationalism prevents those who assent to it from having access to this kind of experience. In fact, we enter into a domain where, on an objective ground certainly, *reality* depends nonetheless upon our liberty. Isn't this always the case, as soon as love steps in? Without any action on my part, the other person exists certainly and I exist equally without him; but that the two of us constitute a united couple, a pair of friends, this rests on our free will. The *being* of our communion is really *created* by our oath—which is explicit in marriage, and implicit most of the time in friendship—which binds us to one another.

This being so, it is up to our fidelity to perpetuate it, even beyond the ordeal of death. Our betrayal alone could end it. There are such friends to whom I feel closer and who have on me a deeper actual influence because they are dead, than others from whom life has simply separated me or with whom I rub shoulders every day. It is enough for me to recollect myself in order to find them as they were and infinitely better, so understanding and so good that before them all masks and all deceits are abandoned, and we live together in such an intimate way as is unknown in this world where bodies keep us apart. Following the proverb, love and friendship are stronger than death. For one who had this experience, the wound that the death of a loved one causes does not contain that incurable venom which poisons the existence of those who limit themselves to the tangible. The well-founded hope that death will not cut all bonds permits us to face it with serenity. To

one who can say with Thérèse of the Child Jesus "I will spend my
heaven doing good on earth," death no longer appears as an incurable break, it ceases to be the greatest suffering.

To the extent that the true love in which I already participate
down here can blossom only in the beyond, I may legitimately
aspire after death—not for itself, but inasmuch as it conditions the
awaited encounter. "I would like to dissolve to *be* with Christ" (St.
Paul); "Come, Lord Jesus, do not delay any longer" (St. John);
"I am dying from not dying" (St. Theresa of Avila). Throughout
the Christian centuries, the same invocation is ever echoed. "There
is a man," says Lacordaire, "whose tomb is guarded by love."
Although he no longer grants us this familiar contact the disciples
enjoyed, Jesus remains present among us. Above all to him goes
the friendship, the fidelity which defies death and the disappear-
ing of habitual appearances. He was foreseeing it himself when he
announced to the apostles: "I tell you the truth, it is good for you
that I go. For if I would not go, the Spirit would not come to you."
The spiritual presence is infinitely superior to the visible presence.

Assuredly, few are the desires for death that spring from love
alone. Very often—as is shown by my friend André Godin in a yet
unpublished thesis—they correspond to a process of disengage-
ment which rather shows a diminution or a deviation of affectivity.
It would be a gross illusion to ascribe any mystical value to dec-
larations which only reflect despair or selfish coiling up. It remains
that among genuine saints, love for Jesus Christ can be so intense
that, without doing anything to hasten the moment of their death,
they await it with a shudder of joy.

We are far, in their case, from the initial horror which constitutes our common lot. Indeed death sets up itself as a judge of our
affections. How different is my reaction toward it according to
whether my attachment gets bogged in the flesh or leaps toward the
spiritual! Death is the great test for love.

II

But, fidelity beyond the grave, is it not illusory? In reality the
dead one, whether or not he remains alive *for me,* is he still living?
Crucial questions, to which, at all times, the spontaneous belief of
humanity, such as it is expressed in the religions and in most meta-

physics, has given a positive answer. One postulate alone, one should notice—which is valid only for certain special disciplines—commands the negation. This postulate they adopt and unduly extend, those who cannot or will not continue with the dead this friendship we have spoken of. In this relation of fidelity, "experience" (if we be permitted to use this ambiguous word) acknowledges the other, not at all as the product of an over-heated imagination, but as real, as acting. And, experience for experience, it is obvious that we have not one proof of an annihilation—how would we?—while thousands of tales from all peoples keep alive the belief in immortality and pretend to relate communications with and interventions of the beyond.

Legends, superstitions? Often, very often, assuredly. But only one well established case would suffice to justify this un-uprootable conviction. Does this case exist?

Nearly two thousand years ago, a man died, posted naked upon a slave gibbet, after atrocious corporeal and moral sufferings. In order to make sure He was dead, although this was indubitable, a Roman solider pierced His heart. With Him was dying the hope of a little group of friends who had saluted Him as being the Messiah, the Saviour of the world. Lamentable failure on this Good Friday evening. All His companions have abandoned Him, as early as the eve, at the moment when He was apprehended by the police. The head of His apostles has denied Him three times, swearing: "This man I do not know." That is another of His friends, the one who sold Him for thirty silver pieces! Now that He is dead, nothing remains of His work.

A few days later, however, this work comes to life again and, after two millenniums of diverse events, continues more alive than ever: it is the Catholic Church.

The origin of this new life: the unshakable triumphant faith, the certitude of the resurrection of Christ. It was not accepted painlessly. Nobody, it seems, was expecting it: after such a death! Some disciples—He will reach them on the road—were returning home commenting with sadness on their deceived hopes; at the same time the women were announcing visions of angels and the apostles had discovered the disappearance of His body. The empty sepulchre did not suffice to convince them. They will have to see Him, to hear Him, to eat with Him, to touch Him in order that the doubts be erased. But these same poor men, who had run away at the sight of a danger that was not menacing them, shall stand up to all the mighty ones. They shall overcome all sufferings. They shall accept martyrdom to attest that He, Jesus, has defeated death and that they have seen Him alive beyond the tomb.

This glorious life, they now remember He had foretold it to them—at a moment when they were not yet ready to understand it—they see clearly that it fits in the web of his life and teaching, they know that it is the token of our resurrection. And in spite of the innumerable faults and failures of those who constitute and direct it, the Church perpetuates through the centuries the faithfulness of the origins, lives from the presence of His living head, the resurrected dead.

This fact, established as it is by the traditions, the documents and the tremendous consequences it still develops in our days—if we do not admit it, it is not for purely historical reasons, for no event possesses more solid proofs, on the historical level. Without here going into discussions of apologetics concerning the person of Christ, we will, in order to elucidate a little the mystery interesting us, build upon the teachings of this fact: A man transcended death. Now, anguish overcomes us mainly when we wonder whether death opens a door upon another life or is a cul-de-sac. Through the example of Christ, we know that death is a road, not an end.

Even after the resurrection of Jesus Christ however, the characteristics of life beyond the grave are not copiously given—and doubtless the mystery must remain an essential condition of the test death is. Let us retain at least what we can learn from it.

If we read the brief pages in which the gospels describe the Resurrection, it does not appear that Jesus "came out" of the tomb as the painters like to represent Him. We only read of an angel who overturns the stone and exposes an *already* deserted sepulchre. Rather than a reanimation of the corpse lying on white stone, one must picture that, on this Sunday morning, suddenly, the pieces of linen that were around the remains dropped, empty, as Peter and John will find them a little later. The mortal body of Christ disappears. But from this moment, for manifesting visibly, tangibly His life and His presence, He will assume the appearance —or better the body—He will want, where and when He will want it. Thus, to spare the disciples a too violent psychological shock, He will not always take a body absolutely identical to the one they had known before His death. Neither Mary Magdalene, nor the disciples of Emmaus, nor the apostles fishing in the lake of Genesareth will recognize Him at once. Surely, through tactfulness, Jesus slightly dissembles himself in order to prepare them for His revelation.

Certainly unique in His theanthropic personality, Christ nonetheless remains, especially for the glorious life, our prototype, "the first-born from among the dead." Without forgetting that He differs from us in His quality of Head of the Church, whose members we are, it is legitimate to infer from His resurrection to ours. And for the sake of our topic, we will limit ourselves to one essential detail.

In the same way as for Him, our "glorious body," our after-death body, will not be, as the one which is ours in this life, *imposed* on us, but will depend on our free will. The one who is resurrected gives himself a body as he pleases. This simple fact opens up, it seems, immense perspectives, thanks to which we might be able to bring out the ultimate meaning of death.

Proposing in a few words the hypothesis which seems the most likely because it joins the diverse streams of metaphysical and religious reflection, we would readily say that death is indispensable so that the fulfilment of man's freedom be achieved.

To be free is to posit oneself, it is to personally determine one's way of acting, better still, one's way of being. Now, it is undeniable that during all his earthly existence, man *is* very little free. Let us say that he *becomes* free. Gradually he frees himself from hereditary, familial, social, etc., determinisms, he accepts or opposes, he guides himself as best he can between obscure forces and he tries, if he truly wants to free himself, to turn life to the best account for his personal ends. But how far this precarious freedom is from the divine freedom in the image of which, still, it was created!

In spite of the infinite distance that separates it from its model, it tends nevertheless to resemble it. Does not human existence give rhythm to a progressively increased possibility of renewal and creation of the self? At first grafted somehow upon another life—that of the mother—(and grafted by an act in which he partook in no way, since he was not previous to this conception), the embryo tries little by little movements that are independent of the material influx. Birth breaks the primitive symbiosis, projects him into a biologically autonomous, but still quite dependent existence. The child has chosen neither his race, nor his family, neither the place nor the time of his birth, neither his country nor his social milieu, nor the language, nor the rules of etiquette, nor the aesthetic criteria, nor the moral principles, nor the religious practices that his education transmits to him, nor his physical temperament, nor his character, nor anything: he did not choose to exist. But once started in the adventure of life, little by little he must take upon himself, abandon, bend, modify all the "given" elements that characterize him. On the biological, intellectual, moral, social, religious level, through a series of weanings, of cries and of engagements, little by little he acquires his autonomy, he chooses the attitude that will define him.

This passage from the "imposed" to the "personal" is most perceptible at the time of puberty. In general, the child is balanced, reasonable; he resembles an adult more than an adolescent does. In the thick of the crisis, the adolescent questions everything. Certainly, one may like in him the charm of his promise and of his generous *élan*, but one must admit that most of the time his body and imagination, his intelligence and affectivity are out of proportion. The gracefulness of childhood has disappeared along with its equilibrium. But if the crisis is well resolved, is there anything more beautiful than a young man, than a young woman, in the full-blown harmony of a healthy body, of a cultivated spirit, of a solid moral life? The difference and the progress are due to the fact that the equilibrium of the child is *received,* passive, moulded with ignorances and immunizations, while the adult, if he successfully comes out of his puberty crisis, raises himself to an active equilibrium he has himself, at least partly, regained.

At the vocation age, when it is time to choose a career, he himself decides, more or less, on the orientation of his life: he actively participates in the creation of his being. It is incumbent upon him, when comes the crisis of the age of 25 or 30, to maintain his ideal in concretely adapting it to the hard conditions of reality which were often ignored by the enthusiastic ardour of adolescence. And at maturity what defines his being, is less his origin and the external circumstances than his personal worth, the line of his action, the family he has founded, the works he has done.

Yet, however deeply he has taken possession of himself, he never works but on a *given* fund: his body with its possibilities and its defects, his character, his civil status, the contingent situation of the world at this moment. In order to be truly "the son of his works," the son of his will and of his freedom, in short in order to posit *himself,* it would be necessary that man could give himself the body that suits him and determine by himself the kind of relations he will have with other beings. To surrender the received body would thus be an indispensable condition of our full liberty.

Now this surrender, is it not what appears most evident in all death? As the butterfly surrenders the cocoon in which it was developing while it was a chrysalis, so when we will reach our definitive stage, we will leave behind this body which was the first and essential condition of our spiritual maturation. We shall give to ourselves, as Christ in His life beyond the grave, the body we will want. The body which is ours during the *becoming* is only somehow the matrix where is formed the *being* I shall be, and which is incarnated spirit. Indispensable during the embryonic life, the role of the matrix ceases at the moment of birth; thus, this body, which I did not choose and cannot dispense with during my *becoming,* shall disappear in order that my *being* be realized. And it shall be up to me, if it would please me as it is, to assume a totally similar one. Identical or different, it will truly be *my body* this time, the one I have wanted. Thus do we see Jesus Christ keeping in His glorious body the stigmata and the mark of the nails at His hands and feet, without being satisfied with simply animating anew the bloodless, torn and disfigured corpse enclosed in the Sepulchre.

What is true of my relation to my body, would it not be true of all the other relations which define my being? At the moment of dying, everything is questioned again (much more radically than at the time of puberty) and I have to choose myself, my definitive attitude toward the universe, others, myself and God. Down here, in the measure in which I rise to spiritual autonomy, I become master of this attitude. Without changing anything in the *"en-soi"* of other beings, it depends on me whether God be *for me* real or non-existent, according to whether I will live as a religious man or

as an atheist. It depends on me whether others be for me brothers
or indifferent ones, according to whether I involve myself *with*
them in the adventure of existence or, alone, I play my mean and
scornful game. It depends on me whether the universe have a
magnificent meaning for our divinization or it seems to me absurd,
nauseating, hopeless, according to whether I relate to it in an
enthusiastic offering and in a joyous service or I break all relations
that would not be of a cold scientific technique or of a sensual
selfishness. It depends on me whether I build myself a sincere,
loving, creative personality or I wither in a sterile lucidity and a
wicked destruction, according to whether I will return to my origins in a fruitful meditation or I will spread myself in introspection
and diversion.

But here below, one must admit, I can only mark a trend: I am
becoming free, I *am* not yet free in the full sense of the term. And
my earthly options seem to be mostly preparatory exercises,
"rehearsals" (as one rehearses a play or a set speech) for the
definitive option; they educate my liberty to spring up. Let us
transpose again on the spiritual level the biological comparison of
embryonic life. In his prenatal existence, the child learns most of
the movements he will need on the day of his birth; his heart gains
its proper movement, he moves head, arms and legs, he even ab-
sorbs and digests what he can. Similarly, if we be permitted this
expression, down here we are "embryos of spirits." During the
terrestrial becoming, we practice positing the definitive act, whatever the time and the conditions, external or internal, of our
human existence. There hardly is any common measure between
the progressive initiation of life and the sudden revelation which
crowns it at death. If the child could remember, he would tell us
the abyss which separates his life in the mother's womb and the
existence birth throws him into, and how little the first one, although preparing it, permitted him to foresee the second. We have
all been through this experience, but none of us ever went to teach
the children still in gestation about it. Without pushing this parallel
too far—which would render it ridiculous—is not our terrestrial
existence from the point of view of our *spiritual being,* what the
prenatal existence was for our *becoming?* Death, according to
the beautiful expression of the old martyrologies is the *dies natalis,*
the day of the genuine birth, where this time, I will make myself

what I want to *be* for eternity. That is why even our deceased friends let the ordeal of dying remain a mystery to us.

Much more than the corporeal birth, the death of each one considered as an act of *auto-position* is a unique event, strictly unforeseeable—since utterly free—for which the experience of others would be of no use: we shall have to act as the creators of ourselves. The platonic formula on "life, apprenticeship of death" becomes, in this perspective, profoundly significant. The chief action of our terrestrial existence is precisely the one which ends it, the one with which the *becoming* ceases in order to make way for *being,* the act of dying.

Yes, it is an act. The witness of a death-struggle would be tempted to see only passivity, failing. This is because he only perceives the failing of the becoming, the downfall of this transitory body which, its role being done, is effectively exhausted. But this sad sight is only the reverse of reality. Breaking the bond that held him to the world of determinisms and constraints, the true self blossoms and freely chooses the relations that shall constitute him. Upon an existential ground which my liberty can neither annihilate nor create (the *reality-in-itself* of God, of others, of the world and of myself), it depends on me to create their *reality for me,* my *being with them* or *without them,* communion or isolation, friendship or hatred. And what matters for me, my *being*—by opposition to my raw *existence*—is precisely this freely chosen attitude. Let us not imagine however an *ex nihilo* creation by an isolated being. The action of freedom in us is essentially a response to an invitation. The artist creates only when attracted by the beauty of the world or by inspiration. Similarly, I create myself as a free "person" only in an encounter with someone else, only in answer to the grace of God.

But I am the one who utters this answer, and it can be a refusal as well as an acceptance, a more or less radical refusal, a more or less generous acceptance. Also there will be an infinite diversity among beings, each one choosing himself in an original, unforeseeable, inimitable way.

If we would like to rank this diversity, in theological terms, we would have to admit an infinity of "degrees" between the highest of heaven and the lowest of hell. That is exactly what it is, in fact. The option posited in the act of dying is in itself definitive, immu-

table. Eternity, everyone knows it, has no common measure with
time: it can be assimilated neither with a very long duration nor
with an instant. Every time we succeed—if we ever succeed in this
on earth—in grasping totality as such (in poetry, love or mystical
ecstasy, for instance) eternity erupts in us. But we fall back, alas!
into temporality; since we apprehend only partially realities that
are themselves particular, we are really obliged to multiply our
imperfect graspings and this "discourse" is at the origin of temporal "becoming." But in the act of dying we will precisely have to
invent our mode of immediate participation with the totality of
existents. The choice made, in full light, there will be no reason
nor any possibility to question it again. Thus, each one of us will
be, for eternity, exactly what he wants to be. God has committed
man to the hands of his own counsel. Each one will make himself
as he pleases. And no one shall regret his choice. The regret would
in fact suppose, as regards the option, a second moment. But if
there was place for a second moment, why would there not be
place for a third moment for a new choice, a fourth one for a new
regret, etc.? This would no longer be eternity, understood as an
immediate participation in the totality of the real, but a single
prolongation of the inconsistency of becoming, a period of experiences and of corrections.

Since each one will be precisely what he wants to be, no one will
regret his choice. However, this does not mean that all will equally
participate in beatitude. As we briefly indicated at the beginning of
this essay, happiness is measured by union, suffering by rupture.
The highest degree of heaven, consequently (we resort to an obviously inadequate spatial representation) will be the one where the
being will have willed himself *with* others to a maximum, in a
loving communion with the whole of reality. And the lowest degree
of hell will be the one where, coiled up upon himself in isolation,
the being will be excluded from others to a maximum, will have
willed himself to be *without*.

With or *without*: all is summed up in the alternative between
these two prepositions. At the heart of all our free acts an option
between the two attitudes these prepositions characterize is tenta-
tively taking place. Metaphysicians will doubtless say that liberty
does not necessarily imply choice. For the infinite being, let us
admit it. But the limited being will always have to choose between

that by which he participates in all others and that by which it is possible for him to shut himself up upon himself. The distinction between the "closed" and the "opened" rules the whole moral and religious order where it defines the two contradictory poles of egoism and charity.

At the moment of dying, a being measures himself. He chooses the degree of intimacy with others (God, the society of spirits and the whole universe) or, on the other hand, he coils up upon himself, whichever seems preferable to him. He takes up for eternity the attitude that pleases him. It is in this total context that one must understand the aphorism: "In death, all men are equal." Not only because all go through the same ordeal, but above all because none of them is handicapped by the circumstances imposed on his terrestrial becoming. The materiality of the acts or the merits "acquired" (like a treasure) will not count much at this moment. What alone will matter will be the fundamental orientation of the soul toward communion or toward isolation. This orientation, every man, whatever be his civil status, his heredity or the conditions of his existence, has little by little adopted by himself.

The fact that at death everything is questioned anew and that the sudden revelation does not prolong in a homogeneous way the progressive initiation, in no way strips the actions, or at least the attitudes, of our terrestrial life of their value. Experience, under its many negative and positive forms, educates our liberty. Sin— which always coincides with the egoistic or prideful coiling up upon oneself—may, through the disgust it generates, open up to communion, just as the normal development of a virtuous life can. But the latter is an infinitely better way (on the condition, of course, that it is not vitated by pharisaism, which still is a form of this subtle self-pride). The being who is oriented toward charity, who all his life searched for a more profound union with God and others, shall blossom spontaneously at the moment when this communion will be offered to him. There is hardly any possible hesitation about the eternal destiny of a genuinely charitable man, and the Church, who forbids herself to affirm the damnation of any one soul in particular, counts innumerable saints whose beatitude she certifies.

As for the soul coiled up upon itself, for it the final option takes on mainly a tragic character. It is absolutely possible for it to be totally converted as it reaches the definitive level of being. But the turnabout will be the more painful—in consideration of the acquired habits—the more this egoism has hardened. And this difficulty, exactly proportioned, constitutes the Christian purgatory (which, in this hypothesis, it is not necessary to think of in a temporal fashion). Finally, it may happen that, despite the totally new conditions of the option, the finite and egoistic beings persists in the refusal of charity and wills himself for ever separated and in hell.

Of this choice, of this double possibility, have we not the shadow of an experience in the profound reaction that provokes in us the belief in a near death? The imminence of danger liberates us from our ties and releases at the same time a strong liberation of affectivity. Now, very often, one witnesses in the being thus shaken, either a conversion from the mediocre to the better, or contrarily an exacerbation of the sensual egoism. The intrusion of the absolute into the human life consecrates and fixes the generally accepted orientation, it does not overturn it. The *Sparkenbroke* of Charles Morgan's novel, if he remains for ever marked by the precocious experience he had in the familial cellar, becomes neither more altruistic nor more religious. On the other hand the *Annick* whose story Jacqueline Vincent tells us in *Comme par mé garde* (*As though inadvertently*), has his innate generosity open up only under the sun of death. Apart from literary references, at the level of our daily existence, have we not all met some of these beings, some consecrating to charity the whole of what they consider as the surplus of a menaced existence, others only racing with greater frenzy toward pleasures and ambitious competition? The very thought of death works like a catalyst and forces us to take a position. Has not the meditation on death always been recommended by ascetics in every period and does it not find a normal place in the development of a retreat? Death provokes liberty, and reveals the depths of hearts.

The two themes developed, meet. Death is at once a test for love and a condition of freedom, for freedom has no other profound significance but to permit love. The Triune God who has created us, invites us to participate in His intimate life, which is charitable communion among the Three Persons. *Invites us*: for how could He be interested by a being who would not have freely chosen to love Him?—i.e., one who would not have personally overcome the temptation of refusal or betrayal. This helps us to understand the sense of this terrestrial adventure.

Every man is born in a *community* which imposes itself on him as a fact anterior to his free will. But the more he becomes conscious of his personal autonomy, the more it depends on him, either to break the relations which link him to others, or, on the contrary, to assume them and deepen them. According to his choice, he will either close himself up in the isolation of egoism and pride, he will live *without* others, or he will open himself up to communion with God and men encountered in faith and love. As in the order of birth, we start with a rich but confused primitive *complex*—whose elements are distinguished by the *analysis* and are brought together again by the *synthesis*—the dialectic is fulfilled in the order of love only when, freed from the imposed *community,* we freely assent to *communion.* But when we say liberty we include the possibility of breaking off along the way. Just as the analysis is indispensable to pass from the confusion of the complex to the harmony of the synthesis, but implies if one stops short (as is the case with these primitive minds set on scientism) the danger of missing both the complex and the synthesis; so liberty alone makes it possible to pass from community to communion, but involves the risk of an individualist isolation which tears one away from the community without introducing him to communion.

Therefore, he who wants to make a success of his life shall simultaneously aspire to the highest freedom and unflinchingly guide this freedom in the direction of charity. With this condition, death for him will be deprived of its sinister character of absolute rupture. It has often been noticed that the primitive man or the little child accepts death with much more ease than most civilized adults. This is because the child and the primitive hardly free themselves from the community. The problem of their destiny and of their strictly personal survival worries them very little. But anguish mostly tortures the already evolved being who stops at the intermediary stage between community and communion. "Deracinated" as the sociologists say, uprooted from the group in which he was born, he has not yet involved himself in a new union, nor built himself a superior milieu in which he will blossom in love.

And when, moreover, he has chosen isolation, death must appear to him as the worst of catastrophes, for it threatens to annihilate this I to which alone he clings. On the contrary, while glancing at the testimony of the saints, we saw that those who raise themselves to genuine communion do not fear death: it will only change the form of their love, it will destroy nothing.

The fanaticism of certain young Hitlerians who were rushing headlong into the carnage in the intoxication of the first battles of 1940 resulted from their over-integration in the community. One cannot help thinking, in this connection, of those animals which thoughtlessly sacrifice themselves for the good of the species. Such a death is unworthy of man.

But the attitude of the one who deserts through egoism is hardly worth more. Without concern for others or for the superior interests at stake in the conflict, he only considers his own well-being. If he uses freedom, it is in the sense of isolation. And he is the one who, unable to withstand the wounds of existence, will commit suicide when the disappointments are too great, when life, from his own individual point of view is no longer worth living.

The Christian, on the contrary, knows that, according to the word and example of Christ, there is no greater love than to lay one's life down for those he loves, than to give it out of oneself, freely, through love.

The submission to death through instinct, the refusal of death through self-love, the suicide through egoism constitute so many crimes. But generously accepted, death confers the supreme accomplishment on those who dispose of themselves with a view to charity. If we wish to measure the abyss between the community which precedes or excludes personal freedom and the communion which follows and crowns it, let us appraise the difference between the gregarious folly of death for the race and the sacrifice of one's life offered by a soldier who exposes himself to danger in order to save a companion or accomplish a mission. But whereas the community negates freedom, voluntary isolation perverts it, which is much worse. Thus the general reprobation which stigmatizes the deserter or the self-murderer is justified (although the act of suicide, even when immediately followed by death is but the penultimate act of existence, the last one being that of dying, which may radically transform the moral orientation).

At any rate, the most human and most Christian attitude in facing life and in the perspective of death, is the progressive opening to the totality of the real, the apprenticeship of an ever more intimate communion with God, others, one's deeper self and the universe. Then, since in charity we will profoundly participate in everything that is, we will be able, like Francis of Assisi, to end our canticle of the creatures praising our sister death.

Laudate sii, mi Signore, per sora nostra morte corporale de la quale nulu omo vivente po' scampare.
Guai a quilli che morrano in le peccata mortali.
Beati quilli que si trovarano in le tue santissime voluntati, ca la morte secunda non li potera far mal.

Be praised, my Lord, for our sister, bodily death, from whom no living man can escape.
Woe to them who shall die in mortal sin.
Blessed those who shall be found in Thy most holy will, for the second death will not be able to do them ill.

O day of Encounter, I await you in peace for I hope, Lord, in your immense Bounty.

Translated by Leo Paré

230   G

Gleason, Robert, S.J.

AUTHOR
       A Theology Reader

TITLE

230   G

Gleason, Robert, S.J.
  A Theology Reader